HERBERT HOOVER: *American Quaker*

By DAVID HINSHAW

THE HOME FRONT

A MAN FROM KANSAS: THE STORY OF WILLIAM ALLEN WHITE

AN EXPERIMENT IN FRIENDSHIP

SWEDEN: CHAMPION OF PEACE

DAVID HINSHAW

HERBERT HOOVER:

American Quaker

FARRAR, STRAUS AND COMPANY · NEW YORK

 Permission from authors and publishers for use of selections from the following books, magazines and newspapers is gratefully acknowledged by the author: *27 Masters of Politics* by Raymond Moley, copyright 1949, Funk & Wagnalls, New York. *Addresses Upon The American Road, 1933–1938* by Herbert Hoover, Charles Scribner's Sons, New York. *Addresses Upon The American Road, 1945–1948* by Herbert Hoover, D. Van Nostrand Company, Inc., 1949. "Let's Go Fishin'" by Herbert Hoover, Crowell-Collier Publishing Co., New York. For quotations from a series of articles by John T. Pace, August, 1949, The New York *Journal-American,* New York. Manufactured in the United States of America by H. Wolff Book Manufacturing Co., Inc., New York. Designed by Stefan Salter.

ff

FOREWORD AND ACKNOWLEDGMENT

My concern to write this biography of Herbert Hoover grew out of our common Middlewestern Quaker heritage and our thirty-five years of association and friendship.

Our common religious heritage and my many opportunities to observe him in action have, I believe, given me a special insight into his motives and methods, principles and purpose. And because of my belief that ideals, *per se,* are a real and vital part of the life of every individual I have given special consideration to the interpretation of the ideals which have colored and given direction to Mr. Hoover's life.

Believing further that a biography of a man should be centered around his most distinctive qualities and traits, I have stressed Mr. Hoover's spiritual, moral and intellectual qualities. After he and his record have been examined and analyzed, they stand out clear and unsullied.

My hope is that my interpretation and description of Mr. Hoover may give fresh hope and strength to those readers who, despite all of today's doubts and alarums, continue to hold fast to their belief that the glamourless and unexciting eternal verities alone hold the essence of man's wisdom, that they fix the course of his highest purpose.

There is considerable information and interpretation of Quaker principles, practices and methods throughout the book. The sources of my information about them comes in part from my being a birthright member of the Society of Friends, from my having attended a Quaker boarding school and a Quaker college and from a lifetime of activity in this religious movement of which I am a member.

The facts on which my presentation and interpretation of Mr. Hoover's record, purpose, character and ideals are based come from many sources. A portion of it is firsthand knowledge gained from a thirty-five year period of association and friendship; another portion comes from mutual friends who have long been associated with him and still another portion comes from top ranking officials in his administration who were my friends. All of this has been checked and rechecked with the printed record of his life, words and works as it appears in the publications listed in the bibliography at the end of the book.

In an effort to check against factual or interpretive errors, the following friends of mine have read the manuscript: Walter F. Brown, A. T. Burch, Perrin Galpin, Hugh Gibson, Ernest L. Klein, Bert Mattei, Jeremiah Milbank, Sidney A. Mitchell, William C. Mullendore, John Richardson, Edgar Rickard, Dr. O. Glenn Saxon, Arch Shaw and Lewis L. Strauss.

In addition Dr. Julius Klein read the Commerce Department Chapter, Dr. Clyde Fisher and Dr. Easton Rothwell read the chapter on the Hoover Institute and Library on War, Revolution and Peace and Charles B. Coates, Vice President of the Citizens Committee, read the Hoover Commission on Government Reorganization chapter.

I am grateful to them beyond measure for their invaluable help in checking errors as well as for their many suggestions. What I most appreciate is the great restraint each one exercised in not attempting to influence me to change the opinions about men and incidents that I have expressed.

Elsewhere in this book is a bibliography listing the source material used for this work. I am especially indebted to the following books and their authors: *Hoover and His Times* by Edwin Emerson, Garden City Publishing Company; *Herbert Hoover: A Reminiscent Biography* by Will Irwin, The Century Company; *The State Papers and Other Collected Writings of Herbert Hoover* by William Starr Myers, Doubleday Doran and Company. For permission to use copyright material, I am indebted to the following authors and publishers: *27 Masters of Politics* by Raymond Moley, copyright 1949, Funk & Wagnalls, New York; *Addresses Upon The American Road, 1933–1938* by Herbert Hoover, Charles Scribner's Sons, New York; *Addresses Upon The American Road, 1945–1948* by Herbert Hoover, D. Van Nostrand Company, Inc., 1949. The article "Let's Go Fishin'" by Herbert Hoover was first published by the Crowell-Collier Publishing Company, New York. The quotations from a series of articles by John T. Pace first appeared in the New York *Journal-American,* New York. I am also grateful for permission to use quotations from the columns of George Sokolsky, King Features Syndicate, and David Lawrence, formerly with the New York *Sun*.

The opinions herein are mine which I am entitled to hold and to express provided I do not unfairly injure others. This I have not done.

To those readers who disagree with my opinions about and estimate of Mr. Hoover, I reply with the words of an artist, who while painting my portrait was told by a mutual friend:

"But Mr. Hinshaw doesn't look like this."

The artist replied:

"That's the way he looks to me."

DAVID HINSHAW

Dunmow Farm
West Chester
Pennsylvania
December, 1949

CONTENTS

Hoover Reconsidered

The sharp contrast between public feeling about President Hoover near the end of his term and that in 1949 is reflected in the recent unprecedented action of the Congress of the United States which was chronicled for posterity and recorded on a large embossed scroll. It reads:

> Resolved by the Senate (the House concurring) that the Congress hereby extends to the Honorable Herbert Hoover . . . its cordial birthday greetings . . . and expresses admiration and gratitude for his devoted service to his country and to the world; and that the Congress expresses its hope that he be spared for many years of useful and honorable service.

The official greetings from the President and the Congress sent Mr. Hoover—enough to crown the career of any man—evidenced the present great warmth of feeling, respect and admiration for him on the part of a substantial cross section of the people of the nation and the world who found many ways to offer their tributes.

These widespread expressions of good will, admiration, appreciation and affection for Mr. Hoover were inspired by the approach of his seventy-fifth birthday on August 10, 1949.

Some of the expressions were contained in the many hundred radio comments about him. These praised him for his fine qualities and commended him for the multitude of varied contributions he has made to his country and to the world. Other expressions about him were printed in over six hundred syndicated and 1510 original newspaper editorials, Democratic and Republican alike, during the week of August 8, 1949. Still other expressions took the form of proclamations or public statements issued by a dozen governors, and others were in the formal greetings extended to him by more than a hundred foreign governments or organizations. Lastly, there were the expressions of affection and admiration in the letters which more than twenty-five thousand of his friends and admirers wrote to him.

His home town, Palo Alto, California, reciprocated this national good feeling toward its most distinguished son (following the example of a dozen or more great European cities) by making him an honorary citizen.

How vastly different all of this 1949 expression of public sentiment toward Mr. Hoover is from that of 1932 is emphasized by the following statement and an incident:

A handful of his old and more devoted friends, men and women whose belief in his integrity of action and purpose had never wavered and whose appreciation of his long years of selfless service had never dimmed, conceived the idea of getting up what they believed would be a smallish birthday party for him. They told him nothing of their plans other than to insist that he postpone a fishing trip in order that he might be present at Stanford University on August 10, prepared to deliver a speech on that date. He did not think much of the proposal but upon their insistence he agreed to do as they wished.

The project had neither committees nor chairmen. A few of his friends in different parts of the country undertook, mainly by letter, to enlist the co-operation of others of his friends and theirs. The idea caught on everywhere. Everyone who was told of it volunteered to co-operate fully in this effort to stimulate others to let Mr. Hoover know what they thought of him while he was still alive to hear it.

One man with the help of a secretary prepared the copy and sent it to the newspapers, magazines and radio stations. He has stated that never in a busy lifetime has he had part in any effort that had the self-starting qualities or the speed or strength this Hoover seventy-fifth birthday celebration idea possessed. It was so alive that it jumped if you touched it. Before any of us realized it the small friendly planned birthday celebration had, with startling speed and strength, snowballed itself into a great movement.

One of the most interesting phases of this undertaking was that the man for whom today's almost universal expression of good will and good wishes was expressed has not changed in character, purpose or ideals during the last seventeen years. He now believes just as passionately as he believed in 1932 in the essential goodness of people, in liberty and freedom; in democracy and in God's unfolding purpose for man. The expressions indicate that public sentiment has caught up with fairness and justice.

The Nation's Press Reappraises Mr. Hoover

There is inspired reading in the Hoover birthday editorial comment for every man and woman who believes that the eternal verities are of transcendent importance in the life of mankind.

They make refreshing reading, too, in this cynical age of doubt and discouragement, because they demonstrate what the most hard-boiled thinking group of men in the land selected and wrote about Mr. Hoover's high integrity and remarkable contributions with unqualified admiration.

This evidence from the nation's clearest thinkers proves that today's editor has not lost sight of man's higher purpose, has not been blinded by half-truths and opportunistic expediences. It gives strong indication that truth, fairness, integrity, selfless service and duty well done still count most with men even though they are not glamorous. But, if the editors are right in today's appraisal of Mr. Hoover, this much seems certain: he's the kind of man you will most need in such a crisis because you can depend upon him. And dependability is the cornerstone of our social structure.

From what the editors say you would find him resourceful, too, far more able than most men to appraise and realize upon your resourcefulness and companionship. At the same time you would find him a brilliant conversationalist and an entertaining companion.

Evaluating Editorial Opinion

I advance no theory that the editorials in the nation's newspapers contain the strained essence of the people's wisdom nor that they unerringly reflect the public thinking of the moment. On the other hand,

I hold a firm conviction, which rests on fifty years of observation and experience, that newspaper editorial writers are the best informed, clearest thinking and most broad-minded men in the communities where they live and work. Because they are human they occasionally make mistakes. Sometimes they are uncertain about what is truth, just as men everywhere have been—even long before the day when Pontius Pilate posed that question. Even so, there is no other barometer in the land which records public thinking, purpose and ideals with anything like the fidelity and the accuracy of the editorials which appear in the nation's newspapers.

It follows, therefore, that the margin of possible error in interpreting public sentiment would be reduced almost to nothing provided (a) the editorials treat the same subject, (b) they are published simultaneously in more than twenty-one hundred newspapers and (c) the papers represent all shades of social, economic and political opinion.

If my estimate of newspaper editorial writers is accurate, then the nation's estimate of Mr. Hoover as gauged by the newspaper editorial columns from one end of the country to the other on or about August 10, 1949, may be summarized as follows:

> Mr. Hoover is a great statesman. His sterling qualities of character and marked abilities experienced an eclipse for a number of years as the result of a malign partisan smear campaign which made him the scapegoat of a cosmic, social, political and economic cataclysm.
>
> He is a man of highest personal and public integrity who possesses admirable moral and spiritual qualities.
>
> He has been a selfless public servant who has rendered distinguished service to the people of the United States and the world.
>
> His patriotism is above question. His love of America and his undeviating adherence to the highest purposes of the American tradition and way of life are inspiring.
>
> His lack of political experience and his refusal to employ demagogic arts caused the public to mistake integrity and rectitude for covert disloyalty or indifference to the people's distress.
>
> Proof of his admirable qualities of character may be found in his not having been embittered by the public doubt of his high purpose and expressed disfavor of him.

The people, rather than Mr. Hoover, are to be commended for today's high public estimate of him and his record, because the sweeping change in the past years of their appraisal of him proves that the judgment of all the people, once they have the facts, may be relied upon implicitly. This augurs well for the continued existence of democracy. It is commendable because it demonstrates conclusively that the people are good sportsmen in that they are fair.

The astonishing, almost unbelievable, aspect of the more than twenty-one hundred Hoover birthday editorials at hand is the near unanimity of the writers in their expressions of favorable opinions of Mr. Hoover. There were a few writers, perhaps twenty-five or so, who clung to their earlier beliefs. This was to be expected because nowhere, not even in heaven, if we accept the story of Lucifer as true, is unanimity possible. When Lucifer found the perfection of heaven boring he left it for a hot spot where he could devote his time to fomenting discord and playing hell generally. From Lucifer's time down to this day every man of woman born is occasionally troubled by the urge that bothered Lucifer. And when so troubled he gives it free expression.

One writer continues to dislike Mr. Hoover's "high collars and his chins." I understand how he feels because I occasionally pass total strangers whose dress or looks make me want to give them a swift kick. I refrain from doing so largely, perhaps, because of the fear of what might happen to me if the habit were to be adopted generally.

A few editors grumbled over their interpretation of the way Mr. Hoover handled the prohibition question. Another one put a black mark after Mr. Hoover's name because of the allegation that Mr. Hoover once had said "prosperity is just around the corner." This complaint is absurd since Mr. Hoover never, in private or in public, made that statement.

Editorial Birthday Greetings

The expression of editorial opinion in connection with Mr. Hoover's birthday was generous in both coverage and content. From the deep South the Birmingham, Alabama, *Age-Herald* said, "The nation might well honor this man." The Huntsville, Alabama, *Times* in saying "the tribute is being paid him from many sources" added that it "befits one who has lived a long life of service in many capacities for the good of the nation and the world."

It was the belief of the Augusta, Georgia, *Chronicle* that "people are just beginning to recognize the solid virtues of this man who is so typically American."

A similar note was sounded in other sections. "For the refreshment of its own soul, the nation can well afford to pause today to pay tribute to Herbert Hoover on his seventy-fifth birthday anniversary," said the Elkhart, Indiana, *Truth*. The El Paso, Texas, *Times* stated that "Mr. Hoover once again stands in high regard. We hope he so continues for many more happy birthdays." The Harrisburg, Pennsylvania, *News* spoke for industrial Pennsylvania and said, "All in all, the world and the United States are the better for Herbert Hoover's seventy-five years of useful living. Not only he but his times may be felicitated on his birthday."

From the Northeast came the words of the Portland, Maine, *Press-Herald,* "His name will endure as a man who served American democracy with ability and unflinching faith." The Salt Lake City, Utah, *Deseret News* sounded the keynote of the hour with, "And so —to a man whose flair has been not for showmanship and propaganda, but for work and sound public service—we are happy to say: Many Happy Returns of This Day."

One of the striking things disclosed in reviewing the Hoover birthday editorials is the way great numbers of editors went beyond comment on this occasion and directed attention to various phases of his career. There was comment on Herbert Hoover the statesman, the justice of his new popular acclaim and reasons for this changed public attitude, as well as comment on him as a politician and upon his selfless service.

Citing that "judgment of him already has softened since he left offices," the Gonzales, Texas, *Inquirer* took up a point which the Grand Rapids, Michigan, *Press* emphasized by stating that "Only a few unregenerate diehards are left to disagree with the bipartisan expression of Congress, which honored Mr. Hoover's anniversary by voicing its admiration and gratitude for his devoted service to his country and the world."

The Louisville, Kentucky, *Courier-Journal,* long noteworthy for its able editorial expression, commented, "Too seldom in this troubled and imperfect world does the right prevail or do we live to see justice done. . . . Unscathed, he has survived a prolonged attack of almost incredible scurrility . . . at last right has prevailed. It was long overdue."

Probing into the cause of the changed public attitude toward Mr. Hoover, the Columbus, Ohio, *Dispatch* concludes, "He has lived down as though they never had touched him the lies, the misrepresentations, the gossip, the libels and the slanders that were manufactured against him for selfish political ends. Through it all he kept, as even now he keeps, his serenity, his faith in the everlasting righteousness of justice and fair play."

As might be expected there was general mention of Mr. Hoover's political qualities. The Dallas, Texas, *News* said, "He was hurt, close associates say. Politically, the naive, the frank, the honest Quaker boy cannot understand how some will do anything in first ward fashion to get elected, then turn around and caress and applaud the attacked. In the Hoover rules, you don't pole-ax a man one month and halo him the next." On this point, the Jacksonville, Florida, *Journal* pointed out that "although he is strictly not a politician, Herbert Hoover is a splendid American."

On two points all editors were in close accord. One is the selfless service of Herbert Hoover to his country and the world and his matchless integrity. The Denver, Colorado, *Post,* one of the first newspapers to urge appropriate observance of the Hoover anniversary, said that "Both as a statesman and as a man he has earned this regard by unselfish public service and impeccable conduct. He enjoys the admiration and respect now of many people who once hated and abused him." The Hartford, Connecticut, *Courant* pointed out that he "has always been what he is today, a fine unselfish public citizen, devoted to the welfare of his country and the world."

The Lewiston, Idaho, *Tribune* hit the nail squarely on the head in these words: "A practising Quaker, he follows the tenets of that faith in his everyday living." Equally direct is the Faribault, Minnesota, *News* in commenting that "more than any other man of his generation, probably, Mr. Hoover has expressed and exemplified the high ideals of the American spirit."

The editorial opinion, as well as comment and direct tributes, could be summarized in the editorial words of *Collier's Weekly,* "We are happy that Mr. Hoover's deserved reward of public esteem has come to him in his lifetime. We salute him on his birthday as a wise statesman, a steadfast guardian of America's great traditions, and a cheerful believer in a future based on these traditions."

The continuity of this objective appraisal of Herbert Hoover is far too long to permit the presentation of it here, or even of excerpts from many of the finer editorials about him. They run the gamut of his words, deeds and actions, discuss his strengths and his weaknesses, his successes and his failures, his ideals and faith, his character and selfless service, his integrity and his solid Americanism. Their significance in the ever unfolding drama of public opinion prompts me to present portions of many of them in Appendix I.

PART ONE

HOOVER'S BACKGROUND AND TRAINING

CHAPTER ONE

Some Close-ups of Herbert Hoover

Jesse and Huldah Hoover, Herbert Hoover's parents, lived in a one-story cottage across an alley from his father's blacksmith shop and agriculture machine agency in West Branch, Iowa.

According to a letter written by an aunt of the future President, "early on the morning of August 10, 1874, Jesse came and tapped on my window and said, 'Well we have another General Grant at our house. Huldah would like to see thee.'"

One of Mr. Hoover's memories of his early years concerns an experiment with boiling tar. What he did might be interpreted as indicative of a scientific turn of mind; actually it likely was nothing more than an expression of insatiable boyish curiosity. He has told that as he watched the bubbles rise on the smelly, thick tar in a kettle back of his father's blacksmith shop, he started wondering whether or not it would burn. He speculated about its ability to put out fire. But the boyish mind refused to guess, since the answers could be learned by lighting a stick in a fire and putting it in the boiling kettle of tar. He got his answer instantly. The flash-fire he started was checked only by the strenuous efforts of his father and the village fire department.

The dramatic and quick answer to his question combined with a severe parental lecture and an old-fashioned spanking fixed this experience firmly in his memory.

Jesse Hoover died of typhoid fever when his son Herbert was six years old. Previous to his father's death, and until the death of his mother when he was nine-and-one-half years old, he lived the life of simple joys and wholesome activities that are the experience of small Quaker boys in a Quaker community.

His first teacher remembers him as a plump, "sweet little boy" who learned quickly and never made any trouble in school but whose greatest interest seemed to be in getting outdoors to play.

In 1927 Mr. Hoover told the Iowa Society in Washington about the old swimming hole under the railroad bridge "which needs to be deepened" because it was "hard to keep from pounding the mud with your hands and feet when you shove off for the thirty feet of a cross-channel swim." He spoke of the "cracker-boxes, triggered with a figure-four, set in the woods to catch rabbits." He and his little friends fished in the creek for "sunfish, suckers and catfish with a willow pole, a line of butcher's string, a cork salvaged from a rubbish heap, an angleworm and a one-cent hook." In the wintertime there was "sliding down Cook's Hill in a home-made sled and thawing out your chilblains with ice-water."

In season there were tasty wild strawberries and wild grapes to be had for the picking; the boy's inevitable collection of birds' eggs; skating in winter over the frozen swimming hole on a pair of heel plate skates, the usual boy circus and what might have been the incipient mining engineer (or natural boy interest) in the collection of fragments of coral, agate or other bright-colored stones from the ballast along the railroad tracks.

One summer the three little Hoover children had a storybook experience when an uncle, the Indian government agent at Pawhuska, Oklahoma, on the Osage Indian reservation, and his wife had them for several months' visit. Their only companions were Indian children. All summer long they hunted and fished, made camp fires and cooked what they caught, if anything; made bows and arrows and generally lived the kind of life every boy longs to live. This experience left its ineradicable marks on him in the form of a love of the outdoors and the smell of campfire smoke, that perfume which cleanses the soul, and spreads the kind of peace which only communion with nature can give to a man's spirits.

In West Branch he and his companions celebrated each Fourth of July with firecrackers bought with money received from old iron they collected.

Apart from these outdoor pastimes and school attendance there was the gentle, tender, home life, with its family Bible-reading at the day's close; when the majesty of the stories of noble men lifted up his eyes and the quiet period of silent worship before the family said "farewells" at parting for the night.

There was, too, the silent grace before meals, a Quaker custom patterned after their silent worship where each member is responsible for the conduct of his own religious exercise. There is a question, of course, of whether or not the little boy understood the meaning of this silent grace any better than did the little Quaker girl in the apocryphal story. She, after listening to the spoken grace by the Baptist minister-father of her companion asked, "What was your father saying?" Her friend answered, "He was thanking the Lord for the food." To which the little Quaker maid replied, "We never do that at home." When asked what her family did, the little Quakeress answered, "We just stick our noses down and smell our plates."

It is possible also that the little boy Herbert did not catch the deeper significance and meaning of the Quaker silent worship custom in the Fifth Day (Thursday) and First Day (Sunday) meetings, as he strove to sit without squirming, after the manner of small Quaker boys since the movement began. But regardless of how little or how much he understood of the meaning of these customs, he did catch an understanding of and a liking for the quietude and for the unity and harmony of family and community living that they helped to beget, as well as for the kindness, patience and tolerance, the peace and the affection that they engendered.

In February, 1884, six months before his tenth birthday, his gentle Quaker preacher-mother died of pneumonia. From her he gained much of his idealism and his faith; from his father comes the source of his love of his fellow man, his sense of humor and his interest in mechanics.

A New Life Begins

Following the death of Huldah Hoover the relatives met in family council and decided to give each of the children a home. Herbert went to live with his uncle Allan Hoover on a nearby farm. He remained there until he was eleven years old, doing farm work in the summer, going to school in winter and performing chores the year round.

A marked Quaker characteristic is an interest in education. This has been made manifest in many ways. Ezra Cornell, the founder of the university that bears his name, was a Quaker. So was Johns Hopkins, and the Brown family of Providence, founders, respectively, of the universities which bear their names. Dr. Taylor, a Quaker, provided more than a million dollars for the founding of Bryn Mawr College. Today ten colleges or universities and more than a score of secondary schools are under Quaker direction. These include: Earlham College, Richmond, Indiana; Friends Central College, Central City, Nebraska; Friends University, Wichita, Kansas; Guilford College, Guilford, N. C.; Haverford College, Haverford, Penna.; Pacific College, Newberg, Oregon; Wm. Penn College, Oskaloosa, Iowa; Swarthmore College, Swarthmore, Penna.; Whittier College, Whittier, Calif.; and Wilmington College, Wilmington, Ohio.

Because he held this characteristic interest in education, one of Herbert Hoover's uncles, a brother of his mother, Dr. John Minthorn, founded a Quaker academy at Newberg, Oregon (now Pacific College). Dr. Minthorn offered to make a home for his nephew and at the same time provide him with better educational advantages than were offered by the rural schools in Iowa. Here, until he entered Stanford University six years later, he fed his doctor-uncle's horses, milked the cows and made himself useful about the place between school hours.

When asked years later what his favorite subject was in school, he replied, "None. They were something to race through so that I could get out of doors."

A Momentous Decision

Dr. Minthorn moved to Salem, Oregon, to open a land office in that city and took his nephew along to serve as office boy when he was fourteen years old. The fact that the land company had mining as well as farm land interests is responsible for Herbert Hoover's career as a mining engineer. Up until the time he met one of the company's mining consultants he had drifted along—now he had his goal. It was that of a mining engineer. To realize it, he selected the newly opened Stanford University as his alma mater.

The fact that his preparatory school work was inadequate—he had only a smattering of Latin, some mathematics and too little work in other subjects—was not an entrance deterrent in the new university, which he entered in the fall of 1891, two months after his seventeenth birthday. Upon arrival there he deposited in a bank his entire fortune of $300.

Fate Steps In

His training in his uncle's office stood him in good stead in that it enabled him to serve as secretary for the great Branner, head of Stanford's geology department. Even better than giving Hoover some income, this relationship brought him closer to the man who helped most to equip him for his life work.

According to Will Irwin* one of Branner's former students in later years asked the great teacher, "What first attracted your special attention to Hoover?"

Branner replied, "A bit of laboratory routine. I'd always employed the working students of my classes as assistants or secretaries. Constantly we received geological survey reports and German scientific periodicals. These, as they accumulated, had to be bound. I'd hand them over to the ordinary assistant and he'd ask, 'How and where?' Send them to a binder in the city I'd say and he'd ask, 'How shall I pack them?' and so on. But with Hoover I'd say get these periodicals bound and the next time I'd notice them they'd be back on the shelves and the bill for binding and shipping would be on my desk."

Fate Enters Again

It was Branner, too, who was responsible, unwittingly in this instance, in helping Hoover to reach the most important decision any man faces in life: that of finding the one woman of all women for his wife.

---

* Will Irwin, *Herbert Hoover, A Reminiscent Biography,* The Century Company, N.Y.

One of Branner's practices was to give a series of university extension lectures at high schools. One year he delivered them at nearby Monterey's high school. A senior, a girl named Lou Henry, was so fascinated by Branner's accounts of the mysteries of the earth that she decided she wanted to enter Stanford University and study under him.

Her parents agreed and she entered Stanford as a freshman in the fall of 1894—Hoover's senior year. She heard from every side accounts of this brilliant student, Hoover. It was Hoover this and Hoover that everywhere. One day Dr. Branner was telling her about some new specimens in a cabinet. "Hoover brought them in from the field," he said. "They've been called carboniferous but I'll eat my hat if they aren't pre-carboniferous. Isn't that your opinion, Hoover?" Miss Henry looked up and saw a lean, immature-looking boy, the great Hoover who should have been a giant according to the legends she had heard. For himself Hoover was even less articulate than usual. Branner soon withdrew but before the young couple parted Hoover had asked permission to call on her the following Friday night and thereafter their fates were fixed.

Here I interrupt the narration to round out the picture of how Mr. Hoover in action met a variety of situations which confronted him through the years. I'll return to the chronological story of his life in later chapters.

A Broken Locomotive

Once, in China, while enroute from Chang Wan Tow harbor to Tong Shang, Hoover was granted permission by an Indian service colonel to ride with the Hindu troops on a British military train. When the wheezy locomotive gave up, Hoover, after finding the Hindu engineer making no move to repair it, diagnosed the trouble and had begun to make repairs with a mechanic's hammer when the colonel appeared and started giving orders. After ignoring the first orders Hoover finally turned to the colonel and said, "Brother, I'm the only person present who can get you out of this fix. Any more of your lip and I'll leave you where you are."

Later, when the engine was unable to pull the heavy train up a grade, the colonel sent word to Hoover by messenger to make more repairs. He went to the engine, uncoupled it from the train, sent word to the colonel that he'd gone in search of help and rode on to his destination in it, Tong Shang, more than one hundred miles distant, where he notified the British military authorities of the hitch in troop movements.

Maintaining His Integrity

One significant episode in Mr. Hoover's life was the position he took in regard to the defalcation of a subordinate in the firm that he had recently joined. This subordinate, by dishonest manipulation of an issue of capital stock of one of the most successful mines the firm managed, had jeopardized the firm's standing. Technically, because this fraud had taken place shortly after he joined the firm, Mr. Hoover's moral and legal liability was fixed at $50,000. He refused, however, to stand on this technicality for the reason, he said, that the firm's honor was his personal honor. Accordingly, he insisted upon paying the full quota of a full partner, or $500,000. This nearly strapped him and he began anew to acquire a competence, for he had to rake and scrape to raise the money to meet this self-imposed half-million assessment. The details of this incident are given in Appendix II.

A 1905 Impression of Mr. Hoover

Mrs. Fred A. Wickett of Palo Alto, California, with her parents, went to Sydney, Australia, in 1905. During the three-week boat trip she had often noticed a quiet young mining engineer, with whom her father had held many lengthy conversations.

Near the end of the trip her father said to her, "Daughter, you have had a pleasant journey and made many friends. In the years to come you may forget their names—but there is one name you must never forget.

"I'll tell you why I like him and have been so impressed with him. It is because I never have met anyone who has such a burning patriotism and love for his country—or any man who has so excellent a mind. More than either of these qualities he has an inner integrity that is sound and real. The country is going to need a man like that and you'll hear about him some day."

Years later at a dinner in San Francisco which was given in honor of Mr. Hoover in commemoration of his Belgian Relief work, her husband, when they were introduced to Mr. Hoover asked, "Do you remember a man named Smith on the *S. S. Ventura* in '05?"

Mr. Hoover instantly replied, "Yes, indeed I do remember Gilbert A. Smith. Does he still carry two watches?"

Hoover's Americanism to the Fore

Mr. Hoover experienced a great lift of spirit when he was able to return to his home land and his own people—to work side by side with them in 1914 at the outbreak of World War I. Walter H. Page, America's Ambassador to England at that time, in a letter published in the New York *Herald Tribune* in October, 1925, gave an oblique glance at the quality and depth of Mr. Hoover's longing for America.

Ambassador Page first stated that Mr. Hoover had been approached by officials of the British government with the suggestion that, if he would become a British subject, the government would be pleased to give him an important executive post and added the hint that if he succeeded in his task a title might await him.

According to Ambassador Page, Mr. Hoover's answer was, "I'll do what I can for you with pleasure; but I'll be damned if I'll give up my American citizenship—not on your life!"

Relief Without Ideology

Mr. Hoover, preparatory to making a public appeal for support of his Russian relief program, called a conference of representatives of many social agencies in Washington. During the discussion one woman expressed her doubts about the wisdom of the project by asking, "Mr. Secretary, aren't we going to help Bolshevism by feeding these people?"

Mr. Hoover banged his gavel angrily and replied, "Twenty million people are starving. Whatever their politics, they shall be fed."

Science and Economics

Early in the year 1920 Mr. Hoover secured funds from private sources with which to finance a study he wanted made of American industrial wastes and how to eliminate them. He took this step before he knew who would be nominated or elected President and long before he could even have guessed that he would become the next Secretary of Commerce.

The following reasons may have had some part in influencing his action: (a) He was a student of history and knew that there would be an upsurge of manufacturing activity following the war; (b) He was a well-informed man about European conditions and felt certain European competition for American products in foreign markets would put us at a disadvantage if our present wastes were continued; and (c) he was an engineer and he loathed slipshod methods.

Perhaps the major influence which prompted him came from his yearning to help improve the lot of the people of America—all of the people. He believed to a certainty that the high standards of living which the American people enjoyed came from the steadily mounting per capita productivity. These standards, he insisted, could be advanced only by improving manufacturing processes and methods and by eliminating waste in materials through standardization of products. He sought also to find ways to reduce waste in our distribution system. This was the efficiency engineer speaking but that the promptings for it came from his moral and spiritual purpose is indicated by his statement that:

> The moral and intellectual progress of the Nation is not the offspring of poverty or low living standards. The incentives to crime decrease with increasing security; the opportunity for education and the growth of understanding are the products of economic progress—not of economic degeneration. Devotion to economic improvement whether in individual effort or in improved methods enlarges the field of leadership; it is not a stimulant of idle or luxurious living. (See Appendix III.)

Holding these convictions he sought to further them by enlisting fifty distinguished engineers, economists and other specialists to make the study. It was completed by the time he became Secretary of Commerce. Its findings and recommendations charted Hoover's course of action. The report estimated that about 30 per cent of American industrial effort was wasted and that without hampering competition or injecting government interference, American industry, by full coordination, could save thirty billion dollars per year.

The Nature of Hoover's "Small Talk"

A pleasant illustration of the kind of small talk Mr. Hoover goes in for occurred early in 1933 when my family and I were White House guests. Following the Sunday dinner the President, myself, and two other male guests, joined by my fifteen-year-old son Robert, retired to the Lincoln study for coffee and cigars.

Instead of joining in conversation with his grown guests the tired and harassed President turned to the fifteen-year-old boy and said to him in substance:

> This is the room, son, where President Lincoln held his cabinet meetings. If you will look carefully up there at that etching of Carpentar's painting of the Lincoln cabinet you will recognize these chairs and that table.
>
> When we came to the White House four years ago we discovered only one of these chairs. Mrs. Hoover found most of the others stored away in the attic upstairs and we had them upholstered. The table had disappeared. We finally found it in the Historical Society's headquarters in Hartford, Connecticut. Nobody knows how it got there. But they sent it back when we asked for it.
>
> The British Army took that mirror over there when it sacked Washington in the War of 1812 and kept it until forty or so years ago. Choate, our Ambassador to England, induced them to return it.
>
> That painting by an obscure Scotch painter, and not a very good one at that, represents America's first official interest in the fine arts. Someone had an idea that there should be some paintings in the White House. Congress fell in with the suggestion and appropriated a few thousand dollars for its purchase.
>
> Now if you will look at the Carpentar etching again you will see that Secretary Seward in the foreground is wearing white trousers.

But if you will go up to the Capitol and look at the original painting you'll find that Seward's trousers are black.

What happened was that Seward's son protested when he saw the white trousers on his father, which Carpentar had painted on him to lighten the picture's foreground. Seward's son insisted, since his father never had worn white trousers in his life, that the painting was inaccurate. But before he had made his protest the plate for the etching had been made. That's the reason why all of the prints of Carpentar's painting of Lincoln's cabinet show Seward wearing white trousers and the original which Carpentar changed after the son's protest has him wearing black trousers.

This account of how an exhausted and troubled President of the United States extended himself to entertain a fifteen-year-old boy shows another facet of the Hoover character. Even his small talk has a purpose and he illuminates it with such an array of fact and interpretation as to make it fascinating and important.

Because he knows so much about so many things I have often felt that he must be a terribly lonely man. Since there are so few people who know enough to make interesting companions for him it has often seemed to me that, except for the saving grace of his warm humanity, he would find most people boring.

Hoover at Close Range

Lord Curzon once remarked that, "Mr. Hoover is the bluntest man in Europe." This quality rests on his habit of brushing aside the little amenities and getting down to the business in hand immediately. He possesses Benjamin Franklin's simplicity and directness but lacks Franklin's suavity of manner. He is without affectation and is wholly unself-conscious. Many people mistake his modesty for shyness. He always refuses to take credit to himself for the things he accomplishes.

He is typically American in appearance; full faced, clean shaven, gentle, with kindly eyes that smile with the mouth and the wrinkles of his face. These with chuckles—I never have heard him laugh aloud—frequently mark a conversation with him. His voice is low and has little inflection. He is of medium height, a stoutish man whose dress never varies except as to color, and that usually concerns its shade of brown or blue. He notifies his tailor to send him another suit, and except on infrequent occasions never stops in for a fitting.

One of Mr. Hoover's most remarkable qualities is his flexibility of mind and his avoidance of getting into mental ruts. His experience has been so varied, his curiosity so insatiable, and his observation so accurate as to make him feel sure of himself when he tackles any problem.

In later chapters I refer to his quality of Quaker stubbornness. He has that, as well as many other Quaker qualities. It should be made clear here, however, that his stubborn quality is really akin to tenacity. He clings tenaciously to his beliefs and convictions, but he is not obstinate.

Circumstance has favored him in that he was born, as Thoreau said of himself, in the nick of time. Great occasions make great men if the human material exists.

Mr. Hoover's Two Dominant Qualities Are Americanism and Quakerism

Mr. Hoover's abiding faith in Americanism and his pride in his country's accomplishments prompted members of the mining fraternity to nickname him Hail Columbia Hoover. Because his Quaker training and humanitarian instincts made him one of those men "to whom the miseries of the world are miseries and will not let them rest," he has devoted his life to selfless service.

How He Works

One of Mr. Hoover's Belgian Relief Commission's associates, Robinson Smith, in an unpublished article written twenty years ago, said that one of the most striking features about that undertaking was that Mr. Hoover at the very start should have hit upon "the leading ideas that controlled its development to the end."

Mr. Smith, in describing the Commission's operating headquarters in London, stated that it consisted of "but six departments, and some of them consisted of one man, its head. Reports and dietetics consisted of one man, who consulted with himself, instead of as between departments. If you had cause to be seen, you were seen and usually at once. . . . No time was wasted by regular daily meetings of the departmental heads. They talked things over at lunch which was served in the office, or if a matter arose that asked for immediate decision from another department, that decision was obtained then and there. It did not wait over until next day. If an important memorandum was being prepared, all departments were consulted, but though Mr. Hoover had a strong committee to back him, he assembled them but twice."

According to Mr. Smith, Mr. Hoover was "a man of many memoranda, since again and again he was forced to urge upon the urgency of the work, which, as prices rose and shipping became scarce, was more and more jeopardized. He was also forced to keep asking for guarantees from the Germans. These memoranda of his are models of lucid exposition. They keep to the point, yet view it from every possible angle, forestalling the criticism to which he knew they would be subjected."

As a usual thing Mr. Hoover dictates his memoranda, walking with his hands jingling coins in his pockets and with concentration written on his face. When the typed drafts are ready he works them over most carefully, filling the pages with interlineations and marginal comments, revising and eliminating with great care. Because he refuses to be satisfied until he has introduced every argument and covered all points, he frequently works over a draft two or more times.

The Intellectual Hoover

During the busy years between the time the Hoovers went to China in 1899 and 1914, when they visited and revisited all continents except South America and Mr. Hoover managed a variety of great enterprises, he and Mrs. Hoover found an outlet for their intellectual energies in an unusual undertaking.

A paper read at a scientific conference aroused Mr. Hoover's interest in Georgius Agricola, a contemporary of Martin Luther, who in 1550 completed his exhaustive treatise "De re Metallica" on mining and smelting. Agricola's treatise was the first word on the subject since the Roman period. But its significance was hidden from the modern members of the mining profession because it was written in Low Latin and also because the technology of the Middle Ages is lost, and therefore the terms Agricola used had little modern meaning.

Mrs. Hoover, an excellent Latin student, undertook the translation part of the project and her husband set up a small chemical laboratory in their various homes scattered over the earth and carried on his "scientific detective work." By constantly comparing their two efforts they were able, after five years of absorbing work, to translate into modern terms all except two or three of Agricola's more involved passages.

They published their translation of the book in 1912 for private circulation among their friends. I am the happy owner of an inscribed copy which in form and appearance, even including wood cuts, is a replica of Agricola's large, vellum-bound original. Today this remarkable book has become an important and valuable collector's item.

Walter Brown once told me of a Sunday picnic party he had enjoyed with the Hoovers in the early 1920's. The two Hoover sons were youngsters then and they and several of their friends went along. The picnic grounds were a woods with a clear brook running through it. While lunch arrangements were being made Hoover and the youngsters were carefully examining the stream for the purpose of finding the best spot for the location of a hydraulic dam.

As soon as the food was eaten the Secretary of Commerce and his young friends took off their shoes, rolled up their trousers and began to roll or carry boulders to the dam site and to put them in place. Hoover helped in all of this and at the same time instructed them in the principles of the undertaking and showed them how the silt the stream carried would seal the dam. The boys gained useful knowledge and a sense of accomplishment from their experience as well as outdoor exercise which undoubtedly was as satisfactory as would have been aimless chasing about the woods or throwing stones at birds. And without being so told they may have caught some understanding of how to give useful purpose to time spent at play.

Helping a Child Dissipate Doubts

Once, after President Hoover's friends the Perrin Galpins had visited the White House, little Stephen Galpin, about eleven years old, told some of his playmates about his wonderful experience. After the skeptical manner of boys, they demanded details to support his claim. "What did you have to eat?" one of them asked. Stephen said, "Spinach and—" but his further account was lost in a ribald chorus of "Yah! Yah! Spinach at the White House! Spinach at the White House!"

When the President learned of his little friend's problem he wrote him the following letter:

February 2, 1933

My Dear Stephen:

This is to certify that you lunched at the White House with me. I have never been strong for spinach myself, and I had meant to tell you that you didn't have to eat it.

In order to make sure that you remember that you were at the White House I am sending you herewith a button which you are entitled to wear as proof thereof.

Yours faithfully,
(signed) HERBERT HOOVER

(Washington Bicentennial Button enclosed.)

How Hoover Spends Idle Moments

According to O. Glenn Saxon of Yale University, who was Mr. Hoover's fishing companion in the Northwest during the summer of 1937, they would drive to some predetermined town when the day's fishing was done. There they would spend the night at a wayside cabin, hotel or at the home of a friend.

Almost every evening, Dr. Saxon relates, local residents, working men and women, garage mechanics, small business men, miners, store owners, clerks and farmers gathered around and discussed the state of the nation or community, economics and politics until midnight or after.

"Mostly it was questions and answers," Dr. Saxon reports, with Mr.

Hoover "talking as one of them without bitterness or political bias, quietly explaining, analyzing and illustrating his points by simple examples, and yet never talking down to them."

Sagas of enduring nature were written in long ago days about great leaders who did this same kind of thing.

CHAPTER TWO

To Him Who Endureth Much is Given the Victory

The phenomenon of the sweeping change in the public's attitude toward Herbert Hoover from the low of the early 1930's to the high of today is not surprising to those familiar with the fickleness of public sentiment. This alternate blowing hot and cold about their leaders by the masses of men is as old as the human race. It likely will not end until men in the mass reach intellectual and spiritual maturity.

Every generation has seen similar shifts of public opinion. My generation saw the public sweep the inspiring and incomparable Theodore Roosevelt forward on high waves of approval, only to plummet him to the bottom of the troughs of disapproval, and then, during his last years, to sweep him again to the crest of the waves with many expressions of admiration and affection. An earlier generation saw masses of men revile the immortal Abraham Lincoln, and then, as hate and prejudice consumed themselves and were replaced by a better understanding of Lincoln's purpose and methods, saw our generation place him on the pedestal which is reserved for only the authentic great of the world. Today men in the mass have measured Mr. Hoover with the spiritual and moral yardsticks of integrity, selfless service, adherence to high principle and unblemished character and have decided that Mr. Hoover is a great and good man. Although he is the same man, they again are seeking his leadership. They have come back to him. He has not come back. He could not because he never went away. It has ever been thus with leaders whose lives are in tune with the eternal verities. It likely will long be thus.

Shifts Puzzle Pessimists

Pessimists who find it difficult to see beyond the ends of their noses are frequently disturbed by such shifts of public opinion. Things, they say, are bad, hence undoubtedly will become worse. Their premise seems unassailable except to the optimist who, to an extent, has what Carlyle calls the time-sense of a geologist and whose creed rests on the indefinable belief that life is worthwhile and that man's visions are God's reality.

The optimist's faith is supported by the historical fact that a return to public favor is reserved solely for those leaders who made honest, courageous and uncompromising records and who served usefully and with high purpose. Further support for their faith is found in the historical fact that the demagogue—whose stock in trade is expediency, whose programs sway with the winds of popular demands and whose easy virtues permit him to compromise principle—regardless of how great his personal popularity may once have been, is never able to regain it once he has lost it. And that, to the optimist, is as it should be.

Some Reasons Why Men Turn Against Their Leaders

A variety of causes and reasons can and do change the public attitude toward a great leader. Sometimes changes come because men are inclined to tire of being good. Usually, however, men in the mass turn against a trustworthy leader only when they are in distress. This happens partly because prejudice and hate are natural first expressions of troubled men whether their troubles are caused by man or by the blind forces of nature. Hungry men think only of their immediate need. Insecure men may trade anything, even their freedom, for seeming security.

Because, in their present stage of spiritual and intellectual immaturity, men in the mass are so constituted that they must personify their causes and principles, so must they also personify their hates. Since it is difficult for them to hate either their own mistakes or the blind forces of nature they look for a scapegoat when they are in trouble.

Even his partisan opponents, who nineteen years ago fabricated and advertised the charge that Mr. Hoover was responsible for the world-wide chaos, misery and speculation which engulfed every nation following World War I, today admit the untruth of their charge. But in 1930 they educated the country to believe that he was the sole cause of their misery. Will Rogers' quip during the depression about the man who, when he found a worm in an apple from which he had taken a bite said, "Damn Hoover," helps to recall how the public generally blamed the President for their misfortunes.

My friend, the late Arthur Guiterman, wrote and sent me the following lines in the late months of 1930, after an evening's visit during which we had discussed the general public's alarming tendency to act upon the opposition's suggestion that it blame President Hoover for everything and anything that went wrong:

If Wall Street grabbed your final cent,
That's right, impeach the President.
If Europe seethes with discontent,
Denounce the cause—our President.
If China lacks a government,
Reprove our laggard President.
If what you loaned is keeping lent,
Charge that against the President.
If industry seems hellward bent,
One can't forgive the President.
You don't see where your money went?
Investigate the President.
If all you had is rashly spent,
You'd best accuse the President.
If malefactors won't repent,
Inveigh against the President.
If all the world is indigent,
Who made it so? Our President;
For droughts and wars are consequent
On blunders by the President.
So give your feelings proper vent
By growling at the President.
It helps us all and pays the rent
To sit and blame the President.

The "Hoover Depression" Myth

Many factors contributed to the defeat of President Hoover in 1932. First and foremost of these was the world depression which destroyed governments, social, political and economic systems and created chaos all over the earth. Another was his inability to dramatize and present, in a way the public could understand and believe, his sound and comprehensive relief and recovery programs. The influence of his Quaker inheritance was responsible for this quality. Another potent factor in the situation which made him trouble was the prohibition question.

A real factor which contributed to President Hoover's political defeat was the wholly discreditable but ably conducted efforts of his political opponents to discredit him by convincing the public that he was solely responsible for their economic troubles. Because the public's troubles were personal and real and because men in distress always look for someone to blame, the people were ready to believe that their troubles were caused by Hoover instead of world-wide social, economic and political chaos.

It is understandable why the Democratic party created and spread the myth of the Hoover-caused depression. The Republican party's orators and press department for years had been claiming credit for the prosperous periods. In the minds of the Democrats there was some cosmic justice in placing on the Republicans the blame for the depression. They were right in the main, but it was hard on Hoover.

The real reason, however, for the initiation of the Democratic party's smear-Hoover campaign was that it wanted to elect its presidential candidate in 1932. So its leaders set to with a will to destroy the Republican party's front man.

The Communists joyously joined forces with the Democrats and introduced their techniques which dragged to a new low level the political attack methods in this country.

Any reader who questions the Communist support of and effective participation in the Democratic party's smear-Hoover campaign is referred to *The Whole of Their Lives* by Benjamin Gitlow, at that time head of the Communist party in the United States. Following his expulsion by Stalin, Mr. Gitlow wrote his book which *tells all* concerning the Communist party's machinations in the United States. Charles Scribner's Sons published it in 1948.

Refused to Deal in Nostrums

Another factor which contributed to President Hoover's unpopularity was that distressed and troubled men and women demanded that their government create a magic formula which would solve their problems. He knew this to be impossible. And believing that it was his duty to help people solve their economic problems he challenged their wishful thinking by counseling patience, co-operation and an uncompromising adherence to American traditions and the American way of life.

As a student of history he knew that this period of distress was not strikingly different in nature from scores of others through which man has struggled, suffered and sacrificed and finally overcome seemingly impossible odds; and that in all of them, including that of the world depression of the 1930's, man has tried to find a magic formula by which he might make his government strong, swift and efficient.

President Hoover created and advanced a recovery program which he believed would enable the people of the United States and the rest of the world to work their way out of their difficulties and, at the same time would best serve the higher purpose of the individual.

The nub of his recovery program was contained in his belief that "it is solely by production of more goods and more varieties of goods that we advance the standard of living and security of men. . . . If we constantly decrease costs and prices and keep up earnings, the production of plenty will be more and more widely distributed. These laws may be re-stitched in new phrases but they are the very shoes of human progress. . . ."* Believing this, he sought to create jobs by giving industry necessary support and by taking steps to tie in the wage scale to the cost-of-living scale. Along with this he initiated a relief program that was fashioned according to the long-established

---

* "Crisis to Free Men," address by Herbert Hoover before Republican National Convention, Cleveland, Ohio, June 10, 1936.

American method of centralized ideas and help and decentralized authority.

At the same time he undertook to strengthen and give direction to the moral and spiritual purpose of the people of the nation. He called upon them to respond with co-operation, neighborly helpfulness, patience and work. Winston Churchill, in a desperate period in his nation's history, when a visible foreign enemy was using every means to destroy his people, was able to enlist, inspire and ennoble them with a "blood, sweat and tears" program; but President Hoover lacked Churchill's dramatic instinct, his perfect sense of timing, his magic with words and his remarkable ability as an orator.

President Hoover suffered still another and even more serious handicap in that he was fighting a subtle, hidden enemy. He knew that this hidden enemy could weaken or destroy the moral fiber of the people without their being aware of its insidious disintegrating force. A people could see a material enemy who struck at their bodies and their houses but only a few of them could sense the presence of this unseen enemy and its power to weaken man's spiritual purpose. Furthermore the great mass of the people believed that they were fighting a domestic economic enemy—never realizing until they had turned Mr. Hoover out of the White House that it had come from every foreign nation whose shores were touched by the seven seas.

That Mr. Hoover held deep and unshakable convictions about those significant principles which have given direction and support to man's evolving purpose there is no question.

One of his abiding beliefs was that men have overcome depressions and confusions "because of some men who stood solid . . . not because they knew the solution to all these confusions . . . [or] even had the power to find them . . . [but] because they held certain positive principles of life, of morals and spiritual values . . . we must hold these verities within some whole nations if the lamp of civilization is to be kept alight." These principles "stand out in simple concepts . . . truth, justice, tolerance, mercy and respect for the dignity and personality of the individual man . . . inspiringly expressed in the immortal words of Christ on the Mount. In these concepts alone, (is) the answer to the world yearning for control of these growing powers over matter."

Basically, his recovery program sought to preserve for the individual citizen a high degree of personal freedom for the exercise of his initiative, effort, movement, expression and worship, and at the same time help him through his troubled period. It follows as naturally and inevitably as night follows day that the man Hoover would cling tenaciously to his faith in these principles of democratic government and the American way of life that the boy Hoover had been taught to regard as almost sacred. Few if any of the men of his youth held any doubts about the inherent soundness of the American experiment in government or in its efforts to provide more complete justice and greater opportunity for the common man than had any other form of government. Mr. Hoover's thoughts are highlighted in the excerpts from his speech "Attitude on Morals in Government," Appendix IV.

His faith in its basic principles was buttressed by his vast business experience, by his varied and far-reaching humanitarian activities, his public service and his observations and reading. The sum total was a determination, come hell or high water, to chart and follow a recovery program which conformed to the best American procedures and traditions. He ruled out resort to European quackeries and nostrums and took the hard course of work, co-operation and patience.

Today, nineteen years later, the complete record of the great depression proves conclusively that President Hoover's domestic recovery program was so soundly conceived and ably administered that by midsummer 1932, it had checked the course of the depression. More than this his measures had so effectively taken hold as to increase industrial output and employment substantially.

This in itself was a notable accomplishment. But he did far more than this in that he cushioned our domestic economy from the repeated shocks of the destructive political, social and economic upheavals which followed one after the other throughout the world for a two-year period.

David Lawrence, editor and columnist, has recently written that his "courageous fight against the depression was virtually won by the time he was leaving office" and pointed out that it was only during the period between election day in 1932 and March 4, 1933 when his successor took over that panic seized the American people. It did so, according to Mr. Lawrence "because of the uncertainty of what the new administration would do." Fuel was added to the flames by the refusal of the incoming administration to collaborate with the outgoing one.

Proof that the United States was solvent and that the frozen assets of the banks could have been liquidated is provided by the subsequent record which shows that the losses to depositors were relatively small. In fact, Mr. Lawrence stated, "it was a higher average of return to bank depositors than had been experienced in bank losses of a half-century before."

Mr. Lawrence also stated in the article referred to above that: "Herbert Hoover's name will shine because his character is unblemished and his record as custodian of the people's funds and the people's interests stands untarnished through the years." (New York *Sun,* August 15, 1949.)

His Quakerism Manifests Itself

One of the causes of his defeat for re-election in 1932, and perhaps it was the major one, came from within the man himself. It was unrelated to his administrative ability, resourcefulness and industry. It was a limitation that came out of his inheritance of the Quaker quality which might be called unemotional stoicism. A friend recently gave me his estimate of Quakers. He likes them, he said, "because of what they do rather than what they say. They don't go around tooting their own horns. There is more example than there is precept in what they do."

This trait, whether in Quakers or non-Quakers, is generally admired and respected in the normal relations of life. The Quakers have tended, however, to become almost secretive about their good works.

Desirous as it would be for all men to find and maintain the happy middle position, the fact remains that they seem unable to do so. Men are largely the product of their environment and training. And Hoover is a Quaker by birth, environment and training. Quaker principles by precept, example and osmosis have become a part of his inner life.

One of the many curious things about Quakers is their difficulty of translating into political terms their ability to crystallize and accelerate public sentiment in spiritual matters. They are distinguished world experts in this latter field, but since the mid-seventeen hundreds most of them have been dubs in the political field.

Previous to 1756, when a *minute* (a *resolution* to non-Quakers) adopted by the Philadelphia Yearly Meeting called upon Friends to eschew political office, the Quakers had demonstrated that they had political savvy. Between 1680 and 1756 they were either in control or else held a dominant place in the government of Pennsylvania. At least four Quakers were colonial governors of Rhode Island, and Quakers served as colonial governors of other provinces. Many of them served with distinctive success in several state legislatures during the colonial period.

Since that time only an occasional Quaker has sought elective office. There have been notable individual exceptions in recent years but most of them were men who, in later life, joined other denominations. This group includes such men as the former Speaker of the House "Uncle" Joe Cannon, former Senator and Governor Joseph M. Dixon of Montana, former Governor and Senator Arthur Capper of Kansas and former Governor Stubbs of Kansas among others.

That quality which makes it difficult or impossible for Quakers to bridge the deep and wide gap that separates spiritual purpose from political action is their refusal as a group "to toot their own horns." The public generally admires and approves this quality when they see evidences of it in spiritual areas. But a large part of that same public, in a democracy, demands showmanship, flattery, detailed and repeated explanations and interpretations from its servants of their actions, methods and purposes. Because of President Hoover's Quaker training and the inhibitions it creates, he was unable to do this in a way the political public demanded.

One of the many newspapers which recently commented on this quality of Mr. Hoover's, *The Missoulian* of Missoula, Montana, spoke of his consciousness "of his own rectitude" and his trust that the record always will show he "did not defend himself vigorously."

Sought What Was Best—Not Public Approval

As President he always strove in the best Quaker tradition to do what he believed was right. That was the test he used. Whether what he did would meet with public approval or disapproval was not a part of his calculations. This fixed Quaker method of operation has grown out of three centuries of determined purpose to do what they believed to be right regardless of public opposition or criticism. As a body, over the generations, the Quakers have come to believe that if they strive at all times to satisfy the prompting of their spirits they can leave explanations of their actions to history.

The Quaker practice of attempting to satisfy the promptings of their spirits, however well it served them as a religious movement, did not well serve one of its members who was at the same time the President of the United States. Being the kind of man he was, he paid the price—as men in like circumstances have had to pay the price—for holding undeviatingly to their principles.

President Hoover was further handicapped by the fact that prejudice and hate—the most readily aroused of man's emotions—were riding high, wide and handsome all over the world at that time.

Those Who Know Hoover Best Admire Him the Most

The best test of a quality of a man is that of learning how those who have long been closely associated with him appraise him. Measured by this test Mr. Hoover is a good and great man. The men and women who have worked with him for thirty-five or more years know him at his best and his worst. They have repeatedly seen how quickly his wrath is aroused against the liar, double-dealer and crook, and can recall countless instances of his indignation over injustice and intolerance. They know from first hand that in disaster, famine, depression and war he has seen man at his worst and has come through all of these holocausts with visions of man at his best. Best of all, they know from a thousand experiences that in his unmatched service to relieve the distress of men in the mass everything he plans and does is for the individual. He serves men but he aims at a man—more especially at a child.

Because he has touched life at so many points Mr. Hoover has the rare and unusual ability of making friends of all manner, kinds and classes of men. He easily gains the friendship of workmen and scientists, educators and statesmen, religious leaders and men of the world.

One reason for this undoubtedly is his deep understanding of and sympathy with the purposes and desires of all men of good will. Another is his amazing knowledge and his rare versatility. His approach is almost unique. One friend has stated that:

> Many times in my long association with Mr. Hoover I have seen examples of his ability to arouse the most ardent loyalty of other men. I recall the incident of a well-known newspaper publisher of upstate New York. This was some months before the Republican convention which nominated Mr. Hoover for the presidency. The publisher, enroute to Florida for a vacation, stopped off in Washington to chat with Mr. Hoover. The conversation had been under way at Mr. Hoover's desk for a few minutes when the Chief reached into the lower left-hand drawer, took two cigars from a box, and placed them on the edge of the desk. Soon Mr. Hoover took one himself and lighted it without saying a word. The publisher, deciding that the other was for him, took it and also lighted up. Then followed an hour or more of serious conversation.

I saw this man a month later.

"Well," he said, "if Mr. Hoover had handed me a cigar when I walked into his office, I would have gone on to Florida. Instead, I spent the next 28 nights on sleepers lining up New York delegates for him."

These old friends and associates like the way he goes about carrying out a job. His engineering training prompts him first to get the facts—all of the facts. A recent editorial in the San Francisco *Chronicle* expressed the belief about Mr. Hoover that:

His has been an undeviating devotion to facts and to those courses of action that spring manifestly from a thorough grasp of facts . . . facts—which is to say, truth,—must be the prerequisites of any other kind of job. . . . The truth, then, has been the dominant objective of Mr. Hoover's life, and this explains much about the man himself. It is axiomatic of such a man that self is relatively unimportant—a means rather than an end.

When he has the facts about a problem or a situation he draws up the specifications. In true Quaker tradition he relies on reason, co-operation and persuasion to gain right, fair and just ends. This method has enabled him to call on the best and highest ideals of his fellow workers and to tie them through loyalty and devotion to common ideals. He has gained it to an amazing extent from these men and women because he has deserved it.

Taking the bad with the good, Hoover's close associates know how taciturn he can be. Some of them have smarted under this gruffness and some have been offended by his grumpiness. Still others have been hurt at times by his sparing use of personal praise. A few have been disturbed by what one of them has called, "The Chief's insistence upon doing things his own way." One of the presidential secretaries, after returning to his office from a difficult session with Mr. Hoover, remarked to a friend: "That man has the richest mind and the worst manners of any living man."

This trait of his has disturbed some otherwise pleasant personal relationships. It seems, to those who know him best, to come from the vast store of information about men and events that he had filed away in his remarkable and unusually retentive brain in such an orderly manner that he can draw upon it instantly at need.

One of his colleagues in World War I, Bernard M. Baruch, once said that of all the men he had ever met, Hoover had the supreme ability of absorbing and assembling facts in order, to plan from them a course of action and to get the desired result. "Facts to Hoover's brain," said Baruch, "are as water to a sponge, they are absorbed into every tiny interstice." And he added that he would rather have Hoover's judgment than that of any other man on any problem that was so complex as to demand an extraordinary grasp of detail.

His Information Not Always Accurate

Once in a while he slips up on a point of information. Such an incident occurred at a small White House luncheon he and Mrs. Hoover gave for the distinguished actress Minnie Maddern Fiske. The topic of superstitions was brought into the discussion and one of us expressed curiosity about the origin of the superstition of not stepping on a crack. The President came up with his answer. It might have come, he said, from little Eva's (of Uncle Tom's Cabin) experience in crossing the Ohio River on ice cakes. Mrs. Fiske turned to the President and said:

> "I'll have to check you there Mr. President. I've played the part of Little Eva hundreds of times and I always went to heaven in a clothesbasket which was pulled up with a rope. You meant Eliza, I'm sure."

The President chuckled and admitted his mistake with a schoolboy "got" grin.

Indifferent to Minor Social Graces

Being the kind of man he is Mr. Hoover often disappoints those who want a man to walk and talk, as it were, with them. His apparent indifference to minor social graces disturbs others. When still a newspaper correspondent, Charles Michelson, of poison-pen renown, complained to a fellow correspondent about Hoover's failure to shake hands with him. This affronted Michelson. Why it should have done so is strange to me. I feel that handshaking other than with close friends is pointless. Hoover may hold the same opinion of it.

Whether or not he does is unknown but of this I am certain: Hoover tries to get down to business without any mumbo-jumbo. That's how he has been able to do more things and do them well than perhaps any hundred of his contemporaries. Hoover's lifetime accomplishments add up to an amazing total. The combined accomplishments of many millions of men now living do not equal his in either service or results. And he started from scratch just as did those men who have done the least.

An Indefatigable Worker

Mr. Hoover has been able to do all that he has done because he has kept everlastingly at work. Work and more work has been his full life. One of his friends has described Hoover's appearance at a conference he had called in 1939 in New York to consider ways to aid the people of Finland. The conference room was filled with former relief work associates when he reached it from the train, immediately after his arrival from California. He greeted these old and close friends with a brief nod of his head which took in the entire group and then proceeded to state the need and the problem which he followed up with a program of action. Next he began to marshal his forces by delegating one man after another to the task of enlisting this one or the other of their old colleagues.

In less than one hour's time the program had been formulated, the staff recruited and the tasks assigned without one moment having been spent on personal greetings.

A striking illustration of the way the work habit dominates all of his waking moments was furnished by his activities in connection with the Reorganization Commission during the period when he was suffering from that loathsome and miserable disease, the shingles. Even at the peak of his suffering he continued to make weekly trips to Washington with one arm in a sling, conferring with members of the task forces, studying reports, outlining courses of action. And then for relaxation he would read Toynbee's history or some other equally sturdy book. Once his nurse insisted that he substitute "whodunits" for Toynbee but he refused to do so.

There was no time for play after he entered the university. He carried two jobs as an undergraduate. One was his studies, the other was the work he did to earn the cost of his education, and earn it as he went along. Life has been hard for him, hard and grim, and as an orphan and ward, it also has been lonely. He wove his own magic carpet with uncountable hours of hard work by day and night over the long years.

The demand which his need, profession and his ideals placed on him while he was earning his living, advancing in his profession and gaining a competence, left him neither desire nor capacity to waste time on what he believed were non-essentials. With him, as with one of my own Quaker preacher-grandmothers, "Life is a very serious thing." This was her reply to the opinion I expressed as a boy to the effect that if a man were honest, fair, kind and helpful he could discard his long face and enjoy life. Hoover came directly under the influence of my grandmother's generation. He had her outlook.

To an amazing extent he has filled "each unforgiving minute with sixty seconds' worth of distance run" and by doing so has made a multitude of contributions to society which will thrill and inspire men for generations to come.

CHAPTER THREE

What Makes Hoover Tick?

The Herbert Hoover who was the world's hero during World War I and in the years following it, the American villain in the early 1930's, and its highly esteemed, elder statesman today, is one and the same man.

This sweeping shift in public opinion about him from the low of the 1930's to the high of today cannot be dismissed with the phrase, "You can't keep a good man down." It does not apply since it was the public, not Hoover, who was down—down in distress and fear and to its baser qualities of hate and prejudice and selfish purpose.

How Mr. Hoover was able, when lied about, to refuse to deal in lies, or where he found the fortitude and courage to stoop to rebuild the broken things to which he had given his life can be understood only by an examination of the customs, practices and principles of the stock from which he comes. His Quaker qualities were the determining influences on his purpose and faith, his thoughts and actions.

They are the key at once to his strength as a statesman and his difficulties as a political leader. Hoover is their product; he is the expression of their purpose. They explain in large measure why the public understands and at the same time is unable to understand him, why he is liked or disliked by masses of men.

There can be no doubt about the accuracy of this observation if Catholic church officials are right in their belief that the Church need have no concern about the continued adherence to its faith of any child; provided that previous to its seventh or eighth birthday the child has been well grounded in Catholicism. The twig so bent inclines the tree, whether in the Catholic church or the Society of Friends or any religious denomination or movement.

Accepting this as a premise, it is easy to believe that Herbert Hoover, the son of a Quaker minister, who lived in Quaker homes and in Quaker communities and attended Quaker schools until he was seventeen years old, believes, thinks and acts in the Quaker tradition.

The Peculiar People Called Quakers

The Quakers are a peculiar people. They occupy an anomalous position in the world. A great many informed people appear to admire, usually from afar, however, Quaker principles, motives and actions. A mass of evidence could be assembled to support this statement. For example, an editorial in the New York *Herald Tribune* of July 19, 1949, ably analyzed and commented upon the strength and weaknesses of the recent Quaker report on American-Russian relations. It expressed sympathy with the Quakers' aims and, after critically examining the report, added: "All men are not yet Quakers; if they were we might more easily repose our faith in one another's virtue and good will."

That editorial appraisal is supported by the fact that although this religious movement is three hundred years old, there are only 145,000 Quakers out of the world's total population of more than two billion people.

In one way or another the world pays tribute to its high regard for many Quaker principles and characteristics. Quakers occasionally are embarrassed by some of these tributes. This is particularly true of the use some commercial concerns make of the term *Quaker*. Their purpose apparently is, by its use, to convince the public of the high quality of their product. For example, there are such products on the market as Quaker whiskey, oats, cigars, oil and what have you. No Quaker owns or manages any company which manufactures these or any other products which carry the word *Quaker,* nor would any member of the Society ever think of capitalizing on his denomination's reputation in such a manner.

No Quaker is flattered by the fact that there are no Methodist, Baptist, Catholic, Presbyterian or Congregational products of the above nature advertised. All good Quakers, on the contrary, are deeply disturbed that non-Quakers should use the name of their Society to denote quality and integrity of product.

Reasons Why Quakers Are Respected

There is something about Quakerism, as it is lived by its more admirable members, that gains the respect of most non-Quakers. A non-Quaker once wrote that members of other denominations looked upon Quakerism as their favorite faith next to their own. Even so, few of them, exceedingly few, ever leave their own faith and espouse Quakerism. One reason for this is explained in a measure by a remark of a friend of mine to the effect that "The Quaker faith is too tough for most people to take on. Most people want a one-day-a-week religion, not a seven-day-week one." He was right in that the Quaker movement is a demanding and high-purposed one which expects its members to strive to make Divine law and human law one. Those of its members who come out of its mold and who grow in the grace of its teachings are almost uniformly kind, even to gentleness, filled with compassion, tolerant, helpful and honest.

The Quakers, as do other denominations, have their share of members who fall short of achieving this purpose.

Quakerism's most distinguished characteristic is that it produces free-wheeling individuals, each of whom is guided by his "Inner Light." The "Inner Light," according to Quaker belief, is each member's direct connection with his Maker. This belief rather than a creed controls the individual Quaker. Its acceptance has tended to produce a body of men and women who, in the face of any odds, insist, with a peculiar brand of stubbornness which is a hallmark of Quakers, upon doing what they believe to be right without fear of consequences.

Hoover Explained in Quaker Terms

By comparing the hows and whys of the Quakers with the hows and whys of the Hoover record a student of psychology might make an understanding explanation of what Herbert Hoover has felt impelled to do in his life and how and why he has done it.

That such an explanation and interpretation would not, however, carry an implication that the Quaker way and the Hoover way are right should be clear without so stating. What follows is an explanation and interpretation based on information about Quakerism and Hoover. I do not try to justify either the Quakers or Hoover. If the Quakers' position is right, time, man's infallible assayer of truth, will justify their position. If their position is wrong, neither time nor whitewash will help justify either their principles or actions. Nor, by the same token, will it improve Mr. Hoover's place in history.

Both Mr. Hoover and I are birthright members of the Society of Friends; both were born in the Middle West, Mr. Hoover in Iowa, I in Kansas; both spent our first years in Quaker homes and Quaker communities, and both were associated with and came under the direct influence of relatives who were Quaker ministers.

A little more than two centuries ago, in 1738, Mr. Hoover's great-great-great-grandfather Andrew Hoover came to America and first settled in southeastern Pennsylvania, later moving to Maryland and still later in 1762 to North Carolina where he died in 1794. He and his wife were German Pietists with Quaker affiliations.

About 1732 my Hinshaw Irish-Quaker forebears also settled in southeastern Pennsylvania, and ten years later moved to North Carolina in search of a warmer climate.

Both the Hoover and Hinshaw families owned slaves until the quickened Quaker conscience caused them to give the slaves their freedom. Both families tried for a generation or more with hired labor to compete with slave labor but found this difficult. Wanting also to escape from the black pall of slavery, both families took part in the great Quaker migration from the South (one of the most dramatic and important but least-heralded religious migrations in the history of the United States) and moved to the Northwest Territory where slavery was prohibited by charter. Jesse and Rebecca Hoover, Mr. Hoover's great-grandparents, were married at the Friends Meeting at West Milton, Ohio, in 1819, the year after they arrived from North Carolina. My great-grandfather, Stephen Hinshaw, and his family left North Carolina in 1831 and settled in Indiana.

Mr. Hoover's grandparents, Eli and Mary Hoover, moved to West

Branch, Iowa, in 1852, and three years later my grandparents, Andrew and Sarah Ann Hinshaw moved to what later became Emporia, Kansas.

Thus for two centuries Mr. Hoover's family and mine have followed trails which crossed and re-crossed. Long, long ago, while a Kansas farm boy, I listened to and was inspired by the stories of how the orphaned son of my grandparents' friends had succeeded in getting a university education. These Quakerly accounts of what he had been able to do (partly because of their paucity in numbers the Quakers are more like a big family than a religious movement, thus almost everything of moment about any Quaker soon becomes the common knowledge of all Quakers) helped in a measure to stimulate me to seek a college education.

Thus he touched my life more than a half-century ago. Although I did not meet him until many years later we did have many common ties. We both learned something of gentle Quaker ways and outlook on life in the homes of our respective parents and grandparents, from the meetings for worship we attended and from our young Quaker relatives and friends. And we occasionally caught glimpses of those things which are not to be seen on land or sea but which, nevertheless, are enduring realities.

This long background of ancestor association should, despite differences in our blood strains, fate's treatment, our callings, activities and accomplishments, enable me to have some special insight into the compelling forces of Mr. Hoover's life.

Twenty years ago I wrote of him in an article in the *Century* (Spring issue, 1930):

> Hoover the Quaker, given to reticence, distinctly modest, quick in sympathy for the oppressed, with great strength and instinctive gentleness and with astounding audacity of the spirit, is full of the manners and methods of his peculiar people. He does not represent Quakerism in its rigid interpretation, but the indelible impressions of childhood have matured into a manhood concerned with things of the spirit, and the fiber of that spirit makes it pliable but unbreakable.

The key to understanding his words, work and life, whether in 1929 or 1949, is contained in that paragraph. Hoover is a Quaker, with an unshakable faith in the moral and spiritual purpose of man and an uncompromising attitude toward any proposals or moves which are designed to by-pass man's higher purpose.

Some people may scoff at the statement that Herbert Hoover's life and works have been dominated by the teachings and principles of Quakerism. Most if not all such scoffers will be non-Quakers, men and women who believe they know more about what a Quaker should be or is like than does any birthright Quaker.

They will say, and with truth, that Mr. Hoover is not a teetotaler; that he smokes and that, occasionally by way of emphasis, he uses profane language, none of which *good* Quakers do. At this point their voices fall, because they have run dry of evidence.

Granted that their points are supported by fact as regards Mr. Hoover, they nevertheless have little significance. I know many Quakers and only a few are above reproach. Nearly every Quaker has at one time or another experienced lapses in one or another of the non-Quakerish practices mentioned above. But such practices barely touch the spirit of the vast majority of the membership—and the spirit, to Quakers, is what is important.

Mr. Hoover, such practices to the contrary, does outwardly manifest the influence of Quaker principles and practices in other and far more important ways. His instinctive gentleness, his stubbornness, his integrity and his undiluted spirituality and high moral purpose combined with his record of selfless service to his fellow men also are manifestations of his Quaker upbringing and its influence on his life.

An informed and close observer could find other illustrations of an outward expression of the principles of Quakerism that live in Mr. Hoover's heart. For example, after the manner of Quakers, Mr. Hoover wears plain, almost drab suits. He eschews loud colors and personal adornments. He uses plain speech to express his thoughts. He relies on logic and reason to support his arguments.

Following his election to the Presidency, Mr. Hoover placed on a fellow Quaker the task of securing necessary funds for the purchase of a site and the construction of an approved Friends Meeting House in Washington in order that the President of the United States might have a place to worship which was worthy of his office. And in true Quaker fashion he and Mrs. Hoover made substantial, but unheralded contributions to the project.

Before the new Meeting House was completed Mr. Hoover moved to insure the presence of a gifted fellow Quaker minister at meetings for worship by arranging for the release from Stanford University of Dr. Augustus T. Murray, long head of the Greek Department of that institution.

Earlier, when as Secretary of Commerce, he had been compassionately moved to help relieve the starving condition of German children, Mr. Hoover called upon his fellow Quakers in the American Friends Service Committee to undertake this work which many people looked on with disfavor and he helped them raise several million dollars for this humane service.

Later, while President, Mr. Hoover again called upon the Friends Service Committee to help relieve distress in our coal mining areas. Again, he helped to find them money for this service.

Following the "broken glass" days of horror in Nazi Germany, during which thousands of Jews were barbarously slaughtered, three Quaker leaders, the great, late Dr. Rufus M. Jones, George Walton and D. Robert Yarnall, traveled to Berlin and by gentle, earnest persuasion secured permission from top Gestapo officials for the Service Committee to conduct relief services for the German Jews. Mr. Hoover again helped to finance their work.

Actually he secured all the money they would need from some of his friends. He had estimated that the Service Committee could effectively use a substantial sum. But when his fellow Quakers met with his contributor friends they stated that they would need only half of the amount of the sum Mr. Hoover had estimated. He fumed to me over "these Quaker friends of ours" who had put him in a false position because, as he said, "Before they get through they will need twice as much as I got for them. Why are they always so infernally cautious?"

Dr. Rufus M. Jones once told me about how, in an interview, Mr.

Hoover had expressed himself with considerable emphasis and heat over some phase of the program; whereupon the venerable Rufus said to him, "Thee had better center down, Herbert." ("Center down" in Quaker terms means to take quiet stock of yourself when disturbed.)

I asked Rufus, "What did he say?" and he replied, "Why he centered down, of course."

His Quakerism Expresses Itself

Mr. Hoover's speeches abound with expressions which support the Quaker belief that spiritual and moral forces are of transcendent importance in the life of man.

Time and again, as in a speech before the Kansas City, Missouri, Joint Republican Organizations, he has pointed out that he believes with all his heart that these moral forces which "affect the character and soul of a people will control its destinies." They transcend all political partisanship "where they enter government." Man's progress, he holds, "is in proportion to the advancement of truth and justice." These are "what we usually call morals," those things the American people "have learned at their mother's knee." Morals include both "money and honesty . . . telling the whole truth . . . keeping one's word . . . fidelity to public trust."

In the same speech Mr. Hoover, after positively defining them, sought to define them further by stating that "they exclude hypocrisy . . . creation of hate. Half-truth, hypocrisy and hate are departments in the art of demagogues. The polite phrase for all this is intellectual dishonesty."

"It is moral standards in government which create sturdy self-reliance and self-respect among citizens. It is moral standards that create perceptions of what degrades the faith of a people in self-government . . ."

Additional Evidences of Quaker Influence

A careful examination of his professional, public and private record will support the statement that he can be classified as a worthy descendant of those early colonial Quakers who, for conscience' sake, were jailed, whipped from town to town at the end of an oxcart, lost their property by confiscation, and, because they believed in freedom of worship, four of them were hanged by the Pilgrim Fathers on Boston Common.

The superb courage, profound humility and tremendous spiritual purpose of Hoover's Quaker forebears colored his life, fixed its purpose and prepared him for possible martyrdom. Right was right to them, and what was right today, they stubbornly insisted with their last breath on the gallows, or as their ears were cut off, would still be right one hundred or one thousand years later. Their steadfast adherence to principle once prompted ex-President Taft to remark that it was dangerous for any man to oppose the Quakers' spiritual or moral stand on any issue because three hundred years later history would prove the Quakers to have been right.

It is unimportant whether or not the Quakers are or always have been right on spiritual and moral questions. The point is that persecution of the early Quakers helped to develop in the movement's followers an unyielding determination never to believe that the means, unless it was spiritual or moral, could justify the end, unless it was right, fair and honest, both today and until after the last tiny star in the firmament would grow dim.

Only those who know about and understand the Quaker's purpose to do what he believes to be right, regardless of what consequences may befall him, will be able to understand how greatly this same purpose influenced Hoover's life and actions.

The Quaker Movement

The Quaker movement, for it is a *movement* and not a religious sect, crystallized into form about 1647 as "Friends of the Truth." This name was shortly after changed to the "Religious Society of Friends," which continues to be the official designation of the body. But because its early leaders bade the members tremble at the word of the Lord, an English justice in 1650 called them *Quakers*. This still is the name by which the movement is best known. Its founder, George Fox, and his supporters strove to revive primitive apostolic Christianity during a period when forms, ceremonies and belief in witchcraft were dominant in England.

Fox conceived a spiritual and social democracy. He sought to make Divine law and human law one, and he taught that the Divine Being speaks directly to the heart of every man—that the Kingdom of God is within, an "Inner Light" that guides men along right paths.

This personal aspect of religious experience excluded both ministers and set places of worship. Dependence upon the immediate guidance of the Holy Spirit led the Quakers to meet for worship in outward silence. They eschewed music during religious services because, they believed, it served to arouse the emotions of the worshippers and thereby to distract the members' direct communion with God. Stained-glass windows and other similar things pleasing to the senses were disdained as were comfortable pews. In an effort to make their religion pure and undefiled they exalted the spirit. And being stoics, they debased the flesh.

Quakerism and Individualism

Holding a concept of religion which is individualistic to its core, the early Quakers created machinery for their movement which best fitted its religious concept. They provided for neither creed nor head authority. The Monthly Meeting, that is an established place where a number of members meet for worship and business at regular intervals, was originally made—and continues to be—the primary executive power of the movement as far as the membership is concerned. Quarterly Meetings, composed of two or more Monthly Meetings, take up the slack between the operations of the Monthly Meetings and the Yearly Meetings. The boundaries of the Yearly Meetings are irregular and somewhat flexible.

Every man, woman and child claiming membership has the right to speak on any question in any of the meetings. Questions about which there may be difference of opinion are decided either by the *weight* of the meeting, that is by the expressed opinion of those members whose judgment over the years has been found to be sound, or else by postponing decision until some future date in order that Friends may have opportunity to search their hearts for the right answer. On every question the Quakers strive to go forward in unity. Perhaps the roots of Hoover's method of action, which relies on voluntary co-operation rather than power, have grown in this particular soil.

How Quaker Ministers Are Made

The regular officers of the Monthly Meeting are elders and overseers, who are appointed by their own Meetings. They have general supervision of the business as well as the membership. There is no formal provision for the training of ministers and no ceremony of ordination. A typical Quaker discipline provides in part that:

"When a man or woman has spoken as a minister so that the meeting is edified and spiritually helped thereby the elders are carefully to consider whether he has received from the Head of the Church a gift in the ministry which should be officially recognized."

The question of controlling the tendency of zealots to speak in Meeting has been a minor problem in Quaker discipline—but Quaker elders have a penetrating directness and a purposeful firmness which, exercised in private interviews with offenders, serves to restrain excessive and trivial speaking. The handling of this problem by timely and sensible intervention is typical of the Quakers in the management of their church affairs.

Some non-Quaker visitors at Friends' Meetings, who are moved to speak, present a different problem. Friends permit them to speak until they run down. Once after such a speaker had told the meeting what was wrong with the world and wherein the Quakers had been negligent about righting his ideas of these wrongs, I turned to a weighty Friend next to me, a *good* man if such ever lived, and whispered, "I'm ashamed of thee, Alfred." He replied, and he meant it, "I'm often ashamed of myself."

CHAPTER FOUR

What Makes Quakers That Way?

The Quaker discipline seeks to clarify and establish as practice certain basic tenets. These deal primarily with integrity, kindness, helpfulness, simplicity and individual responsibility. It makes no provision for divorce.

In their discipline and by precept and example, Quakers also encourage all members to live simply and within their means and to meet all of their just obligations. By not trying to keep up with the Joneses most Quakers have been able to accumulate a competence. This tends to make the improvident envious of them and it has gained for them the reputation of being canny business men. Because they try to be fair and honest in their dealings, seeking neither to take an advantage of the other fellow nor to let him take an advantage of them, they are believed to be shrewd business men. Because a few Quakers have been neither fair nor honest in their business dealings, the reputation of all Quakers has suffered accordingly.

The Heart of the Quaker Discipline

The real heart of the Quaker discipline—that interpretation of principles and practices which more than any other, or even perhaps all other factors combined, serves to create a mold for making Quakers what they are, for better or worse—lies in a dozen or so Queries which, with slight variation in language, have been read and answered once each month in Quaker Meetings for three hundred years.

Every regular attendant of Quaker Meetings has heard these Queries read countless times and searched his own heart for the answers to them while at the same time the other members of the meeting are pondering and answering them. Herbert Hoover's thinking and life have been directly influenced by these probing questions. The Queries and the careful, honest answers, informally by the members and formally by the recording clerk of the meeting, exert a powerful, direct influence on the members of the movement by conditioning them for their responsibilities as members of the meeting, of their own families and of the world in which they live.

Excerpts from the revised Queries which were adopted by the two Philadelphia Yearly Meetings at their 1946 sessions indicate how the Society of Friends seeks to help individuals and meetings to examine themselves in reference to the Quaker goal of conduct.

The first section of these Queries which deals with religious meetings is as follows:

Are your meetings for worship and business held in expectant waiting for divine guidance?

Is there a living silence in which you feel drawn together by the power of God in your midst?

Do your meetings give evidence that Friends come to them with hearts and minds prepared for worship?

Are your meetings a source of strength and guidance for daily Christian living?

Other sections deal in similar manner with such topics as the ministry, participation in meetings, unity within the meeting, education, oversight of the membership, social and economic relationships, civic responsibilities, extending the Quaker message, the home, self-discipline and human brotherhood.

Queries under these section heads seek to learn if the local ministry in meetings for worship is exercised "in the simplicity and sincerity of Truth"; regular and punctual attendance at meetings and the maintenance of "love and unity among you." One asks, "When differences arise, are endeavors made to settle them speedily and in a spirit of meekness and love?"

Education queries seek to encourage Friends to read their Bibles and to study the history of Christianity as well as to provide for the proper education of youth.

The Queries concerned with meeting oversight seek to draw members together with "a spirit of fellowship" by keeping in contact with all members of the meeting, of aiding those in material need and by "counseling" with those "whose conduct or manner of living gives ground for concern."

That Friends are concerned about the community or nation as a whole is indicated by the Query which seeks to learn what individual Friends and the meeting are doing "To insure equal opportunities in social and economic life for those who suffer discrimination because of race, creed or social class." Their desire is to create a social and economic system "which will so function as to sustain and enrich life for all."

The Queries also seek to encourage the understanding of the causes of war and to "develop the conditions and institutions of peace," to carry a full share of responsibilities in the government, local, state and nation and "to assure freedom of speech, and of religion and equal educational opportunities for all."

Under the Self-Discipline section Queries seek to learn if Friends "keep to simplicity and moderation" of speech, living and pursuit of business; about the punctuality in "keeping promises," justness "in the payment of debts" and finally "honorable in all your dealings."

The Human Brotherhood Queries seek to learn if Friends live in the life and power which takes away the occasion of all wars. Do you seek to take your part in the ministry of reconciliation between individuals, groups, and nations? Do you faithfully maintain our testimony against military training and other preparation for war and against participation in war as inconsistent with the spirit and teaching of Christ?

In all your relations with others do you treat them as brothers and equals?

Why Quakers Are Pacifists

Quakers have ever held that all war is inconsistent with the spirit and teachings of Christ. The members are urged to "live in the life and power that takes away the occasion for all wars." This tenet has caused conscientious Quakers much anguish because it brings into direct conflict their law-abiding, good citizen principles and their unyielding belief that it is wrong to take the life of a fellow man who also is a child of God.

Resting their faith as they do on the gospel of love, the Quakers have always borne testimony against war. This has helped to crystallize sentiment against all war and it also has demonstrated over and over again a singleness of purpose and a moral fiber. It has brought tragedy to many Quaker hearts, but they have kept principle above personal considerations in spite of agony and heartaches.

It is out of such a background of principle and pain, of high purpose and heavy heartache, that Mr. Hoover's lofty ideals of world peace were born. And these lofty ideals, a blend of common sense, plain justice and spiritual aspiration, are being applied with hands made tender with sacrifice for the cause. They will be advanced according to sound Quaker practice of precept and example which when harnessed to the power of public opinion have helped to lift a mass-lethargy that seemed immovable.

Other Quaker Principles

The Quaker record, as related to their efforts to establish freedom for worship for all other denominations as well as for themselves, their efforts to abolish slavery, their advocacy of fair treatment for the Indians and their humanitarian activities which recognize neither creed, color nor nationality, have enabled Mr. Hoover and others of his faith to believe that realizable ideals are the most vital reality in the world.

Since oath-taking implied a double standard of truth, the Quakers refused to take oaths. As a result the laws of our land were changed to provide for affirmation as an alternative for any man who tries at all times to speak the truth. This is a simple point to many, a splitting of hairs as it were, but to Quakers who strive to make their word or their checks as good as any bond, it has seemed a most important one.

Out of Quaker teachings and thinking and way of life has also come the quality of tolerance. The Quakers hold steadfastly to the belief that the other fellow has a right to hold such beliefs and to follow such practices as he considers proper and right. The Quaker quality of tolerance is expressed in many ways, most notably perhaps in their humanitarian work, in that they seek to help.

Humility is another marked Quaker quality. The profound humility with which the persecuted Quakers received attacks on their bodies and property furnishes evidence of the group's possession of this trait. On his world food mission trip in 1946, Mr. Hoover and Gandhi met at Delhi. During the meeting Gandhi glanced at the dollar watch fastened to his loin cloth to learn the time, whereupon Mr. Hoover pulled his own dollar watch out of his pocket and showing it to Gandhi remarked, "This is a mark of our common humility."

There is the delightful story of William Penn's remarks when, sitting in judgment on a woman charged with being a witch, Penn asked her, "Dost thou ride a broom in the sky?" The poor, frightened creature, no doubt having in mind the then Puritan practice of burning witches at the stake, affirmatively replied that she did. Whereupon Penn remarked in substance as he dismissed the charge, "That is thy right if thou chooses to exercise it."

Quaker Humor

One other distinctive quality Quakers have is their type of humor. It is unbarbed and gentle and usually comes from a turn of thought. It produces grins or smiles, almost never belly-laughs. Since it has the qualities of the rippling of a clear brook rather than the rush of the cataract it pleases rather than pains. It is never cynical and it never discomforts the other fellow.

A few years ago Mr. Hoover and his son Alan were driving swiftly along a Pacific Coast highway at two o'clock in the morning on their way home from a fishing trip when they were stopped by the whistle of a motorcycle policeman who, having seen Palo Alto on the car's license plate, turned his flashlight on the two unshaven men dressed in fishing togs and remarked, "So you're that man, are you?"

Hoover grunted and nodded, "Yes."

The policeman then said, "Well, if you are damn fool enough to drive sixty miles an hour along this road at 2:00 a.m., it's all right with me. Get the hell out of here!"

This was the sum total of the conversation. Neither Hoover nor his son made any comment until they had traveled several miles when Hoover remarked, "That fellow must have been a Democrat."

Quakerism Devoid of Histrionics

Forty-five years ago I was a student in a Quaker boarding school whose library of over ten thousand volumes did not then contain a single work of fiction. That school, whose graduates entered our great universities, taught no Shakespeare, for he employed fiction to dramatize life. University and college admissions committees permitted the school's authorities to substitute Milton and other classic poets for Shakespeare.

This practice of several generations of Quakers of minimizing the dramatic has tended to reduce the ability of its members to explain their positions on public questions in terms that are always entirely understandable to the public.

The late William Allen White, in a letter to the author dated December 8, 1929, touched on this point indirectly when he said:

> . . . The President has great capacity to convince intellectuals. He has small capacity to stir people emotionally, and through the emotions one gets to the will, not through the intellect. He can plow the ground, harrow it, plant the seed, cultivate it, but seems to lack the power to harvest it and flail it into a political merchantable product. Probably he would fail terribly if he tried to do the other thing. He must be what he is. What he is is important and necessary. . . . The intellectual appeal finally will win. It is a slower process, but probably surer. . . .

Support for Mr. White's theory that Mr. Hoover's appeal is to the intellect is found in the fact that fifty United States colleges and universities and twenty-four foreign universities have conferred honorary degrees upon him. This is a far larger number than have been conferred upon any other living man. Such recognition indicates that his mind and accomplishments are admired by educational leaders throughout the world.

Firsts and Musts of Quakerism

Quakerism appeals to the mind as well as the heart when stripped of what its followers believe to be non-essentials. It holds the following as *firsts* and *musts* for its members: integrity, tolerance, kindness, helpfulness, respect for the individual as a child of God and his guidance by the *Inner Light.*

These Quaker *firsts* and *musts* also are the *firsts* and *musts* of many other religious denominations. But the Quaker way of applying them has made of the movement's members a truly *peculiar people.*

The saving grace of the movement is that its way of life and form of worship has produced an exceptional number of saintly men and women who by precept and example have exerted a determining influence in the spiritual affairs of men which is out of all proportion to the numerical size of the movement.

These brief facts about Quakers and this interpretation of their principles and ways of worship, thinking and conduct, have been presented to make more understandable the principles and thinking which have exerted so great an influence on the life of the Quaker, Herbert Hoover.

Some Reasons Why Quakers and Hoover Irritate Other People

The world seems to admire Quaker principles and looks with favor on Quaker good works but large numbers of people are frequently irritated by Quaker ways of doing things as well as by Quaker positions on public questions. Some people find Quakers exasperating due to their unyielding determination never to compromise what they believe to be their principles. This adherence to his principles caused Hoover, as President, some of his troubles.

Using swear words or beating dumb brutes came under the head of principle with him—but tail-twisting as a means of punishment came under the head of disciplinary method. This is natural, since the Quakers, except for a handful of the best of them, have faults just as do the other two billion or more individuals in the world.

Fearing that my Quaker training and my belief in Quaker principles might make this brief interpretation of Quakerism partial, I wrote ten friends the following letter:

> I am writing a book which touches upon and appertains to my fellow co-religionists, the Quakers, and attempt in it to state what is right as well as what is wrong with them from the non-Quaker point of view.
>
> That the world generally respects good Quakers and their principles seems evident. However, the fact that the 300-year old Quaker movement has only about 145,000 members out of a total world population of more than two billion suggests something else again.
>
> What is that something else?
>
> Would you try to tell me what it is, briefly or at length as you please?

None of these men and women is a Quaker and so far as I know none has any Quaker ancestry. Included in the list were two editors of great metropolitan newspapers, a publisher of one of the larger weekly magazines, a distinguished columnist, a Wall Street lawyer, a Wall Street banker, an official of a radio broadcasting company, a distinguished minister, and a well-known book publisher.

One of them replied in part:

> I should guess that one reason they don't multiply is that they make no effort of proselytizing or missionary work or persuading others to join. . . . Another reason, I assume, is that Quakerism is not so much a creed or organized sect, like other faiths, as a way of life. . . . I suppose you don't "join" democracy, or even Christianity, as such. In this sense, perhaps there are many more Christians who really are Friends than you count. . . .

Another one expressed the belief that:

> The quietness of Quakers is part of their strength, and it is not contradicted by the amount of great human service which they render in an active way. The miss, of course, is the persuasive, evangelistic note. . . . I believe Quakers could go out on the march with a wider evangelistic appeal, not to join Quakers necessarily, but to believe in and follow Christ. You can be too quiet when it comes to expressing your faith.

Another friend offered the opinion that:

> The Quaker religion is too rich for the average man's blood. This is not as paradoxical as it would seem at first ranged alongside the simple, almost austere quality of Quakerism. True simplicity is most difficult of attainment. It is easier by far to overdo than to exercise restraint. . . .
>
> There are some who will say the Quakers are more than simple, they are *naive*. . . . There are Quakers who are naive, true. I find this a virtue except when their own great overwhelming faith leads them into a perilous over-simplification of complex, material problems in a confused and ruthless world.
>
> It is in the unassailable integrity and undiluted spirituality and faith that the great strength of the Quakers lies; and in their devotion to principle before profit . . . it is not in numbers but in quality that Quakerism has its strength.

One friend, as did the others, felt that the Quaker principle of non-resistance was unrealistic. He began by stating his belief that Quakers had

> . . . not grown more numerous during all the years because one of their prime tenets is appropriate for a free minority, but not for a responsible majority. In effect the Quakers have taken on the oriental philosophy of non-resistance. That is a tolerable attitude in a much more diversified world than that which has been in the making during the last hundred and fifty years, at least I think so.
>
> I don't know how Quaker non-resistance would meet the facts of a world in which a Hitler, or a Communist group, intended to conquer all who did not voluntarily submit.

Touching on the same point of numerical size as did my friend above, another one expressed the belief that there were so few Quakers because:

> First, your religion demands responsibility. Instead of the successful formula of repentance and saving souls for eternity, your religion demands the search for truth *and* action, here and now, in this world. This requires effort, and continuing performance, and allows no comforts of procrastination. . . . They must not only think,

but also act. It is a hard combination, and accounts for both the high quality and low quantity of the membership of Friends.

It seems to me you have gone back to the teachings of Jesus, the true, vital Christianity. You live what all decent thinking people want—faith, strength, determination, patience, fortitude, generosity, service—a combination of spiritual search, and earthly realization. . . . Almost alone in the world today, the Friends stand as a group for what is right; for light, for succour, and peace. Thinking people praise, and believe in, and contribute to the cause of the Friends. . . . Why don't they join you, as Quakers? They agree with you, and strive to be like you. But they don't join your church because they see nothing incompatible with incorporating what they know of your religion with their own, and staying in their own church. Human nature doesn't like to reject. We embrace your teachings and example, as we understand them, and stay in the church we already belong to. . . .

Another friend replied:

It has always seemed to me that tolerance in the most real sense is so patently ingrained in Quakers that they do not engage in proselyting. . . . It may be that time will demonstrate the survivorship of the tolerant man as greater than that of the bully—I don't know. . . . The ruthless determinist who has no doubts and is set upon eliminating dissidents has certainly some advantages in dealing with the tolerance of those who feel it unnecessary to exterminate those with whom they do not agree. . . .

There is more example than there is precept in what Quakers do. When they are intolerant it is of their own shortcomings, not the shortcomings of others. . . .

After his first point that the teachers and priests of other religious denominations, with few exceptions, come more nearly living higher ideals than the laity, "who live in a work-a-day world," another friend expressed his belief that Quakers "try to make every member a priest. As there are very few people who can attain such a high ideal it naturally follows that there are very few Quakers." He then added:

Another thing about Quakerism is that it is based primarily on intelligence. It appeals to the ethical and reasonable side of man, and almost entirely leaves out the emotional. Most of us—even the best—like some appeal to the emotions with our religion. We want music, and ritual, and symbols. These the Quaker meeting certainly does not give.

However, I think that to popularize it, would emasculate it. The 145,000 members, due to their high standards and abiding faith, are far more effective than the numbers of their movement would indicate.

The most challenging and pointed reply I received began by stating that the letter was a joint product of the writer and his distinguished wife.

We live (he wrote) in a Quaker region and have Quaker relatives as well as friends, and five of our children have attended Quaker schools. We like to think that in many respects we have Quaker attitudes and follow Quaker ways of life. . . .

Now I can quite understand that the Quaker faith is against militant activity. But it seemed to me . . . it leads to avoidance of the issue. And that often means withdrawal from the realities of life. My wife and myself, who at one time had made up our minds that we were going to become Quakers, decided not long ago that we could not do so.

Finally, we have a feeling that relief projects and the pacifist position, fine as both are, are not enough in the modern world. I believe that many more people would be drawn to the Quaker Movement if it could be aggressive in the promotion of such projects as its splendid study of relations with the Soviet Union, recently announced. There are more jobs like that that need to be done and that I should think the Quakers would do, such as getting behind the world health organization, the food and agricultural organization and other agencies that hold promise of positive results for world peace.

I wonder if the general failure of Quakers to realize their beliefs lies in their self-absorption? We sometimes feel that the good works they do are done not so much for the sake of others, out of a genuine love for mankind, as a desire to provide a means for exercising their own religious principles, and on a lower level to provide a ready answer to criticism. For example, Quaker schools are now gradually admitting Negroes—but only one or two, in a token fashion. It is an eat-your-cake-and-have-it-too sort of prudence. I doubt whether such prudence combines well with true religion.

You will see that our relations with Quakers, while entirely friendly and approving much, in comparison to other religions, have nevertheless become tinged with some amusement and gentle cynicism. They are children of God undoubtedly—but careful ones!

Acting in the belief that the testimony concerning and interpretation of Quakerism which I have presented in the earlier part of this chapter somewhat adequately states the Quaker case, it seems out of place here to comment on any of the points offered by any of my correspondents except one or two in the last letter quoted. I do so only to correct misapprehension.

First, I never have at any time heard any Quaker express the thought that Quakers individually or as a group should carry on "good works . . . to provide a ready answer to criticism." The only expression I ever have heard made by Quakers concerning either the source of their inspiration or the purpose of their humanitarian activities is that it expresses their belief that "love is the greatest power for good in the world." By giving expression to that belief in their lives and by their works Quakers hope to help create oases of good will, which, in God's good time, may serve as bases for universal peace.

The other point I wish to comment on concerns the admission of Negroes to Quaker boarding schools. This question has caused Quakers much heart-searching. They have believed that it was right to do so. They have believed also that they should proceed cautiously with a social experiment such as this which, due to prejudice and custom, inherently carries many problems. Thus, instead of opening their boarding school doors wide to any and all Negro children applicants, they carefully screen the list and admit only those as students who appear to possess qualities which will make them most acceptable. In this careful manner, they seek not to make the world over in a day, but with "prudence" to create slowly and surely an acceptance of the practice by all of their white patrons. The basic principle which my friend failed to take into account is that Quakers strive always to "go forward in unity."

It is undeniably true that Quaker caution or prudence frequently disturbs, irritates, exasperates or causes "some amusement and gentle cynicism" on the part of non-Quakers who are in a hurry to make over a world. Taking their cue from God, the Quakers are not in a hurry to make either mankind or the world over. They stand apart from the world's vast population, compressed into a small group around which the movement's leaders have attempted to create ways and to furnish an outlook on life here and hereafter which will protect its members and principles from the disintegrating influences of *worldly* ways. These influences do make Quakers different, and in some ways not always to their credit, from their fellow human beings. Some of them even become a bit queer, or as a venerable Quaker is reported to have said to his wife, "Every one is queer but thee and me and at times thee is a little queer."

Exalting the individual as they do, the Quakers are quick to protect his sense of self-respect, his most precious gift from his Maker. As a corollary they believe in liberty, that thing a man cannot have unless he gives it to others; which he does not seek unless he has faith in his fellow men. In its significant manifestations the Quaker faith is essentially one of optimism and is premised on the conviction that kindness pays in lasting satisfaction in the human heart. Moreover, they try to enjoy a little bit of heaven on the way to heaven.

It is by and through adherence to such principles that many people are prompted to believe that worthy Quakers hold a fragment of heaven in their hearts.

No one can say exactly to what extent Quaker principles and Quaker ways have colored Herbert Hoover's life and fixed its purpose. But evidences of their pervasive influences exist in many of his speeches and in the great majority of his actions. Whatever his faults and limitations may be they can be traced directly back to the Quaker influence. The same thing holds true of his moral and spiritual qualities as they have found expression in his words and works.

The *boy* Hoover's conception of man's moral and spiritual purpose as set forth in the Ten Commandments and the Sermon on the Mount was broadened by the *man* Hoover's conception to include the principle of liberty envisaged by the Magna Charta and political equality which the American Constitution sought to make a reality. Resting his faith and gathering his inspiration from these four greatest of all human documents, he has gone forth to live and to preach.

Sounding for all the world like an Old Testament prophet, he has repeatedly given testimony of his faith in man's spiritual and moral purpose, and in equality and a free society.

CHAPTER FIVE

Hoover's Professional Career

Previous to 1914 Mr. Hoover was little known outside the mining field. But he was known and respected by the members of his profession all over the world because of his genius as a mining engineer, and his amazing accomplishments in North America, Australia, Russia, Burma and China. These had made him a legendary figure, the Paul Bunyan of the world's mining profession.

The fees he received for his services grew step by step with the growth of his successful operation and administration of his clients' mining properties. In time these fees, augmented with his share of the profits in the properties he directed for clients, ultimately enabled him to earn $100,000 or more per year. Fortunately for him there was only a 1 per cent income tax levied during those halcyon days. This fact combined with his Quaker training which had taught him to live frugally made it possible for him to save a substantial part of his earnings. By the time he was forty years old these had grown into a sizable competence. Despite popular belief, however, he never became a multi-millionaire. As a result of thirty-five years of public service for which he never has accepted, or if accepted has not used for himself, any remuneration whatever for his services, he today has left only about one-fourth of his original competence.

As much a part of him as his Quakerism was the philosophy and the customs of his neighbors of the time and place where he was born and raised. Only those who knew the Midwestern frontiers during the decades which followed the Civil War are able to understand the full meaning of this statement.

Many illustrations could be given which would visualize life in that region in that far away day. A striking one concerns the fact that sixteen years before Herbert Hoover was born, a member of the

United States Senate opposed the admission of Oregon as a state. He argued that the then-existing means of transportation would make it difficult for Oregon's Congressmen, because of that territory's great distance from Washington, to attend sessions of Congress and return to their districts for campaign purposes.

He was right at that moment in a limited way. His stand suggests that he had not grasped the true significance of the American spirit—a spirit unique in the history of nations.

The Seed Bed of the American Spirit

This unique American spirit did not have its origins alone in the vast and varied reach of a mighty land which possessed great natural resources; instead it came largely from the character and soul of its settlers. They came from every land and clime. The vast majority of them were the courageously aspiring of the earth. They sought freedom in all its manifestations, freedom for the individual citizen to exercise his initiative, effort, movement, expression and worship.

The fundamental inspiration of the American spirit was a desire to provide justice and opportunity for each of its citizens. Herbert Hoover was born and grew up in the heart of that America where creeds and breeds rubbed elbows, where ideals of kindness and neighborly helpfulness were generated and lived which touch the universal heart of mankind. His forebears were still under the inspiration of their discovery of a new spiritual inheritance; the concept which places only the Creator above man, which held that the individual's self-respect and dignity out-rank the state in importance. They and their forebears had proved to their complete satisfaction in multiplied instances that man's most precious heritage is above creed, color and national boundaries and that the finest fruits of human nature flourish most abundantly where the soul is free.

A Faith Flowers

Out of their daily lives grew a faith which flowered into a creed. They believed in the dignity and integrity of the individual man as an end in himself; that it is better to be governed by persuasion than coercion; that in the long view all values are inseparable from the love of truth; that knowledge and the power it confers should be used to promote the welfare and happiness of *all* men. Above all else they sought to solve their own and their country's problems through mutual consent and co-operative action.

Hoover knew that the beliefs, qualities and co-operative action of free men, rather than vast areas and great natural resources, were the main source of America's unmatched wealth. Without these beliefs, qualities and co-operative action America could or would have been another China, Africa, South America or Russia. If this be true, it follows that America then and today represents the best and the worst of every nation, because our stock comes from every nation. Fortunately, for the point of view of men and women of good will and good purpose, the best of every nation has been in the ascendancy most of the time in America.

Long Ago and Far Away

The America which existed during Herbert Hoover's boyhood and growing years has gone forever from the land. Great as have been the physical changes which have been made in the country since that time they are of little significance when compared with the changes in the spirits and purpose of the people themselves.

In Mr. Hoover's boyhood the family, community, even the nation, were largely self-contained units. The postman furnished their principal direct contact with the federal government. In one paragraph of his seventy-fourth birthday address, delivered at the village of his birth, on August 10, 1948, he gave a description of his home and community life:

> Here I spent the first ten years of my boyhood. My parents and grandparents came to this village in the covered wagon—pioneers in this community. They lie buried over the hill. They broke the prairie into homes of independent living. They worshipped God; they did their duty to their neighbors. They toiled to bring to their children greater comfort, better education and to open to them wider opportunity than had been theirs.

I am proud to have been born in Iowa. As I have said before, through the eyes of a ten-year-old boy it was a place of adventure and daily discoveries. The wonder of the growing crops, the excitements of the harvest, the journeys to the woods for nuts and hunting, the joys of snowy winters, the comfort of the family fireside, of good food and tender care.

And out of the excessive energy of all small boys, the evenings were filled with accounts of defeat and victory over animate and inanimate things—so far as they were permitted in a Quaker community. . . .

Compelling forces have changed this idyllic, isolated West Branch, Iowa, setting into that of a bustling community whose residents can hear in their own homes the voices of statesmen, crooners or comedians, or the sound of distant battles. In their motion-picture theatres they can see events shortly after they have taken place. By telephone they can talk with London or almost anywhere else in the world. Their automobiles, running on paved roads, have pushed back their horizons to far-distant places and airplanes can wing them toward the sun. The enlarged scope and improved nature of the printing press brings them endless streams of newspapers, magazines and books.

World War I changed not only the speed but the direction of these forces. Their movement and direction first became noticeable about seventy-five years ago, and they were greatly accelerated by World War I. The sweeping social and economic changes they have produced flowed from the test tubes and laboratories through our industrial plants in the production of an ever-increasing stream of goods and the transportation and distribution of these goods. In turn, these have provided comfort and security and greater opportunity for more individuals than have been provided by all the laws of all the liberal governments in the history of mankind. And in seventy-five years these forces, and others, have upped the cost of the federal government from about four-hundred million dollars to over forty billion dollars annually.

The gigantic forces of mass production which have emerged to give practical expression to American genius for organization and invention have created new ways of living and earning a living. They have taken man from the open spaces and Mother Nature and closely surrounded him in cities with human nature. From this has come an increasing interdependence, greater restrictions on man's freedom. And from it has come the greatest of all social problems, that of how to live in cities.

Social and economic complications grew hand in hand with the growth of our industrialism which takes more and more men away from their centuries-long individualism and closeness to nature.

These things and many more are known to Herbert Hoover, but he cannot forget the days of his youth when our nation was great because its people were self-reliant and resourceful, when man trusted man and co-operation was the rule.

Whether or not the swift and sweeping changes which have taken place between his boyhood and his seventy-fifth year make it impossible for the American people to retain their ancient and hard-gained liberties, their self-reliance, industry, initiative, tolerance and helpfulness, only time will tell.

Making Pikers of Horatio Alger Heroes

Mr. Hoover's was a Horatio Alger story such as Alger never dared write because truth does what fiction dares not try to do. Only the barest outline of his mining activities can be given in the limited space of this brief chapter.

A chance meeting with a mining engineer turned his thinking toward this calling. Another meeting, with a member of the faculty of the just-founded Stanford University, decided him to enroll there as a student.

Four years later, in 1895, he was graduated and went out to find a job as a member of a technical staff of a mining company. When he could find no such job he became a laborer in a mine in Nevada City, "Mostly," as he has explained, "because I had to eat." Early in 1896, with a small sum saved from his laborer's wages, he went to San

Francisco and asked the great mining engineer, Louis Janin, for a job. He began as Janin's office boy, but soon graduated to mining engineering field work.

The incident which brought about his rapid promotion came when a client asked Janin to make a hurried report on a mine. Janin asked Hoover to help gather the information for the report. By working under forced draft through two days and nights Hoover himself produced a report that was sufficiently informative and complete as to cause Janin to ask in amazement, "Where did you dig up all of this information?" Hoover replied, "I ought to know every foot and every vein of that mine because I once worked in it as a mucker."

One of his first acts after becoming a member of Janin's regular staff was to rent a house of sorts, furnish it and send for his young brother and sister to join him in his new home. This, too, was in the Quaker tradition which places great emphasis upon home and family life. One of the Queries which is read once each month in all monthly meetings for the members to consider and answer in their hearts runs:

> Are you endeavoring to make your home a place of friendliness, refreshment and peace where God becomes more real to all who dwell there and to those who visit it?

Now in his own home again for the first time since early boyhood, he went to work with a prodigious will. He traveled over Colorado, New Mexico, Arizona, Nevada and California on field engineering missions. Less than two years later, when an internationally-operating British mining firm asked Janin to recommend an American mining engineer, preferably a young man who could introduce California gold mining methods in the new Coolgardie gold district in Australia, Janin recommended the twenty-three-year-old Hoover.

Australia Beckons

One of Hoover's Stanford University lawyer-friends in later years described how Hoover, who did not look a day over eighteen, had called upon him to ask for advice. Hoover reported that the English firm had wired Janin instructions for Hoover to report to London.

The only thing Hoover feared was that his youth would lose him the job.

That it did not do so is another story. He got the job and in less than two years' time this young man reorganized the company's gold mining operation methods in Australia, planned new plants, ordered new equipment and staffed the project with carefully selected experts, a practice he has always followed. At the end of his second year in Australia an unsolicited offer came to him from the Chinese government.

China Now Beckons

China sought the services of a young, progressive, able, scientifically trained mining engineer to take charge of its program of developing natural resources. Her officials combed the world to find the right man and they found Herbert Hoover and offered him a contract that called for $15,000-per-year salary plus expenses.

Hoover took stock of his Australian job. He had staffed the operations with able technicians. The new methods he introduced were working successfully. The equipment was ordered. He had no obligation to remain. Having reached these conclusions he cabled a question to Lou Henry in California. She replied affirmatively. Soon he started back to the States, where Lou Henry and he were married by a friend who was a Catholic priest. Hoover was twenty-four years old when he and his bride hurried off to China a few days later in 1899.

From his base in Peking he traveled into the far reaches of the provinces of Chihli, Manchuria, Mongolia, Shantung and Shansi. In his professional travels in the States he had become familiar with the burro as a transportation aid: in Australia's dry areas the camel entered his life. Afterward he once remarked, "The sight of a camel makes me a little seasick to this day. What those beasts need is a gyroscope." In China he traveled by canal on river boats, or on shaggy ponies over impossible roads, living in camps or native inns.

His exploratory trips discovered no minerals in quantities other than the world's greatest coal deposits in northeastern China. About this time the growing unrest of the giant nation broke into sporadic revolutionary outbursts and later flamed into the Boxer Rebellion. This unrest first slowed down and later ended his work in China. Hoover's restless energy, industry and his genius as a mining engineer—by now clearly discernible by members of his profession—plus his record of constructive accomplishment in China and earlier in Australia, brought him a partnership offer in 1902 from the London mining firm with which he had begun his Australian career.

Now on His Way to Town

During the next dozen years his travels covered the world. He made low-grade mineral deposits, unprofitable under obsolete methods, yield great profits. He maintained offices during these years in San Francisco, New York, London, Melbourne, Shanghai, St. Petersburg and Mandalay. The nature of his work gradually changed from that of expert technician to co-ordinator and administrator of industrial enterprises—a doctor of sick companies. As an executive he strove to eliminate waste. Wherever he worked he blazed a trail for American engineers, American methods and created a demand for American machinery and products.

He became top man of a group of internationally operating mining engineers who worked together in a loose liaison as associates. Later still Mr. Hoover operated a mine located in Burma for a client on the basis of a fee plus share in the profits. This mine had been considered valueless because there had been no successful way devised to treat and recover the rich content of base metals. Hoover solved this problem after exacting research and overcame the mechanical details of the mining and preparation of the ore. Soon thereafter the mine was producing good profits. His share of them added appreciably to his savings. He had earned his competence the hard way. Shortly after he had done this the people of Europe found themselves in the midst of what up to then was the most terrible of all wars in man's long warring history.

Except for one year—1907—and one year during his Australian service, at the beginning of his experience as a mining engineer, he had resided in the United States a part of each of these years. He and Mrs. Hoover maintained a home at Palo Alto, adjacent to their beloved alma mater. In 1914 Hoover's San Francisco Panama-Pacific Exposition colleagues induced him to take on the forlorn job of enlisting the participation of European governments and industries in that city's fair.

By this time Hoover had worked and lived in a score or more foreign countries, adapted himself to their ways and customs; considered and humored their institutions, studied the problems of the people sympathetically and helped them in every possible way.

Always mindful of the Quaker Query which sought to "create a social and economic system which will so function as to sustain and enrich life for all," he gave such thought and treatment to the tens of thousands of men in America, Australia, Russia and elsewhere, who worked in the far-flung enterprises he directed. At no time, anywhere in any of them, did these workers, many of whom belonged to labor unions, ever call a strike in a Hoover-managed enterprise.

The spirit of his sympathetic understanding, now in the bud, was soon to reach full blossom in his first great undertaking of pure kindness.

PART TWO

ENTERS WORLD ARENA

CHAPTER ONE

Hoover Emerges as a World Figure

Chairman of The Commission for Relief in Belgium

When World War I suddenly exploded in the face of civilization in August, 1914, Mr. Hoover was in London. He had gone there as the Commissioner of San Francisco's planned Panama-Pacific Exposition which had been scheduled to be held in 1914. Up to that time he was comparatively unknown outside of his mining engineering profession, his circle of personal acquaintances and Stanford University alumni. Suddenly several thousand American tourists in Europe became familiar with his name. Many of them met this "benevolent casualty" who was termed by the London *Nation,* "the biggest man who has emerged on the Allied side during the war."

Serious dislocations and grave shocks followed one another rapidly after the fighting got under way. Mr. Hoover had left San Francisco for Europe in March of that year and between that date and early July he had gone from one European capital to another on his mission.

Shortly after the Austrian Archduke and Duchess were murdered he began to sense serious trouble. This conviction grew upon him as he went his rounds, talking with old friends or business associates in the capitals he visited. He watched the swift shifts in sentiment and used the knowledge he had gained over the years to appraise the way intrigues, jealousies, hates and armament activities had created frictions that led to war in Europe in the past.

His knowledge of European ways coupled with what he saw going on convinced him that further efforts to interest European governments and industries in the planned San Francisco Exposition were useless. He thereupon returned to London and concentrated on salvaging what he could from his mining interests in Europe.

Fate Calls Hoover

The hand of fate beckoned to him even before the shooting war began on August 3 and directed him to express his instinctive spirit of helpfulness which by birth, inclination and training he was destined to follow for the next thirty-five years.

The job which fate gave him was that of performing the miracle of creating ways to feed, shelter, finance and find transportation back to the States for the more than one hundred thousand Americans who had been touring Europe when war was declared.

They had hurriedly flocked to London from the Continent, but once in London other troubles faced them. Their traveler's checks were uncashable because of war restrictions. They filled English hotels, and due to the war's dislocations of hotel staffs who were being called to the colors and to inadequate or confused food supplies they were almost as badly off as they had been on the Continent, except that they were away from the war zones' dangers. Perhaps their greatest problem grew out of the almost complete absence of a way to get back to the United States since nearly all transatlantic ships had been diverted to war's pursuits.

They were indeed penniless strangers in a strange land. They swarmed into the American Embassy. In desperation, overworked Ambassador Page asked boyish-looking Hoover to assume responsibility for taking care of these frantic tourists. How he answered the Ambassador's appeal was told in a *New York Times* news item on August 6, 1914, under a London dateline. It told of the "admirable relief work of Herbert C. Hoover, a California mining engineer who opened an office of his own in the American consulate and advanced sums of $25 or more in coin to . . . Americans who had nothing but paper money. He declares he will do this until his stock is exhausted."

This news story is the first which treated Mr. Hoover as a public figure.

The hastily created Hoover organization brought order out of chaos with amazing speed. It found shelter and food, money and finally transportation. Within a few days it was handling more than five thousand Americans per day and continued at this rate for six weeks. The money for the tourists came from a London bank which he and ten Americans guaranteed against loss. The Hoover group accepted tourist checks, personal checks or other evidences of credit, to the extent of $1,500,000 which they had little opportunity to scrutinize. Of this sum they lost only about $100.

Ambassador Walter Hines Page wrote President Wilson when Hoover had completed the refugee job:

> Life is worth more, too, for knowing Hoover. . . . He's a simple, modest, energetic man who began his career in California and will end it in Heaven; and he doesn't want anybody's thanks. *

One Good Turn Deserves Another

According to Burton J. Hendrick, "Hoover's private affairs had been disorganized, he had already sent his family home and his one ambition was to get on the first ship sailing for the United States." ** Actually he had engaged passage home for the last week in September, 1914. But higher gods were soon to beckon him. War on the Continent was now under way on a large and desperate scale. Germany's invading armies at the end of September occupied nearly all of Belgium. At the beginning of the war food stocks in Belgium's stores and warehouses were barely sufficient to supply the population in the German occupied area for thirty days. The German occupation cut off sources of supplies for a population which then numbered seven and a half million people who hitherto had imported 80 per cent of their foodstuffs. In retaliation for the British action of bottling up their fleet, the Germans placed a strict food blockade on all conquered territory and pointed out that Germany, with barely enough food for her own people, could spare the Belgians none.

The Allies refused to open even a hole in this blockade for these

* Burton J. Hendrick, *The Life and Letters of Walter Hines Page,* Doubleday Doran, New York, N.Y.
** Ibid.

seven and a half million imprisoned citizens of their ally on the grounds that they were trying to starve Germany into submission. They gave as a further reason for their inhumanity the lack of guaranty that Germany would not appropriate any foodstuffs shipped into Belgium.

In the midst of this desperate situation of millions of innocent people facing starvation, Millard K. Shaler, an American mining engineer in Brussels, learned from a smuggled-in London newspaper how Mr. Hoover had helped to work out and dispose of the American tourists' problems. Shaler hurried to London and sought Hoover's advice on where and how to find food supplies as well as details about shipping them. Hoover told him how to purchase and load his supplies. Shaler next made his purchase and then discovered that British officials would not give him a shipping permit. He thereupon went back for more help. Hoover took him to Ambassador Page.

It was Hoover, *the mining engineer,* who walked with Shaler into the American Embassy in London that day in October, 1914. But it was Hoover, *the humanitarian,* who walked out of the Embassy with Shaler a few hours later. He himself, however, did not realize that this was the case until four days later.

He quickly discovered that he could not forget the desperate food needs of these millions of innocent, trapped victims of war. Their plight gripped his mind, heart and sympathies.

Here he was at the peak of his career. Due to his far-reaching mining interests and operations he was in a position to control a large share of the world's supply of base metals, particularly zinc and lead, which were certain to be fabulously valuable if the war continued. In that case he could have become one of the wealthiest men in the world.

He weighed the problem for three days with Ambassador Page and the Belgians as they discussed details and imagined possibilities. Each night of these three days he balanced the plight and the need of the Belgians against his own problems and as the world knows to its great gladness he cast his lot with the trapped, helpless and starving Belgians.

No man could then have dreamed that Hoover's decision would

open for him a ten-year humanitarian service which is without parallel in history. The records show that when his European Children's Relief work concluded its activities in 1923 the relief operations he directed between November, 1914, for the Commission for Relief in Belgium into July, 1923, purchased, shipped and arranged for the distribution of 33,841,307 metric tons of food, clothing and medical supplies to people in desperate need, the total value of which was $5,234,-028,208.56. (A metric ton is the equivalent of 2,204.6 of our avoirdupois pounds.)

Equally striking, even amazing, is the fact that due to the unimpeachable integrity, remarkable ability and high sense of service of Mr. Hoover and his colleagues no question ever has been raised about improper expenditure of one cent of this stupendous sum.

I step out of the chronologic year and move forward to 1941 for the purpose of whispering the following observation—I whisper it because of its explosive qualities: There is something radically wrong with our political system, our voters or our leaders otherwise we as a nation would not have shunned the services, information or advice during the tragic and fearful period of World War II when Mr. Hoover stood ready to give it.

He once told me that his first move after making his 1914 decision was to resign from his paid executive jobs and to delegate the conduct of his business to his associates. He helped to place many of them in his former positions on the boards of companies and agreed to advise them without charge until they learned the ropes. This marked the abrupt end of his active career as a mining engineer.

The Inspiration for Hoover's Decision

That he should have so decided is not so strange. As a Quaker, therefore, when the opportunity came to help people in desperate need he would do so. The Quakers ever have been noted for their compassion. Its source came from their spiritual purpose to follow the course set by Jesus as He went about healing with His hands. The Quakers, in turn, have sought to heal with love and tender care.

This was the dominant influence which started Hoover on his public service career, which in October, 1949, had covered thirty-five years. The variety and nature of the manifold services he has rendered mankind and his amazing accomplishments in many fields make his a most fabulous career.

Now He Has a Real Job

He brought and gave everything he had to the new undertaking which officially came to be known as the Commission for Relief in Belgium. That there was no precedent for it did not phase him. He had had to create his own precedents all his life. The job called for great organizing skill, one of his many special fortes. It called for common sense and a warm, human feeling. Hoover had both. It required knowledge of international finance. This he had mastered during his successful business career. Diplomacy of a high order was needed and here his fellow Quakers' practice of giving a soft answer to turn away wrath became especially useful.

All of the foregoing qualifications could not have swung the job if its responsible head had not also possessed an intimate acquaintance with Europe and Europeans. Hoover had this. Last and most important of all, the man at the head of this undertaking must possess unquestioned and unimpeachable integrity. This was all-important, otherwise neither belligerent would trust it. Hoover's record for integrity was spotless.

Briefly stated, the herculean task which the Commission for Relief in Belgium undertook was: (a) to persuade the Allied powers and the German powers to give it permission to exist and to function as the provisioning organization of several million Belgians and Frenchmen who were on the verge of starvation; and (b) to organize with lightning speed the financing and purchase of an immense movement of foodstuffs by rail and ship.

Three months after Hoover began his Belgian Relief work, on January 12, 1916, Ambassador Page wrote President Wilson:

> But for Hoover Belgium would now be starved. He's gathering together and transporting and getting distributed $5,000,000 worth of

food a month, with a perfect organization of volunteers. He has a fleet of thirty-five ships flying the Commission's flag—the only flag that all of the belligerents have entered into an agreement to respect. . . . The surplus food being near exhaustion in the United States and Canada, he now has begun on Argentine, where the crop is just coming on. I introduced him to the Argentine minister the other day and the minister said to me afterwards: "Somehow I feel like doing what that man asked me to do." A stone would weep to hear what Hoover has seen in Belgium—pitiful beyond all telling.*

Something New Under the Sun

The Commission for Relief in Belgium began as a purely philanthropic enterprise but was soon receiving the financial support of the Allied and American governments. It was without incorporation or definite legal status or laws. It came soon to have the attributes of a government. Commission ships, flying the Commission flag, operated under an agreed immunity from all belligerent governments accorded no other flag. It made contracts and informal treaties with the governments of belligerents on both sides. Its representatives traveled in occupied regions on its own passports and were granted powers and immunities of great significance. It was neutral as between belligerents but frequently waged controversies with both belligerents. And it received aid and essential co-operation from both. Its contacts covered the world.

It had neither guns, policemen nor soldiers. Its only power was the power of the spirit.

Looking back over the long busy years which separate July, 1949, from November, 1914, when I tried to serve that organization with limited talents for a brief period, until broken health landed me in a hospital for a long siege, I still am moved by the thrill which Herbert Hoover's inspiring leadership brought me in that splendid crusade which had no other purpose than to help millions of innocent war victims.

---

* Burton J. Hendrick, *The Life and Letters of Walter Hines Page.* Doubleday & Company, Inc., N.Y.

Now, after thirty-five years, our attention is apt to become focused on the miracle and the magnitude of the Commission for Relief in Belgium. This prevents our realizing that its leaders faced and overcame crisis after crisis. In the early days of its life new and grave crises almost daily threatened the Commission's existence. We underlings never worried because of our confidence in Hoover's resourcefulness, his determination and his remarkable ability. And he always fully justified our faith.

Troubles Galore

A few illustrations will emphasize this point. In 1914, with the iron ring surrounding them, the Belgians were reaping their crops. The Allies ruled that the Commission must requisition and ration every grain, and it became Hoover's job to accept this ruling and to create regulations and an organization which would satisfy the Allies.

When the Allies learned that Germany was buying livestock from the Belgian peasants to provide fresh meat supplies for its army, the British again protested vigorously. Hoover solved this problem by placing Belgian slaughter houses under the Commission's control.

Next it was clothing. Belgian supplies were running low. The Commission called on America for clothing and Americans quickly answered with shiploads which the Belgians cleaned, renovated and distributed. This Commission project would have passed unnoticed had not the German army been running short of wool for soldier's uniforms. Since it was possible for the Germans to grind up the second-hand wool garments and reweave them into uniform cloth, the British demanded that the Commission supervise all manufacture and sale of cloth and clothing in Belgium. This was done, and another crisis was averted.

Another of the Commission's difficulties, far more complex in nature, concerned the amount of foodstuffs that the British would let through the blockade. The vigilant and determined British officials insisted that only enough food be shipped in to keep the Belgians alive. The crux of the question was: How much is enough? British official opinion differed from Hoover's. In time he won out on this by becoming an unquestioned authority on dietetics. He and his staff turned to expert dietitians for information. Horace Fletcher, of "thirty-two chews" fame was one of these, another was Alfred McCann, a then recognized authority on the subject. Their recommendations were sent to London. In due course Hoover was able to make a scientific estimate of the number of calories per day a man working at hard labor would need and how many a child required. The proportions of proteins, carbohydrates and fats were worked out carefully.

He topped this information off with a careful watch for warning signals from Belgium's vital statistics. At one time they showed tuberculosis was increasing among children. Hoover created a medical commission which recommended more milk for children, a balanced midday lunch for babies and boys and girls. The midday lunch called for the transformation of Belgium's schoolhouses and public buildings into soup kitchens and for providing equipment and food. The Commission for a four-year period provided a noonday meal for 2,300,000 children.

When the war was over Belgian authorities made a careful survey of health conditions. Their report stated that the health of their country's children had never before been as good as it was on Armistice Day, November 11, 1918.

Everybody Helps Hoover

Working through our State Department, Hoover enlisted the active help of Ambassadors Page in London, Gerard in Berlin and Whitlock in Brussels and with their guidance and full co-operation as well as that of American diplomatic officials in other capitals he finally fashioned an operating organization which could stand the shocks of the brute passions of men that then were loose in the world.

The top echelon of Commission officials were all Americans and all, except Hugh Gibson, were mining engineers. The fact that with one exception the Commission's top echelon were mining experts is a case in point. It facilitated their dealings wth the Germans who held all experts in highest esteem.

Once Hoover had gained permission from both belligerents for the

Commission to exist and had found funds for immediate needs, the Commission's activities were rapidly expanded. This required an enlarged staff. Hoover recruited it by issuing a call in late November, 1914 for young Americans who were willing to work for (a) a bare living, and (b) the satisfaction of saving life. The response to his call was immediate and generous. Now he had the necessary personnel.

Hoover then began to enlist his next-to-top leadership. This group came from here and there in his wide acquaintanceship. Now he was ready to buy and ship food supplies and to set up and man food distribution and feeding centers in the areas of need.

With permission for existence obtained, procedures created and personnel recruited Hoover turned his attention to finances. The Commission's first funds consisted of Belgian money on deposit in British banks and a substantial British government contribution. These were supplemented by charitable gifts from the British Empire and America. Before these were all expended Hoover worked out an exchange system that helped unblock Belgium's frozen funds. He added to the Commission's bank balances by selling food supplies at a profit on a rationed basis to those Belgians and French citizens who were able to pay for them and was thereby able to purchase more food for the 55 per cent of the Belgians who were unable to pay anything.

Military Leaders Throw Sand in the Gear Box

The Commission's problem of overcoming the opposition of military leaders on both sides, however, was an even more troublesome one than that of financing the Commission's work.

The crux of the military problem was that the Allies sought through their blockade to starve the Germans into submission. The British insisted that "It's the Germans' job to feed the Belgians." The Germans for their part realized that such food as they gave the Belgians would have to be taken from their own people, therefore they themselves would soon be in need.

These sharply divergent needs and points of view caused continuous problems. Hoover spoke of these in one letter in which he described the "delicate balance" of the Commission's business due to "the complete conviction of the British military authorities that the whole of the effort is to their disadvantage and profoundly to the advantage of the Germans," who, he added, "do not always realize how easy it is to plunge us into difficulties."

Despite the difficulties which both belligerents created for the Commission its work grew quick step by quick step with the fast expanding scope of the military activities and the increasing complexities that were created by growing tensions. The military machines grew more and more ruthless. Along with their ruthlessness they became more adamant in their refusals to give consideration to any purpose other than wholesale murder and starvation.

The Allies' blockade of continental ports, the Germans' "sink on sight" U-boat orders, the tightening of borders and military control of areas made needs for food of ten million Belgian and French people more and more desperate.

Money—Always Money

The Commission's need for funds grew in proportion to the rapid growth in numbers of those dependent on it. It soared from an early $5,000,000 per month to an ultimate monthly requirement of $25,000,000—a larger sum than the United States Government annually spent three decades earlier. An enlarged budget called for more and more ships. It also called for an expanding purchasing organization and a bigger and better distributing organization. It operated on faith much of the time; once it had liabilities of more than $20,000,000 in excess of even its promised assets. But Hoover found the money, somehow, somewhere, and he obtained the necessary official permits for continued existence.

Hoover supplemented Elijah's faith of depending on the ravens with Franklin's belief that the Lord helps those who help themselves. He sought to help himself, that is, the Commission, by appealing to the French whose "hearts bled" over the desperate need of several millions of their trapped countrymen. But French officials refused to admit the principle that their government had any responsibility for caring for these victims. That, they insisted, was Germany's job. But

Hoover was grim, determined and eloquent. The result was that two days after his interviews in Paris he received a check which read, "Pay to the order of Herbert Hoover 25,000,000 francs" (then $5,000,000) with a note which said, "Kindly acknowledge receipt of the enclosed." And another crisis was met.

The major part of the Commission's funds was provided by the Allied and the Belgian governments and the generous people of the world. This crusade of mercy reached and inspiringly moved the universal heart of mankind.

For example, Hoover's laborer mining friends in far-off Australia contributed $70,000. Two old ladies in England, having no money to give, sent Hoover twelve silver buttons cut from their finest gowns. In a note acknowledging their contribution he wrote:

> It is not necessary yet to permit such sacrifice as yours. Your action has led one of us here to contribute £10 to the Belgian cause. So what you have done was not in vain. I return your buttons—all except one, which, if you will allow me, I shall keep as a reminder that there are people like you in the world.

"That there are people like you in the world" inspired millions of men and women everywhere to support Hoover's leadership in this ennobling work; support it with their prayers, their efforts and their means.

How the United States Helped

In the United States the Commission's staff asked the railroads to move purchased foodstuffs without charge. This the railroads did until our purchases mounted into trainload lots of such products as wheat, for example. Later the railroads required us to pay freight charges but they continued to give the Commission's purchases every possible advantage of rates and always gave them shipping priorities.

The American public's direct and principal participation in the European holocaust previous to America's entry in the war in April 1917, was that of supporting the Belgian Relief Commission's noble work. The millers of Kansas contributed a shipload of flour—many other states loaded ships with contributed foodstuffs. The Rocky Mountain Club of New York City turned over to the Commission a half million dollars they had raised for a new club house. Foundations sent ships loaded with food to the trapped and helpless victims of Belgium. Belgian Relief Committees sprung up everywhere to express America's finest instincts of heart and mind. They collected enormous amounts of money and clothing for the Belgians between the fall of 1914 and the spring of 1917.

Between October, 1914, and August, 1919, the Commission's sales and purchase account totaled $928,000,000 with an overhead charge of .375 per cent. Its nearly seventy vessels transported 5,174,431 metric tons of foodstuffs and clothing in 993 overseas passages and 1320 channel crossings.

A firm of certified accountants kept and audited the Commission's accounts. When this firm closed the Commission's books in 1919, it added a voluntary statement that Mr. Hoover himself never had received one cent of its funds either for traveling expenses, services or any other purpose whatsoever. When the French government was presented with a copy of the accountant's report a high official waved it aside with the remark, "We have far more important things to do than that of examining Mr. Hoover's accounts."

Served Without Compensation

It is not at all remarkable, in the light of his Quaker upbringing, that Hoover should refuse any pay for his Belgian Relief Commission services. His own Quaker minister-mother received no compensation for her spiritual ministrations. One of the writer's Kansas Quaker grandmother-preachers felt and answered two calls to minister in Europe and in many parts of the United States, and always at her own expense and without any compensation.

It is a carefully nurtured and closely adhered-to Quaker principle that humanitarian or public service should be given, not sold. Centering their religious faith on spiritual rather than on worldly things as they do, Quakers generally are interested primarily in acquiring only a sufficient competence to enable them to live with decency and dignity and to provide a margin for security. When and as they accomplish this they seek opportunities to serve their fellow men without gain.

Since Quaker principles and practices are a vital part of Herbert Hoover's innermost self and since he had acquired his competence, he could not have done other than to give himself unreservedly and without pay or profit to the Belgian Relief Commission's work.

Having done so he created a pattern and precedent which he continued to follow from that time forward whether in relief work, public service or semi-public service. From 1914 to 1949, Mr. Hoover has never received, or if received—he was legally required to accept his salary as Secretary of Commerce and as President—he has never kept one cent for himself. Apart from, and in addition to his long held beliefs in this regard, was Mr. Hoover's deep feeling that his country had been good to him and he wanted, to the limit of his ability and means, to give himself as completely as possible to its service. Thus his free service was both a point of conscience and principle.

Hoover—the Commission's Works

Necessary and important as it is to present briefly a few highlights of the Commission's method of operation and financing, the really important part of its work was that of gaining and holding the respect and forcing the co-operation of the belligerents on both sides. High purpose, unviolated neutrality, dogged insistence, resourcefulness, ability and common sense of a high order combined with faith helped to solve its problems. Hoover went without let or hindrance from German to Allied headquarters and even to their front lines and always immune to search—the only man so privileged in the entire world.

It was inevitable that Hoover was always the storm center with both belligerents. He demanded special consideration for this crusade in practical idealism. He succeeded because he appealed to the higher motives of the military leaders whose sole thought and effort was centered on the gruesome task of wholesale murder and pillage. But his integrity, idealism, Quaker stubbornness, common sense and the force of his logic helped him to steer the Commission's course past its dangers.

For example, he once hurried to Berlin to remonstrate over U-boat sinkings of the Commission's ships. This had been done contrary to agreement. A high German naval official assured him that it would never happen again. Hoover replied with a parable:

> "Your Excellency," he said, "there was a man once who was annoyed by a snarling dog. He went to see the owner and asked him to muzzle the dog. 'There is no need of that,' said the owner, 'the dog will never bite you.' 'Maybe,' said the man. 'You know the dog will not bite me. I know the dog will not bite me. But does the dog know?' "
>
> "Pardon me one moment, Herr Hoover, I will telephone at once the dog." And he did so.

In another crisis, when Hoover made a veiled threat to a German official, the official replied:

> Mr. Hoover, I will grant your request—not on account of your country, but on account of you and your friends, a small group of eccentric gentlemen who happen to be of American birth. You have worked miracles here in Belgium and the world will not forget you. But don't speak to me of America; for it is not behind you. Your country cares for nothing on earth but money, war profits—only that.

The Commission was not a one-man show even though Hoover was the Commission's chairman and carried the brunt of the work. All of its major and many of its minor problems were debated vigorously in its London, Brussels, Rotterdam and New York offices. But in spite of his insistence of not being played up it did become largely a Hoover show. "Play up Belgium" was his invariable response. Although he demanded that this be done he was its omniscient, almost its omnipotent, head. One possible answer to his amazing success comes partly from the fact that his direct methods knocked the military and diplomatic authorities off balance due to the fact that they were specialists in the oblique approach. He would get what he wanted by his direct approach before they could get started with their oblique one.

The Storm Weathered

By the end of 1916 the privileges which the warring governments had accorded the Commission's staff and work became acknowledged rights. Sources for adequate funds and food supplies had been found. The organization's personnel had been tested by every conceivable trial by fire. All was going well. "It's going along all right at last," said Hoover as he planned to return to the United States and make it his base of operations.

Early in 1917 I had invited him to address a small group. He accepted tentatively, stating that he would be present if he were not called out of the country. A few days before the date of the meeting he telephoned to say that he could not join us because he had to start for Europe the next day on a semi-official mission.

The unrestricted U-boat warfare had curtailed passenger ship sailings to the barest minimum. In February, 1917, the German government proclaimed that only one American ship per week would be "allowed to sail for England." President Wilson promptly handed the German Ambassador his passport. This was the grave situation which in March sent Hoover hurriedly back to Europe. His mission was that of trying to induce the leaders of neutral nations such as Spain and Holland to take charge of the Commission's activities if and when America entered the war.

By the time he had completed this task the United States had declared war on Germany. In April, 1917, the Allied leaders informed the newly formed Council of National Defense that their primary needs were for troops and food. The Council cabled Hoover in Europe and asked him to make a survey of the food needs of our new Allies, and to devise ways and means of supplying them. He immediately began the survey. Shortly after its completion he returned to Washington to enter a new and greater field of public service—and one which would bring into use other of his hitherto hidden, but marked, talents.

Hoover Tells What He Really Thought

His own country was now in the war against the German powers, and with nominal direction of the Belgian Relief Commission's work in the hands of officials of neutral governments, Hoover, for the first time in two and a half years, gave full expression to his true feelings and stated his beliefs concerning Germany's system and purpose. These he summarized as follows:

> For two and a half years we have been obliged to remain silent witnesses of the character of the forces dominating this war. But we are now at liberty to say that, though we break with great regret an association with many German individuals, yet it is our conviction, born of an intimate experience and contact, that there is no hope for democracy or liberalism, and consequently for the real peace and safety of our country, unless the system which brought the world into this unfathomable misery is stamped out, once and for all.

A great crusade had ended, a crusade of mercy which had created a new pattern in humanitarian work, a crusade that was prompted by the heart and managed by the brain.

Now its directing head moved on to another and more important service, that of stimulating and directing the voluntary co-operation of one hundred thirty million people in the effort to produce and save the food supplies which were needed to win the war.

CHAPTER TWO

The United States Food Administration

1917–1919

The United States Food Administration managed to reduce to a minimum the frictions and tensions which inevitably are created in times of total national effort by establishing and enforcing rules and regulations of a centralized authority by the wise procedure of "centralizing ideas" and "decentralizing authority."

Bureaucrats in Washington did not run it. Leaders in the communities where people live and work did that. Mr. Hoover believed in and trusted the common sense and the good faith of the people.

These general observations disposed of, we return to April, 1917. Shortly after war was declared on April 6 of that year, President Wilson cabled Mr. Hoover and requested his early return to the United States in order that the government might have the benefit of his experience and knowledge in handling wartime food problems. He asked also that Mr. Hoover bring along as much detailed and over-all information as he could gather about the food needs of our allies.

Due to the information he had gained as Chairman of the Commission for Relief in Belgium about food sources, shipping facilities, the amounts and kinds of food needed to provide health and life-sustaining diets for a given population, Mr. Hoover was able in a few weeks' time to gather all pertinent data on the subject.

With this in hand he sailed for home in early May. Enroute, he assayed the facts and began to formulate policies for a food program.

Even before his arrival in America the food situation had become precarious. The Allies' heavy and uncontrolled demands for foodstuffs had overdrawn our reserves, prices were rising rapidly and food markets were becoming demoralized. It was evident that Allied food needs—on which victory depended—and our own equally important food needs called for early action.

Congress was even then considering some form of legislation which would provide for conservation of food, protect producers and consumers and at the same time enable us to help our Allies. The exact form this legislation should take, because much of it was revolutionary in nature, required prolonged debate in Congress.

President Wilson, to avoid losing precious time, used his war powers in authorizing Mr. Hoover to take such steps as he could to organize voluntary conservation of food, to co-operate with business organizations on a voluntary basis both to secure conservation and direction of the movement of food supplies to our Allies. It was possible for him to act quickly and effectively along these lines under the newly created Council of National Defense and the Exports Administrative Board, predecessor of the War Trade Board, which under an April 24, 1917 Act of Congress had a Treasury fund of $3,000,000,000 that could be drawn on for the establishment of credits to be used in the purchase of food supplies for the Allied governments.

This setup enabled Mr. Hoover soon after his return home to take an important part in creating and directing our food policies.

As a result of the authority and directions President Wilson gave him, Mr. Hoover and his colleagues, many of whom had been associated with him in the Belgian Relief Commission service, had created a detailed production, conservation, purchase and distribution food program and had parts of it in full operation by the time Congress had finished its debates and sent the legislation to President Wilson. When, on August 10, 1917, President Wilson appointed Mr. Hoover U.S. Food Administrator, the new organization was staffed and ready to move fast.

In this undertaking Hoover followed his lifelong habit, whether in his professional work, humanitarian, or semi-public service, of enlisting the efforts of able men. The Food Administration was soon staffed with such men as well as with ex-members of the Belgian Commission's personnel who were experts in the new field of human helpfulness.

Selected Title of Food Administrator

After rejecting suggested titles of "Food Dictator," "Controller" or "Director" Hoover himself selected the title of "Food Administrator." This was more in keeping with his beliefs in individualism, liberty and co-operation.

The duty of the Food Administration as President Wilson outlined it fell into two parts: first to organize the service of self-denial and to stimulate the food production of the American people for the purpose of supplying our own military and civilian populations and that of the Allies with foodstuffs during the war, and looking ahead, all Europe after the Armistice; and second, to control so far as possible the distribution of foodstuff supplies and to limit speculation. As President Wilson phrased it, America and her Allies were now "eating at a common table."

Outlines Policies and Program

In outlining the policy and program of the Food Administration shortly after it was legally created, Hoover said, in a public statement:

> The Food Administration is called into being to stabilize and not to disturb conditions and to defend honest enterprise against illegitimate competition. It has been devised to correct the abnormalities and abuses that have crept into trade by reason of the world disturbance and to restore business as far as may be to a reasonable basis.
>
> The businessmen of this country, I am convinced . . . realize their own patriotic obligation and the solemnity of the situation, and will fairly and generously co-operate in meeting the national emergency. I do not believe that drastic force need be applied. . . . But if there be those who expect to exploit this hour of sacrifice, if there are men or organizations scheming to increase the trials of this country, we shall not hesitate to apply to the full the drastic, coercive powers that Congress has conferred upon us in this instrument.

Mr. Hoover also held the conviction that government, especially in time of war, should scrupulously avoid tinkering with the complicated machinery of private business. He believed, too, that government should lead, advise, adjust and harmonize—but never, except in instances of wrong doing, should it use its power.

Controlling the Recalcitrant

One of the "drastic, coercive powers" which Congress conferred on the Food Administration was that of cancelling licenses to do business which had been granted under its authority. The licenses included food manufacturers, jobbers, wholesalers and retailers whose volume of business exceeded one hundred thousand dollars annually.

In reporting to President Wilson at the end of the war, Mr. Hoover stated that "99 per cent of American business gave hearty co-operation." The one per cent which did not, such as those manufacturers who exceeded a fair profit and those dealers who diluted their shipments with inferior grain, lost their license to do business. Smaller offenders were disciplined by local food committees. The usual procedure was to fine the offenders and contribute the amount of the fine to the Red Cross.

"Centralizing Ideas"—"Decentralizing Execution"

The Hoover method of enlisting the people's voluntary co-operation met with remarkable success. He avoided the pitfalls which had destroyed the programs of European food "dictators," one after another of whom had attempted to take complete charge of a crop, make prices by law, ration the people and establish and enforce severe penalties for the infractions of their rules and regulations. And every one of them had failed. All of them lost their jobs even in countries where men had been forced to goosestep to the voice of authority for generations.

Hoover looked with horror on any program which commandeered crops from a free people, policed consumers or distributed food cards. Such practices were obnoxious to free men whose greatest accomplishments had come out of their freely given co-operation.

Every plan the Food Administration officials of World War I made, and every proposal they presented to the people, was built around this idea. To carry it out they "centralized ideas and decentralized execution." They believed that their cause was the whole people's cause, therefore their program must be geared to the communities where people lived and they should be made responsible for carrying it out.

The Food Administrator in World War I sent no agents from Washington to the states except for the purpose of giving advice at conferences. Each of the forty-eight states and 3069 counties in the nation had its own food administrator who was a leader in his community, who knew its resources and needs as well as the temper and peculiarities of its people. No ration cards were issued. No enforcement officers appeared to irritate the people.

Produced Needed Fats Quickly in 1917–1918

Hoover's experience and studies in the Belgian Relief enabled him to see that wheat, sugar and fats were first necessities in maintaining the Allied soldiers and civilians. Fats were especially important because of the subtle part they have in rounding out man's food ration. Since the Orient's fats and oils required too long a shipping haul, the only quick and close source was the American hog, whose females produce two litters of pigs each year. These, if properly fed, can be made into two hundred pound hogs ready for slaughter in less than eight months from birth.

Unfortunately the American hog crop was far below normal in 1917, due primarily to abnormally large purchases of the American grain crops by the European governments during the two preceding years. These purchases had limited the available grain for hog feed and consequently greatly curtailed hog breeding. They had helped to drive the American farmer out of the hog business. Since American hogs were the most dependable source of the fats badly needed by our Allies, Hoover's conclusion was that hog breeding should be stimulated.

Having formulated his policy, Mr. Hoover sought men to carry it out. The men he called in for a conference consisted of an advisory board of farmers with representatives from every hog and cattle state. Former Governor Stuart of Virginia was chairman of the group which made the recommendations that the Food Administration carried out.

These recommendations called for agreements between the packers and buyers that they would pay the committee's recommended price for hogs. The price agreed upon limited the packers' profit to 9 per cent of the capital employed in processing and handling the pork. This arrangement gave United States hog growers the greatest profit they ever had made up to that time.

"Food Will Win the War"

This five-word comprehensive slogan sounded a responsive note in the heart of every true American. He could understand it without explanation. Best of all he could do something about it, he himself alone, and by so doing he also could serve.

It caught on quickly everywhere. Rich and poor alike displayed it with pride in the windows of their homes. Nearly every store, restaurant and dining car in the nation placed a poster carrying the slogan in a prominent place. Thousands of billboards heralded it as did the bulletin boards of all factories. Even the Pullman Company broke its heretofore unbreakable restriction and posted it in its cars. It was the central theme of all Food Administration advertising. There is reason to believe that no other slogan has been so completely displayed or so productive of results.

An All-Inclusive, Intricate Job

Hoover's problem was an all-inclusive, intricate one. First he must provide an indispensable minimum of food for all, American and Allied civilians and military forces alike. Types of food essential for growing children must be set apart. Because of transportation difficulties, it was best that Americans should eat the more perishable or bulky forms of food products. The shortage of sugar prompted him to appeal to Americans to forego the pleasure of satisfying their sweet tooth and to volunteer to use no more than two pounds of sugar per month. He instigated wheatless Mondays and Wednesdays, meatless Tuesdays, porkless Thursdays and Saturdays. There was "Victory Bread" which contained more of the wheat grain than ordinary white bread. Twelve rules were given out for public eating places.

The spirit of the Food Administration's crusade filled the news and advertising columns of the nation's newspapers. "Serve just enough" became the patriotic purpose, almost the prayerful rite, of the people.

Millions of citizens who were unable to fight, who longed for a way to serve and sacrifice, voluntarily joined the Hoover ranks. Volunteer pledges that they would not waste food poured in to the Food Administration offices from fourteen million families.

Why Food Would Win the War

The desperate Allied need for food in 1917 was due to the fact that for nearly three years they had switched their efforts from food production to that of killing men. Furthermore, many of their food producing areas had become battlegrounds and many of their farmers were in the trenches or their graves. U-boat activities had sent countless ships with countless tons of food to the bottom of the ocean. Late in 1917 Lord Rhondda, the English Crop Controller, despondent over the food shortage, cabled America: "We are beaten, the war is over." In 1918 he cabled Hoover: "Unless you are able to send us seventy-five million bushels of wheat over and above what you have sent up to January 1 . . . I cannot take responsibility of assuring our people that there will be food enough to win the war; imperative necessity compels me to cable you in this blunt way."

A little later, during the early spring of 1918, the fate of the Allied cause rested primarily on the fulfillment of food shipment schedules from the United States. This statement is supported by the letter to Mr. Hoover dated February 22, 1918 which was written and signed by Lord Reading, Ambassador from Great Britain, Count V. Macchi di Cellere, Ambassador from Italy and French High Commissioner André Tardieu. An extract from it reads:

> We feel that every endeavor must be made to ship at least 1,100,000 tons in March and more if possible. . . . [Failure to do so] would be nothing short of calamity and we most earnestly seek your assistance. . . . We *must* meet and overcome the present crisis. Our excuse for our insistence is the fact . . . that a failure to make ade-

quate shipments in March may produce events of incalculable gravity in both Europe and America.

Appraising the Job Done

Just as the proof of the pudding is in the eating, the proof of a job well done is in the record of what was accomplished.

Expressed in terms of number of tons of food supplies produced and shipped to our Allies, the record shows that the average annual shipments of breadstuffs, meats and fats, sugar and feed grains the United States shipped to Europe during the three preceding pre-war years was 5,533,000 tons whereas in 1917–1918, the first year of U. S. Food Administration operation, these shipments jumped to 11,820,000 tons and in its second year, 1918–1919, they went to 16,301,061 tons.

Credit for this stupendous increase in our exports of food belongs equally to the American farmers and to the wise, understanding guidance and direction of the Food Administration.

Expressed in terms of governmental machinery the U. S. Food Administration's record is equally amazing, and its liquidation program could serve as a model for those present-day war emergency units which four-and-a-half years after the end of the war are still operating at full speed. The World War I Food Administration, whose vast organization reached into every nook and corner of the nation, was completely liquidated within four months after the Armistice was declared on November 11, 1918.

Expressed in human terms World War I Food Administration's record demonstrates that a free people by voluntary co-operation are capable of overcoming any earthly odds. It followed throughout all of its operations the policy of leadership as opposed to that of regimentation and coercion. This procedure enabled it to shift the major burden from the government in Washington to volunteers where the people lived. It issued no orders. What it did issue were requests and recommendations. It did not ration the people. Instead it appealed to them to ration themselves. The people's response to this appeal was inspiring.

The most astonishing, almost unbelievable part of the Food Administration's record is expressed in terms of what its operation cost the taxpayers. The Treasury Department's records of the federal government show that the taxpayers of the United States received back every cent of money advanced the Food Administration by both congressional and presidential appropriation, and on top of that the United States Treasury received from the Hoover organizations an additional sum which was in excess of $52,000,000. This represented the net earned profits of its two subsidiary organizations, the United States Grain Corporation and the Sugar Equalization Board.

Originally the Congress had provided the Grain Corporation with an appropriation of $50,000,000 and the Sugar Equalization Board with $5,000,000, and the President and the Congress had appropriated $10,000,000 for administrative expenses of the Food Administration proper. The Grain Corporation and the Sugar Board by businesslike methods had been able to purchase foodstuffs they sold at a slight—very slight at that—margin of profit to the Allies and at a substantial margin of profit to neutrals, earning profits of over $60,000,000 on total transactions which exceeded $10,000,000,000. The Food Administration proper expended $7,862,669 of its $10,000,000 appropriations on administration.

A detailed breakdown of comparative costs of United States food direction in World Wars I and II would make eyebrow-lifting reading.

Quakerism in Action

The factor which perhaps more than any other contributed to the success of the Food Administration's efforts to enlist the whole people's co-operation was that it advertised a cause and not a man. The one *never-to-be-violated rule* of its publicity department was that all releases to the press should refer to *The United States Food Administration* or to the *Food Administrator,* never to Mr. Hoover by name.

This procedure helped constantly to convince the public that it was their affair, not that of some distant, high-placed official. It helped also to enlist the all-out support of the press.

It was patterned after the Quaker method of playing down the individual for the purpose of playing up the cause. They follow it because it is difficult and often impossible to advertise both the individual and the cause without discounting one or the other of them. By following this method they have had an influence on men's thinking far out of proportion to the size of the Quaker membership. By following it they have had remarkable success in crystallizing and accelerating public opinion.

Hoover's sure instinct on how to reach the public heart and his rare ability to hitch ideals, intelligence and enthusiasm together and make them into a perfectly matched team is the hard core of the answer of how he alone of all of the food administrators or "dictators" of the warring nations held his job from start to finish of World War I.

He once stated, in a speech before the Young Republican League of Colorado:

> . . . While the inspiration to reform comes from the human heart, it is achieved only by the intellect. Enthusiastic hearts have flooded us with illusions. Ideals without illusions are good. Ideals with illusions are no good.

Man could really make something of this earth if he approached the solutions of his problems with high ideals and advanced his programs with intelligence and enthusiasm!

Comparison of World Wars I and II Food Administration Records

One of the most disheartening truths of life is that man, both individually and en masse, seems unable to learn and apply only such facts of life as they gain from their own experience.

A graphic illustration of this point can be found in the comparison of our government's food programs in World Wars I and II. Its World War I food production, distribution and price controlling program had been both universally popular and remarkably successful. Every fact, to the smallest detail of policy and procedure was available for use. So was the man who directed it, as also were a host of his assistants. Both the facts and the directors of the World War I program were ignored as though they never had existed.

In their stead was placed a multitude of executive order created governmental organizations with conflicting authority that were manned by men whose primary qualifications appeared to be that they knew little or nothing at all about the field of their endeavors.

In the midst of the war, in my book *The Home Front* (G. P. Putnam's Sons, New York, 1943), I pointed out:

> The administrative incapacity or inexperience of many reformers in high official position prevented their knowing when they were doing things which would infuriate the people. These officials, who were flanked by lawyers and former college professors and other professional theorists, felt secure in their own conceit and high purpose. They also, at the same time, doubted both the people's capacity and patriotic purpose. To meet this situation, they sought to blueprint and regulate to the last detail the activities of one hundred and thirty-five million people. Their imaginations far outstripped the common-sense or understanding of their employers, the people.
>
> Free men, and especially free Americans, do not like to be bossed or shoved around; they prefer to have public needs explained to them and their co-operation invited. The bossy activities of little men in Washington, therefore, irritated every adult in the nation. Senator Harry F. Byrd, of Virginia, as reported in the press in early December, 1941, emphasized the plight of five million farmers and other small truckers throughout the country, all of whom, to do business, must digest the Office of Defense Transportation's instructions, 24,000 words of fine print, in order to present their case for a "transportation certificate of war necessity" in connection with gasoline rationing.
>
> Senator Byrd also stated that a statistical report sent him revealed that in the three preceding months eighty-nine companies had received 3,479 separate questionnaires or requests for reports of one kind and another, or an average of 164 for each company during the quarterly period. "It took those companies an average of 495,480 man-hours per year to comply with the requests," Senator Byrd said, "and a breakdown showed that 64 per cent were duplicates in some degree and 34 per cent were outright duplicates." And in February, 1943, Senator Byrd reported that the rules, regulations, and interpretations of OPA alone totaled eleven million words.

Senator Arthur H. Vandenberg, of Michigan, speaking on the same subject, expressed the belief that it was impossible for business concerns to furnish much of the information the government demanded. Because of this, he said, the flood of questionnaires from government departments "strikes positive terror to the hearts of citizens who wish to be totally loyal, yet who find their loyalties channeled into maddening inquisitions."

Asserting that it was up to Congress to find out who is responsible for this "pattern of needlessly intimate inquisitions" which seems to proceed "on the theory that the American people will behave only when placed in a strait jacket," Senator Vandenberg cited an example of what is making the nation "quiz-dizzy." He said he had been told that a farmer in Michigan had to fill out a four-page report before he could buy a pair of boots. And he had been told of a case which took a firm nine months, at a cost of $55,000 to answer government questionnaires.

One Washington, D. C., department store received five volumes, containing 13,423 fine printed pages of OPA rules and regulations. The store had to engage a staff of twenty-seven people, which devoted all of its time in trying to keep up with OPA rules.

The Pure Oil Company, according to a statement of its president, Henry M. Dawes, in the annual report issued in late February, 1943, had been forced to spend between 8 and 10 per cent of its earnings for the year to compile statistics, questionnaires and information for government and "quasi-government" authorities:

> To attempt to arrive at any exact figure for this cost would be to indulge in the same passion for statistics that has created the problem.
>
> Such a mass of uncoordinated, immaterial and irrelevant data is being assembled in connection with our industry as can never be digested. Voluminous questionnaires are issued that are rarely scanned and seldom briefed, and which for the most part demonstrate things already admitted.
>
> The cost in money is, however, insignificant as compared with the injury that is done by the diversion of manpower and the confusion

of thinking which results from too much concentration upon unrelated and inconsequential details.

The Truman Committee, investigating the fuel oil situation in early December, 1942, reported that the oil program had "bogged down in a formula of complex calculations by experts who disdain simple percentage-cut procedure." The Associated Press reported that, according to the Truman's Committee's findings, the price-administration formula fixers went back forty-three years in their exploration of temperature statistics and came up with a procedure that ignores wind velocity; that old weather standby, humidity, and also ignores the thickness of walls. Thus it provided many homes with uninhabitable allowances.

The slide rule experts used their laboriously acquired and unessential information as the basis for their calculations on the amount of oil necessary to heat a given number of square feet in a given county instead of assuming that the average householder had not deliberately wasted money in previous years by purchasing fuel oil he did not need, and cutting his allotment on a percentage system based on the need for reducing consumption in his area.

Such exact knowledge of the use of slide rules and science and such paucity of understanding of the ways of men were to be expected of men inexperienced in life outside classrooms and textbooks. There was the published story of the request of a food dehydrating firm which wrote the WPB requesting a priority for a one-hundred-foot conveyor belt. According to the story, a WPB official in reply asked what proportion of the firm's output went to meet war needs. The company replied, "60 per cent," whereupon the WPB official reportedly answered, "We are granting you priority for a sixty-foot conveyor belt in consideration of the fact that 60 per cent of your output goes to the war effort."

There also was a newspaper story which stated that a representative of a large chain-grocery firm had called upon the OPA to inquire if the price ceiling on potatoes applied also to seed potatoes. He was told by the OPA official, "I don't know. I've never seen seed potatoes growing, so I don't know what seed potatoes are."

Senator Butler of Nebraska charged, in late December, 1942, that the directions of a twenty-four page OPA pamphlet (each of the first twenty pages contained three columns of fine print) on how to cut up a beef to be sold wholesale were so "specific as to be incomprehensible." He added, "The whole thing is nutty. It just shows what a bunch of young lawyers can do when they meet up with a beef chart." (These young lawyers and their theorist collaborators arrogantly continued to exercise their power until late March, 1943, when OPA Director Prentiss M. Brown stripped them of their veto powers and according to news reports reduced the number employed by the OPA from 2,700 to 100.)

An avalanche of detailed orders, report forms, and questionnaires was sent to millions of citizens to tell them how to do things they had spent their lives doing well. Many government reports, Senator Byrd stated, "are so fantastic in their demands and so absurd in the information requested as to be almost unbelievable."

Senator Joseph C. O'Mahoney, Democrat, Wyoming, pointed out in a speech he delivered in December, 1942:

> Between January 7, 1941, and April 12, 1942, the President issued 500 executive orders. They were not written in the halls of Congress on the responsibility of men chosen by the public and known to the public. They were written in private by anonymous experts. They were not subject to public hearing nor were they analyzed in public debate. They did not become known to the public until issued—and then they were effective. . . .
>
> Some of them were intended by their authors to remake the world, others to remake the industrial and economic organizations of our own country. All of them were conceived in private and were promulgated before the persons who must obey them had any opportunity to comment on them, much less to suggest amendments. . . .

Millions of citizens believed that these detailed, voluminous regulations and orders boded no good for free institutions. Millions were irritated by the implication they carried, the implication that their government servants trusted neither their good sense nor their honest purpose. The people's irritation was further increased by the incompetence and inefficiency of many of these servants. Each of these things served to create a certain amount of disunity, to divert the people's attention from the nation's compelling need—namely, unanimous and universal co-operation in the war program.

The irritations caused by bunglers or by willful officials created public bad temper. But anxiety did not come to live in hearts and homes until greater numbers of our armed forces were sent to faraway bases and battle fronts. The people did not shrink appreciably from the heartache, suffering, sacrifice, and destruction. This they accepted as inevitable. But they just as definitely refused to accept as either inevitable or necessary the loss of human lives which resulted from official incompetence, reform unabated, or politics as usual. The result was that the people registered their temper and attitude November 3, 1942.

The election day returns revealed many things, among them that the people were surfeited with politics-as-usual and reform-as-usual during the war. It was brought out in the defeat of "rubber-stamp" members of Congress. It also revealed that they were tired of "the autocratic orders of pinhead autocrats," as one Democratic senator expressed it; that they were tired of reforms which were forced upon them in an arbitrary and capricious manner by officials in important government posts who misused their great wartime powers to change our system of government.

This official practice and attitude had too definitely made the nation's war a *New Deal* War; and on election day, therefore, the people voted to make it an *American* War. They rebelled against irritating regulations which they believed to be senseless. Their ballot-box mandate to the Administration was to drop reform, favoritism, and partisan practices; to strip officialdom of incompetents, and to organize and man the government for efficient conduct of the war.

This belated but emphatic national protest against the government's maladministration of the war program carried the most dangerous threat the people had yet made against Hitlerism. This was true because the sole election issue was greater, more vigorous, and more efficient conduct of the war. It was a vote of no-confidence in bureaucratic fumbling and red tape; a demand from the people for value received.

Because the people always expect their government to express their noble and just purposes, and never to reflect their baseness or weakness, they characteristically voted "agin" the bad, rather than "for the good." But a miracle took place in the voting booths of the land on election day. The animus which millions of voters felt toward the administration when they entered the voting booth ran down their pencils and spent its force on their ballots. They left the booths with civic hearts cleansed of partisan poisons for the moment.

According to a telegram the New York State Food Merchants Association sent the Secretary of Agriculture on February 27, 1943:

> Black market threatens the entire retail food distribution picture unless a practical attitude is immediately taken by OPA pricing executives. Recent price controls on butter are rapidly helping to make this item as popular as meat with "foodleggers," and the ceilings on fresh vegetables are an open invitation to black market operators to enter this field.
>
> As we see it, the only solution of the problem, as long as OPA cannot set prices on all commodities at the farmer's level, is to allow each level of distribution a fixed percentage of mark-up over its cost.
>
> Our customers can't eat theories. Please help us give them butter, meat and vegetables without the necessity of paying off graduates of the prohibition era. The success of point-rationing is also threatened if these perishable items cannot be distributed through normal business channels.

The Administration's misguided and improper farm policy had created shortages in fats, oils, oleomargarine, cotton seed, and dairy products, before Herbert Hoover's crusade aroused the public to its weaknesses. Neglect or lack of official foresight had reduced the supply of milk to a point which would threaten the public health. Factors which were creating a reduced milk supply included a shortage of labor, price ceilings on hay and other feeds which made profitable shipment impossible, price ceilings on dairy products, and limited transportation facilities.

Farm leaders bitterly denounced such OPA officials as the ones who held that milk prices must be kept uniform, otherwise the "little steel" formula would break down. This "over-emphasis on price instead of supply will yet make us a nation of undernourished men, women and children," said one farm organization official. According to advocates of this school of thought, there is but one sure way to avoid inflation, and that is to provide an abundant supply. Do that, and ration the goods produced so that equal treatment will be assured to everyone, and you will need price-fixing only to prevent profiteering. Some government officials, however, in the spring of 1943, sought to roll back prices and then proposed subsidies to meet farmers' increased production costs.

At the Midwest Governors' Conference held in Des Moines, Iowa, in March, 1943, Governor Dwight Griswold of Nebraska stated:

> There are no trick formulas by which the farm wartime problems can be solved. Let us solve them as best we can right in our own states. In Nebraska we intend to find our own help to plant and harvest crops. It will be difficult, but our own boys who are in the front lines throughout the world have far more difficulties to face.

Despite the wisdom of Thomas Jefferson's observation that "were we directed from Washington when to sow and when to reap we would soon want bread," the bureaucrats of Washington harassed the farmers of the nation with an almost ceaseless flood of questionnaires or regulations. These questionnaires demanded detailed and complete information which few farmers were able to provide, and which, even when provided, was of little value to the government. The regulations, mostly, if not entirely, drawn up by young lawyers who had never been on a farm, seriously handicapped farming operations. And they served, too, to exasperate the farmers by their revelation of the regulating officials' ignorance of the simple farming facts of life. There was the story, perhaps apocryphal, but illustrative, of an OPA economist who refused to approve the program presented by California poultrymen. He would not do so, he said, because the poultrymen had failed to include possible profits to be made from eggs which the capons and broilers would lay!

Hundreds of thousands, if not millions, of farmers were handicapped in their food production works by the ODT's centralized office gasoline allotments.

One farmer wrote his congressman,

> "I've yet to hear anyone say he isn't ready and willing to do whatever is for the best interests of our beloved country. We all want to do that. But we do object to our servants in Washington telling us so many times, 'You must and you cannot' when the you-musts and the you-cannots make neither sense nor reason."

The *Vineyard Gazette* of Edgartown, Mass., editorially stated that:

> "It is certainly time to cut the red tape which puts so many hindrances and devilments in the way of production on our farms. We like the spirit of another island farmer who sent back a long, complicated form without filling it out.
>
> " 'I can't understand this,' he wrote. 'Here is what I need extra gasoline for'—and he stated plainly what his situation was—'and if you don't want me to have it, or if you want me to sell my herd, just let me know.' "

These were the almost unanimous complaints and recommendations of the working chairmen, who came closer to the problem than the far-distant officials who used slide rules to get their answers.

The World War I Food Administration trusted the people and appealed to their patriotic purpose. It issued no orders. It had no centralized authority. It gave the full power of interpreting and enforcing its policies to local officials in the communities.

On the question of comparative costs of the two programs there can be only surmise. The World War I program cost to the taxpayers is known. It cost them $52,000,000, less than nothing. God alone knows how much the World War II food program cost the taxpayers because it is hidden in a maze of triple-entry bookkeeping records which are buried deep in the files of a host of evanescent subsidiary or conflicting organizations.

CHAPTER THREE

American Relief Administration

1918–1921

All information concerning food conditions in central Europe that seeped through the military lines during the weeks just ahead of the Armistice on November 11, 1918, was foreboding. Food reserves had been reduced to the vanishing point, current supplies were extremely low. The next harvest was at least ten months away. Commerce and transportation were at a standstill. Gold was gone. Stable governments did not exist and the paper money of instable governments was worthless. A promise to pay by a government which did not officially exist (and most of them could not until a peace treaty was signed) had no food purchasing value.

Without help from the outside, approximately two hundred million men, women and children in central and eastern Europe would face starvation. Without outside help at least half of them would die, or else, because of malnutrition, be susceptible to destructive diseases.

Allied government officials realized that this desperate, gigantic situation was too big and too complicated for private charity to handle. While they debated ways and means of action, starvation, which knows no time schedules, moved ahead with its destructive forces.

The Allies had their own ideas, calling for a joint operational program. To this Mr. Hoover said no. His reasons were set forth in a cable, dated November 7, 1918, to Joseph C. Cotton, the Food Administration's London representative, in which he said:

> For your general advice this government will not agree to any program that even looks like Inter-Allied control of our economic resources after peace. After peace, over one-half of the whole export food supplies of the world will come from the United States and for the buyers of these supplies to sit in majority in dictation to us

as to prices and distribution is wholly inconceivable. The same applies to raw materials. Our only hope of securing justice in distribution, proper appreciation abroad of the effort we make to assist foreign nations, and proper return for the service that we will perform will revolve around complete independence of commitment to joint action on our part.*

Four days later in a memorandum to President Wilson, Mr. Hoover presented at length his views about what should be done and how. He had prepared the memorandum following President Wilson's action in commissioning him to start for Europe at an early date for the purpose of formulating and advancing a broad relief program.

On November 12, President Wilson prepared a "to whom it may concern" memorandum wherein he approved the program Mr. Hoover had prepared and also stated that the United States Food Administrator "will proceed at once to Europe to determine what action is required" and then outlined the possible fields of action.

Back of Mr. Hoover lay forty-four years of hard work and remarkable accomplishment; ahead of him? No one knew what. Now, however, he was no longer sailing uncharted seas. He knew more about world food sources and production and distribution than any other living man. He knew how to find and get food supplies transported. He knew how many calories were needed to sustain life and he knew the right proportion of carbohydrates, proteins and vitamins required to make a balanced diet.

Supplementing and complementing this comprehensive knowledge was a tried and trusted army of experienced associates who stood ready to respond to his call for help. Topping all this was his intimate knowledge of Europe and the food needs of Europeans.

No longer, as in the early days of the Commission for Relief in Belgium, did Hoover have to rely heavily on common sense, unyielding and unselfish purpose and stubborn determination. First, the Belgian job and next his work as Food Administrator, had given him prestige among the great as well as the little people. Now he spoke with the

* *American Food in the World War and Reconstruction Period,* by Frank M. Surface and Raymond L. Bland, Stanford University Press, 1931.

voice of authority. Now he represented a powerful nation which had the food, and money to pay for it and the heart and the urge to help relieve starvation. Everyone, except a handful of high officials of our European Allies, was anxious and willing to co-operate.

The food supplies they needed were in America, thanks to the people's full co-operation with his Food Administration's food saving, stepped-up food production program.

The job Hoover faced, nevertheless, was an almost insoluble, impossible one. Germany was starved and some Allied officials held that the starving condition of her people was a good thing. The Austro-Hungarians were in a worse condition than the Germans; Poland and the Russian provinces which Germany had overrun were even worse off and all southeastern Europe disorganized and hungry. A cold winter blanketed Europe. On top of all this Allied officials refused to withdraw the blockade against the Central Empires until peace terms were conclusively made.

Armed with Presidential authority Mr. Hoover sailed for Europe on November 18, 1918, just one week after the Armistice, but before leaving Washington he had with Presidential authority completed arrangements for the War Department to ship 140,000 tons of foodstuffs and the Grain Corporation to ship an additional 120,000 tons to Europe.

His first problem upon arrival was to try to effect some agreement with the Allies for the distribution of these supplies, since the relief of Europe must from necessity be handled as a joint responsibility of the Allied and associated governments because of economic blockade, political and other problems. But at no point in any place, Mr. Hoover insisted, would the United States enter into any arrangements by which it would lose control of supplies which had to come from and be financed by the United States. United States UNRRA officials, following World War II, would have found it to the advantage of the taxpayers of the United States as well as to the people they were supposed to help had they studied and followed Mr. Hoover's American Relief Administration program and course.

To this the Allied governments were opposed. They held that since the Central Powers were a common foe, all Allied and associated governments' resources should be pooled. Mr. Hoover advanced additional reasons to those in his cable to Cotton for his refusal to accept their proposal.

One was his belief that the job to be done was so tremendous and difficult that it could best be done with executive power centered in one head. A joint inter-Allied commission, he held, would be inefficient and troublesome in situations which required prompt action and frequent swift changes in policy. In addition he was adamant on the point that the United States would not participate in any organization in which the distribution of its supplies and funds could be determined by a majority vote of representatives of other countries.

Almost immediately upon his arrival in Europe Mr. Hoover had sent missions to various parts of Europe to make first-hand studies of food needs and requirements. Following this he established resident missions in each country to which relief supplies were to be sent.

Meanwhile negotiations continued with the Allied governments on a *modus operandi*. In due course, on December 31, 1918, the four associated governments agreed to create a Supreme Council of Supply and Relief which on January 11, 1919, named Mr. Hoover Director General. Later, February 24, 1919, his work became the Food Section of the recently formed Supreme Economic Council.

Even before he had won these open battles Mr. Hoover and his staff were fighting the hidden battles of starvation with thousands of tons of food supplies.

Men's Minds, Not Food Supplies, The First Problem

How to get around the Allied refusal to lift the blockade became Hoover's first problem. This had to be done quickly because starvation cannot be halted by debate or negotiation. He looked for a loophole in the Allied position and soon found what seemed to be a possible one. He proposed that the Allies lift the food blockade for the four northern neutral nations of Denmark, Holland, Norway and Sweden and permit them to buy food and exchange it with the Germans for other products. On Christmas Eve the Blockade Committee said *yes;* seven days later it said *no.*

Days and weeks passed but the Allies would not relent. Even in America there was open opposition to any proposal that contemplated helping our recent enemies despite their desperate need. Hoover disposed of the American opposition with a bristling statement. He stated that the point of view of his Western upbringing was "not to kick a man in the stomach after we have licked him" and then his tender heart took over from the he-man and he added, "We have not been fighting women and children and we are not beginning now." Next the Hoover with vision stepped in and pointed out that:

> . . . no matter how deeply we may feel at the present moment, our vision must stretch over the next hundred years and we must write now into history such acts as will stand creditably in the minds of our grandchildren.

The Allies Yield—But Grudgingly

This statement and his effective arguments, supported by the more humane Allied officials, helped to get permission from the Supreme War Council to sell the Germans such foodstuffs as they could manage to purchase. Less than one week after receiving this permission, Hoover signed an agreement with the German delegates in Brussels. Even before the signing he had flashed messages by radio to the seven seas in search of food-laden ships, with orders to change their ports of destination and hurry to various Continental ports with their life-saving cargoes.

One of those little known but dramatic incidents in human affairs comes into this story here. It concerns the Germans' agreement to pay for these food supplies with gold. The Germans were to ship the gold to a New York City bank which had agreed to advance 90 per cent of its purported value to the American Relief Administration. Later, when the boxes containing this gold were opened in the vaults of the bank in New York City, they were found to contain United States gold double eagles. These had been a part of the one-billion dollar gold indemnity which Germany had levied on France at the end of the 1870 Franco-Prussian War. During the years between 1870 and 1919 these United States gold pieces had lain hidden in vaults deep under Berlin. Now they came back home on an errand of mercy.

Advice Sought on Peace Problems

Although Hoover was not a member of the United States Peace Commission, he was constantly being asked for counsel and advice during the proceedings. His primary concern was about "the gaunt realities which prowled outside." Because others shared his earnest concern he had some voice in the discussions. His opinions carried great weight, both because he represented the U. S. Food Administration and because of the fact that he was chairman of the Grain Corporation. He also was head of the continuing Commission for Relief in Belgium. Added to these operations he headed the American Relief Administration, then emerging to carry on an urgently needed job. Within a short time he was also Director General of Supplies and Relief under the Supreme War Council. Moreover he was recognized by the responsible representatives of every nation as the world's foremost authority on sources of food supplies and equitable distribution of them. When the latter office was dissolved through his own action, he was made head of the Supreme Economic Council.

General Pershing once defined Hoover's place in the scheme of the armistice period by saying, "Mr. Hoover is the food regulator of the world."

John Maynard Keynes (later Lord Keynes), an English delegate to the Peace Mission, wrote:

"Mr. Hoover was the only man who emerged from the ordeal of Paris with an enhanced reputation. . . ."

His further remarks are contained in Appendix IV.

A Sad But Inspiring Story

The details of the American Relief Administration and its disheartening battles against delay, hate and greed make a long story. It was forced to meet attacks from some quarters which contended that it was too soft with the defeated enemy. These and other charges against the ARA have been recorded and disposed of by historians. For the most part they were effectively answered on the spot by the ARA's heroic and almost superhuman efforts to abate hunger. They will be retold a thousand times in the years to come after the manner of men who relive great and fine deeds.

The inspiring way Hoover's resourcefulness enabled the ARA to overcome blockades, curb greed, soften hate and feed the needy—all of the needy, whether friend or enemy, regardless of his color, nationality or creed—gave the world many years of peace which it might otherwise not have had.

As he wrestled with the problem of rehabilitating Europe, Hoover also wrestled with another complex and challenging question. It was how to help the Russian people without aiding their Bolshevik movement. In a lengthy letter on the Russian problem of March 28, 1919, to President Wilson, he said in part:

> It simply cannot be denied, that this swinging of the social pendulum from the tyranny of the extreme right to the tyranny of the extreme left is based on a foundation of real social grievance. The tyranny of the reactionaries in eastern and central Europe for generations before the war, the sufferings of their common people, is but a commonplace to every social student. . . . The poor were starved and driven mad in the presence of extravagance and waste.

It is possible that World War I might not have been in vain if the "gaunt realities" that Hoover clearly discerned hovering over the Versailles peace conference had been given more consideration.

Next He Helps Feed Russia

The chronology must be broken here for the purpose of including in this chapter the ARA's relief work in Russia. Two years after its major work was completed in Europe (the work with children went on for years) Russia faced a severe famine. The Russian people were hungry, terrified and without funds. Maxim Gorki, Russian novelist, issued an appeal for American aid in July, 1921. The still-intact American Relief Association had a cash balance of about $7,000,000.

Then Secretary of Commerce, Hoover replied to Gorki and indicated that the ARA stood ready to help the Russian people under certain reasonable conditions. One of these, he stated, was that of the release of Americans then being held in Soviet prisons. He asked also for full liberty of travel for relief workers. And he insisted upon equal treatment in food distribution for all Russians regardless of class. He volunteered assurance that the undertaking would be non-political from the American angle.

The Gorki-Hoover exchange launched negotiations and within a month, on August 20, 1921, an agreement for the project was drafted in Riga. Because of its historical significance and because it completely refutes later Communistic propaganda to the effect that the ARA discriminated against Communists in the distribution of relief, the complete text of the Riga Agreement between the ARA and the Russian Socialist Federative Soviet Republic is presented in Appendix VII.

Americans responded generously to Mr. Hoover's call to help Russia's starving millions. Congress released the sum of $20,000,000 from the accounts of the Grain Corporation. The Kremlin consented to add to these sums about $11,000,000 from Russian gold reserves. In all, about $78,000,000 was found for the Russian aid program. Estimates placed the number of lives this program saved at about fifteen million. Millions of men, women and children were inoculated against typhus, paratyphoid, diphtheria, smallpox and cholera by Hoover relief mission workers; the greatest, to that time at least, anti-epidemic inoculation in history. In all, 150 shiploads of food and supplies amounting to 833,875 tons were sent to the needy in Russia by the Hoover mission.

Upon completion of this work Hoover urged Americans to continue helping Soviet children. "I would rather," he said in this connection, "have implanted the love of the American flag in the hearts of millions, than to have added to the American Navy all the battleships that the Atlantic can float."

The Soviet government officially presented Mr. Hoover a decorative scroll expressing extravagant appreciation of his and the ARA's "entirely unselfish efforts" whereby "millions of people of all ages were saved from death." The complete text is given in Appendix VIII.

Mr. Gorki, in a letter to Mr. Hoover, wrote: "Permit me to express my feelings of gratitude to all citizens of the United States of America and complete satisfaction with the humanitarian work of the American Relief Administration of which you are chairman. . . ." Further extracts from his letter are contained in Appendix IX.

These expressions failed to stop or even to discourage the critical charges of American Communists that Mr. Hoover's relief activities were unfair to their European brethren. Mr. Hoover's comments on these charges are contained in Appendix X.

The Men of the ARA

The roster of the American Relief Association carried the names of several hundred men of good will and good purpose, men from all walks of life and from almost every church group and some from no church. But every mother's son of them was exhilarated by an opportunity to be helpful to their fellow-men in need. Just as their church affiliation was unknown so was the group's denominational religious content unknown. That its spiritual content ran high has never been questioned. Its members were, moreover, free-wheeling individualists, resourceful, able and full of enthusiasm (in the Greek meaning of the word, *from God*) about their mission.

They traveled on passports which also carried a special pass with Hoover's signature. Border officials examined these passports in a desultory fashion until they came to Hoover's signature; then promptly and with a sharp salute and marked deference they would wave the Hoover men on their way.

One ARA relief train which was hurrying to meet an emergency in the Balkans was blocked at the border by an army officer of one of the countries it had to cross. When diplomacy failed, the doughboy in charge of the train covered the obstructing officer and guards with his automatic and ordered the engineer to get going. Will Irwin in *A Reminiscent Biography* reported that the doughboy said in a Vienna newspaper interview, "Those wop kings and generals don't mean nothing in my life. I'm working for Hoover."

Guerrilla factions in one country actually surrendered, not to the United States of America but to the *United States Food Administration,* and stopped fighting. When his troubled lieutenant later reported the incident to Hoover in Paris, fearful that he had overstepped his authority in taking the surrendered swords of the two leaders, Hoover asked him where the swords were. The lieutenant replied that he had brought them along, whereupon Hoover told him, "You keep one of them as a souvenir and give me the other one and I'll try to settle it."

Where railroad ports of entry or warehouses had been damaged beyond use the Hoover engineers put them in operating order in jig time. Wherever food was needed they managed to get it there and if railroads or waterways for vessels did not exist they used horses, oxen, camels or rowboats to move it. When there was no coal to furnish motive power they found coal.

During the Armistice period alone, during which all Central Europe's normal transportation facilities were either almost hopelessly crippled or non-existent, the resourceful and able ARA staff found or created transportation for and directed the distribution of 1,684,456.6 metric tons of food stocks which had a value of $363,211,835.48. Following the armistice period they delivered and distributed far greater amounts.

Used American Slang for Telegraphic Code

Because they were working in many different countries which held different ideologies—nearly all suspicious of each other—the ARA started its work with its own telegraphic code. But the suspicious Allies forbade its use and insisted that all of its messages must be sent in plain language. The Hoover men got around this code problem by using American slang to hide their secrets. Tom Gregory's wire which reported on an important conference he had held with an obstructionist Austrian archduke said, "Archie on the carpet 3:00 P.M. through the hoop at three-five."

The ARA men actually became the economic directors of Europe during that stagnant, disorganized, black-hopeless period which followed the Armistice. Their common sense, their American know-how, their resourcefulness and their unbeatable Yankee spirit prevented the deaths from starvation of more than ten million men, women and children beyond question—some estimates say twenty million. In addition, their fine spirit and methods revived the hopes and purpose of many times that number of men and women.

Sharing such deeply satisfying spiritual experiences, it is not surprising that even now, thirty years later, this group of practical idealists hold an annual dinner-meeting. These gatherings are grand occasions—and until the years began to sap their vim and vigor they were boisterous affairs. Mr. Hoover has attended many of these reunion dinners and usually speaks briefly. In a somewhat serious vein at the reunion in 1925, he said:

> In all this long period of association in a common task, there has been little time for cultivation of friendships, little time to sit down and talk.
>
> It is perhaps better that the Generals should never see the front. These emergencies could only be met by implacable courage and resolution in which the death of individuals could not count as against the interest of the masses. The summoning of human sympathy and human interest by intimate personal contact with human misery and dangers of this situation might have clouded the judgment of the men who have directed its many activities.
>
> The ARA has been an organization of discipline, discipline not based upon orders but on the single-minded devotion of men to a great purpose. It has been the inspiration of human service and not the discipline of an army. Its success has been based upon the evolution of responsibility, not upon the petty plans of organization and installation of the red tape of regulated functions. . . . (ARA *Journal*, 1925.)

Mr. Hoover summed up in a nutshell in those three paragraphs his own record and philosophy. Repeat some of the phrases, "there has been little time for cultivation of friendships, little time to sit down and talk. . . . It is perhaps better that the Generals never see the front. . . . The ARA has been an organization . . . based on the single-minded devotion of men to a great purpose. . . . Its success has been based upon the evolution of responsibility, not upon the petty plans of organization and installation of the red tape of regulated functions. . . ."

The American Relief Association was and is Hoover at his best. It helped to bring him to the crest of a fruitful life. Upon his return to his home in Palo Alto, Hoover was besieged with callers, communications and insistent invitations to speak at a multitude of places.

Finding it impossible to handle the demands in an ordinary way, he prepared and distributed a statement which was in the form of a burlesque of an engineering report. It said in part:

> I plan to adhere to the following rules for one month:
>
> *First—*
>
> (a) That I will reply to no telephone calls, and my secretary has directions to explain in the most amiable manner that I am spending a month with two vigorous small boys. . . .
>
> (b) That I do not myself read any communication that exceeds one page. . . . These rules are solely for my own good.
>
> (c) That I must decline the honor of speaking at public meetings to which I have received invitations. . . . I am not a spellbinder and I am satisfied that the American people will be gratified to find a citizen who has retired from public office who wants to keep still . . . this rule is for the public good. . . . My family is building a palace containing seven rooms and a basement, a kitchen, and a garage, all on the university campus. The old cottage is good enough, but we all think we can build a better house than anybody ever built before, and every American family is entitled to this experience once in a lifetime. . . .

In those terse sentences, the warm, human, and humorous Hoover reveals himself to be the man his friends know and love.

[illegible] has been so conspicuous. [illegible]
[illegible] of mind is a great quality. [illegible]
[illegible] upon the evolution of [illegible]
[illegible] and translation of the old type of [illegible]

PART THREE

THE FRUITION

CHAPTER ONE

Secretary of Commerce and Roving Quarterback

1921–1928

When Mr. Hoover took the oath of office as Secretary of Commerce early in March, 1921, he became a public servant in the strict sense of the word in that he was the head of an established, continuously operating government department instead of director or administrator of an emergency, short-lived organization as heretofore had been the case.

He was now *a part* of the public service, not merely *in* it.

President-elect Harding had offered him some range of choice as to the cabinet post he would prefer to fill. As was his custom, previous to making a decision he canvassed the situation thoroughly, consulted with men who had served as cabinet members, and particularly with men who had previously served as Secretary of Commerce. Although the Commerce Department was down the list in importance, everything he learned about its potentialities for service pointed his thinking and predilections toward it. There, he believed, he would find opportunity to use his talents as an engineer and to advance his beliefs as an economist. There, too, he might best capitalize on his varied world-wide experiences for the benefit of his fellow countrymen. As an engineer he looked upon it as an engineering job. As a humanitarian he believed that it offered an unparalleled opportunity to help raise the standard of living of those who work for their livelihood.

The basic tenet of Hoover's economic thinking was that above everything else American business needed a lifting purpose. This need he believed took precedence over its struggle for material success. He wanted no "evanescent, emotional, dramatic crusade." What he sought was "a finer regard for the rights of others, a stronger devotion to obligations of citizenship . . . the organization of the forces of our economic life so that they may produce happier individual lives." He sought also greater security in employment, as well as the comforts of living, wider possibilities in the enjoyment of nature and enlarged "opportunities of intellectual life."

As an economist with humanitarian impulses he wanted to "work our machines heartlessly but not our men" in order that goods could be sold at lower prices, thereby placing them within reach of more people. If this were done, he believed, more jobs would be created and more people could enjoy greater comfort. The production of more goods and more varieties of goods and services would, he held, "advance the standard of living and security of men."

As an engineer with humanitarian impulses he expressed the belief that the structure of betterment for the common man must be inspired by the human heart—but he held "it can only be achieved by the intellect."

Such a structure, he stated before the 1936 Republican National Convention, can be built only "by using the mold of justice, by laying brick upon brick of scientific research; by painstaking sifting of truth from the collection of fact and experience. . . . That great structure of human progress can be built only by free men."

This was the philosophy, the ideal and the purpose of a free man that guided his efforts to serve free men.

In an address before the Annual Alumni Banquet of Stevens Institute of Technology in 1939, Hoover restated this conviction by first saying that engineers sometimes have bright economic thoughts that statesmen are slow to get, and added:

> . . . Many years ago we announced right out loud that the way to lift the standard of living was to eliminate waste and otherwise reduce the costs of production. We said thereby prices would come down and the people could buy more and employ more people on the job. We said that thereby hours could be shortened and wages increased. A few years later the economists also announced the discovery of this idea. But even with these reinforcements it is apparent that the lawmakers have not yet heard of it. At least, they are busy

increasing waste and putting costs up by a variety of devices. Thereby prices go up. And people buy less and that throws other people and even themselves out of jobs. Public orators then blame it on "technological" unemployment, with an accusing finger pointed at the engineer. . . .

His Motives and Beliefs

Hoover's knowledge of what to do and how he would try to accomplish it as Secretary of Commerce came out of his observation, training and experience. From his inner self came his belief that what he sought to do was right. He knew all too well that the despairing people of most foreign countries looked upon free America as the hope of the world. To him there was no undertaking more important than that of helping in every way possible to keep America the hope of the world; because by so doing his country, through example and leadership, could improve the lot of the world's despairing millions. His ultimate purpose was that of enabling man to realize his glory and fulfill his promise.

His studies, observations and experiences told his subconscious if not his conscious self that courage, enterprise, initiative, energy and related qualities of character quickly disappear if they are not exercised; that brain cells become atrophied when unused just as fish which live far below the surface suffer a hereditary blindness. So he wanted to make America stronger by strengthening the individual citizen.

He knew from firsthand experience that masses of men in many countries frequently followed leaders, who spoke in the name of truths they held as absolute, only to lose their freedom. He had stood by helplessly and watched the inability of constructive statesmen to penetrate the soul of the multitude, to understand its dreams and to denounce philosophic abstractions. Throughout his life he had successfully met situations by the use of concrete proposals which the people could understand. Experience had demonstrated that this method would work miracles when it was coupled with ideas which represented the invisible spring from which social and economic progress comes. And he realized that civilization and constitutions disappear when these springs go dry.

Whether or not exactly these thoughts and beliefs ran through Hoover's mind when he became Secretary of Commerce, the record shows that his method of operation and the multitude of his successful accomplishments while holding that office were related to or else inspired by them.

While serving as Secretary of Commerce he stated that his objectives had but one purpose, that of maintaining the

> American standards of living for both workers and farmers, and to place production on a more stable footing by enlarging consumption and export markets through reduced production and distribution costs.

The full story of his varied activities and accomplishments as Secretary of Commerce would require many volumes. It will be possible here only to highlight briefly a few illustrations.

Encouraging Ethical Practices in Business

Implementing his ideas, Hoover created an entire division in the Department of Commerce whose duty was to work out a "code of ethics" with trade associations which sought to eliminate abuse and unfair competition in each trade. He neither sought nor wanted governmental police power. Instead he asked business to create and follow better ethical standards. Each code was defined and adopted as applicable to its special trade. To make certain that the codes had no single element of violation of the antitrust laws, Hoover enlisted the co-operation of the Federal Trade Commission. In an effort to assure confidence, these codes were promulgated by the Federal Trade Commission as standards of fair practice. No force was attempted or implied. Their adoption was entirely voluntary. Since these codes covered the larger part of the business activities of the country, they were gradually becoming a part of its business customs until the next administration attempted to make them compulsory. When that happened these codes of ethics lost their moral lift and as a consequence their popular support.

He held that the "publication of the codes of ethics by many associations" which advanced service as the primary purpose and which condemned "specific unfair practices" while at the same time they insisted upon "a higher plane of relationships between employer and employee" were all indications of "improving thought and growing moral perceptions" and were a "strong beginning of a new force in the business world."

At the same time he expressed the belief that if all of the co-operating trade associations would "accept as their primary purpose the lifting of standards" and would co-operate together for "the voluntary enforcement of high standards," then we as a nation would have traveled far on the "road of the elimination of government from business."

Tackling the Job of Eliminating Business Waste

One of the many facts established by the year 1920 on the elimination of waste in industry was that manufacturers of nearly every kind of product were turning out an unnecessary number of designs and sizes. Paving-brick manufacturers, for example, were producing sixty-six different sizes of brick. This great variety of bricks contributed nothing whatever to either the beauty of our cities or to the reduction of cost in the manufacture of brick. The study showed that replacement needs of buildings constructed of odd sized bricks required the producers to have and keep special machinery in working order and to tie up capital in stock of odd or little-used sizes for no useful reason.

Hoover's engineers first got the facts. When presented to the leaders of the industry everyone was happy to co-operate. Working through his newly created Division of Commercial Standards, a conference of representatives of brick producers, manufacturers in related fields and municipal officials (the consumers), was called. Out of it came an agreement, mutually and voluntarily approved, that the paving brick manufacturers would reduce the number of sizes of bricks from sixty-six to eleven.

The next group to be called in for a conference consisted of architects, building-brick manufacturers and contractors. They readily agreed to reduce building-brick sizes from forty-four to one. Following the building-brick people came the manufacturers, distributors and consumers of beds, springs and mattresses who gladly consented to reduce the sizes of their products from seventy-four combinations of lengths and widths to four. This was a great boon to retailers because they would no longer be required to go to the expense of tailoring odd sizes to fit the customer's needs.

The word about the remarkable understanding and fairness of this new activity began to spread throughout the business world and the manufacturers of other products came in and asked for guidance. One of these was the lumber industry. This was a major undertaking because of its vast size and the far-reaching implications in conservation of our forests.

Entirely by voluntary agreement, Mr. Hoover, during his first six years as Secretary of Commerce, was able to get eighty-six different industries to eliminate wasteful practices of their products and produce better goods. In human terms this meant more work at better pay and better products at lower prices for an ever increasing number of people. And it also brought the investor surer and bigger returns.

Completely Reorganized Department of Commerce

Among other things Hoover completely reorganized the entire department. His efforts lifted it from the most obscure department to that of almost equal rank with that of other cabinet posts in service to the public. Executive orders greatly expanded its scope by assigning bureaus from other departments to it. Congress also imposed new duties on it. In addition each of its divisions grew steadily in efficiency and usefulness under officials of the highest type.

One of the department divisions which he rejuvenated was the Bureau of the Census. He made it into the greatest fact-finding institution in the world. Now its revamping and compiling of statistics enables it most helpfully to guide workers, farmers, manufacturers, and business men in their plans and programs. B. H.—meaning before

Hoover—this department's principal activity was to count noses every ten years and to total the number.

Another division he transformed was that of the Bureau of Fisheries. Under him it became a practical, live, useful body instead of a purely research organization into aquatic life. One of this division's important accomplishments was that of saving the Alaskan salmon industry from destruction.

The Bureau of Mines felt his purpose by expanding its activities to include safety inspection of mines. This new activity has helped directly to decrease mine accidents.

The Bureau of Patents came to life under his guidance and prodding and cut the time lag for passing on inventors' applications from eighteen to six months.

One of his most important accomplishments was that of reorganizing the Foreign Trade Service of the United States. American exports were greatly increased under his leadership and with the co-operation of manufacturers and merchants. Increased sales of American products abroad gave steady jobs to additional United States workmen and added to the prosperity of all groups.

He had a special interest in this division because of his belief that our strong position in foreign trade rested on our ability to produce enormous quantities of moderate-priced goods by machine methods. He held that:

> If we keep on delivering an honest product, made American-fashion, packed—with due regard to climate—American fashion, foreigners will realize finally that our goods, in spite of their unfamiliarity, are better and cheaper.

How useful the services of this reorganized, revitalized department were can be found in its record. Individual requests by merchants and manufacturers for specific information and services increased from two-hundred thousand to more than two million annually. Under its guidance foreign trade grew 35 per cent above the prewar total. It did this while the foreign trade of other ex-belligerents barely reached prewar levels.

Leadership in the 1921 Unemployment Crisis

Hoover met the after-war collapse and unemployment which followed it throughout the world by calling an unemployment conference in 1921. To it came the country's leading employers and labor leaders. The conference group charted and launched a co-operative campaign calling for increased employment through public works and a general cleanup campaign. The purpose was to make certain that more individuals were able to earn some income each week. Increased employment by these means soon brought increased buying, and the wheels of production started so rapidly that within six months our employment problem had disappeared, whereas that of foreign nations was met by doles and continued failures.

Tackled Another Phase of Business Waste

Another of his many projects was the inauguration of a nationwide effort to eliminate industrial waste. He sought to do this by stimulating co-operation between manufacturers, merchants, transportation and consumers. The object was to decrease production costs, stabilize business and reduce prices to consumers. The program had many facets. It sought to reduce business booms and slumps by establishing better co-operation between shippers and the railroads, reducing seasonal employment, enlarging the use of electrical power, increasing salvage of waste materials. It supported further scientific research, commercial arbitration and reduction of labor strife. Waterway transportation was in the program as was also the establishment of standards, grades and qualities of products. This latter move sought to protect the consumer.

Stabilizing the Construction Business and Reducing Home Building Costs

One of Hoover's Commerce Department projects was carried out by a nationwide committee with representatives from the construction industries. It included men from such groups or trades as material manufacturers, contractors, realtors, labor and public officials. High on the committee's agenda was consideration of the seasonal operation of construction industries. Out of its deliberations came ways to add fully fifty days to the construction season, extending it into the winter months. By doing so it stabilized prices, brought workers increased earnings and at the same time decreased building costs. And it stimulated the demand for more building construction.

Holding the conviction that home ownership would help improve social and economic conditions and that home building was one of the great necessities both for the comfort and security of the people, as well as an important aid in the maintenance of employment, Hoover directed a nationwide movement to this end. He initiated the better-homes movement in communities all over the land. He made a further contribution by bringing about standardization and simplification of dimensions in building materials, thereby reducing their cost to home builders. This, in turn, stimulated home building. Residential building grew from 27.8 per cent of our total annual construction in 1920 to 48.7 per cent in 1926.

Encouraged Zoning

Related to, but apart from his home ownership program, was a zoning program for communities. Recognizing that the unsupported home maker would be without the protection of zoning restrictions, Hoover created a commission on zoning. He hired experts to make a critical examination of the problem, propose remedies and prepare a "zoning primer" which contained all of the basic information on the subject that any municipal official or public-spirited citizen needed. The national real estate boards gave this primer wholesale distribution. In five years' time twenty-eight states had used it as the basis for new zoning laws and 580 cities, towns and villages, which contained about half of our urban population, adopted zoning regulations based on the facts and recommendations which the Department of Commerce made available.

The Commodity Division

One of Mr. Hoover's early discoveries as Secretary of Commerce was that businessmen had no one in Washington to whom they could turn for an intelligent discussion of their industrial problems—no experts comparable to those at the service of farmers in the Department of Agriculture or labor leaders in the Department of Labor.

He corrected this situation by enlisting the collaboration of industry. The ultimate result was that the Department of Commerce recruited a corps of able men to head eighteen new divisions in the department.

The Civil Service collaborated splendidly in building up this new group; a group which served as an invaluable vehicle for the interchanging of ideas, advice and guidance between industry and the government. As a result, whenever an industrialist had problems of any sort with the rest of the government he was able through these new agencies to get advice as to procedure.

Encouraged Trade Association Movement

Mr. Hoover vigorously encouraged the trade association movement with a view toward bringing countless numbers of small industrialists together to overcome their mutual problems. He placed the services of the department at the disposal of industry far more effectively than could have been done by depending upon individual contact with tens of thousands of single plants. Previous to Mr. Hoover's action one could almost have counted on the fingers of two hands the number of really soundly organized and effective trade associations. When he left the department the total number of such associations went well over two thousand.

Tabulated and Analyzed International Balance of Payments to U.S.

Before Mr. Hoover became Secretary of Commerce there had never been any attempt to tabulate and analyze the *international balance of payments* of the United States. The old fiction that our international operations were simply interchanges of goods had become widely entrenched among casual thinkers on such subjects. No systematic and thoroughgoing analysis of the great number of invisibles ever had been made. Theretofore the government had only the roughest guesses as to the amount spent by American tourists abroad, or paid abroad as interest to foreign investors, ship owners, insurance companies, and other interests. Mr. Hoover brought together a group of experts in these fields who made the first exhaustive analysis that had ever been attempted. This was carried on and enlarged from year to year. It has now become a permanent fixture of our national statistical setup.

Analyzed the Distribution of Major Commodities

The Commerce Department had not previously made more than a casual routine statistical attempt to analyze the process of distribution, the identification of markets within this country, the migration of industries, the changing mechanisms of distribution, and similar factors which made up the commerce of the nation. Mr. Hoover changed this by bringing out the first of an impressive series of marketing atlases which analyzed the distribution of major commodities. Much of this work was done in close collaboration with the industries which contributed substantially toward the cost of the effort. There had been no precedent for such a governmental relationship between industry and government. This not only resulted in a much more complete and useful job, but also assured the very active determination of each industry to get a maximum benefit out of the results.

Analysis of the Causes of Bankruptcy

Another important contribution Mr. Hoover made was that of the first thoroughgoing analysis of the causes of bankruptcy among small businessmen. Previously, only wild guesses and more or less demagogic charges and countercharges dealt with the subject of the causes and results of failures among small grocerymen, restaurant owners, druggists, etc. Following the general example of the medical profession and the law in studying the causes of difficulty from actual cases of "infirmity" Mr. Hoover organized an elaborate and periodic study of thousands of records in the bankruptcy courts in selected areas. The information secured threw a wholly new light on the entire situation and proved to be an invaluable guide not only to the interested industries but to the department.

Monthly Conferences with Business Paper Editors

One important "institution" Mr. Hoover launched was that of a series of monthly conferences with the editors of business publications. These were held throughout his entire administration as Secretary of Commerce. They operated on a question-and-answer basis and yielded much valuable information as to the industrial and commercial problems of the country. They also offered a splendid channel for disseminating the information and reactions of the department throughout the business life of the nation. These conferences became a major medium not only for the guidance of the department as a real service agency but also for the business press of the country in its information and editorial guidance of tens of thousands of business establishments from coast to coast.

Battle with Foreign Raw Material Monopolies

A major spectacular feature of Mr. Hoover's service as Secretary of Commerce was his battle with foreign raw material monopolies whose chief market was the United States. The opening gun in this battle sounded when the British government, through the Stevenson Act of 1923, put the price of crude rubber up to fantastic figures—from 35¢ to more than $1.25 per pound. There was no economic justification for this action. Because rubber production was so heavily concentrated in British hands it seemed impossible to break this ruthless exploitation of the American consumer who was by far the largest buyer of the product. Mr. Hoover, however, organized a vigorous campaign for the stimulation of non-British sources of rubber, e.g., Dutch, Indonesian and other planters, possible new plantations in Liberia and Brazil (Firestone and Ford), the stimulation of a greater use of reclaimed rubber, and above all the sharp encouragement of efforts toward synthetic production. His action saved the United States' rubber users $700,000,000 per year.

It should be stated in fairness that the British were not the only offenders in the attempt to create an artificially high price for a natural product. Mr. Hoover found it necessary to launch a simultaneous effort to protect American buyers from similar ruthless exploitation by the Dutch quinine monopoly, operations with Chile in nitrate, Brazilian coffee, Japanese camphor, silk, etc. This campaign went on for years on a wide front, all under Mr. Hoover's direct supervision and direction and became in the end one of his principal achievements in the department.

Important as were all of his major projects, they did not outrank in usefulness the administrative devices which he created and used within the department itself. The administrative devices which helped make the entire department's machinery run smoothly included:

1. Weekly meetings with division chiefs during which he answered questions concerning government policies, and also acquainted them with his own vast store of information on a multitude of business problems in all parts of the world.

Out of them came closer collaboration and a closely-knit, effective government team.

2. This unity of purpose and effort, which rested on reason and information made the Department of Commerce under Hoover the most efficient and the least expensive of the major agencies of our government.

3. Mr. Hoover revitalized and gave stimulus to all of the divisions in the Commerce Department with an extremely small front office staff "that included only a solicitor, a chief clerk and two or three secretaries." The entire budget for Mr. Hoover's front office staff was less than $100,000 annually whereas in recent years it has run into several million dollars annually.

Worse still is the fact that these later big budgets for the front office staff have meant the encirclement of the Secretary of Commerce with a vast coterie of intermediaries, buffers and subordinates who completely isolate him from the department's working staff. This wall of supernumeraries around the secretary is largely responsible for the demoralization and the innocuous functioning since Mr. Hoover's time of what then was the most efficient and smooth-running department in our federal government.

Standardizing Specifications for Federal Government Purchases

Another of Hoover's undertakings was to establish the Federal Specifications Board. Its duty was to unify the diverse buying specifications of the various federal departments. Its work brought both savings to the government and stability to manufacturing. This program was later extended into co-operation with state, municipal and institutional purchasing agents at the request of various governors and mayors. Here, too, it helped further to reduce the taxpayer's burden. Business in turn adopted many of these specifications for its own purchases, to the mutual benefit of consumer and producer.

Waterways and Aviation

Operating on the principle that any improvement or strengthening of the nation's economic system is beneficial to the nation as a whole, Hoover injected new life into the movement which sought development of midwestern waterways. This program visualized them as a single great transportation system which were to be interconnected and completed as a whole along modern lines.

Among other duties, Hoover served as chairman of the President's St. Lawrence Waterway Commission and directed a survey and report on the project by Canadian and American joint engineering commissions.

Aviation was then in its swaddling clothes, but looking ahead Hoover saw its potentialities. He launched an investigation and study of the development of commercial aviation in foreign countries, and at the same time called for the preparation of plans for aviation development in the United States. He co-operated with Congress in creating the Commercial Aviation Division of the Department of Commerce. This division pioneered the way for developing commercial aviation under federal government encouragement.

Radio and Merchant Marine

In 1927 he served as president of the International Radio Conference which was composed of representatives from seventy-four nations. This conference unanimously agreed upon treaties which protected the radio listener as well as the lives at sea by controlling international radio communication.

Still another activity which Hoover carried on for four years was the promotion of radio broadcasting. He sought to prevent interference through voluntary regulation, with the aid of annual conferences. This ultimately led to the enactment of the federal law which secures the control of radio wave lengths to the people through the federal government.

Hoover also had a prominent place in the program which sought to encourage American merchant marine development. Department of Commerce agencies supported congressional measures designed to build up the merchant fleet.

Foreign Debts, Hoover Dam, Academy of Sciences and Other Activities

As a member of the War Department Commission he opposed the cancellation of foreign government war debts and he helped work out the settlement formula which, for some years, yielded larger annual payments.

He served as chairman of the Colorado River Commission and worked out an agreement and a seven-basin-states recommendation which settled the twenty-year dispute over water rights—a dispute which had blocked all development of the basin. Out of this came what now has, with justice, been renamed *Hoover Dam.*

He served as chairman and active director of the national drive to raise a fund of $20,000,000 with which to assist and encourage scientific research through the National Academy of Sciences.

Disaster called upon him to serve as director of the Mississippi flood relief. This activity provided for the rescue, care and rehabilitation in their homes of 650,000 American citizens who were victims of the disaster.

An investigator for a foreign board of trade, with wide-eyed astonishment at the Commerce Department's collection of current facts, estimates and statistics on which the Department based most of its work, asked, "How do you make your people open up their books in this manner?" He was told, "We couldn't, even if we threatened them with jail." What this foreigner, who had lived and worked in a country where official orders instead of responsive co-operation were the custom, did not understand was that Americans readily follow leaders they trust.

That remark holds the touchstone of Hoover's spirit, the source of his strength, the explanation of his almost unmatched success in many fields; he believes in the essential goodness of people and in their promptings to be fair and decent.

The quality, scope and nature of Hoover's services as Secretary of Commerce had been valuable and varied. Since they also were in keeping with the American ideal of progress through leadership and voluntary co-operation his name soon began to head the list of Republican candidates for the presidency in 1928.

He had the respect of all of his cabinet colleagues and the support of most of them. His first chief, Harding, once had remarked, "Hoover is the damnedest smartest man I have ever met." His chief of the moment, President Coolidge, publicly stated:

> Measured by accomplishment and ability Herbert Hoover holds commanding rank. If five Americans were to be selected on the basis of merit and ability to devise remedies for the present condition of the world—Herbert Hoover's name would head the list.

The scandals of the Harding administration never touched either Secretary of State Hughes or Mr. Hoover—among other members of the Harding cabinet—who held themselves aloof from the group of poker playing, convivial members composed of the President, Fall, Daugherty and perhaps others.

Mr. Hoover's suspicions or fears of wrong-doing were first definitely aroused during President Harding's Alaskan trip party in the summer of 1923. The Hoovers' names were not included in the original list of those who were to be members of the presidential party. Later President Harding telegraphed Mr. Hoover on the West Coast and invited him and Mrs. Hoover to join the party which they did at Tacoma, Washington, on July 3, 1923.

Shortly thereafter, on shipboard, President Harding asked Mr. Hoover's advice about whether to expose or try to hush up any scandal should one occur in the administration. Mr. Hoover replied that it should be exposed and thereby vindicate the integrity of the administration. Beyond asking his question President Harding did not reveal what was on his mind.

After Harding's death, which occurred a few days after he had sought Mr. Hoover's advice, and Calvin Coolidge had become President, both Mr. Hughes and Mr. Hoover, when they learned about the irregularities which later led to criminal indictment, urged President Coolidge to dismiss Attorney-General Daugherty. President Coolidge, despite the urging of his Secretaries of State and Commerce, refused to do so until he had definite evidence of Daugherty's participation in criminal activities. He later removed Daugherty.

Mr. Hoover has stated that he is convinced that President Harding had no knowledge of the criminal activities of some of his appointees until shortly before his death and that it was such knowledge which eventually caused Harding's death.

The 1928 Pre-Convention and Fall Campaign

The Republican party aspect of the 1928 presidential race went through a period of confusion following President Coolidge's enigmatic statement of August 2, 1927, "I do not choose to run for President in 1928." Speculation filled the air waves, newspaper columns and gatherings of people for many months as to exactly what the President meant. Did he mean that he would not run? Could he have meant that he would run if drafted?

Many of the party's leaders who were ardent admirers and supporters of President Coolidge read the latter meaning into the cryptic statement. One of them, an astute politician, the late J. Henry Rorabach of Connecticut, told me about this time that he was for Coolidge first, last and all the time because Coolidge's nomination meant a sure victory with a minimum of effort. This, he said, would permit him to take a longer vacation and be free of worry. Moreover, he added, "Coolidge is a known quantity politically. He plays ball with the organization. And he stays put. I'm not so sure about some of these other fellows."

This statement by Mr. Rorabach epitomized that of many other party leaders.

Nursing the wish in the hope that it might become the father of the thought, the majority of the Republican leaders continued to insist that the party should draft President Coolidge.

Whether President Coolidge meant that he would not accept the nomination under any circumstances, whether he nursed the hope that he would be drafted, or whether he wanted the tender of the nomination, no one positively knows or ever can find out.

When President Coolidge and his Secretary of Commerce met in Washington a month after the President's Black Hills statement Mr. Hoover told his Chief that, despite the persistent urging of many friends that he become a candidate, he (Hoover) would prefer to continue as a member of the cabinet under Mr. Coolidge. When President Coolidge failed to indicate exactly what he meant by his cryptic statement, Mr. Hoover made a public statement to the effect that President Coolidge should be renominated.

So far as I have ever learned, President Coolidge, between the time he made his statement on August 2 and the meeting of the Republican National Committee in Washington in December, 1927, made neither a private nor a public statement which would reveal the hidden (if any) meaning of his statement. He did, however, tell the National Committee members at their December meeting, "My statement stands." And he encouraged party members to begin considering other candidates.

The situation rocked along without much apparent change until February, 1928. By this time a small host of Republican senators had either announced their candidacies for the presidency or else were toying with the idea of making the race. This group included Willis of Ohio, Goff of West Virginia, Watson of Indiana, Steiwer of Oregon and Curtis of Kansas. Former Governor Lowden of Illinois shied his hat into the ring and some of Vice President Dawes' friends were trying to throw his hat in.

When the time came for filing in Ohio, Mr. Hoover queried the President again about his intentions. President Coolidge stated to Mr. Hoover that he would not file nomination petitions in Ohio. He indicated further that there was no reason why Mr. Hoover should not do so if he wished.

This Mr. Hoover did in a formal letter dated, interestingly enough, on Lincoln's birthday, February 12, 1928.

I can personally testify that there has been nothing like the Hoover pre-convention campaign in 1928 before or since in American politics. Wall Street, for there then was a potent Wall Street political influence in the country, and its allied financial interests were against Mr. Hoover. With few exceptions the Republican senate leaders opposed him. This was true in the main of Republican State Chairmen and National Committeemen as well as lesser party officials. Only the great mass of Republican voters wanted him nominated.

It should be stated here that the later techniques of the Democratic National Committee—the Michelson-directed "Smear Hoover" campaign—were originated and perfected by old-guard Republican leaders in the 1928 pre-convention campaign. One issue they raised and wore threadbare was that Mr. Hoover was not a member in good standing of the Republican party.

The bases for this charge were:

1. In the 1918 congressional campaign Mr. Hoover as United States Food Administrator, while the war was still on, in public letter had called for the election of a Democratic congress to support his Chief, President Wilson. This, his opponents held, was partisan heresy.

2. In 1920 Mr. Hoover, along with former President William Howard Taft, Charles Evans Hughes and a number of other distinguished Republican leaders had advocated that the United States become a member of the League of Nations in opposition to the position taken by other equally distinguished Republican leaders. His position on this question created some bitterness toward him in Republican ranks.

3. In 1920, when many Democratic party leaders tried to snare Mr. Hoover into their party (just as in 1948 they tried the same tactics with General Eisenhower) Mr. Hoover remained silent to their im-

portunings about his party membership. Democratic party leaders in Michigan went so far as to enter Mr. Hoover's name as their party's presidential candidate in the primaries. Mr. Hoover was advised by astute Republican leaders to lie low. One of these was the late, great Oscar S. Straus, Theodore Roosevelt's Secretary of Commerce and Labor. Mr. Straus held that Democratic advocacy of Mr. Hoover for president would enhance Mr. Hoover's desirability with the Republicans for this office.

4. According to Mr. Hoover's Republican opponents he had once been a British subject, therefore was not constitutionally eligible to serve as President. Their evidence rested on nothing more than ignorance and wishful thinking. They were ignorant about British registration procedures, and being so, they built a house of cards on the fact that Mr. Hoover had once leased a house in London, resulting in his name being automatically placed on the voting list for local offices in accordance with British law. Even when conclusively proven wrong they persisted in referring to him as "Sir Herbert."

The fact that Mr. Hoover had served with high distinction as Secretary of Commerce for nearly eight years under two Republican presidents took some of the fretful winds out of the sails of his hidebound partisan opponents. Other of their fretful winds were dissipated by former Senator William E. Calder who, as president of the National Republican Club, stated that Mr. Hoover had been a member in good standing of that organization since 1909 and added that membership in the Republican party was a prerequisite of membership in the club.

Mr. Hoover's senatorial opponents also tried by covert means—they had to project this charge indirectly because many of them had been either members or buddies of the "Ohio gang" of Harding's days—to link Mr. Hoover with the Harding Cabinet scandals. But this could not be made to stick because Mr. Hoover (along with Messrs. Hughes and Mellon) had never at any time been involved even indirectly with the wrongdoers.

They tried, too, to create an issue by peremptorily demanding an accounting of what they called Mr. Hoover's convention "slush fund," but this collapsed when the state groups supporting Hoover proved that the implied charge was without substance.

One other contention of Mr. Hoover's opponents was that he and Mrs. Hoover had been married by a Catholic priest. Mr. Hoover's quick admittance of this fact took care of that one.

Mention should be made of the fact that Mr. Hoover did have the able support of some stalwart men whose Republicanism could not be questioned. This group included, among others, his former cabinet colleagues Harry New and Hubert Work; Congressman Theodore E. Burton of Ohio; Senators Lenroot of Wisconsin, Sackett of Kentucky, Metcalf of Rhode Island; Ex-Governors Goodrich of Indiana and Proctor of Vermont; Ex-Congressmen James Good of Iowa, Ogden Mills of New York, David H. Blair of North Carolina. There also was Walter Brown of Ohio, but with the Bull Moose mark against his name. Many other Republican leaders of varying degrees of importance also entered the fray on Mr. Hoover's side.

However, the party's professional politicians, big and little, were inclined to be unenthusiastic or disapproving of Hoover's candidacy. Their opposition, as previously stated, came largely either from personal political ambition, uncertainty about the brand of Hoover's Republicanism, or doubt about his ability as a vote-getter. Many politicians have little imagination. They follow routine organization methods and strive always to name good vote-getters to top places on the ticket in the expectation that such men will carry the weaker candidates to victory. Well known and popular as Hoover was as a man, there was no existing information about what kind of a vote-getter he would make. Since he had never before been a candidate for public office no one could tell whether or not he had the ability to command partisan loyalty or to arouse public enthusiasm which could be transformed into votes. Lacking imagination as they did, and being wedded to tried organization methods, the local municipal, county and state political leaders were inclined to look on Hoover's candidacy with fishy eyes.

The factors in Mr. Hoover's favor were: (a) his name was held in reverence in a majority of the households of the nation and the people trusted him; (b) the enthusiasm of Hoover's relief work associates (whom the politicians derisively called "Hoover's Boy Scouts" and "Girl Scouts") went up and down the land to preach the Hoover gospel; (c) the naturalized citizens who originated in those countries where Hoover had directed relief programs; (d) the nearly unanimous support given Hoover's candidacy by trade associations, business, social welfare, civic, church and other groups; (e) newspaper and magazine support; (f) the able help of several experienced Republican leaders.

Despite the pall caused by President Coolidge's continued silence regarding his own wishes and despite the hurt and injured queries and attacks of the old-guard Republicans; the Hoover workers had corralled over four hundred delegates by early May and their snowball was rolling faster and getting larger every day. President Coolidge continued to emulate Brer Rabbit and "kept on saying nothing." The old-guard attacks grew in intensity. Mr. Mellon, the key man in the Pennsylvania delegation, while friendly to Mr. Hoover kept his own counsel.

John Richardson of Boston and a member of the Massachusetts delegation is my authority for the statement that a reporter met his state's delegation upon its arrival in Kansas City and stated that William M. Butler, then Chairman of the Republican National Committee and a close friend of President Coolidge, was launching a draft Coolidge movement. Mr. Richardson immediately called upon Mr. Butler and asked him the truth concerning the report. Mr. Butler did not deny it. Decisive action by Mr. Mellon, however, halted Mr. Butler's efforts.

Shortly before the convention proceedings began Mr. Mellon in Kansas City advised Mr. Hoover in Washington by telephone that he intended to recommend to his fellow Pennsylvania delegates to vote for Hoover on the first ballot. The "Stop Hoover" movement thereupon died in its tracks. Mr. Hoover received 837 of the convention's 1084 votes on the first ballot.

Employing new forces which were beyond the control of local and state party leaders and using new techniques which enabled him to play rings around them brought Mr. Hoover the nomination. But it did not endear him to them. Previously these regulars, who made politics their business, had distrusted his non-adherence to their conception of the party faith. Now they added dislike of him to their distrust. As long as things went well in Washington their dislike and distrust were curbed, but if evil days fell upon the Hoover Administration they would be ready to desert him.

That was exactly what happened in 1932.

In his reply to the telegram which notified him of his nomination Mr. Hoover said: ". . . My country owes me nothing. It gave me as it gives every boy and girl, a chance. . . . My whole life has taught me what America means. I am indebted to my country beyond any power to repay. . . . The government is more than administrative; it is power for leadership and co-operation with the forces of business and cultural life . . . the Presidency is more than executive responsibility. It is the inspiring symbol of all that is highest in America's purposes and ideals."

Following his nomination Mr. Hoover made an effort to gain the active support of all groups within the Republican party, of which there were many. His success in this was notable with the exception of Senator George W. Norris of Nebraska. Shortly after Mr. Hoover was nominated Senator Norris sent an emissary who made a reciprocal support proposition to the presidential candidate. Mr. Hoover answered that he would discuss this only with Senator Norris. Later Senator Norris called and baldly offered to support Mr. Hoover for president if he, in turn, would promise to support Norris for senator when he next was a senatorial candidate.

Mr. Hoover stated to Senator Norris that he could not conscientiously enter into any such arrangement.

Not long after this interview Senator Norris publicly announced that he would support Governor Smith.

All other Republican leaders, big and little, however, participated in the campaign in support of the Hoover candidacy.

Mr. Hoover himself made seven major addresses. This was the limit he believed he could make because full use of the radio was being made for the first time in this campaign; therefore, he would have to prepare a wholly new speech for each of these occasions.

This statement makes it necessary for me to digress slightly from the subject and discuss the preparation of Mr. Hoover's speeches. So far as I know, and my direct knowledge on the subject covers a period of thirty or more years, Mr. Hoover has never used the services of a ghost writer to prepare any speech of major importance that he has delivered during that period. He insists upon writing his own. Having been trained as an engineer rather than as a writer, many of his speeches during the earlier years of his public life were too heavy in content and too sparsely sprinkled with easy phrases and sentences to make them wholly understandable by the great masses of men. Added to this is the fact that until after he left the Presidency he never had adequate time to prepare his speeches so that they sounded the way he talks. During these later years of comparative leisure he has developed a terse, in places a pungent, style that is clear, forceful and arresting. But no ghost writer ever taught him that. It came out of himself. Along with it he developed a writing style which, for an engineer or for any other professional man outside the top writing craft, is distinctive and of an unusually high quality.

Related to Mr. Hoover's method of preparing his speeches and his writing style is that of his delivery of formal speeches. For many years this was poor to bad because of his necessity of reading them. For many years his method was to face downward toward the copy and thus give the appearance of talking into his vest. He changed this by using a holder for the copy which held it about even with his eyes. Mr. Hoover never has been able to deliver a major speech after the manner of former Senator Albert J. Beveridge of Indiana, who was able to prepare a speech, read it once and then to visualize it word by word, sentence by sentence, paragraph by paragraph and page by page from its opening to its end. I learned this one time when, during a walk we were taking previous to his delivering a major speech, Beveridge asked me to remind him when we returned to our rooms to make a substitution for a certain word on page six, line seven. At my expressed astonishment over his ability to tell just where the word in question was that he used in the speech he told me of his amazing ability to retain from one reading a complete and clear picture in his mind of the entire speech. Since such a feat of memory was not one of Mr. Hoover's accomplishments, he has had to read his speeches and use sincerity, conviction, common sense, logic, force and penetrating understanding to get his message over to his audiences.

Mr. Hoover presented his program for the country in his campaign speeches. This included the advancement of social reform; taxation reform and business regulation in support of the competitive system; the conservation of natural resources; reform of the judicial system and effective enforcement of all laws; preservation of peace and strengthening of international co-operation; helping agriculture; strengthening the collective bargaining rights of labor and the reorganization of the federal government for purposes of efficiency and economy.

It was reasonably clear, unless the Hoover workers made some major mistakes, that he would be elected. They made none.

That phase of the campaign which most pleased the close and more intelligent followers of both Governor Smith and Mr. Hoover was that neither of these gentlemen at any time in the campaign said anything about the other which could be interpreted as personally derogatory of the other's character, ideals or integrity or that in later years could prevent the establishment of the genuine friendship which they came to enjoy.

Between his election and taking office Mr. Hoover carried out what he then referred to as "good neighbor policies" (a term which his successor's administration later copied and gave wide usage) by making a trip with Mrs. Hoover to several Latin American countries in an effort to help create good will for and confidence in the neighborly qualities of the United States. He did this because he had become convinced while serving as Secretary of Commerce that the countries of the Western Hemisphere could be mutually benefited through the creation of stronger, more friendly ties.

Immediately upon his return from this epoch-making trip he immersed himself in the problems of selecting the top echelon personnel for an administration which all too soon was to become burdened with more grave, gigantic and threatening problems than had ever before been the lot of any peacetime administration in the nation's history.

CHAPTER TWO

The World Economic, Social and Political Situation in 1929

Up to this point I have dealt with the background, circumstances, activities and incidents which directly related to Mr. Hoover's character, ideals and experiences. This chapter detours from the course of previous chapters in presenting a brief survey of the state of the world when he became President. Much of the factual information is derived from a recent study by Dr. Harold G. Moulton of the Brookings Institution, entitled *Controlling Factors in Economic Development.*

This course seems advisable since it will be possible thereby to highlight the great variety of complex and nearly insoluble problems which confronted not only the President and the people of the United States but the heads as well as the people of every other government in the world in 1929.

Many of the disturbing factors prevailing in 1929 were international in character while others were manifestations of domestic trends in particular countries.

Basically, what had happened was that World War I had thrown the economic and financial organization of the entire world completely out of balance. During the century preceding the first great war the world economic and financial system, in the terms of classic economists, was in a state of balanced equilibrium. The more important factors in this situation were (a) all important industrial countries were on the gold standard; (b) government budgets were either balanced or if not balanced were not far out of line; (c) international trade, service and credit organizations fairly readily controlled foreign exchange rates and held them within narrow and automatically self-correcting limits; (d) debtor and creditor countries, through export and import of products, had established means of balanced payments to meet their particular situations under the gold standards.

The world-wide economic and social equilibrium which had been developed over the course of a century and was being maintained previous to the outbreak of World War I in 1914 had experienced many disturbances. The following among other factors helped to cause these disturbances:

1. Increased agricultural production which had been made possible by man's overcoming the "niggardliness of nature" and by the opening of vast new productive areas which, with constantly improving methods of farming and of cheaper transportation, combined to throw trade out of balance.

2. The permanent tendency in some of the older civilizations such as India, China and some European nations for the population growth to outrun the supply of productive natural resources.

3. The phenomenal advance of science. The rapid and sweeping technological advance was felt especially in the fields of agriculture, mining, petroleum, chemistry, electricity and manufacturing. Society became dynamic and the material well-being of all classes was thereby improved.

The changes which these new factors created in the way men lived and worked and believed also made useful the creation of large scale business enterprises which soon grew into big corporate organizations. Bank credits grew with expanding economy. Stable monetary and fiscal systems were a prerequisite to extensive credit operations. This led, following Great Britain's creation in 1916 of the single gold standard, to the adoption by 1900 of the gold standard by all leading nations.

An indication of how difficult it was to maintain this balance of economic and financial equilibrium in only one country, to say nothing about the immensely greater and intricately difficult job of maintaining it in all of the countries of the world, is given by the record of business depressions in the United States alone for the period between the years 1819 and 1913 inclusive, of which there were twelve. Their approximate dates and duration are as follows: 1819, twenty-four months; 1825, twelve months; 1833, nine months; 1837, seventy-two months; 1857, eighteen months; 1866, eighteen months; 1873, sixty-six months; 1882, thirty-six months; 1890, nine months; 1893, forty-eight months; 1907, twelve months; 1913, twenty months. The United States went through the economic wringer five different times during the first forty-six years of the above period and was in the trough of these depressions for an estimated total of 135 months, whereas it had seven such discouraging experiences during the following forty-seven years, the combined total of which was 209 months.

This glance backward indicates that depressions were recurring more frequently and lasting longer during the last half of the nineteenth century and the earlier part of the twentieth than ever before. The phenomenal advance of science is largely to blame for the increasing recurrence of depressions. Its new miracles almost daily confounded and delighted us. Speed became the essence of our national life.

During the thousands of years of recorded history previous to 1819, man's ways of living and earning a living had been changed in only four major instances by forcing him to make social, political, economic and financial adjustments. These followed the invention of the wheel by some nomadic genius on his way out of the forest, thus transforming man from a hunter into a grower and creating the fundamentals of governmental and social organization; the discovery of gunpowder by the Chinese which facilitated wholesale murder; movable type by Gutenberg which made universal literacy possible; and the harnessing of steam by Watt and his successors which made fast, dependable, cheap, all-year-round bulk transportation possible and at the same time shifted loads from the backs of men to engines. Aside from these four, man produced in these thousands of years no major scientific or mechanical things which materially changed the structure or purpose of his life, social organization, or his government.

Almost suddenly, around the middle of the nineteenth century, man's great awakening and change began to manifest itself. There was railroad development and growth which made industrial expansion possible.

The harnessing of electricity, that mysterious force which had intrigued man since the dawn of creation, was effectively accomplished commercially only two months before I was born, when Edison opened his Pearl Street station in New York City and began the production and distribution of electrical energy. Since then it has become every man's Lamp of Aladdin.

Electrical impulses transmitting the human voice over the telephone, and the radio, the Morse Code through telegraph instruments and pictures by wire have made world-wide communication almost instantaneous. As an essential of the automobile electricity makes transportation swift (too swift some of the time) and mobile, and as a source of power it moves great trains or cranes or lights a bulb easily and quietly.

This electrical energy, trinity of communication, transportation and power, is swift and universal. It, perhaps more than all other forces combined, has created the new social, economic, industrial and governmental problems which bewilder man today.

The invention of the internal combustion engine, which gave us the automobile, has further disorganized, complicated and transformed our social and economic life.

Some of the other scientific discoveries and inventions which have helped to make international economic and financial equilibrium more and more difficult to maintain are the Bessemer process for manufacturing steel, perfected in England in the 1860's; Eli Whitney's cotton gin which came more than a half-century ahead of the Bessemer process; McCormick's reaper which launched the agricultural revolution; and Oliver Evans' invention of milling and textile machinery which led to the early industrialization of America. Together with less important discoveries and inventions, they made the effort of a man walking a wire across Niagara Falls look as easy as falling over backwards when compared with that of society's maintaining the international economic and financial equilibrium during the period just preceding World War I.

Then came the great war in 1914.

And with the war came economic, financial, social and political forces which broke into millions of fragments the mechanical structure and credit system that Western civilization had been busily constructing for nearly one hundred years.

War expenditures quickly used up the accumulated wealth of the belligerents and forced them to mortgage their future through domestic and foreign borrowing on an unprecedented scale. The balanced equilibrium now belonged to the limbo of the past due to the undermining of currency foundations in some countries and the excessive accumulation of currency reserves in others.

In time this developing situation transformed many European nations from creditor to debtor nations and by the same action changed the United States and other neutrals from net debtor to net creditor nations.

A further dislocation was introduced at the war's end by the victor's levying of stupendous reparations assessments on the losers.

Compensating Shifts Absent

The possibility of reestablishing the old economic and financial procedures, now as tipsy as a drunk man, seemed a remote one because the war-caused sweeping financial shifts were not followed with corresponding shifts in the producing and consuming power of the involved nations. This situation existed because war borrowings had been used for destructive purposes and was made even worse by the destruction of many industrial plants and areas, and the transformation of plants manufacturing peacetime articles or goods into plants for manufacturing war materials.

Contributing further to the imbalance that had been created in European countries by either the destruction or reduction of output of manufacturers was that of war-stimulated gigantic expansion of both industry and agriculture in the United States and some other nations.

One further factor which made the war-created dis-equilibrium even more difficult was the European territorial adjustments which followed the war's end. Many old and several new nations were confronted with difficult problems when they sought to create financial and economic procedures which would enable them to achieve economic independence. These boundary shifts, which carried confinement of commerce procedures within additional restricted areas, seriously affected the economic life and recovery of a large portion of continental Europe for many years to come.

Since the stupendous cost of the war could not be financed by the levy of current taxes there was, as a consequence, a colossal growth in public debt—which unhappily was not accompanied by a corresponding increase in taxpaying capacity. This was especially true of central European countries.

These external trade and financial maladjustments doing with internal fiscal and monetary deterioration were soon manifested in currency depreciation of most foreign currencies which, while the war was in progress had been checked by control devices.

During 1919 and 1920 the United States stepped into the breach with loans for relief and rehabilitation under Mr. Hoover's direction, as has been described in the American Relief Administration chapter.

During the immediately succeeding years, as supporting credits declined and reparations became a greater burden than the central European governments could carry, the economic and financial structure of central Europe suffered a rapid disintegration. This was checked for a time with the help of a series of co-operative stabilization plans which in turn provided for substantial reductions in reparation payments, as well as by substantial loans to the central European governments.

Several countries, principally Great Britain, France, Sweden and the United States, following the stabilization efforts of the middle twenties, granted large credits both to the central European countries and to other countries throughout the world in an effort to correct the world-wide economic imbalance.

Actually what happened was that the people of the United States (who represent 6 per cent of the world's population) and their free enterprise system were carrying the other 94 per cent of the world's people through war-created economic morass, just as they are doing today.

One of the ill effects which came from the easy flow of United States money across international boundaries was the creation of tariff barriers which the beneficiary countries erected for the purpose of achieving economic self-sufficiency. This trend became sufficiently pronounced by 1927 to prompt the League of Nations Assembly to call a world economic conference for that year. It concluded that "The time has come to put a stop to the growth of customs barriers and to reverse the direction of the movement." The growth was checked temporarily, but by 1929 the movement for higher protection again had gained momentum in Europe.

Another factor in the situation which carried serious repercussions in a large and important sector of United States economy was that the rapid improvement of the agricultural situation in European countries was not accompanied by corresponding adjustments in our output of farm products from the enormously war-stimulated high. The result was a persistent decline in their prices and especially for those which heretofore had been exported in quantity, such as wheat, wool, cotton and sugar. Products from other countries, such as silk, sugar, coffee, rice, tea, cocoa, jute, hemp and flax, also suffered severe price declines as accumulated stocks gutted terminals and warehouses.

Added to all of this was the effect the legacy of war hysteria and war-created dislocations and needs had upon European government budgets in their use of public funds for relief and reconstruction, unemployment and their development of home industries in the effort to achieve economic self-sufficiency. The growing European expansion of both public and private credit left a trail of powder which led directly to a great mountain of TNT. Only a spark was needed to blow skyward all of puny man's efforts to "fix" things instead of concentrating on trying to work his way out of his troubles.

The World Economic and Financial Situation in 1928

A brief examination of economic and financial conditions of the world, apart from Europe and the United States, shows that a business depression was well under way in various areas considerably before it hit the United States in the fall of 1929.

It struck Australia and the Dutch East Indies with considerable force in late 1927 and Brazil the following year. It soon struck Canada, the Argentine and Egypt, and in Europe it struck Belgium, Finland, Poland and England.

These facts place in a strange and unpleasant light the statement Presidential candidate Roosevelt made in a speech in early October 1932 that the economic bubble—

> "burst first in the land of its origin—the United States."

It merits quoting only because it sharply brings out the differences which exist between getting elected to office and writing a historical record.

The Economic and Financial Situation in the United States

Speaking generally the period between 1922 and 1929 in the United States was one of great and well sustained prosperity. A "buyers' strike," which began in May, 1920 was followed by a sharp depression that involved "a precipitate decline of prices and a drastic liquidation of commercial credit." Recovery from this situation began in late 1921 and continued with only slight interruption during the next seven or eight years.

During this period an extensive outpouring of credit stimulated a vast expansion of foreign trade. There was an enormous upsurge in construction and the automobile industry experienced a phenomenal growth. The radio industry developed from scratch and flourished greatly. Inauguration of an installment purchase plan stimulated sales of a great variety of products. Federal, state and local governments expanded their highway and public building construction programs enormously. Commercial bank credits were easy—far too easy for speculative purposes. The federal government budget was balanced and its war debt was being gradually reduced. Income tax rates were reduced. Technological advances served to increase employment.

Weak spots in the situation were created by a fast and vast growing reservoir of funds seeking investment. This condition stimulated the flotation of foreign government securities. And it encouraged speculation in stock exchange securities, land and commodities.

As a result of all this speculative activity the stock market in the United States was in a highly vulnerable position. Its vulnerability was made all the greater by the weak spots in the world economy. A substantial decline in the market could cause a panic. Thus it was only a question of time until the complex and delicate world economic and financial mechanism which had been so carefully created would disastrously break down at some point and bring disaster with it.

As I have mentioned, that breakdown had occurred in Australia, Netherlands East Indies, Germany, Brazil and Finland between one and two years before its effects were seriously felt in the United States.

The world depression which followed the break in the collapse of the stock market in the United States in the fall of 1929 had three distinct phases.

The first phase of it, extending from 1929 to 1931 was expressed in (a) a drastic decline in the price of securities by as much as 60 per cent; (b) a sharp drop in the price of foodstuffs by nearly 50 per cent and raw materials to the same or greater extent; (c) a drop in world trade which amounted to 40 per cent in terms of value; (d) sharp decreases in the price of manufactured products and a far greater one in the price of agricultural products. In the United States industrial production declined 30 per cent and the flow of international loans and short term credits nearly dried up.

The next section presents the major steps President Hoover took to cushion the shock to the country of the impact of the disintegrating economic and financial forces. As a result of his measures many observers saw trends of orderly readjustment in 1930.

The Second Phase of the World Depression

These trends disappeared, however, when the depression entered its second phase in the spring of 1931 as a result of the collapse of the economy of central European governments. They had been operating, largely, on borrowed money. In an effort to meet restricted borrowing conditions they sought to balance international accounts by drastically curtailing imports and increasing exports. When the precarious credit and financial position of the central European countries became disturbingly evident in the second quarter of 1931, French investors withdrew a substantial volume of short-term funds from Germany. When the source of other foreign credits dried up, as a direct result of the German-Austrian customs agreement (which was construed as a violation of the peace treaty) gold soon began to flow out of both Germany and Austria. This led directly to the failure of Austria's largest bank.

The fat was now in the fire.

Doubts rose everywhere over the ability of the capitalistic system to withstand the new strains.

President Hoover, almost alone and by main force, met the situation by establishing a moratorium which suspended reparation and war debt payments to the United States by foreign governments for one year and by arranging for the Bank of International Settlements to make large new short-term loans to Germany, Austria and Hungary.

The disquietude which the central European and South American situation created in the minds of men everywhere soon placed new strains on British economy. Runs on the Bank of England precipitated a foreign exchange and monetary crisis resulting in the British government's abandonment of the gold standard in September, 1931.

The Third Phase of the World Depression

The action of the British government in abandoning the gold standard immediately placed new strains upon United States economy, where all foreign long-term debts to the United States were in default and American short-term claims against other countries were frozen.

As a result of this, foreigners immediately began to make large withdrawals of short-term claims. These consisted principally of bank deposits. American gold soon began to flow abroad, and in October, 1931, alone, $338,000,000 left the United States. The domestic situation was further weakened by the increase of internal hoarding of both gold and paper money.

One additional result of Great Britain's abandonment of the gold standard was that this action precipitated a wholesale breakdown of the international monetary standard. Within eight months' time twenty countries had followed England's course.

The new struggle with which the world's economic and financial leaders were faced was the maintenance of financial solvency. Within sixteen months twenty-three countries authorized general tariff increases and fifty countries increased the tariff on individual items or groups of commodities. Many of them also established quantitative restrictions in the form of import quotas, and thirty-two of them imposed licensing systems to protect themselves from products of the nations which had suspended gold, depreciated their currencies and cut their export prices sharply.

The situation was further troubled by the fact that several Latin American countries and most European governments defaulted outright on all international indebtedness. In some instances current payments on account of commercial transactions were "blocked" or suspended. The result was that a considerable part of international trade soon was expressed in the forced long-term loans by exporters in one country to importers in another.

This bilateral balancing process served to divert commerce from its accustomed channels of economic advantage and "robbed the trade process of much of its necessary flexibility, and served to intensify the vicious interaction between trade shrinkage and financial and monetary disintegration."

The accompanying shrinkage of industrial output and of corporate earnings together with increasing pessimism led to renewed drastic declines in prices of securities.

The wholesale shrinkage in values produced a grave debt crisis. Previous to the depression long range decline in agricultural prices had created a difficult farm-debt problem. Other debts also were becoming increasingly burdensome, especially those in the field of urban mortgages. The railroads were troubled with the threat of wholesale bankruptcy as were many public utility and industrial corporations, because of their inability to refund maturing bonds, as had been their previous custom. The stability of the insurance companies was threatened by the decline in value of the securities in their portfolios, and municipal government units which had been borrowing with unwise prodigality for many years began to find it increasingly difficult to meet their interest obligations.

This situation led to a tremendous increase in the mortality rate of country banks, whose resources were deflated by the decline in value of their security holdings. Also, the decline in the value of securities started a race for liquidation in the larger city banks, which further demoralized the security markets.

The net result of all this was to create a fear of the soundness of the nation's financial condition which naturally created a new flight of funds from the United States to other countries. In the first six months of 1932, the net outflow was $620,000,000.

Bottom of the Depression Reached in Mid-1932

In his study *Controlling Factors in Economic Development,* Doctor Moulton points out that:

> The most striking fact pertaining to the great depression was the comparative shortness of the acute stage—the quickness with which recovery followed collapse . . . sustained recovery began in India and Australia as early as the fourth quarter of 1931. In the third quarter of 1932 improvement began in the United States, Germany, France, Finland, Japan, South Africa, and New Zealand, while in the fourth quarter there was an upturn in the United Kingdom, British Malaya, Belgium, and the Netherlands. The index of industrial production in the United States rose 9 points—from 58 to 67—between July and October 1932. This improvement, however, proved short-lived and it was followed by a new decline during the banking crisis in early 1933. By March, 1933, the index of industrial production had declined to 60.
>
> It should be emphasized that while in many countries a turn was evident in the second half of 1932, the recovery movement remained somewhat sporadic in character and moderate in proportions until the spring of 1933. Perhaps the safest statement would be that in general the bottom of the depression was clearly reached in the summer of 1932, but that a strong and broad forward movement did not begin until nine months later. . . .

The largest percentage drop was in the United States, followed by Canada and Germany. The smallest decline was in Japan and the Scandinavian countries. . . .

Further extracts from this study are contained in Appendix XI.

PART FOUR

THE PRESIDENCY 1929–1933

CHAPTER ONE

Hoover's Basic Philosophy

Before he took the oath of office as President, Mr. Hoover stated that he "conceived the Presidency more than an administrative office; it is a power for leadership bringing coordination of the forces of business and cultural life in every city, town and countryside. The Presidency is more than executive responsibility. It is the symbol of America's high purpose. The President must represent the nation's ideals and he must also represent them to the nations of the world."

After four years in the White House he still regarded the Presidency "as a supreme obligation."

A basic tenet, if not *the* basic tenet of his faith in the American way of life (a phrase which he originated) was "voluntary co-operation within the community." It included perfection of the social organization, care of those in distress, advancement of knowledge, scientific research, education and the many phases of economic life. "This," he held, "is self-government outside of government; it is the most powerful development of individual freedom and equal opportunity that has taken place in the century and one half since our fundamental institutions were founded."

He believed that it was in the further extension of this voluntary co-operation of all the people in all of the nation's communities, along with a growing sense of individual responsibility, rather than an extension of government into our social and economic life which would find the correct "solution of many of our complex problems."

The function of government, as he saw it, was to encourage and build up this co-operation "and its most resolute action should be to deny the extension of bureaucracy."

The primary conception of the American system, he held, is in the co-operation of free men, not "the regimentation of men." It was founded "upon the conception of responsibility of the individual to the community, of the responsibility of local government to the state, of the state to the national government."

It was designed, he once said, to maintain this "equal opportunity to the individual and through decentralization" to bring about and maintain these responsibilities. "The centralization of government will undermine responsibilities and will destroy the system."

Mr. Hoover's economic policies which had been clarified and defined during his nearly eight-year period of service as Secretary of Commerce were as follows:

He supported with complete fidelity the American tradition of free initiative and enterprise; open opportunity and freedom from any attempt of interference by either individuals, groups or the government.

His support of a free economy rested on his deep philosophical belief that the spiritual freedoms of the race—free speech, press and worship; self-government and all of the other essential practices of a free people, such as the predetermination of prices in free markets under competitive forces, are able to exist only in a free economic system. The one exception he held about freedom was that no group, through monopoly, exploitation, abuse or pressure, should infringe upon the rights and freedoms of other groups.

He had firmly, and over a long period of years, opposed collectivist doctrines and their encroachment upon freedom with their attempted regimentation of the individual through coercion. His opposition to these doctrines rested upon their inevitable destruction of democracy by the autocratic spirit of their bureaucracies.

As he appraised history he believed that by far the greatest progress of humanity had been made during the three periods of free men—Greece, which had produced logic, art and our philosophical foundations; Rome, with its growth of self-government, law and peace; and the modern period of the Western World from which had come freedom and democracy and its collateral blessings of scientific discovery, invention and humanitarianism in government.

Out of his Quaker training and beliefs and also from the neighborly helpfulness of people in the pioneer communities where he was born and reared, he had gained a conception of America's true social philosophy which was "a special social system of our own. We have made it ourselves from materials brought in revolt from conditions in Europe." We have lived it and "constantly sought to improve it" though we seldom have "tried to define it." This social system of ours, he believed, "abhors autocracy" and fights it rather than argues with it. Nor was it capitalism, socialism or syndicalism. It wasn't even a "cross-breed of them."

To him the social force which held his interest was "far higher and more precious . . . than all these." Its source, infinitely more enduring, was the belief that "each individual shall be given the chance and stimulation for development of the best with which he has been endowed in heart and mind; it is the sole source of progress; it is American individualism."

The rightfulness of it, he held, "can rest upon either philosophic, political, economic or spiritual grounds."

His driving purpose was to develop and release the power for accomplishment of each individual in the nation, to stimulate "initiative and individuality" to direct their efforts toward "economic progress" so that poverty might be further lessened. "Intellectual, spiritual and moral progress is not the product of poverty," he once said.

In his book, *American Individualism,* he held further that "Instincts, character and the divine spark in the human soul [his fellow Quakers call it *The Inner Light*] are the property alone of the individual." It is his belief that there can be no human thought or impulse to action "which does not arise in the individual. A free people maintains as many potential centers of enterprise, leadership and intellectual and spiritual progress as there are individuals." To him it would be as absurd to talk about abolishing the sun's rays, "if we would secure our food, as to talk about abolishing individualism as a basis of a successful society."

Once in speaking of Theodore Roosevelt, Mr. Hoover said:

> His was a virile energy, an abundant optimism and courage, a greatness of vision and a faith in his country's future which knew no boundaries of limiting doubts. These qualities within him and

his strength were unconsciously developed in communion with nature. He lived much in the open; he loved the mountains, the woods, the streams and the sea. From them he gained a spaciousness of outlook. . . .

That Mr. Hoover had a clear concept of his duties and responsibilities as President few men will deny. In addition to his adherence to American principles of government and the American way of life and his experience in public service, he had sought to prepare himself for his new, vast responsibilities by carefully studying the records, messages, state papers and other pertinent documents of each of his predecessors in that high office.

Early in his administration he remarked to me that he looked upon the White House as the most effective sounding board in the world for the presentation and interpretation of those principles which advance the true well-being of mankind.

Always, all his life, in everything he has done, he has gone forward, thinking like a pessimist but operating like an optimist. "Progressive men never go backward." he has said. Nor can he "conceive of a wholesome or economic system that does not have its roots in religious faith. No blind materialism can for long engage the loyalties of mankind." Economic aspiration, which strongly marks the American system, he has said, "is not an end in itself." It is only one of many instruments which help to accomplish the profound purposes of the American people "which are largely religious in origin." This country, he believed, "is supremely dedicated . . . to pursuit of a richer life for the individual."

As for freedom, he held that "man's vigil and his quest have been to be free" throughout the centuries "To embody liberty in workable government, America was born."

Hand in hand with his belief in liberty went his belief in the free enterprise system. "I know," he said, "it is inseparable from intellectual and spiritual liberty. Because it is the only road to higher standards of living. Because it is the only system under which morals and self-respect of men can survive."

Mr. Hoover stated the broad principles on which his faith in the

American way of life rested and by which its purposes might be effectively advanced and strengthened in his acceptance speech August 11, 1928.

After stating that the points of contact between the people and the government were constantly multiplying and that wise governmental policies become more vital every year in ordinary life, he pointed out that "as our problems grow so do our temptations grow to venture away from those principles upon which our republic was founded and upon which it has grown to greatness" and then he added the admonition that *"we must direct economic progress in support of moral and spiritual progress."*

Peace had been made, he stated, and the healing process of good will was extinguishing the fires of hatred. Domestically the true test of our progress was in "the security, comfort and opportunity that have been brought to the average American family." But most of all he liked "to remember what this program has meant to America's children. The portal of their opportunity has ever been widening." In speaking of poverty with its grinding by undernourishment, cold and ignorance; and fear of old age of those who have the will to work, he expressed the belief that we in America are nearer to the final triumph over it than "ever before in the history of any land." In his judgment there was no guaranty against poverty that is equal "to a job for every man. That is the primary purpose of the economic policies we advocate."

He held, however, that "economic advancement is not an end in itself" because successful democracy "rests wholly upon the moral and spiritual quality of its people." He believed with all his heart that "our growth in spiritual achievements must keep pace with our growth in physical accomplishments" and that "material prosperity and moral progress must march together" if we would make the United States the "commonwealth so grandly conceived by its founders." The only way our government can match the expectations of our people was "to have a constant regard for those human values that give dignity and nobility to life." These, not size, wealth and power alone are what "fulfill the promise of America's opportunity."

Equal opportunity, he held, was the right of every American. "Only from confidence that this right will be upheld can flow the unbounded courage and hope which stimulate each individual man and woman to endeavor and to achievement. The sum of their achievement is the gigantic harvest of national progress."

As opposed to this concept, he pointed out, socialism bids all to end the race equally; provides neither training nor umpire while despotism selects those who should run and those who should win.

He wanted "to see our government great both as an instrument and as a symbol of the nation's greatness" as measured in moral and spiritual welfare and happier homes.

CHAPTER TWO

Credit and Debit Pages in President Hoover's Ledger

When Mr. Hoover became President on March 4, 1929 a vast majority of the American people would have agreed upon the inclusion of the following items on the credit pages of his qualifications for this high office:

> He was a sincere and able apostle of intelligent and responsible citizenship.
>
> His fixed habit of using voluntary agreements rather than coercive laws as instruments for improving the nation's social and economic life were in the best American tradition.
>
> He had exceptional administrative ability.
>
> His clearly demonstrated spiritual and moral qualities and his humanitarian instincts were inspiring.
>
> His unwavering adherence to the principles of the American way of life gave all true Americans fresh pride in their country.

The many evidences of his belief that only moral and spiritual values are permanent, and his steadfast adherence to the principle that freedom is a product of the spirit combined with his belief that the finest results are gained by appealing to the higher qualities of men and women were listed on the credit pages of his ledger.

He had demonstrated in a variety of capacities, and especially as Food Administrator and Secretary of Commerce, that he could blaze great and useful trails to new, vast areas which were of incalculable value to the better development and growth of a democracy and its people.

Many other items could be added to the credit pages of his ledger, but the above list includes most of the major ones.

One segment of the population, that composed of business men, both big and small, was jubilant over Mr. Hoover's election. They and their forebears had been longing to have a successful business man for President ever since George Washington's administration, the only one previous to Mr. Hoover's which had been headed by a business man.

"Now," they said, "we'll have more business in government and less government in business. What this country needs more than anything else is a man with business experience for President."

Political and social scientists were open-minded on the point, with reservations. Their reservations concerned their contention that because the purposes of government and of business are strikingly dissimilar a man, regardless of his business administrative ability, might not, by this token alone, necessarily possess qualifications which would enable him to be a success as an administrator of public affairs. This, they held to be true because governments exist to render common services whereas business units cannot long exist without earning profits.

Furthermore, they held that the business public, that is the managers and investors, are interested primarily in earning and paying regular dividends and to increase the value of the securities. Given those two things the investing public largely leaves the managers of their business concerns alone.

Our voting public, on the other hand, requires, over and above able honest administration, a great amount of repeated explanation, interpretation and justifications of the what's, why's and how's of its administrators' activities.

The existence of the differences between the purposes of public affairs and business affairs and those between the business and the voting public caused the social and political scientists to be both skeptical and hopeful over Mr. Hoover's election. Their attitude was much like that of "Sockless" Jerry Simpson, who, previous to the election days when he suffered many defeats in his efforts to become a member of Congress, would say, "Of course I haven't a chance to get elected." But, waving his arms he would add, "Great God, what if I were to win!"

So it was with some social and political scientists about the election to the Presidency of Herbert Hoover, the successful business man: "Of course he can't succeed. But, Great God, what if he did!"

Debit Items

Leaving the political and social scientists and returning to the general public's items on the pages of Mr. Hoover's ledger we find the following which concern his political qualifications.

The first deals with what might be called the Voters' Basic Requirements of Public Officials, which the public senses but has not expressed concretely. They are:

1. To be able to see the right thing.
2. To have the courage, capacity and the honesty to carry it through without swerving.

The voters unhesitatingly gave Mr. Hoover top passing marks on these two points, but not on the following:

3. To be able and willing to explain over and over again, if necessary, what he has done in such simple terms that his constituents could understand what he did and why he did it.

Another debit item, in the eyes of the general public, concerned Mr. Hoover's ability to match wits and strategy with the professional politicians with whom he would have to deal. Summarized briefly, the reasons on which the public's doubt rested were:

Mr. Hoover was open and above board in his dealings, whereas professional politicians follow devious ways.

Mr. Hoover was devoid of tricks which long have been the professional politician's stock in trade.

Mr. Hoover dealt in principles whereas professional politicians deal in compromise.

Mr. Hoover would promise no more than he believed he could perform. The professional politician, on the contrary, if he believed that it would gain his party votes, would promise the moon.

Hoover's Primary Interest in Ideas a Question Mark

Another of his qualities which created some doubt in the public mind about his qualifications for the Presidency, a doubt it sensed rather than understood and expressed, was that Mr. Hoover's primary interest seemed to lay more in the field of ideas than in men. That was what the prescient William Allen White expressed indirectly in the part of his letter to me which was quoted in an earlier chapter, where he said Mr. Hoover's appeal was to the intellect rather than to the emotions.

Because of his deep interest in ideas and because also he was a first-rate scientist in the mining engineering field, his natural inclination as well as his training prompted him first to look for facts and then to assay them. A good scientist must be well educated, self-effacing and have a single-minded devotion for his task. Trained as a scientist in the exact physical sciences, Mr. Hoover sought to bring the same training and approach to bear on the inexact social, economic and political sciences. It is possible that voters feared his absorption in this effort might prevent his realizing that most people feel rather than think; are swayed by emotion instead of being guided by facts and that rabble-rousers, slogan coiners and self-seekers move them far more easily and surely than the Pasteurs, Farradays, Curies and the Edisons inspire them.

Some day, no one knows how far away that day is, the voting public may be more influenced by the assaying and presentation of facts than by an appeal to their emotions. The distance from us of that day will mark the extent by which Mr. Hoover was ahead of his time.

Twenty years after he entered the White House, in August, 1949, a large number of newspapers discussed the quality of Mr. Hoover's political aptitudes and in doing so they expressed some of the questionings of the general public in 1929. The following four quotations are fairly representative of these editorial expressions.

The Charles City, Iowa, *Press* expressed the opinion that:

> . . . As President, Mr. Hoover, who was totally unfamiliar with precinct type of politics and all forms of political trickery, never was able to gain the support of regular or old-guard Republicans . . . his liberalism wasn't radical enough to suit the progressive Republicans. . . .

The Miami, Florida, *Herald* stated:

> Just the thought of his going around kissing babies to get votes is too ludicrous for words. Dignified, a little shy, never an enthralling speaker . . . he never caught the public fancy either as a cabinet officer or President. . . .

The Bellville, Illinois, *News-Democrat* held that:

> . . . He is not now and never was a politician. Had he been, honesty and forthrightness in dealing with problems as well as reporting to the people would not have become the hallmark of his public character. . . .

It was the belief of the Streator, Illinois, *Times-Press* that:

> . . . Hoover's intrusion into the realm of politics was not to his liking and his nomination and election to President was on a plane far above partisan consideration. His interest was only in the opportunity to serve his fellow men. . . .

The Final Debit Item

Another debit item which should be included here, although it represented the opinion of a minority of the voters at that time, concerns what was popularly believed to be Mr. Hoover's position on the Eighteenth Amendment. All professional wets and many other citizens who believed that this amendment improperly restricted their liberties were disturbed over what they interpreted to be Mr. Hoover's stand on this question.

This subject will be discussed in a later chapter that deals with the Wickersham Commission.

CHAPTER THREE

Politics in Action

It is possible that a man who had been trained in politics at the precinct and county level, and who had no Quaker conscience to live with (a terribly troublesome creature) by stooping to conquer could have welded the old-guard Republicans and the progressive Republicans into an effective working unit. A politician with flexible principles might have performed the miracle with tongue-in-cheek promises and an easy attitude toward the qualifications of appointees.

The President could not bring himself to do either of these things. His political experience at the precinct and county level was *nil.* Insofar as he was a politician he was one at the statesman level. His primary interest was in questions and policies which were directly concerned with the long range, high-purposed development of the nation and which fix the destiny of a people.

With all of his acuteness in so many fields of human endeavor, and his understanding of men in almost all other walks of life, Mr. Hoover never acquired the ability to measure and cope with professional politicians. This is understandable because these men are a race apart who from a thousand experiences have created an unwritten science. They have learned how to mix together and make an attractive whole of personal ambition, greed (for money or power), likableness, plausibility, sophistry and a tiny bit of altruism. With them the end too frequently justifies the means. They use logic, reason and duplicity when necessary, and emotion at all times.

They were something new in Hoover's life and he never found any instruments with which to measure or appraise them. This being the case it was inevitable that many of them would mislead him and some of them, in the guise of friendship, would betray him. During the four years of his presidency there were four different chairmen of the Republican National Committee. Never in any other activity did he encounter such difficulty in finding the right man for the job.

These shifts in the Republican National Committee chairmanship, aside from being manifestations of Hoover's unsure hand politically, served to prevent the stabilization of Republican party politics.

Through his service as Food Administrator and as Secretary of Commerce, President Hoover had been able to make many good friends and supporters in both Houses of Congress. On March 4, 1929, however, he had far more strength in the House, which is closer to the people, than he did in the upper body. These friends in both houses, until the Democrats gained control of the Lower House in the 1930 elections, were able to enlist enough voting strength to pass the legislation he requested.

An analysis of the Senate membership on March 4, 1929 shows that it contained forty-two regular or old-guard Republicans who seldom saw eye-to-eye with the President on political questions, and many of whom considered politics to be a game of strategy and manipulation, one where now-you-see-and-now-you-cannot-see which of the three shells covers the little pea. Their support of the President's programs was erratic and sporadic much of the time.

One reason for the old-guard Senate Republican opposition to the President was that five of their number had been Mr. Hoover's opponents for the presidential nomination in 1928. These included Curtis of Kansas, Goff of West Virginia, Steiwer of Oregon, Watson of Indiana and Willis of Ohio. Curtis was now vice president and Willis was dead. The remaining three and their close friends in the Senate carried the pre-convention feuds over into the new administration. Had their recalcitrant attitude toward him been confined to the Senate that would have been bad enough. They made the situation worse by spearheading the old-guard political leaders' opposition to a Republican President. Another reason for their opposition was that the President was too much of a liberal for them to accept him.

His record, moreover, demonstrated clearly that he was a social and economic reformer at heart. They were fearful that he might also become a political reformer. And this they could not tolerate.

It is possible that as President, by using patronage, promises, threats and browbeating, he could have wheedled a recalcitrant Senate during his first two years (the House co-operated splendidly with him during that period) and forced his programs through.

Over the years, as the nation grew from immature provincialism to world stature, and as it grew in numbers, size and strength it was transformed from its original nearly wholly agricultural to its present industrial nature. These growths and changes carried with them new concepts, duties and responsibilities for the Presidency. Gradually our presidents became broader policy-makers in legislation concerning foreign affairs and the nation's economic life. Mr. Hoover greatly broadened the President's job by having it include social and cultural services. To this concept he gave new significance to more recently initiated presidential duties of advancing social and economic reforms. All of these latter activities had changed the Founding Fathers' concept of the Presidency.

A still more recent development of the presidential office concerned the occupant's place as party leader. This involved him with both patronage and policy problems.

If, as in Mr. Hoover's case, the occupant succeeded another member of his own party, he would have little patronage to dispense unless he were to turn his predecessor's appointees out of office. Such action would be sure to create a break in party ranks and cause much recrimination. As an alternative, the pressure on the new President to select a nominee for one of the few available positions would be such as to cause additional troubles for him, since he might make one man happy and a thousand men bitter by such action.

This was what happened with some of the old-guard party leaders, who lacking the courage to fight him openly, tried to get even by covertly encouraging opposition attacks and by failing to defend his administration.

Mr. Hoover sincerely believed in the independence of the legislative branch of the government and sought to work with the Congress. This, however, could not be done when the Democrats gained control of the house in 1930 and were hell-bent to destroy him politically. But that is another story and will be told later.

He sought to work with Congress up to the point of employing patronage and promises to gain its support. Once, for example, a group of the President's and my political and personal friends in a Mid-western state threatened to make him a lot of political misery over his refusal to name one of their group to the federal district bench. They had first tried to enlist me in their cause but I would not enlist. Later as their letters gave evidence of fast-rising temperatures it seemed well for me, as a friend and well-wisher of both theirs and the President's, to try to bring them together in amity.

The President listened patiently to my recital of my friends' arguments and contentions and then said something like this:

The man our friends want appointed isn't up to the job and I can't appoint him. Their claim that the attorney general's office is prejudiced against their man is all bosh. I sent one of the most able investigators in the government out there on a confidential mission. I told him to make a thorough check on the qualifications of their candidate. This man reports only to me. His report was an unqualified *no* on their man. That settles it as far as I am concerned.

I'd like to go along with our friends in this. They are fine people and I need their support. But I won't try to hold them in line by appointing their man.

I can't do it because I'm convinced that the quality of the federal judiciary must be built up. I've been here in Washington for a dozen years and seen how previous administrations have been pushed and high-pressured and mauled by politicians into making inferior judicial appointments. I am determined to make only top appointments to the federal bench regardless of what it may cost me in friendships or political support. If I name only the best qualified men for the District Court bench it can serve as a training ground and feeder for the Circuit Court which in turn can and should do the same thing for the Supreme Court. There are not in the whole country today more than half a dozen men who rate appointment to either higher court. I want to get this procedure established regardless of how much political support it will cost me.

Only professional party politicians could object to the President's purpose. They did so with vociferous indignation and threatened varied reprisals if he would not do as they wished in just this one instance. "Let him," they told me, "follow his principles on other appointments if he wants. We don't care. But he'll appoint our man, or else."

Some time later in his administration the President nominated the distinguished citizen and great jurist Charles Evans Hughes for the position of Chief Justice of the United States Supreme Court. Because of an old grudge he held against Hughes, Senator Borah opposed confirmation of Hughes and, unbelievable as it now seems, enlisted some of his senator friends and recalcitrant opposition senators to join him but the Senate confirmed the appointment. When word reached Mr. Hoover of the birth of a granddaughter, he remarked, "Thank God she doesn't have to be confirmed by the Senate."

A short time later, in April, 1930, President Hoover nominated Justice John J. Parker of the Fourth District Circuit Court to fill another vacancy in the Supreme Court. Before naming Parker the President had asked the attorney-general to make a careful study of the decisions Judge Parker had rendered over a twenty-year period. They showed, the attorney-general found, unusually high legal competence.

The President had been led to consider Parker for the vacancy for two reasons: the first was that the South at that time had no representative on the Supreme Court and second, he believed that the Circuit Court should serve as a training ground for the Supreme Court.

Because Judge Parker was a nominal Republican, and because he had served on the bench for twenty of his twenty-five adult years, and therefore could not have been active in politics, the President, before naming him queried southern political leaders on their judgment of Parker. Ten southern Democratic senators and seven southern Democratic governors urged the Parker appointment as did leading lawyers and judges of the South.

Satisfied with Judge Parker's qualifications, the President named him. William Green, President of the American Federation of Labor, seeking to publicize his organization's opposition to a particular law, raised his voice in anguished opposition to one of Judge Parker's decisions relative to this law despite the fact that the decision followed closely the Supreme Court's decisions on the same law.

A Negro association joined the opposition with the charge that when he was twenty-one years old Mr. Parker had allegedly made some remark (which he never had made) which dealt with white supremacy in the South.

When the labor and Negro lobbies threatened reprisals on senators who voted for Parker's confirmation, many of them ran to cover like scared rabbits. Partisan opponents joined in the battle. The President needed one additional vote for Parker's confirmation but he was unable to get it, even from Republican senators, on the grounds that any senator who voted for Parker would face election troubles from labor and Negro pressure groups. Following the Senate's refusal to confirm Judge Parker's nomination, the President named Owen J. Roberts, whose nomination was confirmed.

It would be difficult to estimate the number of the clashes President Hoover had with regular Republican leaders over appointments, or to realize what it cost him in party support when he refused to name anyone to public service whose sole recommendation was that the applicant had been a good party worker. Pressure exerted by politicians to make him do their bidding in such instances made him distrustful of them. It seemed to irritate him also to have to deal with men whose honest purpose he doubted.

Related to but somewhat apart from this same point is the fact that the professional politician's oblique approach to questions concerning policies or appointments also tended to throw Mr. Hoover off-balance. It is strange that this should have been the case because the professional politician's approach is quite similar to that of military leaders, and as mentioned earlier, Mr. Hoover played rings around the military leaders on both sides in World War I by catching them off-guard in their oblique approach with his direct approach. It is possible that the difference in quality and extent of integrity that political and military leaders possess accounts in a measure for his difficulty in dealing with politicians and that of his highly successful dealing with military leaders.

So much for the forty-two old-guard Republican members of the Senate on March 4, 1929. What about the fourteen "Progressive" Republicans and one tag-along Farmer-Labor member? They were members of the "farm bloc." Their thinking and action was left of center. The President's views on social, economic and political questions were not sufficiently radical to win their support. But his views on these questions were too liberal for the regular, or old-guard group. His liberalism did not endear him to this group of fifteen senators for several reasons.

The President had an international outlook, whereas Senators Borah, Johnson (of California), La Follette, Norris and others in the group were isolationists at heart and by practice. They were in reality a pressure group and (except for their isolationist outlook) fought always to gain advantages for their agricultural minority. Mr. Hoover sought to be President of all the people.

Another basic reason for their inability to work together was that they and he were temperamentally poles apart. Most of them were emotional, he was unemotional; they felt, he reasoned; their stock in trade was causes, his were facts and figures.

Moreover President Hoover's natural reserve made it impossible for him to jolly them to smooth their ever-ruffled feathers. If it could be said that politics is one of the minor branches of harlotry it should also be stated that, politically, Mr. Hoover held a frigid desire to live a virtuous life.

It was impossible for him ever to follow the announced policy of Mike Sutton, who in the long-ago frontier days, while making a successful race for mayor of Dodge City, Kansas, announced that, if elected, he would be like "Caesar's wife, all things to all men."

President Hoover's difficulties in working with these progressive Republicans began early in his administration. The first break in the ranks took place in the summer of 1928, when he refused to make a political trade with Senator Norris of Nebraska, and Norris became his bitter political enemy.

Senator Borah told Mr. Hoover that Senator Norris was an unprincipled demagogue, but this did not lessen Norris' nuisance value.

This emotional-pressure sectional group was bound to the Republican party with easily breakable ties. This was also true in the main of their Republican constituents. The territory they represented, which roughly speaking was the middlewest and northwest, while normally Republican, had also during the previous fifty years been the nation's seed bed for Greenbackers, Populists, Bryanites and Bull Moosers. It was intransigently committed to a type of militant liberalism. Remove one of its senate leaders, say Kenyon of Iowa who was appointed to the federal bench, and you would get a "wild man" Brookhart in his place.

Insistent as they were for a considerable amount of social attention, political consideration, and a lot of walking and talking in their direction with them, these things alone or combined could not have held them in line. They were political insurgents by instinct, by nature and by voter mandates.

They slipped off the Hoover reservation several times in his first eight months as President. Having found these excursions to their liking they soon established their permanent camps in the political no man's land which lies between the Republican and Democratic parties.

Their breaks with the President troubled many mutual friends. One of these friends was the late William Allen White of Kansas. When others deplored, White acted. It was natural that he should have done so because he always seemed ready and willing to step into a buzz saw and come out twins.

In November, 1929, Mr. White prepared a statement on the President Hoover-farm bloc senatorial situation which he was willing to make public if President Hoover approved.

My part in the project was to show the President Mr. White's proposed (but never issued) public statement. My conference with the President developed several good reasons why the statement should not be given to the press. Quotations from a portion of it will help refresh the reader's memory concerning that troubled situation.

Republicans are facing the menace that shattered the party in the days of Roosevelt and Taft. A mended plate splits on the old crack. We are duplicating in many ways the blunders of two decades ago. Then a conservative occupied the White House and the majority of his party was clearly liberal. Now, we have a liberal President trying to lead a reactionary Congressional organization while the liberal congressional insurgents are hurrying past the red traffic lights. The liberal program is in danger. The Progressive Senators holding aloof from the White House may force the President to work only with conservatives who distrust his program and make his task hard. With liberal support it should be easy. For certainly President Hoover's eight months in the White House have cinched his saddle to ride and lead the Republican party—all of it.

His attitude on world peace has given him world leadership. . . .

Hoover clarified the atmosphere of party politics by his letter of rebuke to the Southern patronage brokers.

He must use the machinery of politics as the party has made it. He can follow no council of perfection. . . .

Here we stand twenty years back, duplicating the insurgency of 1909; but here we have all the cards in our own hands—we who believe in the liberal Republican cause. We have a militant Senate minority which with Hoover might become a majority. We have a great leader in the White House with the people behind him. The possibilities for a real forward movement in the American government are so obvious that the present situation seems tragic. The liberals of the country have nothing to gain by martyrdom. One generous gesture from the group lead by Borah, Norris, Capper and Norbeck will win more in substantial progress today than years of sizzling at the martyr's stake. . . .

Only the President can call order out of chaos. And to him and his leadership the Progressives should rally to save their cause. The Republican party is their refuge and strength. No such opportunity has confronted Republican progressives since Roosevelt [Theodore] left the White House. . . .

It is the plain duty of Congress and particularly the high visioned leaders of Congress who for twenty years have been looking for such an hour as this to turn to Hoover and consolidate their victory. He and they have everything in common. He and they together can realize the ideals of 1928. (From author's personal files.)

It seems clear today that Mr. White's earnest appeal, had it been made public would no more have checked the world-wide gathering forces of economic, social and political simoon than a straw could have checked the force of the tornadoes which frequently occur in the region the farm bloc senators represented.

It is easily conceivable, based on the sweeping change in the public's attitude toward him during the past seventeen years, with any kind of fair break in domestic and world economic conditions during his Presidency, that Mr. Hoover could have left the White House with a record that would have secured for him a recognized place as a towering political leader and statesman.

CHAPTER FOUR

Administrative Appointments, Policies and Program

Of great advantage to Mr. Hoover when he became President was his acquaintanceship or friendship gained from nearly fourteen years' service in Washington as Food Administrator, American Relief Administrator and Secretary of Commerce.

These acquaintances and friends included the permanent and transitory government officials as well as the political, social welfare, labor, industrial and financial leaders of the nation, and hosts of leaders great and small in other fields of endeavor.

In addition to his knowledge of personnel he also had had many opportunities to get a close-up inspection of the operation of governmental machinery. Topping all this he had had an important part in making that machine operate smoothly and efficiently.

His intimate knowledge of social, economic and political conditions in many other countries, his varied war experiences and his studious exacting mind had enabled him to develop a conviction about governmental operation and a working philosophy about its needs and purposes.

Appointments

This combined knowledge, along with that of his judgment of men made his task of selecting his policy making and immediate executive staff a comparatively simple task.

Two striking commentaries should be made about the considerably more than one hundred men and women he named for these positions.

1. They and their subordinates collected and expended more than $25,000,000,000 of public funds during the four years of the Hoover Administration so honestly and capably that despite the frantic and

probing efforts of a succession of investigating committees under the direction of the succeeding hostile administration no evidence was ever produced which impugned either the integrity or the capability of one of them.

That is a record for the big book.

2. Except because of death or promotion almost every one of President Hoover's appointees held his job for the full four years of the administration. There were no resignations because of differences of opinion, improper activities or quarrels.

That, too, is a record for the big book.

Policies and Program

President Hoover had definitely in mind what policies and programs he would seek to establish and initiate when he entered the White House. He was thwarted by foreign factors in carrying out all of them just as another President, Woodrow Wilson, had been thwarted in carrying out his policies and programs by foreign factors. The great world depression impeded President Hoover's efforts and World War I interfered with President Wilson's.

In the field of foreign relations President Hoover tried to lead the people of the nation from their position of spiritual and intellectual isolation, to which they had clung stubbornly for several years, into the world arena in an effort to have them make a real contribution in the establishment of world peace.

To this end he sought to create a realization in the public mind of the new interdependence of nations. He did this in part by speeches. He said, for example, in his inaugural address, "The United States fully accepts the profound truth that our own progress, prosperity and peace are interlocked with the progress, prosperity and peace of all humanity. . . . We not only desire peace with the world but to see peace maintained throughout the world. We wish to advance the reign of justice and reason toward the extinction of force."

He also made specific recommendations to the Congress for action which was designed to advance this program. These included proposals for our participation in maintaining peace.

What he did was prompted by his conviction that "Peace is not a static thing. To maintain peace is as dynamic in its requirements as is the conduct of war."

Implementing his broad policies of international co-operation as an aid to furthering peace, he sought to: (a) improve and strengthen better relations with Latin American countries. His first move in this direction occurred when he made his post-election trip to Latin America; (b) reorganize our diplomatic service; (c) Advance adherence to the World Court, and increase the number of direct treaties which specified arbitration and conciliation; (d) bring about better non-political co-operation with the League of Nations; (e) reduce friction with Great Britain; (f) seek, with co-operation of other nations, to restrain Japan; (g) limit land and naval armaments throughout the world; (h) increase co-operation in the economic fields; (i) obtain a moratorium on, as well as revision of, intergovernmental debts; (j) create a world economic conference to stabilize currencies and reduce trade barriers.

One of those seldom-recorded footnotes of history was recently given me by my friend Raymond Moley. Mr. Moley, who was head of the Roosevelt "braintrust" during the 1932 campaign, said that after he had carefully examined all available material about President Hoover's foreign policy he said to Governor Roosevelt, "There is no issue on foreign affairs because Hoover's conduct of it is good, so what's the use of your making a speech on it?"

After he and Governor Roosevelt discussed the subject completely the Governor remarked, "Yes, you are right, Ray. There's no speech for me there."

The result was that the presidential candidate of a major party made no campaign speech on foreign affairs, a subject of paramount importance.

Domestic Reforms

When the complete history of the Hoover administration is recorded and interpreted it will show that its Chief originated more new governmental policies to correct business abuses than had any of his predecessors. It undoubtedly will show also that as President, Mr. Hoover initiated more steps designed to advance the nation's economic life and to speed up social progress than any of his predecessors. He did all of these things within the framework of the Constitution and with constant and complete regard and respect for the ideals and practices of free men.

As he viewed the domestic scene he saw that extremely little had been done by the federal government in the way of reform since the early days of the Wilson administration. Inaction in this field, combined with the nation's growth, had produced many strains.

In his judgment there was urgent need to introduce reforms in the following fields:

1. *Reform in judicial procedure and law enforcement.* This was needed, he insisted, in part because of "the additional burdens imposed upon our judicial system." He wanted "to re-establish the vigor and effectiveness of law enforcement." This was necessary, he held in his inauguration address, because "The most malign of all these dangers today is disregard and disobedience to law." He could not accept a widely-held thesis that "laws are made for those who choose to obey them" because "ours is a government of laws made by the people themselves." Again, he said, "the very essence of freedom is obedience to law . . . liberty itself has but one foundation and that is the law."

By perseverance in early 1932, he secured legislation which vastly improved federal procedure in criminal cases which he said "realizes in part a quarter of a century of demands for reform. . . . It will increase respect for the law."

President Hoover also instituted sweeping reforms in the related fields of law enforcement, in appointments to the courts, by raising the standards of judges and prosecuting officers, by reorganizing the Federal Bureau of Investigation, by furthering the adoption of the Lindbergh Kidnapping Law, by a complete overhauling of the prison system which included a national board of parole, placing all prison medical services under the Public Health Service, establishment of a boys' reformatory and a reformatory for women, classification and segregation of prisoners, provisions for instructions and employment for prisoners and a probation system.

2. *Reforms and Progress in the Social Area.* The Hoover administration broke far more new ground in this field than perhaps all previous administrations combined.

These included: (a) the White House Conference on Housing which considered better housing, better homes and slum-clearance because the President held that "next to food and clothing the housing of a nation is its most vital social and economic problem." Later in his administration the President induced the Congress, after eight months of inaction, to create the Federal Home Loan Banking System as an aid for home owners. He also secured authority for the RFC to make loans for slum-clearance. (b) Education, which the President held to be "the only door to equal opportunity." The Democratic majority in the House refused to approve his recommendation for the creation of the office of an assistant secretary for education. He did create a nationwide committee for the abolition of illiteracy through the operation of an adult education program. (c) Indian Bureau reform. This was close to the President's Quaker heart because his people—ever since that time in 1680 when William Penn bought his land from the Indians instead of driving them off by force—had always been interested in the welfare of Indians. He secured amendments to many laws which governed the Indians and their property and provided them with better protection from exploitation, and he improved their educational and health services. (d) An attempt to advance both social security and old age pension programs, but due to the depression, Mr. Hoover made little progress. (e) Committee on Recent Social Trends.

Acting upon the realization that the first third of the twentieth century had "been filled with epoch-making events and crowded with problems" which urgently demanded attention the President first sought the facts. He wanted to make doubly sure that (a) certain human rights, which had been infringed upon by the mechanization of industry, should be restored; and (b) that government should take the leadership in humanitarian fields.

In keeping with his invariable demand for facts which are secured by scientific inquiry he instituted a thorough and complete investigation in the entire field of social problems of the nation—the first one ever undertaken. First he secured the funds for the project by private subscription and next appointed a distinguished group of social scientists "to examine and report upon recent social trends in the United States with a view of providing such a review as might supply the basis for formulation of large national policies looking to the next phase of the national development."

The committee secured the co-operation of several hundred specialists in different fields and after three years' work produced the first thorough foundation of social fact ever presented as a guide for public action.

Upon issuing the committee's report on January 2, 1933, President Hoover said:

> . . . The significance of this report lies primarily in the fact that it is a co-operative effort on a very broad scale to project into the field of social thought the scientific mood and the scientific method as correctives to undiscriminating emotional approach and to secure factual basis in seeking for constructive remedies of great social problems. The second significance of the undertaking is that, so far as I can learn, it is the first attempt ever made to study simultaneously all of the fundamental social facts which underlie all our social problems. Much ineffective thinking and many impracticable proposals of remedy have in the past been due to unfamiliarity with facts in fields related to that in which a given problem lies. The effort here has been to relate all the facts and present them under a common standard of measurement.

The 1930 White House Conference on Child Health and Protection

President Hoover, in a public announcement on July 2, 1929, said that he had "decided to call a White House conference on the health and protection of children." He added that the conference would be composed of representatives of "the great voluntary associations together with the federal, state and municipal authorities interested in these questions."

The purpose of the conference, he stated, "will be to determine facts as to our present progress and future needs." The subjects were to embrace "problems of dependent children; regular medical examination; school or public clinics for children; hospitalization; adequate milk supplies; community nurses; maternity instruction and nurses; teaching of health in schools." Also included were facilities for playgrounds and recreation, voluntary organization of children, child labor "and scores of allied subjects."

He added that the sum of a half-million dollars to cover the estimated cost of the conference and the follow-up work required to carry out its conclusions had been provided by private sources.

On November 19, 1930, President Hoover delivered one of the most notable addresses of his career to an audience that packed Constitution Hall to its rear aisles. He was tired and haggard that night. I remember thinking then how much better he would have spoken had he dismissed the wrangling politicians who were badgering him about patronage until nearly seven o'clock, and gone to the White House to rest for an hour before dinner so that he might come refreshed and vigorous to speak to this great audience and to the ten million or more radio listeners.

The pertinent and inspiring paragraphs and the Children's Charter which he sponsored appear in Appendix XII.

CHAPTER FIVE

On the Subject of Hoover Commissions

A lifetime practice that Hoover, the scientist and engineer, carried into the White House was to secure all of the facts concerning any problem and then, with the facts in hand, assay them and plan his course of action.

This practice deserves comment here because it became the source of many jibes during the depression. A reason for this, perhaps, is that since great masses of people feel rather than reason, it was possible to arouse their prejudice by sneering at anyone who charted his course by information and reason.

In Volume II, page 158, of *The State Papers and Other Collected Writings of Herbert Hoover* (William Starr Myers, Doubleday Doran), there appears the following item (no date, evidently early in the month of April, 1932).

COMMISSIONS AND COMMITTEES

In a business so vast and complex as that of the Federal Government a large part of the research work necessarily is carried out by special commissions and committees, delegated to investigate a given subject and to report to the President or to Congress. They also act for the coordination of Government activities, recommended policies, represent the Government abroad or at national functions and exercise semi-judicial or semi-legislative powers delegated by the Congress.

A great majority of these commissions are created, not by the President, but by the Congress upon its own motion. All of the commissions created by the President are for temporary non-administrative purposes as are also a large number of those created by the Congress.

The number of commissions set up under recent administrations are:

	By Congress	By President	Total
President Roosevelt			107
President Taft			63
President Wilson	75	75	150
President Harding			44
President Coolidge	74	44	118
President Hoover	22	20	42

A full list of the commissions and committees created under previous administrations was published as a Senate Document at the request of Senator Watson.

Of the committees or commissions created by President Hoover himself none has entailed appropriations by Congress; all were temporary and all but three or four have completed their useful tasks.

Speaking on this subject at Johns Hopkins University in 1920, Mr. Hoover stated that he sometimes felt that public questions could be divided into two classes.

In the first class he included those problems in which "sufficient facts, figures and concrete experience can be amassed to give certain indication of the course of constructive action."

The second class of public problems, he held, were those which arise out of "sheer complexes of political, economic and social currents, in which solution at best is more largely pure judgment guided by adherence to national ideals."

The solution of these, he believed, depended upon a common judgment, the development of a common mind "flowing out of the common sense of the people." This was the proper approach to their solution, he believed, because the greatness of America "has not grown out of a police court mind."

Some years later President Hoover, in an address, stated that one of the anxieties of his audience undoubtedly concerned his appointment of commissions and committees, and then added: "You have been misled into the impression that I shall soon appoint one every day. That is wrong—I shall probably need to appoint two a day."

He pointed out to his audience that his conception of government firmly convinced him that we have arrived at a time in our history, due to "the increasing complexity of our civilization and the delicacy of adjustments, when we must make doubly certain that we discover the truth."

Because of this, he insisted, it is necessary for us to make the fullest possible use "of the best brains and the best judgment and the best leadership in the country" before we make final decision regarding policies which affect the welfare of the whole people. "And I propose to do it."

He went on to say that in his judgment "The most dangerous animal in the United States is the man with an emotion and a desire to pass a new law. He is prolific with drama and the headlines. He is not the road to the fundamental advance of liberty and the progress of the American people at this time in our history."

The most effective antidote to this dangerous animal, he said, was that of placing him upon "a committee of a dozen people whose appetite is for facts." He believed, he said, that the "greatest catastrophe that could come to our country is that administration policies or legislation or voluntary movements shall be encouraged or enacted upon the basis of the emotions, not upon facts and reason."

The President of the United States, he added, is confronted with a thousand problems, which in a measure do not fall within the scope of governmental agencies, concerning which "truth must be searched from a multitude of facts; where individual and regional experience must be had; where new ideas must be recruited from the kaleidoscope of a great shifting mass of humanity; where judgment must be distilled from many minds; where common agreement must be secured from conflicting forces; where assurances must be given the people of the correctness of these conclusions; where their exposition must be secured."

The subjects, he said, covered the whole range of human thought concerning which he did not claim for himself "the combined knowledge or judgment of the technologists, the philosophers, the scientists, the social thinkers, the economists, and the thousand callings of our people."

The commission or committee method of securing and assaying the facts and of helping to gain public acceptance of their conclusions he believed to be "a vital means of government by the people and for the people, now that the people have ceased to live the simple life."

Holding such views, he sought to bring to the inexact social, political and economic sciences some of the qualities and strengths of the exact physical sciences. Can it be that he was a hundred years ahead of his time?

Can it be in the present stage of the people's political development—democracy and political parties as we know them are both less than three centuries old, and only a brief period in man's long existence—our political leaders to be greatly successful must possess and nicely balance the use of political "umph" and the use of full information and reason?

CHAPTER SIX

Reforms in the Regulation of Business

At the time Mr. Hoover became President the federal, state or local governments had, for decades, been extending their regulation of business activities. The conduct of banks, railroads, communications, electric power companies and other similar types of business were all covered and the anti-trust acts provided regulation for other types of business.

President Hoover's knowledge of the government led him to believe that some of the existing regulations contained weak spots. These weak spots and the tendency of the times to yield to the socialistic effort to put the government into business instead of regulating it, prompted him to seek reform of (a) the anti-trust laws; (b) regulation of electric power, railways, banking and securities sales and stock exchanges.

The reforms of the anti-trust laws sought by the Hoover administration were designed to conserve our natural resources both in the areas of "preventing wasteful practices; in conditions of destructive competition which may impoverish the producer and wage earner."

It sought also solution of the problem "inherent in our anti-trust laws" that derived from their "blanket exemption of trade unions." Certain of these exemptions were justifiable, but no exemptions should be permitted the unions to "enter into conspiracies to limit individual effort, to prevent use of labor saving devices and to act in collusion with employees for these evil ends, or to use their funds for political purposes." One reason cited for the administration's stand on the latter point was that "the building and electrical trades were increasing the cost of homes by 25 to 35 per cent with no benefit to themselves in wage rates or hours."

Many infractions of these laws were stopped by criminal prosecution.

Little headway was made in reforming the anti-trust laws since as the depression deepened competition increased and so ended for the time being most of the violations.

In his first message to the Congress on December 3, 1929, the President recommended the creation of a real Federal Power Commission with specific authority for the general regulation of interstate power but interlocking with the regulating commissions of the several states. This latter point was stressed because approximately 90 per cent of the electric utility industry's generation and distribution of power was intrastate in character "and most states have developed their own regulatory systems . . . to encroach upon their authorities and responsibilities would be an encroachment upon the rights of the states."

A strange and conflicting combination of forces and reason combined to defeat his program. They give particular emphasis to the pre-woman suffrage political aphorism that politics makes strange bedfellows. In this instance the power interests and the radical members of Congress joined in a holy crusade to defeat President Hoover's recommendations by preparing milk and water legislation. They worked together hand in glove although the ends each sought were totally different. The power interests wanted no regulation. Senators Norris, Borah and their followers wanted legislation that would force the government into the power business.

In his second annual message to the Congress President Hoover again recommended legislation for the "effective regulation of interstate electrical power" which "should preserve the independence and responsibility of the states." But the power-radical and Democratic opposition was too great to overcome.

When the Congress passed the Norris bill which provided for the expansion of the Muscle Shoals plant to sell power to the public and to go into the business of making fertilizers, the President vetoed it on March 3, 1931 with the statement that he was "firmly opposed to the government entering into any business the major purpose of which is competition with our citizens."

The tragic phase of the refusal of the radical and Democratic members of Congress to adopt the regulations the President recommended is that had they done so in 1930 they could have prevented enormous losses to the investing public. The Insull "Empire" of holding companies, for example, was largely built after Congress turned down the President's recommendations.

Railway Reorganization

In an effort to improve the railroad situation the Hoover Administration initiated moves to make a reality of the Transportation Act of 1922. This act provided for the consolidation of the one hundred separate railway companies into larger systems for the purposes of improving their financial stability and decreasing their operation cost.

The weakness of the 1922 act was that it carried no mandatory powers. Since the Interstate Commerce Commission had been unable to make progress and since also the government itself was of two minds on the question, nothing had been done previous to the advent of the Hoover administration.

The President called a conference of the presidents of the railroads in the so-called "Trunk Line Territory," that is roughly the area bounded on the south by the Mason and Dixon line and on the west by the Mississippi River and requested them to work out the details for a voluntary consolidation. This they did by December 31, 1930. The radical bloc in Congress, led by Senator Couzens of Michigan and supported by the Democrats defeated the proposal. Their evident purpose was to keep the railway industry demoralized in the hope that eventually the government would have to take them over.

Socialism was in the air then, as it is today.

Reform of Bankruptcy Laws

The force of the continuing depression had so highlighted many weaknesses in the nation's bankruptcy laws as to make reform of them urgent, not so much because of fraud and crime as because of the important social and economic implications of the existing laws.

The Constitution held bankruptcy to be of such national importance in the social and economic order as to make its supervision a federal government function.

The operation of the bankruptcy laws existing during the depression provided little opportunity to business men in financial trouble to keep their concerns operating. And they created bitter problems for farmers and home owners as well.

President Hoover sought, by his proposed reform of the existing laws, to: (a) eliminate fraud in bankruptcy practice; (b) provide for conciliation and adjustment of debt with the aid of the courts; (c) protect those in financial trouble during the negotiation period; (d) create a system of conciliators under the courts for farmers, home owners and small debtors; (e) provide against speculators buying up debts in order to seize property; (f) provide for a two-thirds rule to bind security holders in corporations under safeguard of the courts. The purpose of this latter was to safeguard against the current hold-ups by minorities and a forced sale of properties which all too frequently were purchased by speculators.

In a message to Congress in December, 1931, the President urged it to make provision for these reforms. Two months later he sent Congress an exhaustive report which detailed the need for early action. In this report he stated that the number of bankruptcy cases had increased from 23,000 in the fiscal year of 1921 to 53,000 in 1928 and to 65,000 in 1931. The liabilities involved had increased from $171,000,000 in 1921 to $830,000,000 in 1928 and to $1,008,000,000 in 1931. He stated that a sound bankruptcy system should work first to relieve honest but unfortunate debtors, second to effect a prompt and economical liquidation and distribution of insolvent estates and third to discourage fraud and needless waste of assets by withholding relief from debtors in proper cases.

Despite the indisputable evidence that the need for the reforms the President urged was both urgent and great, the Democratic leaders, whose fixed idea was to defeat Hoover in 1932, bottled up his recommendations in committees during the winter session of 1931–1932.

The President again returned to the subject in a special message to the Congress on January 11, 1933, in which he stated that he had addressed the Congress on February 29, 1932 on "the urgent necessity for revision of the bankruptcy laws." He pointed out that the process of forced liquidation through foreclosure and bankruptcy sale of individual and corporate debtors who through no fault of their own were unable in the present emergency to provide for the payment of their debts in ordinary course as they mature—"is utterly destructive of the interests of the debtor and creditor alike."

He added that if the process were allowed to take its usual course "misery will be suffered by thousands without substantial gain to their creditors. . . ."

The House finally passed a bill but the Senate held it up. On February 20, 1933 the President appealed to the Senate for quick action. It acted, but before doing so, hamstrung the bill. (Early in the Roosevelt administration Congress passed the kind of legislation Mr. Hoover had asked for.)

Had the Democratic majority in Congress passed the bill with the reforms President Hoover requested in December, 1931, it would have kept many thousands of concerns out of bankruptcy, eliminated enormous waste and fraud and prevented the destruction of public confidence and it would have made readjustments possible for hundreds of thousands of small-business men, farmers and home owners.

His proposal was just and fair. The obstructing Democratic leaders were the culprits but the public held Hoover responsible for this tragic inaction.

Development of Natural Resources

Having been born in the Middlewest and reared in the Far West, and having worked throughout the area as a mining engineer, President Hoover was familiar with its natural resources, needs and potentialities.

As President he advocated several changes in the federal government's policies regarding conservation of overgrazed ranges, the expansion of the Reclamation Service to include the construction of great multiple-storage dams which would serve as flood protection, provide water for irrigation purposes to people on both public and private land, improve navigation and to produce hydro-electric power as a by-product.

In this connection he recommended as immediate objectives the Grand Coulee Dam on the Columbia River, the Shasta, Friant and Pine Creek dams in the central California valley, the Cove Creek Dam in Tennessee and the exploration of possible dams in the Missouri River headwaters.

He applied to these undertakings the formula he had so successfully worked out for what Congress has renamed the Hoover Dam (an executive order issued by Secretary of Interior Harold L. Ickes of the Roosevelt administration had, for reasons easily surmised, arbitrarily changed the original name of Hoover Dam to that of *Boulder* Dam).

While Secretary of Commerce, Mr. Hoover, by long and able negotiation, had worked out an agreement between seven states for the construction and the operation of the projected dam, under which the states should administer the irrigation projects in their territories and take all revenues except those from sale of power. By this method it would be possible to provide good administration by state and local governments and equally important, keep the federal government out of business except for water storage and the sale of electric power to existing power distribution systems.

It was not, however, until June 25, 1929, that a sufficient number of states had ratified the interstate compact, thereby making it operative. On that date the President issued a proclamation which made it effective. Thus, the first of the nation's great dams came into being—to assist rather than to destroy private enterprise. The Hoover Dam, under federal legislature, and financed by the federal government, as worked out by Mr. Hoover, was a self-liquidating project. The electric power it generated was sold to public utilities and thereby did not compete with them.

Although it was more completely Mr. Hoover's handiwork than that of any other man, the Roosevelt administration failed to invite him to be present at the dedication ceremonies even "as a bystander," as he wistfully expressed it.

President Hoover sought also to integrate the development of certain river drainage areas as a whole for flood control, navigation and other purposes. Along with this he sought to develop our inland waterway systems.

To initiate this broad program the President sent a lengthy message to the Conference of Western Governors which was held on August 27, 1929 in which he presented his ideas in detail.

The Western governors approved the President's suggestion that a joint range commission be created, and on October 18, 1929, the President appointed as members of it a distinguished group of citizens with James R. Garfield, Secretary of Interior under President Theodore Roosevelt, as chairman.

The commission's areas of activity included the study of the entire question of public domain as to overgrazing, water supply and conservation of oil, coal and related problems.

The commission completed its study and made its recommendations, which were of a far-reaching and invaluable nature, on September 29, 1931, which the President embodied in recommendations to the Congress in early 1932.

The necessary legislation to carry out the commission's recommendations was introduced and favorably reported by the House Committee but depression legislation sidetracked its passage.

Oil Conservation

Four days after he became President, Mr. Hoover publicly stated that:

"There will be no leases or disposal of government oil lands, no matter what emergency they may lie in, or government controls except those which may be mandatory by Congress. In other words there will be complete conservation of government oil in this administration."

When the over-drilling of new pools in different states produced a flood of oil, the President sought, through Federal government leadership, to induce the major oil producing companies and the executives of the states in which most of the new oil was being produced (six in all) to take remedial action. In opening the conference Secretary of Interior Wilbur stated that the "position of the federal government is not to interfere with the rights and duties of the states, but to lend such aid as it can. . . . This administration has no desire to concentrate the forces of government in Washington. It has every desire to co-operate with the states."

The conference produced state conservation legislation and also produced conservation agreements among owners of the larger pools where the federal government also had holdings. The state legislatures of Oklahoma, Kansas, New Mexico and Texas adopted conservation measures, and California's legislature also adopted similar legislation which was later defeated by referendum. Conservation was another Hoover objective. During its four years in office the administration extended the area of national forests by two million acres and national parks and monuments by more than three million acres. The latter represented a 40 per cent growth in four years.

Public Buildings and Highways

During the thirty years from 1900 to 1930 the federal government had expended not more than $250,000,000 for public buildings. By November 4, 1931 the President was able to announce the government had completed, had under construction, or let contracts for 817 projects, as employment aids, the total cost of which would be $319,506,269.

The foregoing did not include the San Francisco Bay bridge, initiated by Hoover while Secretary of Commerce. The army engineers disapproved of the suggestion at that time. As President, he again broached the question, secured approval, and eventually the RFC advanced $75,000,000 for its construction.

As an employment aid, the Hoover administration increased annual federal aid to states for highway construction from $105,000,000 to $260,000,000 thereby providing work for an additional 170,000 men. Highway construction jumped from 7900 miles in 1929 to 16,000 miles in 1932.

Aviation, Radio and Merchant Marine

Since the administration's aviation policies and actions are discussed in later chapters the subject does not need to be treated here other than to state that the real development of aviation industry in America began with the Hoover presidency.

The radio industry, like that of aviation, was still in its swaddling clothes in 1929. The Radio Commission had a temporary status and was handicapped by its regional concept. In his first message to Congress on December 3, 1929, the President recommended the reorganization of the commission and the enaction of legislation to prevent the "danger that the system will degenerate from a national system into five regional agencies with varying practices, varying policies, competitive tendencies and a failure to attain its utmost capacity for service to the whole people of the nation."

The President directed government officials to find a solution of the problem which on the one hand would avoid government ownership and operation of broadcasting facilities and on the other hand permit the creation of a private monopoly. When the concerned officials reported, after several months of effort, that they could find no solution, the President directed the attorney-general to start legal action to bring about the dissolution of the then so-called "radio manufacturing trust." This legal action checked the growth of private monopoly.

Although he, as President, had no control over the operations of the Shipping Board, which was an instrument of the Congress, President Hoover was able by his control of the awarding of mail-carrying contracts to force an increase in the number of tons of merchant ships built in 1929 from 128,000 to 213,000 in 1932. The Board's new shipping construction tonnage fell to 66,000 in 1934 and to 63,000 in 1935.

CHAPTER SEVEN

The Hawley-Smoot Tariff Bill

In the issue of August 10, 1949 the Sheboygan, Wisconsin, *Press* editorially stated that in his first campaign for the Presidency Mr. Hoover "promised tariff revision to benefit the farmers. . . . Instead of limiting tariff revision to farm products, he signed a bill which *revised tariff schedules to new highs.* (Italics author's.) He signed the bill against the advice of economists . . . who foresaw the disaster that would follow . . ."

On August 11, 1949, the Fayetteville, North Carolina, *Observer* editorially said that it was Mr. Hoover's "misfortune to have gone along with the super-high tariff wing of the Republican party."

Governor Roosevelt, while a candidate for the Presidency in 1932 called the Hawley-Smoot bill a "wicked and exorbitant tariff" and charged that the United States "was sealed by the highest tariff wall in the history of the world."

Inaccurate memories and irresponsible campaign charges such as these make interesting, even astonishing, collectors' items in that they indicate why the general public is so little to blame for some of its fantastic misconceptions concerning governmental operations.

Evidence in the files of the United States Tariff Commission should be far more dependable than either faulty memories or loose campaign charges. This evidence conclusively establishes the fact that the duties collected under the *tariffs established in the Hawley-Smoot tariff law* when set against those collected in a comparable year under the old law *were only 2.2 per cent higher and that 93.73 per cent of this 2.2 per cent increase came from tariffs collected upon products of agricultural origin,* and the balance from commodities of non-agricultural origin. A statistical estimate of the new schedules by the Tariff Commission revealed that the average duties collectible under it would be about 16 per cent as compared with 13.83 per cent under the prevailing law.

By comparison the average level of tariff under the Dingley law was 25.8 per cent; the Payne-Aldrich 19.3 per cent and the Fordney-McCumber 13.83 per cent. Further comparison of the Hawley-Smoot tariff level with that of the Roosevelt administration, against which no popular outcry ever has been raised, shows that the latter in effect increased tariffs by 59 per cent through devaluation of the dollar. The Roosevelt administration also made great increases in tariff duties by removing from the free list such great imports as crude oil, gasoline, lubricating oils, coal, coke, lumber, copper and whale oil. The percentage of the free list—duty-free goods coming in—of the Hawley-Smoot Bill was 66.5 per cent whereas in 1936 a Democratic Congress had lowered it to 57 per cent.

The threatening bark of the opposition was far more frightening than the actual gentle bite of the rates of the Hawley-Smoot tariff law; written because President Hoover had been elected on a platform that promised a tariff revision designed to give relief to the farmers of the nation.

It has been well said that our tariff question is "complicated by deep-seated tradition, emotion and intellectual dishonesty in both political parties."

In the case of the Hawley-Smoot tariff legislation the progressive Republicans and a large majority of the Democrats each wanted some tariffs on industrial goods. It was inevitable that there would be some increase (the sole question was how much) in industrial tariffs since the regular Republicans also wanted them.

The record proves that the slight increases in tariff duties under the Hawley-Smoot bill had no part whatever, as has been charged, in serving as the beginning of a world movement to increase tariffs. As a matter of fact forty—count them—other governments had already imposed higher tariffs before it became law. An earlier chapter has told of the concern of League of Nations' officials in 1927 over the fast-growing number of governments which even then had imposed high tariff duties.

A desire for self-sufficiency in a period of international fear had caused these governments to impose higher tariff duties as an aid to national defense. American industry was in a fairly sound position but this was not true of American agriculture.

The farmers of the country, and especially those of the South and of that vast area which lies between the Allegheny and the Rocky mountains, had been in acute financial distress ever since the early 1920's.

Another factor in the agricultural situation included market gluts of farm products when the government discontinued its wartime purchasing levels. Another was the drop in European purchases from inability to pay for the farmers' products. Still another came from new competitive foreign areas which had come into being during the war. At the same time increases in industrial wages were being translated into higher prices for agricultural machinery and everything else the farmer had to buy at a time when farms were being mechanized rapidly while the reduced markets for agricultural products paid the farmer a lower price for his products.

Carrying out his party's platform promise, President Hoover issued a call on March 7, 1929 for a special session of the Congress and set the convening date as April 15. He specified that the special session's purpose would be to revise the agricultural section of the existing tariff law which would "further agricultural relief and legislation for limited changes in the tariff [which] cannot in justice to our farmers . . . be postponed."

The President summarized the situation in his message which carried the call for the special session by saying:

> An effective tariff upon agricultural products that will compensate the farmer's higher costs and higher standards of living has a dual purpose. Such a tariff not only protects the farmer in our domestic market, but it also stimulates him to diversify his crops and to grow products that he could not otherwise produce, and thus lessens his dependence upon exports to foreign markets. . . . It seems but natural, therefore, that the American farmer, having been greatly handicapped in his foreign market by such compe-

tition from the younger expanding countries, should ask that foreign access to our domestic markets should be regulated by taking into account the differences in our costs of production.

President Hoover sought first to strengthen our agricultural economy with the new tariff law. Collaterally with that purpose he sought also to take tariff schedule-making out of the field of politics and place it in the field of economics where he believed it belonged. It was the duty of Congress to determine whether the policy should be for high tariff rates or low ones, but the schedules of rates should be made by a permanent non-partisan commission composed of economists who would fix the rates after they had gathered and assayed the economic facts.

His basic tariff policy was that of establishing and maintaining duties which would express the "difference in the cost of production at home and abroad" by taking from foreign producers the advantages they then were enjoying by "paying lower wages to labor." He sought by this to protect the American workman as well as the producer. This policy was first enunciated in the 1912 Bull Moose platform. Mr. Hoover's tariff policy not only provided for the maintenance of competition after protecting American standards of living but provided also that the tariff should be based on national policy instead of the log-rolling "local issue."

In the contest between the President and the Congress, the President firmly held to two points:

1. That "no provision for flexible tariff, no tariff bill."
2. That unduly high rates, if enacted, would be revised downward by the concurrently created Tariff Commission.

The contest between the President and the Congress continued throughout the long, disturbing, anxious months of 1929 until the legislation was enacted June 15, 1930 during the period when the economic world was collapsing. President Hoover unyieldingly insisted that "the revision must be limited" and that the bill carry the provision for the creation of a Tariff Commission with effective powers to "lower or raise the tariffs on a proper basis," with all of its proceedings "to be open to public hearings and in judicial form."

Through this new commission he sought to do away with "the orgy of greed and privilege which surrounded constant change by Congress."

Opposition to President Hoover's moderate position by old-guard Republican senators was led by Grundy of Pennsylvania, who voted against the bill, proof that Hoover did not "go along with the super-high tariff wing of the Republican party."

Further evidence that President Hoover did not "go along with the super-high tariff wing" of his party is furnished by the following incident which concerns the President and Senator James Watson of Indiana, then Republican leader in the Senate, and as such the man responsible for gaining support for the President's policies in the Senate.

I visited Mr. Hoover just after the incident happened. Only the day before, he related, Senator Watson had telephoned and asked for a private conference. His reason for wanting it, he said, was to discuss the status of the Hawley-Smoot tariff bill. Senator Watson had added that he thought some compromises could be worked out but that it would be better for the Republican party if no word leaked out to the public that he had discussed these with the President. The best way to prevent a news leak, he suggested, would be for him to enter through the east gate and see the President in the White House residence since in this way he could avoid being seen and questioned by the newspaper correspondents who were stationed in the White House executive offices.

To all of this, the President agreed, not because he considered the Senator's reasons sound, but because Watson wanted it done that way.

Up to this point, he said, he had no complaint. But, he added, he had nothing but contempt for what Watson next did. Five minutes after Watson had hung up, a newspaper correspondent friend of the President's who was stationed on the hill telephoned to inquire why Mr. Hoover had invited Watson to a secret, private White House residence conference.

The President asked his newspaper friend, "How do you know anything about this?" and he reported the correspondent as saying:

Senator Watson confidentially sent word to all correspondents that the President had just asked him to the White House for a private, secret conference but he did not know what it was all about. His guess, Watson told the newspaper men, was that the President must be about ready to go along with the Senate's tariff bill program.

The President finished telling about Senator Watson's attempted double-cross with a bear-like growl, "How are you going to deal with a man like that, huh?"

Senator Watson, a master of political intrigue, obviously sought to put the President at a disadvantage on the tariff fight by making him appear ready to compromise. Once he had worked the President over and softened him up Watson then would be ready to spring his compromise proposals on the public.

How T.R. Handled a Similar Situation

A great political strategist, who could play politics as a game and who also was a major political statesman, Theodore Roosevelt, once was the intended victim in an identical manner of "Uncle Joe" Cannon, the then-Speaker and old-guard Republican leader of the House. T.R., however, immediately sent for the newspaper men when he was told about Cannon's misleading announcement, and said to them in substance:

> The Speaker of the House of Representatives telephoned and asked me for a secret, private conference in the residence. He requested the privilege of entering by the east gate. I granted his request. He did not state what he wanted to discuss with me. I suggest that you gentlemen gather at the east entrance in twenty minutes and ask the Speaker why he had requested a secret, private conference with me and then ask him what he wanted to discuss with me.

The correspondents gleefully followed T.R.'s suggestion much to Speaker Cannon's discomfiture. This red pepper experience forever cured Speaker Cannon of sucking eggs in T.R.'s henhouse. Had President Hoover given Senator Watson similar treatment he also might have been cured of a bad habit. But only a man long schooled in politics who enjoyed it as a game could meet the situation as T.R. did.

The only three bad features about the Hawley-Smoot tariff legislation were: (a) Its passage gave the President's political opponents an excuse to make grave, though baseless charges. (b) Its demands upon his time and energies prevented his using his total efforts to devise ways to help soften the blows the collapsing world economy was striking at our domestic economy. (c) While the long and difficult negotiations produced a Tariff Commission with revision powers, the President's unyielding insistence for a Tariff Commission with teeth served to sharpen the conflict between him and many Republican senators. In the end he signed the Hawley-Smoot bill and thereby made it law. He won his battle but his victory greatly weakened his forces for the coming political war in the 1930 congressional elections.

CHAPTER EIGHT

The Wickersham Commission and the Bonus Army

One of President Hoover's major problems outside the depression field which had wide voting-public repercussions concerned the enforcement provisions of the Eighteenth Amendment or dry law.

It is a matter of record that when the prohibition law was enacted Mr. Hoover did not believe it was a practical reform. But as President he had but one duty—to enforce it. Personally he would have been happy to believe that mankind had advanced sufficiently to give up all use of alcoholic drinks but he had no illusions about the inability of the federal government to suppress the drinking habit.

Before the adoption of the dry law he had not been a teetotaler although he had long believed that the human race would be better off without alcoholic beverages. While the law was on the statute books he refrained from drinking, just as did many other good citizens who believed that disregard for some law served to destroy respect for all law. He held that it was a citizen's duty to discourage its violation. In addition, he believed, as he stated publicly that "our country has deliberately undertaken a great social and economic experiment, *noble in motive and far reaching in purpose*. It must be worked out constructively."

The prohibition amendment's fatal defect was that its enforcement was made "concurrent" between the federal government and the states. The assumption of its sponsors apparently was that the public powers of municipalities, counties and states would be responsible for its enforcement and the federal government would be charged with controlling interstate commerce, imports and conspiracies which crossed state borders.

Evidence abounded that local and state police authorities did not carry out their enforcement duties. The "grave abuses" which grew from their failure troubled Mr. Hoover, who was outspoken against the return "to the old saloon with its political and social corruption" as well as against enduring "the bootlegger and the speakeasy with their abuses and crime. Either is intolerable."

In a number of his 1928 campaign speeches Mr. Hoover emphasized some of the dry law's inherently complex enforcement problems. He stated that if elected he would appoint a Commission to (a) study the entire question of enforcement of this and other laws and to secure all pertinent facts concerning it; and (b) to recommend improvements of the nation's law enforcement machinery.

Governor Al Smith, the 1928 Democratic nominee for President, who from long years of political experience had developed his political faculties to such an extent that he seemed able to absorb pertinent facts as a sponge does water and had a sixth sense which enabled him to formulate policies by ear, required no commission to help determine his stand on the prohibition question. He was *agin* it. He wanted it repealed. Raised as he was in the tough give-and-take school of precinct and ward politics, he had learned how to present and debate a question in the manner that would catch the crowd's fancy, and his listeners' votes. With this training and equipment Governor Smith went up and down the land preaching repeal, pointing up the arguments against the dry law and firing the indignation of that segment of the public which opposed it.

On the other hand, Mr. Hoover's lifetime need for data with which to formulate a public policy prompted him to seek all of the facts to help him determine the stand he as President should take on the Eighteenth Amendment.

Holding such views, President Hoover appointed a Commission in May, 1929, with former attorney-general George W. Wickersham as chairman.

At its initial meeting in the White House on May 28, 1929, the President pointed out that:

> The American people are deeply concerned over the alarming disobedience of law, the abuses in law enforcement and the growth

of organized crime, which has spread in every field of evil-doing and in every part of our country. A nation does not fail from its growth of wealth or power. But no nation can for long survive the failure of its citizens to respect and obey the laws which they themselves make. Nor can it survive a decadence of the moral and spiritual concepts that are the basis of respect for law, nor from neglect to organize itself to defeat crime and the corruption that flows from it. Nor is this a problem confined to the enforcement and obedience of one law or the laws of the federal or state governments separately. The problem is partly the attitude toward all law.

It is my hope that the commission shall secure an accurate determination of fact and cause, following them with constructive, courageous conclusions which will bring public understanding and command public support of its solutions. . . . I do pray for the success of your endeavors, for by such success you will have performed one of the greatest services to our generation.

During the period the Wickersham Commission was struggling with the question, former Secretary of State Elihu Root, one of the country's foremost authorities on constitutional law, was a White House guest. The President recited the varied and serious problems connected with prohibition enforcement and asked Mr. Root's advice as to whether or not he should recommend the repeal of the Eighteenth Amendment.

The following are not Mr. Root's exact words but it accurately reports the substance and nature of his reply:

The Amendment should never have been adopted. But it was. You are under the most sacred of oaths to uphold the Constitution. While you can veto any other legislation you do not have that power in relation to amendments to the Constitution. That distinction was made for the definite purpose of holding alterations of the Constitution away from the President who is solely an enforcement officer in its relation. Furthermore, this law expresses itself in criminal proceedings. If you were to recommend repeal you would be nullifying the Constitution because from that day no judge and no jury would convict. You must not do that. Your sacred duty is to enforce the law with every power you can exert. The futility will become more evident daily and the people finally will demand its repeal.

The Wickersham Commission made an exhaustive study of the subjects assigned to it. Its initial report indirectly damned the law and at the same time recommended against repeal action by the President. Subsequent reports, however, revealed that considerable division existed within the Commission regarding methods of handling the problems of enforcement. This division reflected the country's sharply divided opinion about the amendment itself.

The Commission's report did help greatly to clarify public and legislative thinking on court procedures and upon police practices as well as upon preventive measures in respect to crime and its suppression.

In his August, 1932, acceptance speech, President Hoover publicly stated his official position on the situation which had been created by the adoption of the Eighteenth Amendment in the following paragraphs:

> We must recognize the difficulties which have developed in making the Eighteenth Amendment effective and that grave abuses have grown up. . . . An increasing number of states and municipalities are proving themselves unwilling to engage in such enforcement. Owing to this . . . in large sections an increasing illegal traffic in liquor. But worse than this there has been in those areas a spread of disrespect not only for this law but for all laws, grave dangers of practical nullification of the Constitution, a degeneration in municipal government, and an increase in subsidized crime and violence. I cannot consent to the continuation of this regime. . . .
>
> It is my conviction that the nature of this change, and one upon which all reasonable people can find common ground, is that each state shall be given the right to deal with the problem as it may determine, but subject to absolute guarantees in the Constitution to protect each state from interference and invasion by its neighbors, and that in no part of the United States shall there be a return to the saloon system with its inevitable political and social corruption and its organized interference with other states.
>
> American statesmanship is capable of working out such a solution and making it effective.

Now, seventeen years later, with emotion under control and indignation fires nearly out, the question may properly be asked:

Had you been in Mr. Hoover's position what would you have done?

The Devil Tries a Trick—the Bonus Army

This time the devil pulled a gadget out of his bag of tricks and with the help of some of his Communist first cousins was able to add another serious problem to the President's already overloaded pack. Together, the devil and the Communists used President Hoover's veto of the bonus bill to rouse the veterans' indignation. They used the argument that the President had been unfair to the veterans—despite the record which showed that he had initiated a series of efforts which extended direct help to several hundred thousand needy veterans. When he became President there were 367,000 disabled or destitute veterans or dependents who were on the Federal government's benefit rolls and 853,000 at the end of his term.

The Hoover administration in addition had built twenty-five new hospitals for sick and disabled veterans, with an increase in bed accommodations from 26,000 to 45,000 and had hospitals under construction which would accommodate 7,000 more.

Everything President Hoover had done to help wounded or needy veterans was ignored by a small group of their number who might be termed "professional money-hunters." These men, encouraged by Democratic members of Congress, demanded an immediate loan of 50 per cent on their "bonus certificates" or half of the $3,400,000,000 bonus which had been voted them in the early 1920's with the provision that their "bonus certificates" be paid at the end of twenty-five years. Meanwhile the Treasury was paying $112,000,000 annually into a fund for this purpose.

Congress passed the bill and the President vetoed it on February 26, 1931, on the grounds that it would make too great a drain on the Federal treasury. Congress passed the bill over the President's veto.

The following fall Senator Robinson and Speaker Garner, Democratic leaders in the Senate and the House proposed that the entire bonus be paid in cash. The American Legion, at its annual meeting in Detroit, Michigan, in response to the President's appeal, refused to endorse the legislation.

Professional veterans, with open encouragement and help from Democratic members of Congress continued to advance a variety of unsound and absurd veteran benefit proposals and thereby served to create a tense situation which in turn brought about the Communist-inspired and directed Bonus March on Washington.

How the Communists Engineered the Bonus March

Those veterans who joined the bonus march because they believed they had a just grievance, and the readers who may doubt the accuracy of the flat statement that it was Communist-inspired and directed, are referred to: (a) the FBI report which the government later made public, (b) Benjamin Gitlow's book, *The Whole of Their Lives,* published by Charles Scribner's Sons, New York, 1949. Mr. Gitlow was the head of the Communist party in the United States in 1932. (c) The articles of John T. Pace which were published in the New York *Journal American* and other newspapers in late August, 1949.

The bonus march was organized and promoted by the Communists and included a large number of ex-convicts and other disreputable characters. John T. Pace, then a Communist leader, but later a deputy sheriff of Centerville, Tennessee, has publicly told of his part in this Communist-inspired and directed attempt. He reached Washington, he stated, in June, 1932, as leader of a thousand veterans from the Middle West and although he had been named "by the Communist party as leader of the left-wing group I did not make a move without consulting Emmanuel Levine" who, he had been told by his Communist superiors, "was the boss."

Pace has stated that Levine, "a veteran Communist agitator, told me that Moscow regarded this bonus march as a real propaganda opportunity to bring about a revolt and hatred against President Hoover" and added, "Levine said to me the *'veterans have some fascist misleaders who don't want violence—your job is to keep them stirred up and our party must take over.'* " (Italics author's.)

Pace told how he, under Levine's orders, led "a delegation of several hundred Reds down Pennsylvania Avenue to seize an abandoned government building near the capitol," a seizure they had carefully planned. The illegality of their act, in Levine's words, would "provoke the cops and get some action." When Pace protested against violence he reports Levine as having said, "Comrade Pace, in every revolution some workers must die," and furthermore Moscow wanted violence because that would force Hoover "to call out the army and once the army steps in we'll have a full-scale revolution going."

Under Levine's orders, Communists were sent to Anacostia flats "where several thousand legitimate veterans . . . were camped. They did not want violence so Levine told me to provoke it. I sent Communists into their ranks with orders to throw bricks at cops and even at our own Red marchers to provoke trouble. . . . We succeeded in bringing several hundred legitimate veterans to our buildings. . . . The Communist program . . . ran like clockwork . . . so many were to be arrested each day . . . we were to defy police efforts to evict us from the buildings we had seized."

Shortly after the agitators and their duped veterans had forcibly and illegally seized and occupied the buildings in question for the purpose of creating an incident, the carefully planned-for incident occurred when the Washington, D. C., local police authorities ordered the veterans to quit the buildings. This they refused to do because their refusal would precipitate a riot. The riot occurred.

The police, in self-protection, shot and killed two men and wounded others. Several police were wounded. The Washington, D. C., police authorities, in an effort to prevent further bloodshed, now appealed in writing to the President to send federal troops to help preserve order since the police were greatly outnumbered. The President thereupon gave the Secretary of War specific orders to confine the army action to that of restoring order in the city, and to allow the men to return to their camps outside the city. The army exceeded the President's orders.

The federal troops *restored order without firing a shot or otherwise injuring a single individual.* Order was restored and the majority of the "bonus marchers" returned to their homes with funds provided for this purpose by Congress at the President's request. About two thousand bonus marchers refused to leave Washington. They had come for the purpose of trying to fan flames of hatred and their job was not finished. A government checkup was made of those who remained. It revealed that nearly nine hundred had never been members of our armed forces and further that nine hundred of the others who remained in Washington were ex-convicts!

Several members of these two groups admitted that they had engineered the "march" and inspired the marchers. They had thereby made dupes out of the genuine veterans and out of millions of Americans as well.

Currently (July 1949) Eleanor Roosevelt, in a magazine article referred to Mr. Hoover's having ordered out troops in the bonus incident and thereby raised a conflict with his pacific Quaker principles. When he did that, Mr. Hoover was first the President of the United States and second a Quaker. As President he was under oath to defend and uphold the Constitution. This included maintaining order. Mrs. Roosevelt's implied doubt about Mr. Hoover's principles serves the Communist agitator's purpose, namely, that of destroying the reputation of democratic leaders. If they are able to do this they will at the same time undermine the public's belief in the principles of liberty and free government.

The bonus Communist agitators and their millions of unwitting—or otherwise—American citizen allies fanned the flames of hatred against the President of the United States. By fomenting greater unrest and uncertainty in the public mind they helped materially to destroy public confidence in the eventual re-establishment of social stability and economic recovery and of Mr. Hoover's fitness for the presidency.

CHAPTER NINE

Banking Reform Proposals and Air Mail Contracts

The Hoover Administration's policies and programs in the two areas of banking reforms and air mail contracts require special consideration because of (a) the false political charges that as President Mr. Hoover coddled the banks; and (b) the baseless charges of "collusion, lawlessness and graft" in the Hoover administration's air mail policies and contracts.

Banking Reform Recommendations

In his first regular state-of-the-union message the President urged Congress to create a special joint commission which would include members of Congress and administration officials for the purpose of investigating the entire banking system of the nation and to make recommendations for constructive legislation.

The weakness of the nation's banking system lay in the fact that there were 24,000 independent banks in the country, 15,000 of which were state chartered banks which operated under the laws of the state in which they were located and inspected and regulated by state officials. One of these was The Bank of United States, chartered by and operated under the laws of the state of New York and solely under New York State inspection previous to its failure on December 12, 1930. The failure of this New York State bank which had 400,000 depositors with $180,000,000 in deposits at the time its doors were closed, jarred the structure of the nation's banking system and caused a fresh run on all the banks. Later investigation proved that the failure was caused by fraud and the gross negligence of New York State banking officials.

An indication of the weakness of the nation's banking system is furnished by the record, which shows that during the three "prosperous" years of 1926, 1927 and 1928, there were net failures of 199 national banks with deposits of $177,000,000 and 1387 state banks with deposits of $362,000,000.

What could be expected during a depression period of a banking system with that kind of a "prosperous" period record?

The Congress ignored the President's 1929 urgent request to create a joint committee to study the nation's banking system and recommend constructive legislation.

Faced with congressional inaction, President Hoover repeatedly, but without success, asked Congress for drastic bank reform legislation along the following lines:

1. To cause every commercial bank to join the Federal Reserve System.
2. To establish inspection of all commercial banks by the Federal Reserve System.
3. To secure gradual separation of promotion affiliates from all banks.
4. To prohibit extension of long-term credits by demand deposit banks.
5. To separate savings and long-term loan institutions from demand deposit institutions.
6. To establish state-wide branch banking by national banks under suitable regulations with provisions that no new branches be established where there were adequate facilities except by purchase of existing banks.

Legislation to accomplish these ends would have enabled the banks of the nation to do their part in helping the country through the great depression, and would have prevented the subsequent national bank moratorium.

Air Mail Contracts

One administration project had an important and far-reaching influence in developing and strengthening the nation's aviation industry. Its constructive air mail program enabled our country to maintain supremacy of the air in World War II.

The Hoover administration's aviation policy and program was formulated and developed following a conference between President, the Postmaster-General and the Secretaries of War, Navy and Commerce.

Out of their surveys and studies this group reached the conclusion that, for military protection purposes as well as for creating continuous transcontinental services east and west and north and south, the country needed four major east-west transcontinental lines and eight major north-south continental lines with certain secondary feeding lines.

Much of this I learned at the time from Postmaster-General Brown, who, as an old friend, had discussed his problems with me. The substance of what he told me, is about as follows:

> The government must get more for the money it now pays the air lines. As it now stands a lot of little operators are making good profits because there is no competition. Each carrier has an exclusive contract to carry the mail over his route. That's all he is interested in. And if we leave things the way they are these air carriers will be living off the government forever. I'm not blaming them. But I'd blame myself if I can't find a way to make the government subsidy we give them help us to develop the entire aviation industry. To my way of thinking that's the only way we can justify the air mail subsidy.
>
> If we can use the air mail contracts to bring about the creation of twelve or fifteen strong, well-financed competitive companies we could soon change aviation history in this country. It would improve the service and it would force the manufacture of better planes. When that is done more people will want to fly. All of these things will build up a stronger aviation industry. And we will need that if we ever get into another war.
>
> The Hoover administration's long-term objective is to make the United States secure in a military way. The civil branch of the government must help the military branch do this. This means the Post Office Department. The way we can best do that is to compel air mail contract carriers to fly planes that will also carry passengers. If we do that we will stimulate the aviation industry to improve the planes they are building. Not one of the air mail carriers today is carrying passengers. Why should they? There is only one carrier for

each route and each one is making a profit. The government is paying the bill. Unless we can stimulate competition they will always live off the government.

As we study the problem it will be my job to make them carry passengers. That's the surest way of getting better planes, lower rates, and of building a better aviation industry.

When I tell the carriers: no contracts unless you carry passengers they insist that I will force them to kill people. One air mail contract carrier official told me when I refused to yield on the point, "All right, Walter Brown, the blood will be on your head."

The next morning he came in and asked if I would fly the first trip on his line that carried passengers. I told him that I'd fly the first trip on every carrier, and I will.

We need scores of new landing fields and rows of beacon lights up and down the land and the development of the radio beam. Those are things I want to get out of the government's air mail subsidy. The "Watres Act" which I helped write will enable me to do some of these things, with the help of a few shot-gun weddings in the industry.

The Hoover administration consolidated air routes into a carefully planned national system of commercial airways and it brought about a greatly improved type of plane, thereby made flying popular. The new planes also were built to facilitate express service. Their speed, safety and reliability were greatly improved and the whole science of aerodynamics was advanced so swiftly that it may be said with assurance: the aviation industry in the United States dates from the Hoover administration.

The dollars-and-cents part of its program shows that for the fiscal year ending June 30, 1929, before its program went into effect, domestic commercial aviation companies flew mail 10,200,000 miles and were paid $14,600,000 for this service at a cost of $1.42 per mile. The air mail receipts reduced the government's subsidy to a net of $1.26 per mile.

In the fiscal year ending June 30, 1933, under the Hoover administration's let contracts, the aviation companies flew mail 35,900,000 miles and were paid $19,400,000 for this service, or about 54 cents per mile.

Air mail receipts brought the net cost down to about 26 cents per mile. The number of passengers carried in 1929 was 165,200 and in 1933, 550,000. The number of aviation company employes stood at 15,000 in 1929 and at 35,000 in 1933—all of whom were in some capacity highly trained war personnel material. It has been estimated that the government would have needed to spend five times the cost of the Hoover administration's aviation program to build up the same organization through the military department.

An additional public benefit which came directly out of this program was that it fostered the passenger and express service which should in time reduce the subsidies to the actual sum represented by air mail receipts.

CHAPTER TEN

New Lows in Political Vilification

A few months after Mr. Hoover became President, the Democratic National Committee created and staffed a press division in Washington with the late Charles Michelson in charge. John J. Raskob, Chairman of the Democratic National Committee, and other men of great wealth raised over one million dollars for Michelson's work.

Mr. Michelson had a brilliant newspaper record as chief of the New York *World*'s Washington bureau for a dozen years. He knew the ins-and-outs of Washington politics and he had many friends among the correspondents as well as government administrative officials and members of Congress of both parties. In addition he was a Democrat and an extreme anti-Hoover Democrat at that. Among his qualities were imagination, mischievousness and a touch of malevolence. Al Smith was his hero and he could not easily forget his disappointment over Smith's defeat.

The *Literary Digest* in the May 26, 1934 issue stated in an article that Michelson began to create news by linking a big Democratic name to every political story.

Actually what Mr. Michelson did was to project Tammany Hall's technique and morals to the national political scene. Belittlement by the use of cynical sneers, vilification by innuendo and false charges by indirection were his stock in trade. It encouraged him to look down, never up. Its sole purpose was to help win elections, never to inspire and encourage men to help create the good society.

Two major factors contributed directly to the success of Michelson's effort. The first of these was President Hoover's Quaker-produced sensitivity. Every individual who has ever come under the direct influence of Quaker ways of thinking, living and worshipping gradually develops a sixth sense which enables him to catch overtones that many non-Quakers miss. In their worship, for example, Quakers attune themselves and wait for the Spirit to speak to them. It follows, therefore, that they must develop or cultivate their extrasensory perceptions, if they are to catch the message the still, small voice whispers to them.

Coupled with that is the instinct or educated trait of Quakers to be fair, kind even to gentleness, and honest in their expressions about others. A good Quaker feels that he has committed a sinful act if he makes a cruel, unfair or untruthful statement about a fellow man; and it is a double sin if he says this wilfully for the purpose of wounding a fellow man's feelings.

I have never discussed this subject with Mr. Hoover, but I feel certain that the below-the-belt partisan attacks which Michelson directed must have greatly troubled him and by doing so interfered with his efforts and purpose to serve all of the people to the best of his ability.

Eighteen months after Mr. Michelson began to play his art of mixing mud-balls for Democratic big-wigs to throw, Frank Kent, distinguished political correspondent and columnist and a friend of Michelson's, in an article in *Scribner*'s magazine in September, 1930, stated that Michelson's goal

> was to "smear" Hoover and the Hoover administration. That is what he is there for and all he is there for. That is his job, and it would be hard to imagine a man with his heart more completely in it. It would have been a genuine pleasure for Mr. Michelson to "smear" the Hoover administration if he were not paid a cent. To get $25,000 a year for doing something you yearn to do anyhow, to have the tools . . . furnished free of charge, to have no real opposition or competition, to be able to hit without getting hit back, why, that is ideal. At least, so it seems to Mr. Michelson, who has had, this year, about the best time of his life. . . . It has been his pleasant task to minimize every Hoover asset and magnify all his liabilities. To sum up, the whole aim and idea of Mr. Michelson's employment is to put Mr. Hoover "in bad" with the American people. That is what he was hired for, and for the first year at least he certainly has earned his money. The Michelson effort has been to paint a picture

of Hoover as an inept, bewildered, weak, and unworthy man without sense of direction, backbone or power of decision. If he has an admirable quality it has not been mentioned among the millions of written words that have flowed from Mr. Michelson's fluent typewriter in the past 18 months. On the contrary, Mr. Michelson has discovered more faults, failings, and flaws in Mr. Hoover since March 4, 1929 than anyone ever suspected before, more in fact than seems possible for one man to have. These discoveries Mr. Michelson has not kept to himself. This is distinctly not what he is paid for. His employment is to get into the daily and weekly press of the country as much stuff putting Hoover and the Hoover administration in an unfavorable light as he can. His success in this direction has been extraordinary and unprecedented.

Mr. Michelson had the utmost co-operation from his Democratic party mouthpieces, who were plainly delighted with his pithy and timely speeches; speeches having their names over his well-written words, mouthing his ideas as their own. As a result, they "hit Mr. Hoover with practically everything save the office furniture. Every move he had made has been followed by the firings of a Michelson publicity barrage. He has been shot at from all sides and with guns of every calibre. And it has been effective. No one doubts that."

The sum total of Mr. Michelson's efforts was, as phrased by the Democratic Speaker of the House and 1932 Vice Presidential candidate John N. Garner, to "whittle Mr. Hoover down to our size."

Michelson occasionally put a stone in the center of one of the mudballs he mixed for someone else to throw but this proved to be a dangerous thing for the thrower. Some instances of this nature follow:

1. He sought to revive the story circulated in the 1928 campaign that Mr. Hoover had robbed the Chinese in a mine deal. This charge was effectively given the direct lie by Tong Shao-yi, twice Prime Minister of China and the responsible official of Mr. Hoover's Chinese assignment in a formal statement declaring that Mr. Hoover had acted honorably and in China's interest. Conclusive evidence which establishes the integrity of Mr. Hoover's Chinese operations may be found on page 54, of the Appendix.

2. A pamphlet issued to its speakers in the 1932 campaign by the Michelson office of the Democratic National Committee stated: "First and indelible his [Hoover's] early record is clouded by his former partnerships which contracted cheap Chinese coolie labor in South African mines" and went on to point out that Mr. Hoover had engaged in the slavery of human beings.

President Hoover, in a speech delivered at Cleveland, Ohio, on October 15, 1932, departed from his theretofore unbroken practice of ignoring the Michelson-Democratic Committee attacks by stating that:

> No South African concern with which I ever was connected ever employed a single Chinese laborer. But more important than this, I have in the files in Washington from the man who first penned those lies, a statement under oath humbly and abjectly withdrawing them.

Unfortunately, truth seldom if ever, catches up with untruth. Unfortunately, also, as demonstrated by the results of Michelson's efforts, Hitler was right when he said, "The bigger the lie the more likely it will be believed."

3. John N. Garner, Democratic Speaker of the House, on December 22, 1929, acting as the mouthpiece of the Michelson "smear" machine charged that President Hoover was connected with sugar tariff lobbyists. The Democratic members of the Senate Tariff Lobby Investigating Committee avidly began to search for evidence to support the charge. The fairness and integrity of its members prompted them to report after a careful investigation on January 14, 1930, that "There is no impropriety nor anything open to criticism on the President's part."

4. Another Michelson mud-ball which carried a rock was the planted story in the New York *World* concerning a reported "Second Tea Pot Dome Scandal." The story was ballyhooed in scare headlines. It rested on the fantastic and unsupportable charges of a discharged employe of the Interior Department who claimed that public holdings of shale oil lands of enormous value were being practically given

away. A searching inquiry proved that no trace of irregularity or impropriety existed. After the lies had been broadcast in newspaper headlines the New York *World,* in which the story was originally planted, made an unqualified apology.

5. Two other 1932 campaign canards which grew like a green bay tree in the fetid soil of public antagonists that the Michelson committee had been so long creating concerned children.

One of them was prepared by Mr. Michelson's office and issued as instructions to its speakers by the Democratic National Committee. It informed them:

"How the President has failed the children.

"His real interest in the nation's children may be gained by his recorded effort to emasculate and disrupt the Children's Bureau."

The other was made in a speech by the Democratic candidate in which Governor Roosevelt charged that during the Hoover Administration, "attempts have been made to cut appropriations for child welfare. . . ."

"The United States Health Service states that over six million of our public school children have not enough to eat; many are fainting at their desks; they are a prey of disease and their future health is menaced."

President Hoover directly challenged the truth of the Governor's charge in a speech he delivered at Indianapolis, Indiana, on October 28, with the statement that:

> I have a letter from the Chief of the United States Health Service that no such statement as that quoted by Governor Roosevelt has ever been put out by the Service.

The President also quoted from an address made a week earlier by the president of the American Public Health Association (not a government official) in which the following statement was made:

> . . . by and large, the health of the people as measured in sickness and death has never been better despite the depression.

As to the Children's Bureau, President Hoover stated that during the first year of his administration its appropriations had been increased from $320,000 to $368,000; the second year to $399,000 and in the third year he recommended an appropriation for it of $395,000. But, he added, "The Democratic House of Representatives reduced this by $20,000."

Because fathers and mothers (the vast majority of whom are voters) are moved easily, quickly and deeply by any official neglect of their children, indifference to their needs or discrimination against them, they were more ready to believe the baseless Democratic party lies concerning President Hoover's care of their children than his truthful answers.

By challenging the accuracy of such charges the President forced his opponents to drop them. But the harm, in the loss of many votes, had already been done.

Unable to discover a single instance of dishonesty in the Hoover administration's conduct of the public business, the Michelson office decided that it was safer to peddle innuendo. It was far safer to belittle him and just as effective, to take the President's statements out of their context and twist them, with diabolic ingenuity, into half-truths which made him appear to be an inhuman monster. The Michelson staff patterned their methods after the manner of small boys who stick pins in live insects and, with delight, watch them squirm. They gleefully watched the Hoover administration officials squirm. In time they found it safer to spread such rumors, for example, as the one about the sign over the gate of a California ranch which it was alleged Hoover owned, and which purportedly read, "No white men wanted here." They even arranged for the surreptitious distribution of a photograph of such a sign without being deterred either by the fact that Hoover owned no California ranch nor by the other fact that there was no such sign over a ranch owned by one of Hoover's friends (to whom the President had loaned some money for its purchase) nor by the final fact that *only* white men were employed on the ranch in question. None of these facts served to deter the Michelson office from spreading this cleverly concocted lie, the purpose of which was to plant the poison in the public mind that Hoover discriminated against white workers; and there were millions upon millions of white workers who were voters.

Today's readers who either look back on or read for the first time of Michelson's success in belittling Mr. Hoover, and by belittling, to destroy him politically for the time being, are almost certain to wonder why the Hoover administration permitted this to be done.

There are several possible answers. In my judgment the principal ones are:

1. The people were in distress. For whatever reason, they wanted a scapegoat and the President was the most available candidate. A major part of Mr. Hoover's difficulties as President stemmed from this situation.

2. The Democratic National Committee, through its press agent, Mr. Michelson, made the most of this situation. "The table was spread, all we had to do was eat," he said.

3. There was no one in President Hoover's official family who possessed Michelson's ability as a phrase-maker, his imagination, his malevolence or who was so wholly devoid of a sense of fairness or honesty. Even had there been a man of similar abilities and lack of principles available, President Hoover would have refused to make use of his talents.

4. It is far easier to indict successfully than it is to alibi convincingly.

5. Making interesting copy out of alleged wrong-doing is as easy as falling off a log, whereas the task of putting enough lilt into copy about drab duty done in grim serious fashion so that it will make the news columns requires the artistry of a genius.

6. The failure of the old guard as well as Republican members of his own party to co-operate with him added somewhat to his difficulties.

7. Finally, there was the President's own point of view, revealed by the following statement which Hugh Gibson gave me. Mr. Gibson revealed that once when President Hoover was "being subjected to a particularly scurrilous and outrageous campaign I remarked to Mrs. Hoover on the calm with which he took it. She answered in a matter-of-fact way, 'You see, Bert can take it better than most people because he has deeply engrained in him the Quaker feeling that

nothing matters if you are "right with God." That was dinned into him so thoroughly as a youngster that even if unconsciously, it helps him at a time like this.' "

President Hoover's Quaker training to ignore all canards and innuendoes except those which specifically concerned his integrity or the integrity of his administration. He clung to the belief that the dignity of his office required him to "accept in silence hideous misrepresentations and unjustified complaint."

CHAPTER ELEVEN

The Typhoon Strikes Our Shores

Unmistakable signs and portents had been evident throughout the world for several years that a cataclysmic economic, social and political typhoon was slowly but unmistakably forming. The people of one country after another felt the lash of its fury and the destructive force of its tidal waves.

The storm struck the United States with great force in the fall of 1929 and there followed in its wake the most severe world depression of all history.

The roots went back to World War I. The war killed or crippled more than forty million of the finest youth of that generation, destroyed over three hundred million dollars' worth of property and savings, and placed mortgages on future generations through borrowings which created staggering tax loads. In scores of nations these heavy taxes destroyed industries, paralyzed commerce and wiped out currencies. These were the natural, inevitable consequences of such colossal wastage. A bad peace treaty created dislocations by transfer of huge populations from their former economic settings. Twelve new nations were carved out of three old empires. And these twelve and several old nations built new high tariff walls twelve years before the Hawley-Smoot tariff bill was enacted.

New national fears and suspicions were made manifest through enormous standing armies, a sword which cut two ways; for support of these millions of soldiers placed a heavier tax load on the taxpayers and at the same time withdrew these same millions of soldiers from productive work.

Furthermore, the repercussions of the war upset many governments. Three hundred million people in China; a similar number in India and one hundred sixty million in Russia were in revolution or near-revolution. Other revolutions followed in Portugal, Spain, Brazil, the Argentine, Chile, Peru, Ecuador and Siam. Still others were attempted in a dozen other countries. One effect of these revolutions was the repudiation by these countries of part or all of their domestic and foreign debts. Another effect was their greatly reduced purchases of American goods.

If wealth, as Henry George defined it, "consists of natural products that have been secured, moved or combined, so as to fit them for the gratification of human desires," it becomes evident that the involved nations had destroyed the sources of wealth along with their destruction of property. Many of Europe's industrial plants, moreover, had been destroyed. The machinery of many others had become obsolete. Transportation was badly crippled on the Continent. Our own railroads were in chaos as a result of government operation. Stocks of natural products were low or non-existent. Millions of men who formerly had helped to "secure, move and combine" these natural products were either crippled or dead. Malnutrition and the impact of the war had left millions of other men, women and children with inadequate bodies and unsettled minds. Over and above all of these catastrophic evils was the fact that the war had torn all of these and millions more loose from their spiritual and intellectual moorings. All over the world men were on the loose. They forgot God. They discarded or blasphemed age-old truths which epitomized the wisdom of the race.

One other unsettling war-created factor, but of a different nature, was that the Great War, as have all great wars, speeded up and improved many methods of producing goods. The war-caused shortage of manpower had forced engineers to create ways to shift from men to machinery an ever increasing part of the job of producing and manufacturing war material. These technological advances helped in a measure to change man's way of working and living and to an extent to sever long-established social, economic and political ties.

These and other factors and evils served to disillusion and dishearten the people of Europe.

The War Did Still More

War needs and dislocations enormously stepped up the production of rubber in the East Indies, coffee in Brazil, sugar in Cuba, cocoa in Latin America, copper in the Congo, wheat in Australia and the Argentine, cotton in Egypt and many American farm products. The enormous overproduction of these food and other supplies, far beyond boom rates of consumption and almost infinitely beyond the consumption rate of destroyed national credits and non-existent money, created gluts in the market. Following the immutable law of supply and demand this overproduction brought about a collapse in prices. It carried bankruptcies as well as the destruction of buying power for American goods along with it.

These combined war dislocations forced one country after another in Europe to go off the gold standard. It was this condition, and not "reprisals" against the Hawley-Smoot tariff law of later years which caused foreign countries to impose direct or indirect restrictions of American goods.

Just as in all situations where one thing after another goes wrong and thereby serves to throw other things out of joint, the upset world conditions forced the panic-stricken nationals of troubled countries to dump American securities on our markets.

World Speculation on the Loose

Added to all of the foregoing was the orgy of world-wide speculation which followed the war. This was made possible by the constant inflations of credit and currencies. The National Bureau of Economic Research has reported that the speculative bubble had already broken in eleven countries with a combined population of six hundred million people before our own speculative boom crashed in the fall of 1929. The bubble did not burst "first in the land of its origin—the United States" as Governor Roosevelt stated in the 1932 campaign. "The major collapse abroad" preceded, and did not "follow the United States collapse."

President Hoover had sensed the inflationary dangers to American economy which were inherent in a decision the Federal Reserve Bank of New York made in 1925. This institution, in co-operation with various central banks of Europe, undertook to expand credit by manipulating discount rates combined with *easy money policies* and open market operations. The claimed purpose was to strengthen Europe. The end result was an orgy of speculation, world-wide in extent. Mr. Hoover protested against this action in November 1925. In doing so he referred to the American-British financial understanding and then commented upon the then-existing speculative madness in the United States. He prophetically added:

> As to the effects of these Reserve policies upon the United States, it means inflation with inevitable collapse which will bring calamities upon our farmers, our workers and legitimate business . . .

Later statements and warnings by Mr. Hoover on the rise of speculation concerned the "safety of continued prosperity [which] will depend on . . . caution and resistance to . . . speculation . . . our bankers can check the dangers of speculative credits . . . not since 1920 have we required . . . a more capable administration of credit facilities than now."

For the moment, Mr. Hoover won to the extent that the *open market* operations were discontinued in February 1926. But in July 1927, while he was away from Washington directing relief for Mississippi flood victims, the Federal Reserve Board, in conjunction with banking officials of Great Britain, France and Germany, agreed to enter upon a determined policy whose purpose was that of inflating credit. They did this on the theory that it would help Europe.

The Reserve Board later assured Mr. Hoover that it would immediately stop the snowball it had started down the mountain when and if unhealthy speculation became evident. The Reserve Board's conceit was greater than its powers, for it possessed none of those of Joshua who commanded:

> Sun stand thou still upon Gibeon; and thou moon in the valley of Aj-ă-lon; and the sun stood still, and the moon stayed . . .

Sought to Curb Speculation

Two days after he became President, Mr. Hoover conferred with Federal Reserve Board officials and requested them to take immediate action in an effort to reduce credit for speculative purposes. Also at his suggestion, Secretary of the Treasury Mellon issued a statement on March 15, which sought to encourage the public to buy bonds instead of stocks. Governor Young of the Federal Reserve Board appealed to the banks of the country to co-operate in restricting credit for speculative purposes.

The Chairman of the Committee on Banking and Currency of the House and Charles E. Mitchell, president of the National City Bank immediately expressed open opposition to President Hoover's policy. Mr. Mitchell defied the Administration's program by offering large credits for stock market operations. On April 20, members attending the annual meeting of the American Newspaper Publishers Association were reported as having expressed "grave doubts" about the Reserve Board's action. The fever of speculation meanwhile continued to rise and gambling in the stock market continued unchecked.

As a result of the President's insistence, the Reserve Board publicly announced in early April, 1929, that unless the banks of the country voluntarily restricted credit for speculation it would adopt other methods to stimulate such action.

In May, President Hoover refused to approve the proposal that the United States join the World Bank because he suspected that it would be used either to inflate or deflate credit. His judgment was that the United States should not be a party to any effort which would support stock market gambling throughout the world.

By June, 1929, the speculation situation had become so bad in the United States that the President instructed the Department of Justice to close the mails to bucket shops and market tipsters for the purpose of ending their efforts to stimulate purchase and sale of stocks.

These steps took the federal government as far as it could go under existing laws in the direction of correcting the abuses of the New York Stock Exchange, which operated under the New York State law.

Birthplace, West Branch, Iowa

About 5 years of age, with older brother Theodore

Stanford University, Sophomore year, 1893

Stanford geology class. Hoover second from left

With his police dog, King Tut. Washington, 1928

Inaugural address, March 4, 1929

HARRIS & EWING

With Ramsey MacDonald, White House, 1929

Fishing in Florida, 1933

INS

Mr. and Mrs. Hoover, Stanford, California, 1938

Boyscout Broadcast with Theodore Roosevelt, Jr., 1939

Hoover Library Tower, Stanford University

Opening the Hoover Library, Stanford, California

At the Hoover Library, June, 1941

Hoover and Ralph Lutz, of the Hoover Library

At the Bohemian Grove, California, 1945

In mining clothes at Pioche, Nevada, 1946

With General Mark Clark, food mission, 1946

INS

In Poland, World Food Mission, 1946

When, more than a year later, New York State Governor Franklin Roosevelt still had made no move to control either the activities of the New York Stock Exchange or to check the sale of bonds of foreign governments (nearly all of which were issued by banking institutions with offices in New York), President Hoover on October 10, 1930, moved again into the situation by calling officials of the New York Stock Exchange together, and in language that put the fear of God in their hearts—which is said to be the beginning of wisdom—warned them that unless they put the Stock Exchange house in order he would find ways to do it for them. He admitted that the federal government then had no authority to regulate the Exchange; nevertheless, its responsible officials and its members either would reform Stock Exchange rules and enforce them and the conduct of its members—or else. His *or else* implied positive federal government regulation of the Stock Exchange unless it acted promptly. They moved at a snail's pace, talked much and did little.

The President's administrative steps helped the situation for a period. It soon again grew worse because the prevailing high rates in the call money market brought a flood of funds from private and foreign sources. When these fresh funds became available they gave fresh and strong impetus to the speculative madness.

The Bubble Breaks

The bubble was soon to burst at home as it had done abroad. The aftermath of the end of the speculative boom in many areas served to create a sharp rise in European discount rates in September, 1929, which, in turn, first made our own stock markets feverish and later served to destroy our house of cards.

It is possible that the shock to our economy might have been far less had the eventually-bound-to-happen European depression taken place two years earlier, as it almost certainly would have done if the Federal Reserve Board had followed Mr. Hoover's first urgings in 1925 to curb easy credits.

The deliberate inflation of credit, however, delayed the European collapse by as much as perhaps eighteen months. By so doing it permitted a wild spree of speculation to reach unmanageable proportions. This served to make the depression in the United States cut far deeper and last much longer.

Abnormal Strains Placed on Our Economy

The world-wide character of the depression placed a terrific strain on our economy and contributed enormously to the complexity of our problems. These factors forced President Hoover to adapt his policies to meet the new forces of disintegration and destruction as they occurred.

The first period of our domestic economic crisis extended from the beginning of the stock market crash in October, 1929, and the collapse of central Europe in May, 1931.

Even before the moans of stock gamblers had lessened appreciably, the cries of troubled farmers began to be heard. They, too, had bought on margin, that is, had placed mortgages on their farms at inflated values and bought more high-priced land, farm equipment or luxury items. And all of their purchases were made at inflated prices with small down-payments. A majority of wheat and corn farmers of the Middle West and cotton farmers of the South, led astray by high war-time prices of their products, had gone far beyond their financial depth because of their belief that prosperity would last forever. Their troubled chickens began to come home to roost in the early twenties. From that time on the farm bloc group in the Senate was their mouthpiece.

CHAPTER TWELVE

Weathering the Storm

Statistical records clearly separate the depression of 1929–32 into three distinct stages. The first stage followed the collapse of frenzied stock speculation, first in foreign countries and later in the United States. The second and worst stage was the fearful impact on our national economy of the financial collapse of Europe. The final stage came after the 1932 November presidential election when public fear over the prospect of a complete change in the nation's monetary policy by the incoming administration prepared the way for an economic collapse and ended in the bank panic of 1933.

Weak Spots in Our Economy

There were three or four weak-to-bad areas in our economy in 1929. These included: first, speculation in stocks; second, war-inflated prices of farm land, much of which was mortgaged; third, an out-of-balance farm-industry price condition; and fourth, the weakness of the nation's banking organization. The latter was geared to boom conditions and was inadequate when it met depression conditions.

State chartered banks—forming the vast majority of our banking units—were the weakest link in the banking chain. They operated under forty-eight different kinds of regulations. During 1930, 1931 and 1932 there were 773 failures of national banks with total deposits of $721,000,000 whereas 3,604 state banks with total deposits of $2,031,000,000 folded. The total deposits of bank failures, both national and state, during these three years were approximately 5 per cent of the average total deposits for the period.

Meeting the Farm Problem

The President expressed his belief to me about this time that the farmers could work their way out of their difficulties, provided a better system for marketing their crops could be created. Our farmers, he said, were production experts, the best in the world. Their marketing methods and machinery, however, were poor to bad. They sold their products individually. This practice placed them at the mercy of the ups and downs of economic changes as well as those of the manipulators and speculators in farm products. This bad condition could be remedied, he believed, with the help of better marketing methods designed to get them top market prices for their products and protect them from speculators. He had, he said, created the Federal Farm Board to do just that and induced the Congress to provide it with a half-billion dollar revolving fund. This sum was to be used to advance the co-operative marketing system of farm products.

Not long after he told me this I reported the gist of his remarks to the late William Allen White in answer to some critical comments White had made about the Hoover farm program. White listened intently and then remarked, "If he would only tell these things to the people they would support him enthusiastically."

That, however, was not Hoover's way. He was and always has been a man of action whose action was based on a knowledge of realities. He did things. He did not talk about them. He had not learned that information and explanation for the public must be ground exceedingly fine and fed to the voters with a spoon.

The parable of the duck and the hen is appropriate here. The duck asked the hen, "Why is it that men everywhere sing praises over your egg-laying abilities but never even mention mine? And yet I lay as many eggs as you do and my eggs are bigger and richer than yours. Why they don't sing my praises I can't understand." The hen replied, "That's easy. Whenever I lay an egg I cackle to tell the world about it. But when you lay an egg you slip quietly off the nest and go for a swim without uttering a quack."

Hoover, without cackling about it, directed the Farm Board on October 24, 1929, to advance funds to existing co-operatives for the purpose of helping to cushion the drop in the prices of farm products. As a result, wheat prices by December 31, 1929 reached their pre-

October 24 levels, and cotton showed a drop for the same period of only 6 per cent.

Other Economic Dangers Threaten

By November 15, 1929, when surveys of the nation's economic situation foreshadowed the coming of other serious dangers, the President invited business, industrial and labor leaders to a White House conference. He wanted the hard facts they could give him about business conditions and unemployment. He wanted to secure their co-operation in helping to stabilize economic conditions, reduce unemployment and maintain industrial peace in the belief that co-ordinated individual effort could check the depression; and he held it to be his duty to provide leadership and encourage action.

He explained the purpose and spirit which prompted the calling of these conferences in an address he delivered at Indianapolis, June 15, 1931. He held that these moves to mitigate the depression and to expedite recovery were the first extensive and positive ones ever undertaken for such purposes by the federal government. What he had sought, he said, was to organize co-operative action of the nation's constructive forces and to stimulate every element of initiative and self-reliance in the effort to preserve our democracy against dictator government. In conclusion he said:

> There is no sudden stroke of either governmental or private action which can dissolve these world difficulties; patient constructive action in a multitude of directions is the strategy of success. This battle is upon a thousand fronts. Some people demanding abrupt change . . . in our American system. . . . Others have indomitable confidence that by some legerdemain we can legislate ourselves out of a world-wide depression. Such views are as accurate as the belief we can exorcise a Caribbean hurricane by statutory law.

On November 18, 1929, the President put into action a second time the proposal he had originated in 1922, namely, that the government should expand useful public works and construction during depression periods as aids in stabilizing employment and business. He announced the call of several conferences with industrialists, labor leaders and bankers with the statement: "Words are not of any great importance in times of economic disturbance. It is action that counts."

The first of these conferences was held with the presidents of nearby railroads on November 19, 1929. The major topic discussed at this meeting dealt largely with the maintenance of normal construction work. The press statement issued at the close of the meeting said in part:

> The railway presidents were unanimous in their determination to co-operate in the maintenance of employment and business progress. It was stated that the railways which they represented would proceed with full programs of construction and betterments without any reference to recent stock exchange fluctuations; that they would canvass the situation as to further possibilities of expansion, and that amongst these particular railways it appeared that the total volume of such construction work already indicated an increase during the next six months over the similar period of last year.
>
> It was agreed that the whole question should be taken up at the meeting of the railway executives convening in Chicago next Friday, with view to securing co-operation of all railways in the United States.

Two days later the President called a White House meeting of the leading business executives of the country. First he outlined the situation as he saw it by saying that it was more serious than a stock market crash and further that no one could measure the possible depth of the disaster. His judgment, he said, was that since the stock boom and collapse were world-wide, and since Europe still had a long way to go before recovering from the war, the depression would last for some time because inflated values would have to be liquidated. His primary concern, however, he pointed out, was that of unemployment and human distress, and the maintenance of social order and industrial peace.

The third problem he presented to the conference was that of helping bring about orderly liquidation of securities in an effort to prevent panic. He stressed the point that the industrial policy in previous depressions had been to liquidate labor. He vigorously opposed this as a policy because he refused to consider labor as a commodity. Labor to him meant homes.

In this, as always, when dealing with problems and situations, he began and ended with the individual. He sought to enlist business leaders to participate in a program that would protect the individual worker, by not stepping wages down any faster than the drop in values. To accomplish this he called upon industry to maintain wages and expand construction work. He asked also that available work should be spread among all employes by temporarily shortening the work-week of individuals. And finally, he called upon each industry to relieve the distress of its own employes.

Having stated his views and requests the President asked his conferees to state their views frankly, especially as to what action they felt the government should take in stimulating co-operative action. The discussion made clear that the industrial leaders favored the President's program. They agreed to put it into operation when and if it was approved by labor leaders.

The afternoon of that same day, November 21, the nation's top labor union officials met with the President. The following press statement covered the agreement reached at both meetings:

> The President was authorized by the employers who were present at this morning's conference to state on their individual belief that they will not initiate any movement for wage reduction, and it was their strong recommendation that this attitude should be pursued by the country as a whole.
>
> They considered that aside from the human considerations involved, the consuming power of the country will thereby be maintained.
>
> The President was also authorized by the representatives of labor to state that in their individual views and as their strong recommendation to the country as a whole, no movement beyond those already in negotiation should be initiated for increase of wages, and that every co-operation should be given by labor to industry in the handling of its problems.

The purpose of these declarations is to give assurance that conflicts should not occur during the present situation which will affect the continuity of work, and thus to maintain stability of employment.

Other Business Leaders Called to the White House

The next group called for conference by the President were the leaders of the building and construction industries. On November 22, 1929, they agreed to help maintain and stimulate their industries. On November 23, the President telegraphed the governors of the forty-eight states and the mayors of every city and urged them to expand public works programs in every practical direction. The nearly unanimous affirmative response to this request was heartening.

Three days later, in response to the President's call for a conference, the leaders of the national farm organizations met with him, as did Secretary of Agriculture Hyde, the directors of the Farm Board and the Chairman of Federal Land Banks. The farm organizations agreed to co-operate fully in carrying out the program he presented.

Following a meeting on November 27, 1929, with representatives of the public utility industry, all except Samuel Insull of Chicago (of ignoble fame, who held that there was nothing wrong with his industry) approved the President's program.

The net result of the President's conferences with these different groups was their agreement to undertake and carry out a constructive program during 1930 which would require a total expenditure of more than $3,000,000,000.

Meanwhile the Farm Board had moved to avert any early collapse of farm commodity markets. The *New York Times,* on February 12, 1930, editorially expressed the opinion that: "Indication is that the patient at the end of January has begun to recover."

CHAPTER THIRTEEN

Hoover Administration Relief Policy and Program

Not one of the many unprecedented and grave problems which confronted President Hoover caused him greater difficulties or more heartaches or created more widespread criticism and animosity toward him than that of depression relief. It was strange that the public misjudged him, because by instinct he was sensitive to human suffering and held an impelling impulse to help relieve it wherever and whenever possible.

It was not strange, however, that his relief principles, policies and methods were bitterly criticized, because hungry men think only of the present and their immediate need; jobless men, who cannot find work, become panicky. Furthermore, his political opponents made political capital of human distress by constantly criticizing all that he did and the way he did it.

The Hoover relief program included help for every individual who needed it, had opponents other than Democrats. These were the advocates of big government, regardless of party affiliation. This group was especially critical of the President's insistence that local and state governments should direct relief activities.

Nevertheless he continued to advance his policy of decentralized relief work activity. He stoutly contended that this was the only sure way to guarantee fair, honest and efficient administration of relief supplies and to prevent graft; and, still worse, the corruption of the electorate. The local committees, composed of members of all political parties and groups responsible for relief direction, would not tolerate either graft or corruption.

He dwelt at length upon this latter point during a visit in which I had expressed the belief that the country could well afford to spend a billion dollars in such an effort even though some of it were to be wasted.

He replied in substance: "I will use every dollar of cash this government has and every dollar it can borrow to help take care of every individual in need but that's not the way to do it."

Some years later, in a speech made December 16, 1935, before the John Marshall Republican Club of St. Louis, Mr. Hoover restated his position in the following paragraphs which concisely give his administration relief policies and program:

> It also became my duty in 1930 to see that relief was organized for our unemployed. Organization of relief upon a nation-wide basis was practically unknown in the world before those experiences. It therefore fell to me and my colleagues to pioneer in methods. We had to learn what basis would best and most sympathetically protect those in distress and still place the least burden on those who had to pay for it. I spent long, weary days listening to arguments whether to have direct money relief, or relief in kind, or public works or made-work or "boondoggling," or centralized administration or decentralized responsibility. We tried out these alternatives. Out of those poignant experiences we learned certain fundamentals. We quickly learned that there were four types of persons who rush into relief. There were the starry-eyed who periodically discover that relief is needed and that everything up to date is wrong. There were those whose major passion was sociological experiment upon a mass of distress. There were those who would make profit from misery. There were always those present who do not neglect the political possibilities of relief. But there were the sterling, solid men and women in every city and hamlet who willingly served and sacrificed.
>
> We learned that relief was an emergency operation, not a social experiment; that the object was to serve the people in genuine distress and nobody else. We learned that the dreamers cannot effectually conduct the grinding tasks of relief; that politics must be shunned as a plague. We learned that centralized bureaucracy gives the sufferers more red tape than relief. We learned that we must mobilize on a voluntary basis the best hearts and brains in every

community to serve their neighbors. We learned that there must be complete decentralization to them of both authority and administration. We did not have to learn that local self-government and local responsibility was the basis of American life. . . . (See Appendix XIII.)

Although stung by false charges that he was indifferent to human misery, he publicly took notice of them only once. He did this in a speech at Fort Wayne, Indiana, October 5, 1932, by saying that:

> I shall now say the only harsh word that I have uttered in public office. I hope it will be the last that I shall have to say. When you are told that the President of the United States, who by the most sacred trust of our nation is the President of all the people, a man of your own blood and upbringing, has sat in the White House for the last three years of your misfortune without troubling to know your burdens, without heartaches over your miseries and casualties, without summoning every avenue of skillful assistance irrespective of party or view, without using every ounce of his strength and straining his every nerve to protect and help, without putting aside personal ambition and humbling his pride of opinion if that would serve—then I say to you that such statements are deliberate, intolerable falsehoods.

Perhaps, if he were faced anew as President with relief problems similar to those in 1930, he would, in the light of changed social conceptions and practices, change his methods somewhat. But in 1930 he was breaking new ground. The relief activities he initiated and carried out were without federal government precedent. Undoubtedly, if he had the same job to do over, he would cling to his "centralized ideas —decentralized responsibility" principle because of his conviction that the local committee way of administering relief is the correct way. Because they "used existing officials; they engaged their own tested organizations; they employed their own trusted citizens. . . . They knew the problem of the man next door better than anyone in Washington. . . . They adapted these needs to the individual families. Their stewardship was under the limelight of their own community. They gave spiritual aid and encouragement."

Not one of his presidential predecessors had ever believed that the federal government had any responsibility or obligation to take part in "mitigating business depressions or in the restoration of recovery."

On October 17, 1930, he, therefore, announced a new national policy when he stated that "as a nation we must prevent hunger and cold to those of our people who are in honest difficulties." Only forty-three years earlier in 1887 President Cleveland had refused to approve legislation which was designed to provide aid for drought sufferers with the statement that "though the people support the government, the government should not support the people."

President Hoover was in complete agreement with his distinguished predecessor on the point that the federal government should not directly extend aid to individuals. He believed that if this method were followed it would inevitably lead to greater centralization of power, to the creation of a political oligarchy through corruption of the electorate and to the unnecessary expenditure of vast sums of public money by an inefficient bureaucracy. Combined, he believed these would undermine the social and political structure of American life.

His relief program—what he did, how and why he did it—as now seen in its entirety and in perspective—appears to have been as follows:

1. The federal government must assume leadership in the program and make certain that it was inaugurated in every community.
2. The mobilization of the nation's voluntary forces into a co-operative effort with non-partisan committees operating in every state and local community. These were to be created to administer relief—or made work. This method, which had worked so successfully in another form in the Food Administration's decentralized authority, left to the leaders of the local communities the solution of the problems and the administration of relief. He believed that this method would quicken neighborly hearts to distress, develop a sense of social responsibility, prevent waste of public funds, insure that political capital could not be made of human distress and provide adequate help for everyone who required it.

Because he also believed that jobs were more important to an individual's spiritual and moral purpose than dole, he encouraged the expansion of railway, utility and construction work, urged that wages should be maintained until the decreased cost of living justified reductions and that employment should be staggered for the purpose of giving some income to the greatest possible number of wage earners.

He also took vigorous and far-reaching steps to expand federal, state and municipal public works. He insisted that support for direct relief be provided out of public funds by local and state governments with this important reservation: when these sources could no longer carry the load alone the federal government should supply supplementary money or commodity support for the state or local governments to administer.

The President created national "emergency relief organizations" in 1930, 1931 and 1932. The successive chairmen of these national relief committees, Colonel Arthur Woods, Walter S. Gifford and Newton D. Baker had the co-operation of governors of the states, mayors of cities and other local officials and leaders. They formed more than three thousand local relief committees which mobilized and organized the vast number of agencies of self help in the communities. In 1930 only one governor believed that federal aid was needed in his state.

The President "accredited to those who advocate federal charity a natural anxiety for the people of their states." He publicly pledged in a press statement issued in February, 1931, that if the time ever should come when—

> the voluntary agencies of the country together with local and state governments are unable to find resources with which to prevent hunger and suffering in my country I will ask the aid of every resource of the Federal government. . . . The American people are doing their job today. They should be given a chance to show whether they wish to preserve the principles of individual and local responsibility and mutual self help before they embark on what I believe is a disastrous system. . . .

All partisan or Communist charges that the people of the United States were either starving or else living on starvation diets during the early 1930's are completely refuted by reports of public health officials. These show that the mortality rates during 1931 were appreciably lower than in the two previous years and that infant mortality was lower in 1931 than for any previous year on record.

Meeting the Need

Through congressional approval of his recommendation the President allotted from the Farm Board's surplus commodities for relief (to be distributed through the Red Cross to local committees) 85,000,000 bushels of wheat (20,000,000 barrels of flour sufficient for 6,000,000 families for nine months) and 250,000,000 pounds of cotton—which provided garments for 4,000,000 families.

When unemployment increased to 10,000,000 in early 1932 the President requested Congress to provide $300,000,000 in funds to be loaned by the federal government to the states on the basis of need rather than population. The relief so provided was to be administered through state and local committees. Congress delayed forty-seven days before adopting the legislation.

In another of his efforts to create jobs, President Hoover launched a $750,000,000 public construction program. He also provided an additional $1,500,000,000 for construction of public enterprises of a self-sustaining character.

Nature Delivers a Body Blow

Up to this point the President had been confronted with man-made troubles. They had been varied and bad. In the summer of 1930 nature stepped in to take his measure. It did this by carrying out the most widespread and severe drought in recent history. Its worst effects were experienced in the areas of the Potomac, Ohio and lower Mississippi River valleys and in the northwest. About one million families and twenty million head of livestock were affected.

The President's early moves were: (a) to induce the railroads to haul feed to the drought sufferers at a 50 per cent reduction in rates; (b) to call the governors of the drought-affected states to Washington for a conference with federal and Red Cross officials responsible for drought relief; (c) to direct that the federal share of highway construction funds be applied to drought areas as a means of giving employment to drought distressed farms; and (d) to order the speeding up of governmental waterways and flood-control projects to relieve unemployment in drought areas.

He directed the Federal Land Bank and the Farm Board to expand their credit facilities and he headed a Red Cross drive for $10,000,000 to aid the sufferers. In his annual message on December 2, 1930, he recommended an appropriation of $30,000,000 for seed and feed loans to farmers. The government's total seed and feed loans, administered by the local committees, amounted to $47,000,000, 75 per cent of which ultimately was repaid.

Puts the Brakes on Immigration

In an effort to conserve jobs for our own unemployed, President Hoover issued instructions on September 6, 1930 to immigration officials to temporarily stop all immigration to the United States (amounting to about 250,000 individuals per year).

On October 6, 1930, the President made a speech at the annual meeting of the American Federation of Labor in which he reported on his stewardship:

> In his invitation that I should address you on this occasion, President Green spoke in terms of high praise of the benefits to labor from the nation-wide co-operation initiated at the White House last November for mitigation of the effects of the present depression.
>
> At those White House conferences the leaders of business and industry undertook to do their utmost to maintain the rate of wages. They also undertook in case of shortened employment to distribute work as evenly as possible over their regular body of employees. The leaders of labor undertook to urge effort in production and to prevent conflict and dispute. . . .
>
> We have now had nearly a year in which to observe the working of these arrangements. These, the first undertakings of this character in our history, have been carried out in astonishing degree. There are, of course, exceptions, but in the large sense our great

manufacturing companies, the railways, utilities, and business houses have been able to maintain the established wages. Employers have spread their employment systematically. For the first time in more than a century of these recurring depressions we have been practically free of bitter industrial conflict. . . .

Organized Labor Approved President's Program

Evidence that labor union officials, who had participated in and cooperated with the President's depression aid programs, believed that what he had done was commendable is contained in a report of appreciation which the executive council of the American Federation of Labor made at that body's 1931 annual meeting. This report stated:

> Realization of the pernicious effects of wage reductions has prevented a widespread liquidation of wages such as we had in the depression of 1921. Growing adherence to the high-wage principle, strengthened by the President's stand against wage cuts, has brought effective support from the leading industrialists of the country.
>
> In the full year of 1921 there were ninety-two wage cuts per hundred firms reporting to the Bureau of Labor Statistics, while in the full year of 1930 there were only seven firms per hundred firms reporting.
>
> Although wage cuts have increased in 1931, there still has been no widespread tendency toward a liquidation of wages such as we experienced in 1921.
>
> In the first seven months of 1931 the number of cuts reported per hundred firms was twelve compared to fifty-four in 1921.

Congressional Seesaw Continues

The nub of the issue (aside from its political partisan phases) between President Hoover and the Congress was locally directed relief versus direct federal government dole.

Hardly a day passed when Congress was in session that one or more Democratic party leaders did not make a speech prepared by the party's able ghost writer. In all of these the President was attacked as being heartless, inept, blundering or incapable. When Congress was not in session these or other leaders would issue statements to the press, prepared by the same ghost writer, in which similar charges were made.

As examined today in the light of results they accomplished two things: the first was what they ardently desired, namely, to destroy Mr. Hoover politically; the second, which even they could not have wanted to happen, was the shattering of the faith of the people in their leaders and in their government. They sowed the wind. We today are reaping the whirlwind.

It is possible that some of his partisan opponents admitted in their private consciences that the President's relief program was right and adequate, they nevertheless continued to stuff the legislative hopper with bills that called for the federal government to take over all relief work. In the face of popular demand that he go along with these congressional proposals, he continued to oppose them. On February 22, 1931, he said in a radio broadcast:

> The moment [that] responsibilities of any community, particularly in economic and social questions, are shifted from any part of the nation to Washington, then that community has subjected itself to a remote bureaucracy. . . . It has lost a large part of its voice in the control of its own destiny. . . . Where people divest themselves of local government responsibilities they at once lay the foundation for destruction of their liberties. . . . At once when the government is centralized there arises a limitation upon the liberty of the individual and a restriction of individual opportunity . . . can lead but to the superstate where every man becomes the servant of the State and real liberty is lost.

Sought to Mobilize and Stimulate Individual Effort

Every move the President made was designed to mobilize and stimulate individual effort which, when joined with many millions of individual efforts, could create a force so powerful that it would serve to check the depression and thereby enable us to work our way out of our difficulties.

On October 18, 1931, he spoke of our problems and our purpose as a nation. In it he dwelt on spiritual and moral values, of the individual's place in American life and in the following words, voiced his philosophy:

> I would that I possessed the art of words to fix the real issue with which the troubled world is faced into the mind and heart of every American man and woman. Our country and the world are today involved in more than a financial crisis. We are faced with the primary question of human relations, which reaches to the very depth of organized society and to the very depth of human conscience. This civilization and this great complex, which we call American life, is builded and can alone survive upon the translation into individual action of that fundamental philosophy announced by the Savior nineteen centuries ago. Part of our national suffering today is from failure to observe these primary yet inexorable laws of human relationship. Modern society cannot survive with the defense of Cain, 'Am I my brother's keeper?'
>
> No governmental action, no economic doctrine, no economic plan or project can replace that God-imposed responsibility of the individual man and woman to their neighbors. That is a vital part of the very soul of the people. If we shall gain in this spirit from this painful time, we shall have created a greater and more glorious America. The trial of it is here now. It is a trial of the heart and conscience of individual men and women. . . .

Hindsight Versus Foresight

One of the weaknesses, perhaps the fatal weakness of President Hoover's domestic relief program, was its drabness. It had neither fireworks nor dramatics, but was ably and honestly carried on in a serious business-like way. It successfully provided food, shelter and clothing for the distressed people of the nation. On the other hand, it failed also to give them that which might be called emotional sustenance. Their spirits needed aid and guidance as much as their bodies did.

Had President Hoover's nature, training and beliefs or freedom from other problems enabled him to have sensed the importance of the fundamental human need of people in distress for moral and spiritual sustenance, and had he sought to restore their spirits by giving them a sign, as it were, of his deep and earnest purpose to help them, the story of the people's reaction to the Hoover administration's adequate relief program would today be written in wholly different terms than it now is recorded.

Because hindsight is better than foresight it now is easy to see and believe that could President Hoover have pushed aside grave political and economic problems and sidetracked his administrative duties for a period of three months or so in the fall of 1931 and given to a domestic relief program the same brilliant leadership, imagination and resourcefulness that he gave to both the Belgian Relief Commission and American Relief Administration jobs, he most certainly could have created a type of relief organization which would have done in its way for those in distress what the RFC did for the financially distressed business institutions. Had he created a relief administration corporation that would have served as a rallying ground for the public conscience and altruism of the nation and harnessed those forces to the job of meeting a national emergency it could have silenced his critics even though it might have done no more or done no better than did the voluntary committees he created and inspired; but today it seems certain that such activities would have served as a reassuring sign to all the people that their leader was doing everything possible to help them.

Perhaps he went as far as he could at the time in establishing new social concepts and in creating new precedents and new procedures and responsibilities for the government in relieving distress as the people would let him go. Certainly this is true: Mr. Hoover's relief record as President, which was planned and carried out within the provisions of the Constitution, was so far ahead of that of any of his predecessors in its social implications and purpose as to make it almost revolutionary.

CHAPTER FOURTEEN

A Variety of Activities, Problems and Situations

Some of the minor problems which the government faced during the first two depression years are presented in this chapter since it would be difficult to list them chronologically.

Hoarding of money by our citizens was one of these problems until the administration lessened its effects by organizing and conducting an educational campaign which sought to discourage the practice. It also directed the Federal Reserve System to issue $1,500,000,000 in currency above normal. These actions would have controlled the domestic situation had not foreign factors appeared to upset it. These foreign factors consisted of large sums of nervous money which shaky governments or their frightened citizens sent to the United States. At one time they had here $1,393,500,000 on deposit or invested in short-term bills. Then when conditions grew worse here they would again grow jittery and withdraw these deposits. This seesaw of foreign deposits and withdrawals made our own recovery more difficult.

One major shock which checked our recovery, one that jarred the world sufficiently that men everywhere who run and read could understand, was that caused by the British Government's default on gold payments. The implications of this new and dangerous threat to world economic stability was recognized by well-informed people. The effect it had on the members of a foundation's executive committee which was considering how best to invest a half-million dollars of funds illustrates that point. When our meeting opened, a fellow-member and prominent New York City banker told us the news and added, "How can we decide on anything today, gentlemen? No one can even guess what will happen next now that Great Britain has gone off the gold standard." Millions of men all over the globe held the same opinion. Britain's default pulled the thin rag carpet out from under Europe's slowly improving economy and its repercussions demoralized the economy of the rest of the world.

The President used every resource and device in his efforts to keep America from being dragged to the bottom of the world's economic pit. He invited thirty of the nation's financial leaders to confer with him, Secretary and Undersecretary of the Treasury Mellon and Mills, and Eugene Meyer, Governor of the Federal Reserve Board, on October 31, 1931. He presented to them the memorandum which is highlighted in Appendix XIV.

The RFC Is Born

He next asked the nation's bankers to form a credit pool of $500,000,000 for support of distressed banks. Most of the bankers present looked with favor on the proposal. He wanted capital, he said, which would be readily available for banks which were under pressure. He added that if the banks could not do this he would ask for emergency legislation which would ease the situation. At the President's request the bankers formed the National Credit Association. He stated that he wanted also to provide working capital for financially starved business enterprises. In late August 1931, he told me of this plan, then in the making, and expressed his belief that America could work her way out of her troubles provided our production machine could be kept operating and thereby furnishing jobs for working men. Sensing Britain's difficulties he publicly announced plans for this project six days before Britain slid off the gold standard. The project was named the Reconstruction Finance Corporation (RFC).

Soviets Rig Wheat Market

Going back one year to November 1, 1930, he was brought face to face with another and mighty contestant. This one ushered in the second phase of the world-wide catastrophe. The tip-off to the new troubles came with the collapse of European grain markets. Their prices dropped to an equivalent of about fifty cents per bushel in domestic markets. A panic was prevented by quick action of the Farm Board.

Discovery was made in the fall of 1930 that the Soviet government had sold a great amount of wheat short on the Chicago Board of Trade. Five days later a vice president of Amtorg (Soviet commercial agency in the United States), resigned and publicly stated the purpose of the Soviet government's raid was to create disorganization and disturbance. President Hoover took steps to prevent similar future raids by foreign governments in American markets.

Insurance Company Officials Hold Back

When insurance company officials were reluctant to make any promise other than not pressing mortgage foreclosures, the President created a plan for a Federal Land Board mortgage foreclosure program. *The object was to aid every man in every possible way who was doing his best to meet his obligations.*

Europe Goes Under Again

Following the 1930 elections the President's troubles with the Democratic Congress increased sharply since the Democrats now had a majority in the House. The Democrats were determined to destroy him politically. Even in the face of Democratic obstruction tactics the President continued to project and advance domestic recovery and relief programs. He sought also to create ways to meet the new foreign economic crises which were battering constantly against our economy. Mr. Hoover's appraisal of this situation as of the spring of 1931 is contained in Appendix XV.

In early 1931 panic abroad began to spread swiftly. Prices of securities and commodities shot downward. This in turn depressed our markets. One government after another defaulted on its public debts; revolution in Spain dethroned the king; the Soviet government continued to dump wheat on world markets and thereby depress its price to the harm of our wheat growers. American banks were weakened by central European governments' defaults on short-term loans. These loans aggregated approximately one and one-half billion dollars. And all central Europe was on the verge of complete economic collapse.

In an effort to alleviate the demoralized foreign situation, the President proposed suspension of all payments of inter-governmental debts for one year. The essence of his proposal was that we should, as a wise creditor, give debtor-governments time to recover a semblance of their national prosperity as well as to "be good neighbors." His proposal was conditional on a like postponement for the same period by other creditor governments. Since the proposal could be carried out only with the consent of Congress, he presented it to Senator Robinson, Senate Democratic leader and Congressman Garner, incoming Democratic Speaker of the House. Both of them disapproved his proposal.

Despite Robinson's and Garner's refusal to co-operate, the President continued to seek congressional support. In the end he secured enough promises to insure approval and publicly announced the proposal. The editor of a great London newspaper called it "the greatest thing since the signing of the armistice."

France alone of the group of creditor nations balked. But finally, after much filling and backing, face-saving and technical obstruction, the government of France reversed its earlier stand. But the French reversal was not made until after forty days of delay during which the central European and German situations rapidly deteriorated.

Europe Still Feverish

All Europe continued feverish but the worst seemed to be over. In late July, at a cabinet meeting, the President stated that the situation still was full of danger although there was the chance that "the prairie fire now put out on the continent may have caught in England." In one day French gold withdrawals from London totaled $125,000,000. The Bank of England raised the discount rate. Europe now began a further restriction of imports. This caused commodity prices to drop in the United States. The price of wheat on the Chicago market fell below any previous low. The price of cotton dropped to 6.70 cents per pound. Livestock went to half-century new lows. Money hoarders took $80,000,000 per week out of circulation.

The world was next filled with apprehension by an almost unbelievable incident—mutiny in the British Navy over that government's attempt to reduce sailor pay. This immediately precipitated heavy withdrawals of gold from the Bank of England. It created a frenzied panic which rocked European commodity markets and carried disturbing repercussions to our domestic commodity markets.

The Devil Pulls Out Another Gadget

His satanic majesty pulled another gadget from his bag of tricks before President Hoover was able to create ways to meet the new attacks on our economic stability by inspiring Japan to invade Manchuria.

The President was alarmed by Japan's gangster conquest of Manchuria, which began on September 18. Believing that Japan's actions, if unchallenged, carried an ominous threat to world peace and stability, he sought to enlist the governments of Great Britain and France to join with the United States in taking steps to check Japan's lawless move. The failure of foreign government leaders to appraise events as accurately and to see as far ahead as did Hoover, permitted Japan to set the pattern for dictator conquest which made World War II inevitable.

Meanwhile presidential measures were easing the worst strains. By mid-February 1932, industrial output and employment were on the up-turn. Hoarded currency began again to return to the banks. Prices of wheat and cotton stiffened. Gold withdrawals dropped to the vanishing point.

Congress Adjourns and the Sun Comes Out

Coincident with the adjournment of the Congress on July 16, 1932, the world depression hit solid bottom. Recovery began at that point. The Dow Jones average of thirty leading industrial stocks shows that they reached their lowest level, 40.56, on July 8, 1932. Two months later, September 8, 1932, their average had climbed to 81.39, after which they began to drop. The September 8 date coincided with the news of the outcome of the Maine elections which foreshadowed the defeat of President Hoover. The average of these thirty stocks continued to drop until February 27, 1933, when it reached its next low of 49.08.

The nation, under President Hoover's leadership, had weathered five major crises. The first was created by the stock market collapse in the fall of 1929; the second came from the Austrian and German banking crash which occurred in June, 1931; the third followed England's departure from the gold standard in September, 1931; the fourth was created by the flight of the dollar from the United States in February, 1932; and the fifth by the refusal of the Democratic Congress to cooperate with the President on a recovery program during the first six and one-half months of 1932.

By midsummer 1932 the power of the destructive world economic forces was spent. Every country had gone through the economic wringer. Now people everywhere could start afresh and begin to work their way out of their difficulties. Signs of recovery were unmistakable everywhere outside the United States. At home, where a presidential election was in the offing, they advanced zigzag fashion with some forward movement and a great deal of zigging and zagging.

It is an academic question whether or not a president who had easy principles and who had been trained in the harlotry-phase of politics could have gained support for his program from an opposition Congress which looked with glazed, unmoving eyes on the coming national election.

CHAPTER FIFTEEN

Budget and Reorganization Problems with Congress

The collapse of the speculative boom in the United States, which followed its collapse throughout the world, the shocks and dislocations on our economy, combined with loss of some public support by consideration and enactment of the Hawley-Smoot Tariff Bill, enabled the Democratic party to gain control of the House in the 1930 elections. The elections also reduced the regular Republican membership in the Senate to thirty-six with the support of twelve "Progressive" Republicans and one Farmer-Laborite. The Republicans were able to organize the Senate, but they were not able to get a working majority.

The Democratic candidates had promised as voter bait that they would present a program which would redeem the country from the depression.

Previous to the convening of the new Democratic Congress in December 1931, President Hoover conferred with Senator Joseph Robinson of Arkansas, Democratic leader in the Senate, and John N. Garner, newly designated Speaker-to-be of the House, and reviewed with them the gravity of the domestic situation. He expressed his sincere desire to co-operate with them and added that he would go the limit in supporting any constructive program they offered. All he sought, he stated, was to do what was best for the country.

These two Democratic leaders told the President that it was his "responsibility to propose a program and ours to criticize it."

Later, when the Democratic members of Congress continued to obstruct, oppose and criticize, the President requested Republican House Leader Snell, Congressman Hawley and others to arrange a conference with Speaker Garner and Democratic House Leader Rainey, and present to them the dangers which were threatening the nation in an effort to gain their co-operation in support of any constructive program.

Snell, Hawley and their colleagues at the conference, at the suggestion of President Hoover, promised to give the Democrats full credit for their help, even proposing that they introduce their full share of the measures. But Garner and Rainey would agree to nothing. In reporting by letter to the President, Congressman Hawley said: "Mr. Rainey stated that he would not sponsor the legislation as proposed by you nor would he urge the committees having jurisdiction of such legislation to consider and favorably report thereon. When I urged that the welfare of the country and its people required the prompt enactment of remedial legislation as proposed by you he gave as the reason for his refusal 'We intend to beat him, Hoover.' He repeated this in other words . . ."

The determination of the Democrats to play politics and their refusal to support a constructive program left the President two alternative courses of action, that of waging a constant battle with the Democratic-controlled Congress and that of doing his best to cooperate, consult, explain and plead.

Because of his firmly held belief that no President should undermine the inherent independence of the other two branches of government, he followed the second course.

That the crisis was so grave he dared not, because it would arouse public fears to the point of panic, try to enlist public support for his program. Thus he was unable to obtain the popular support which conceivably could have forced the obstructing and recalcitrant Democratic leaders to place country ahead of party. Instead they dumped a great variety and a vast number of ill-considered proposals into the legislative hopper in both Houses.

The Democratic recovery program consisted largely of the following items:

1. Reduced the Tariff Commission to a mere statistical body under the control of Congress.
2. Passed an inadequate revenue bill which left the budget unbalanced.
3. Passed a bill instructing the Federal Reserve System and the Treasury Department to fix prices at averages prevailing during

the years 1921–1929 by constantly shifting the volume of currency and credit—in short, creating the rubber dollar.

4. Defeated the administration's national economy measure to reduce ordinary expenditures by $250,000,000 by cutting the savings to less than $50,000,000.
5. Passed the Garner-Rainey pork-barrel bill which sought to increase public expenditures by $1,200,000,000 for public works.
6. Passed a bill for the cash prepayment of the soldier's bonus which called for the immediate expenditure of $2,300,000,000.
7. Passed a $2,000,000,000 fiat money bill.
8. Passed the Rainey bill which provided for direct personal banking for any conceivable purpose and for every conceivable security and which would have put the government into destructive competition with private business but for the President's veto.
9. Passed a bill which called for the expenditure of $322,000,000 for miscellaneous odds-and-ends.
10. Passed a bill which authorized the President to reorganize the government and eliminate useless government bureaus and departments and then voided the purpose of the bill by later refusing to approve his recommendations.

Hoover Sought Congressional Co-operation

When the world was staggered by the crisis created by the British collapse in October, 1931, President Hoover movingly called upon Congress for unity and co-operation outside of politics. He took counsel with both Democratic and Republican leaders. Some Democrats responded splendidly, but the main body of the opposition tried to sabotage the Hoover program by delay. Their purpose was political victory in 1932.

This Democratic partisan purpose explains why in a great crisis Congress required 46 days of dawdling debate before it passed the legislation for creating the RFC. The President had asked that this new and useful instrument of government be given widespread powers for the purpose of checking the depression. When the opposition finished working the RFC proposal over, that wholly new and valuable organization came out of their debates with limited resources and scope. Two hundred and twenty-one days later the opposition grudgingly provided it with the powers, vital to agriculture and employment, which the President had originally requested.

On December 8, 1931, the President asked for an increase in the capital of the land banks and an entire revision of the land bank system, thereby enabling these institutions to meet farm mortgage emergencies. The Democrats delayed forty-four days before they were willing to put this proposal through the legislative hopper—forty-four days of delay which cost thousands of farmers their property through foreclosures.

On December 8, 1931 the President proposed the creation of Home Loan Banks to (a) relieve the pressure on home owners and (b) to stimulate home building. Two hundred and twenty-two days later —more than seven months—and after thousands of mortgages had been foreclosed on homes, they passed an attenuated bill.

To meet the contraction of credit which had been caused by foreign withdrawals of gold, the President asked for an act which extended the "eligibility" paper of the Federal Reserve System. This the opposition did after eighty days.

On February 29, 1932 the President outlined a comprehensive reform program of bankruptcy laws. He sought to adjust the burdensome debt of farmers, home owners, railways and business. The Democratic Congress dawdled for an entire year before acting.

Recognizing the need for a drastic reform of the nation's entire banking system, President Hoover called for legislation to make deposits safe as early as December, 1929, but he never was able to secure its adoption.

The President in late 1931 also asked for legislation to provide loans on the assets of closed banks for the purpose of facilitating distribution to depositors and at the same time to conserve the assets of the closed banks. The Democrats did not act on this request while he was in office.

He also asked for revision of railroad regulation designed to strengthen railroad service credit and finance but was able to get only token legislation.

Summed up, the Democratic leadership in Congress, with the support of all but a handful of that party's more patriotic members, adopted and followed delay and obstructionist tactics in the face of the impending crisis. They refused to approve the President's recommendations. They failed to offer an acceptable program of their own. Their purpose, as stated by their leader, was to "scrutinize" the President's program. So they "scrutinized" and dawdled while the world was falling apart and need and fear stalked the land.

Budget Problems

In his second annual message of December 2, 1930 President Hoover gave Congress the first official notice of budgetary difficulties. In it he stated that estimates of receipts and expenditures, which had been made a year earlier at a time when the severity of the depression could not be forecast, now presented a different picture. Instead of a surplus of $123,000,000 the revised estimates of decreased receipts of $430,000,000 and increased expenditures for construction work, and for veterans' services of about $225,000,000, would adversely change the earlier budget estimates by $655,000,000. He expressed the belief that economies which could be effected in governmental operation would substantially reduce this sum.

By October 1931 the government was faced with a further drop in government revenues of over $2,000,000,000 from the pre-depression normal. Estimates indicated that there would be a deficit in the following year's budget of $1,500,000,000 at a time when expenditures for relief must be increased. On the following November 6th he announced at a press conference that he would propose a $350,000,000 cut in government expenditures in an effort to help bring the budget into balance. He recommended that additional appropriations be confined to necessary federal government activities which were designed to avoid public distress, to meet unemployment and agricultural problems.

On December 8, 1931, in his third annual message he reported to

Congress that after allowing for drastic reductions in expenditures there was an indicated budget deficit of $1,417,000,000 which he recommended should be handled by a further reduction in expenditures and an increase in taxes. He reported also that federal government expenditures for public construction for that calendar year were expected to reach $780,000,000 as compared with $260,000,000 in 1928. Altogether the Hoover administration expended nearly $2,400,000,000 on public works construction as an aid to employment of workers.

Instead of considering and acting upon the President's recommendations to balance outgo with income by legislating to provide for reduction of operating expenditures and additional revenues, Speaker Garner, on January 1, 1932, announced that the House Ways and Means Committee would first consider tariff legislation. On January 8, through a press announcement, the President, after stating that "we cannot squander ourselves into prosperity" stressed the need for legislation which would permit reduction of expenditures and for legislation which would produce additional revenues.

President Hoover repeatedly called on the Congress for legislation which would authorize him to consolidate departments and agencies and thereby eliminate duplication of services and waste, but the Democratic Congress granted him only piecemeal authority. Can it be that their niggardliness in this respect so greatly troubled the consciences of those men who were still members of the Congress in 1947 that they felt compelled to join in inviting him to head the government Reorganization Commission which Congress had created that year?

Back in 1930, 1931 and 1932, many of these same Democratic members of Congress and their colleagues listened with deaf ears to Mr. Hoover's pleas for authority to reorganize these same departments, for the same purpose—namely, that of reducing government expenditures through elimination of duplication and to tone up the government service by making it more efficient.

President Hoover's repeated requests that Congress levy new taxes also went unheeded. He asked for the adoption of a national sales tax on certain articles. Fiorello LaGuardia, then Congressman and later Mayor of New York City, spearheaded the opposition to this proposal and defeated it. He accused the President, among other things, of trying to shift the burden of government deficits on the backs of the poor so that he could protect the rich. Later, as Mayor of New York City, when he needed additional revenues, Mr. LaGuardia forced the adoption of a sales tax on the people of that city—the identical tax President Hoover had proposed previously.

Once, when I chided the mayor about his complete flip-flop in the sales tax as an equitable and substantial source of public revenue, he admitted that he had been wrong ("my greatest mistake") in opposing the President's sales tax proposal. "Greatest mistake" or not, his anguished cries over what he as congressman called "the iniquities of the sales tax" and his serious charges against President Hoover concerning the proposal helped to heighten as well as spread the hue and cry against the President. It colored the distressed public's feeling about him as an unfeeling man who was indifferent to the needs of the poor.

In the light of the public's present indifference to sixteen years of unbalanced budgets it seems certain that President Hoover hurt his public position by his repeated and earnest insistence that the Congress should provide him with legislation which would enable him to balance the budget.

Be that as it may, he expressed his belief on March 25, 1932, that a balanced budget was:

> . . . the keystone of recovery. It must be done. Without it the several measures of restoration of public confidence and reconstruction which we have already undertaken will be incomplete and the depression will be prolonged indefinitely . . .

Prophetic words?

At one time President Hoover recommended, for the purpose of securing prompt action and unity of effort in balancing the budget and at the same time protecting "the vital service of the government"; that the two Houses of the Congress delegate members.

> . . . who together with representatives of the Executive, should be authorized to frame for action by the present Congress a complete

national program of economy and to recommend legislation necessary to make it possible and effective.

The President made this proposal, he said, because he was "convinced that only by such unified non-partisan effort . . . can we attain the success so manifestly necessary in the public interest."

This proposal was jeered to death by Senator Joe Robinson and other Democratic leaders on the grounds that it was "another commission."

On May 5, 1932, the President sent another pointed message to the Congress in which he said, "The most essential factor to economic recovery today is the restoration of confidence." The public confidence "had been diminished," he declared, by the tax measures passed by the House, by its action in approving legislation which would increase government expenditures and its "virtual destruction of both the national economy program proposed by the Executive officials and the Special House Committee on Economy."

On May 6, following a whirlwind attack by the Democrats on his message of the previous day, the President issued a public statement in support of his message. In it he said:

> The issue before the country is the re-establishment of confidence and speed toward recovery by ending these delays in balancing the budget through immediate passage of revenue measures and reduction of government expenditures. It is not a partisan issue. This was one of the most important steps of the non-partisan program for restoring stability proposed by me and patriotically accepted by the leaders of both political parties last December. Effective programs, projects, estimates, and possibilities for both economy and revenue have been presented and are known in every detail.
>
> This is not a controversy between the President and Congress or its members. It is an issue of the people against delays and destructive legislation which impair the credit of the United States. It is also an issue between the people and the locust swarm of lobbyists who haunt the halls of Congress seeking selfish privilege for special groups and sections of the country, misleading members as to the real views of the people by showers of propaganda.

What is urgently required is immediate action upon and conclusion of these questions. This is a serious hour which demands that all elements of the government and the people rise with stern courage above partisanship to meet the needs of our national life.

Editorially discussing Congressional obstructionist tactics, the *New York Times* said:

A Democratic senator, Mr. Harrison, calls upon the President to bring order out of chaos. The budget is not balanced. Tax plans have gone astray. "If ever there was a time," he says, "when the President ought to speak out to his leaders in Congress, it is now." But the President has been speaking out to his leaders and appealing to his adversaries, vigorously and consistently since Congress convened five months ago. On the importance of Federal retrenchment and the necessity of balancing the budget he has spoken in no less than 21 messages, statements and addresses. . . . Responsibility for the chaos which now exists in Washington rests upon those members of Congress who have blocked the President at every turn and bolted their own party leadership.

As though in cynical reply to the President's appeal, Senator Walsh of Massachusetts proposed the issue of $2,000,000,000 of fiat money. The House passed the Patman Bonus Bill of $2,400,000,000 to be paid with fiat money. The House then passed the Garner $2,300,000,000 pork-barrel bill. These congressional proposals and measures for increased expenditures, combined with the refusal of the Congress to approve the President's economy proposals, served further to destroy public confidence, create tensions and stimulate increasing uncertainty and fear. Together they further postponed the start toward real recovery.

The President had repeatedly asked the Congress for, and failed to get from it: (a) banking reform; (b) authority to make loans to liquidate banks; (c) reform of bankruptcy laws; (d) regulation of interstate transmission of electric power; (e) revision of railway consolidation laws; (f) revision of the anti-trust laws in respect to natural resource industries; (g) authority to create a new world war debt commission; (h) an increase in revenues by about $400,000,000; and (i) a reduction of expenditures by an additional $300,000,000.

He did wring from the Congress: (a) ratification of the international debt moratorium; (b) creation of the RFC with resources of up to $3,500,000,000 for the support of banks, insurance companies, building and loan associations, railways, and authority to make loans for productive work and for employment relief, agricultural credit banks, and to states; (c) legislation to expand the Land Banks; (d) expansion of "eligibility" paper of the Reserve Board; (e) Federal Home Loan Banks; (f) reduction of Federal expenditures by $300,000,000; (g) limited authority to reorganize government departments in the interest of economy; (h) increase of public works construction for employment purposes aggregating over $700,000,000 in one year; (i) drought relief; (j) appropriation from Farm Board's commodity stocks of large amounts of wheat and cotton for people in distress.

Extracts from the copies of letters I wrote about this time throw an interesting light on what was going on back of the scenes during those troubled days.

The first one dated January 9, 1932, said in part:

> I lunched with the Hoovers Monday and found the President very tired. He invited me to go to the office after lunch where we discussed several situations at considerable length. One of these concerned his inability to get permission from Congress to carry out his governmental reorganization program. He passionately wants tc eliminate the waste and the ineffective operation of the federal government first to reduce its cost and second to tone up the whole service. But to date the Democrats in Congress have blocked him. At one point he showed that he still has his old whimsical trait (but his face is haggard and shows signs of getting hard) by remarking that he was about convinced that about the only way to perpetuate our democratic form of government would be for us to put a dictator in power for a six months' period about once every fifty years; give him unrestricted authority to scrape all the barnacles off the ship of state during that time—and then he added: We should station an army close by to Washington somewhere in Virginia, over which the dictator would have no authority, and give it sealed orders to start marching toward Washington the last day of the dic-

tator's six months' period of service. This would give the dictator time to get away safely.

One paragraph from another letter, dated May 18, 1932, said:

> The relief plan which Senator Robinson [Democratic Senate leader from Arkansas] presented Monday of last week was one of those trying to beat the gun propositions. Robinson had to move fast if he were to get Democratic credit for a relief plan the President already had nearly perfected and was almost ready to announce. When Robinson got the confidential information that the President would soon make some new relief program recommendations he used them all as his own in a hurriedly prepared speech. You may remember that Robinson said in his speech that he would supplement it with a public statement the following day, meaning of course that he had not had time to finish the job then.
>
> The guess is that Harvey Couch leaked. At least the President had discussed his plan in detail with the RFC, and as you know Couch and Robinson are old friends and both are Arkansas Democrats. (From author's personal files.)

These two excerpts indicate which way the wind was blowing. The Democrats tied the President's hands on the budget and reorganization and stole his relief program. Their evident purpose was to prevent his getting credit for anything.

It is somewhat remarkable that Governor Roosevelt, in the 1932 campaign, charged that spending of President Hoover's administration (note the Governor did not say *the Democratic Congress during the Hoover administration*) was "the most reckless and extravagant pace I have ever been able to discover in the statistical record of any peacetime government anywhere, any time." It was, he said, "shocking," "spendthrift," "appalling," "bankruptcy."

The Hoover administration's four year financial record shows that its total deficit was $3,479,541,003, of which amount $2,397,267,363 has since been repaid from recoverable loans. This leaves a net deficit for the four Hoover administration years of $1,082,273,640.

This record could hardly be called "shocking," "spendthrift," or "appalling" when compared with the record which followed it.

CHAPTER SIXTEEN

The 1932 Campaign and Post-Election Doldrums

There had been so much traffic for three and one-half years in the "dark alleys of inspired propaganda" in which "ideals and men [were] assassinated with poisonous whisperings" that President Hoover was unable to check and overcome it during a brief two-months' campaign period.

In addition he had to meet politically damaging statements such as the following Governor Roosevelt made in a speech delivered October 25, 1932:

> The crash came in October, 1929. The President had at his disposal all the instrumentalities of government. From that day until December 31, 1931, he did absolutely nothing to remedy the situation. Not only did he do nothing, but he took the position that Congress could do nothing.

How could a President answer such a charge? The dignity of his office prevents his use of the short ugly word the people readily understand. A recital of all that he had done to help carry the people, the government and the world through social, economic and political catastrophe would have sounded like an alibi.

In a speech he delivered on September 29, Governor Roosevelt charged that:

> We are spending altogether too much money for government services that are neither practical nor necessary. And then in addition we are attempting too many functions. We need to simplify what the Federal government is giving to the people.
>
> I accuse the present administration of being the greatest spending administration in peacetime in all our history. It is an administration that has piled bureau on bureau, commission on commission. . . .

Bureaus and bureaucrats, commissions and commissions have been retained at the expense of the taxpayer.

Governor Roosevelt returned to this subject on October 19. He next stated that "our credit structure is being impaired by the unorthodox federal financing made necessary by the unprecedented magnitude of these [the Hoover administration's] deficits."

Limited by the kind of language which should appear in print I can only say: *Great Caesar's Ghost!*

President Hoover's 1932 campaign speeches were among the most effective he ever delivered. But they came too late. Mr. Michelson and his staff, public distress and the hamstringing activities of the Democratic Congress had done more harm during the previous three and one-half years than he could overcome.

The Democrats' twin objective was to defeat Hoover and elect a Democratic administration in 1932. They succeeded. At the same time, and perhaps unwittingly and without design, they accomplished something of infinitely greater moment, a something the effects of which continue in full force today; namely, the destruction of the people's faith in the integrity and high purpose of a President of the United States and in their government officials.

There was a definite turn for the better in the economic situation during the summer of 1932. Cotton and wheat prices advanced more than 20 per cent in August and September; the Federal Reserve Board's index of industrial production moved upward from 56 in July to 68 in October. The American Federation of Labor reported that 714,000 unemployed men had found jobs between July 1 and October 1. Department store sales moved upward 8 per cent during the same period. Daily average freight car loadings jumped from 80,000 in early July to 96,000 during the first two weeks of October. Moody reported net earnings of 63 principal railroads increased 95 per cent in the third quarter of 1932 over the second quarter. Standard Statistics' index of 351 industrial stocks moved from 34 in July to 56 in September. Bank and business failures fell off perceptibly in August and September.

The *New York Times* (June 16, 1934) stated that "The change for the better in the last half of 1932 is beyond dispute. That this evident revival of confidence was suddenly reversed in February 1933 is equally true."

This improved situation began to disintegrate shortly after President Hoover's defeat in the November elections.

An Objective Appraisal of the Situation

The following paragraphs from an editorial which was published in the Toledo, Ohio, *Times* on August 10, 1949 contain a clear and accurate report of the Washington scene between early November, 1932 and March 4, 1933:

> But that was not all, not by any means. After the election of 1932, Mr. Hoover was subjected by Mr. Roosevelt to the most cruel, most unjust, most bitter, most coldly-calculated campaign of political destruction ever before known. At Mr. Roosevelt's bidding, the slogan of the Democratic members of Congress, then in the majority, became: "We will save the nation, but not Hoover."
>
> Mr. Roosevelt ordered Democratic leaders in the Senate to confirm no Hoover nominations. He directed them to reject the President's proposal for a manufacturers' sales tax, for which Mr. Hoover made a personal appeal before the Senate alone. He ordered them, in fact, to pass nothing Mr. Hoover recommended.
>
> Thus, in January, the Congress, on Mr. Roosevelt's orders, refused to accept the bank-conservator bill, which had been carefully prepared to bolster up the banking institution. Yet, five days after Mr. Roosevelt was in office, the Democrats, at their leader's request included that selfsame bill, word for word, in the emergency banking act of March 9, 1933, because they could not prepare a better one.
>
> Mr. Roosevelt left unanswered for days Mr. Hoover's request to join him in a statement that would allay public fears. He didn't reply until he was forced to, and, then, only to refuse to co-operate. "We will save the nation, but not Hoover."

Post-Election Disaster

President Hoover, in an address to Republicans which he delivered at Glendale, California, on November 12, 1932, said in part:

The majority of the people have decided to entrust the government to a new administration. The political campaign is over.

I asked for unity of national action in the constructive measures which have been initiated during the past three years for care of distress to protect the Nation from imminent dangers and to promote economic recovery. If we are to continue the recovery so evidently in progress during the past few months by overcoming the many difficulties which still confront us we must have continued unity in constructive action all along the economic front. I shall work for that unity during the remaining four months of this administration. Furthermore it is our duty after the 4th of March to co-operate with our opponents in every sound measure for the restoration of prosperity.

I am making early return to Washington in special concern that the measures and instrumentalities which we have in motion on an entirely non-partisan basis shall continue to function vigorously and contribute their utmost. . . .

In his fourth annual message to Congress, December 6, 1932, with its "Information on the State of the Union" together with recommendations of measures for consideration, President Hoover stated that during the previous year the nation had remained at peace, public service had been rendered with devotion, industrial peace had never before been so widespread, education and service had made great strides, public health had reached its highest point and domestic tranquility and acceptance of the results of the recent election "furnish abundant proof in the strength of our institutions."

With grim Quaker insistence he continued in his final annual message to appeal to Congress to revise the nation's banking laws.

Recognizing how closely domestic recovery was linked with world recovery he again informed Congress of this close relationship and stressed the need for co-operation with foreign nations in many measures if recovery were to be achieved. He stated also that the government had taken steps to co-operate with foreign nations in an effort "to secure rapid and assured recovery and protection for the future." Extracts from this last annual message on the state of the nation, banking reform and world co-operation are contained in Appendix XVI.

It was natural that the public should look to President-elect Roosevelt for the nation's future policies. And being the kind of good citizen he was it was just as natural that President Hoover should seek, as he directed administration officials by telephone from Palo Alto the day after election, "to explore the avenues of constructive action which might be pursued within the area apparently outside of conflict between the incoming and the outgoing administrations." He issued these instructions because he believed that it was vital to the public interest that the recent rate of progress should be maintained if possible.

It was to that end President Hoover worked unceasingly until March 4, 1933 without being able to secure the President-elect's cooperation.

On November 12 he telegraphed his successor about one of the first problems to arise. It concerned what action the government should take on the question of foreign government debt payments. The question had been projected by the British Ambassador who had stated that his government ". . . earnestly hope the United States government will see its way clear to enter into an exchange of views at the earliest possible moment." The British Ambassador also requested a suspension of the installment on his government's debt ($95,000,000) which would fall due on December 15. After having learned that other debtor governments were to make similar requests President Hoover asked for a personal conference with Governor Roosevelt for the purpose of learning his views as to policies since negotiations begun at that time would extend into the incoming administration.

The two principals, with aids, met on November 22, at the White House. Apparent agreement as to policy was reached. It was also agreed that the two men should issue their own memorandums. This they did. Following the publication of the President's and the President-elect's separate memorandums the following editorial comment concerning them appeared:

The Detroit *Free Press* said:

It is highly unfortunate that Governor Roosevelt was unable to bring himself to meet the President half way. The refusal of the governor to co-operate actively with Mr. Hoover and his subsequent statement that the matter at issue was "not his baby," are indicative of the lack of largeness and vision more disquieting in a person about to become the Chief Executive of the nation. . . . Mr. Roosevelt had an opportunity unique in the history of the American presidency, and he failed to grasp it.

The New York *Herald Tribune* in its November 24 issue made the comment that:

Americans are so accustomed to having Mr. Hoover do the right and courageous thing that his admirable statement on the debts will hardly occasion surprise. It covers a complex issue, endlessly bedeviled by national prejudices and selfishness, clearly, fairly, and with a minimum of words. . . .

It may be recalled that during the campaign there was heat and resentment in Democratic quarters when it was argued that a change of administration inevitably meant marking time for a number of months. Mr. Hoover has now done his utmost to prevent such a delay in respect to the debt issue. Mr. Roosevelt has felt unable to aid him. The delay must ensue.

On the same date the Baltimore *Sun* said:

[Although foreign debts] may not be legally his baby until the fourth of March . . . it seems to us that Mr. Roosevelt might wisely have given thought to the possibility that this baby, which is not now his, may soon develop into an unruly stepchild, permanently lodged under his roof, and disposed to play with matches.

The principal debtor governments made their December 15 payments with the exception of France, which offered the view that the President-elect did not regard payment of the December 15 installment to be a necessary condition for opening negotiations for debt adjustment.

This recital of the President-elect's failure to co-operate is related to the banking crisis that shortly was to engulf the nation.

President-elect Refuses to Co-operate on Economic Conference

An even greater cause for public disquiet and uncertainty followed President Hoover's telegraphic appeal to his successor on December 17, for his views on and co-operation with the Hoover-arranged World Economic Conference. The President made the further request that the President-elect join him in the selection of "such delegation."

Distorted published versions of the exchange of views between the two prompted the President to give out the complete correspondence on December 22, with the statement:

> Governor Roosevelt considers that it is undesirable for him to accede to my suggestions for co-operative action in the foreign proposals outlined in my recent message to Congress. I will respect his wishes. . . .

The President-elect's refusal to co-operate on the Economic Conference impeded and delayed world recovery and the return to stable money standards.

Hoover Continues Budget Balancing Efforts

Following the election, President Hoover continued his three-year effort to get the Democratic Congress to balance the budget, but it refused to do so. A reasonable assumption is that it was saving this for an accomplishment of the incoming President (who did not balance it during the next twelve years) as indicated by his March 10, 1933 message to the Congress in which he said:

> For three long years the Federal Government has been on the road toward bankruptcy. . . .
>
> With the utmost seriousness I point out to the Congress the profound effect of this fact upon our national economy. It has contributed to the recent collapse of our banking structure. It has accentuated the stagnation of the economic life of our people. It has added to the ranks of the unemployed. Our Government's house is not in order, and for many reasons no effective action has been taken to restore it to order.
>
> Upon the unimpaired credit of the United States Government rest

the safety of deposits, the security of insurance policies, the activity of industrial enterprises, the value of our agricultural products, and the availability of employment. . . . National recovery depends upon it.

The effect of the failure to balance the budget upon the growth of the banking crisis is undoubted. The responsibility for this dates back to December 27, 1932, when the events began that prevented budget balancing.

Garner Plays Hob With Recovery

Speaker of the House and Vice President-elect John N. Garner, on January 4, 1933, threw more sand in the gear box of the nation's economic and financial machine by securing the passage of a resolution which commanded the RFC to make public all loans it had made prior to July 21, 1932.

President Hoover used his best efforts to stop this Congressional action, as also did Jesse Jones and former Senator Atlee Pomerene of Ohio, both Democrats and both members of the RFC board. But hell-bent for destruction of the already defeated Hoover, Garner and his fellow Democrats ignored the President's protest as well as those from other leaders and passed the legislation. Chairman Pomerene of the RFC later publicly stated:

> The banks which got RFC loans were good banks. The loans were amply secured as the law required. Requests for loans did not mean that the applicant banks were unsound, but some silly persons construed them that way. *It was the most damnable and vicious thing that ever was done. It almost counteracted all the good that we have been able to do.* (Italics author's.)

On February 20, President Hoover appealed to the Democratic majority to repeal the legislation by saying:

> . . . This publication . . . is exaggerating fears and is introducing a new element of great danger. It is drying up the sources of credit . . . is forcing payment by distressed creditors to replenish bank funds. It is causing the hoarding of currency.

New currency hoarding and runs on banks which stemmed directly from this "outrage" started a new bank panic which closed many banks and in turn affected the stability of a larger number of other banks. This was particularly true of the banking situation in Michigan which now became alarming.

A critically sick economy is not able to stand serious shocks. But our critically ill economy already was receiving premonitions of a still more severe shock.

Inflation and Currency Devaluation Rumors Afloat

Writing many years afterward, on August 11, 1949, about this troubled situation, the editor of the Cumberland, Maryland, *News* stated that:

> There are at least two valid indictments in this field which we believe history will sustain against Mr. Roosevelt:
>
> (1) The evil slump downward, which American affairs took in the Autumn of 1932, was precipitated when word got around that he intended, if elected, to take the country off the gold standard. His spokesmen, Carter Glass among them, denied this on his behalf. But everybody with gold in the bank took it out, so that the depression began to look like a cataclysm.
>
> (2) Mr. Roosevelt's vicious sense of drama led him, in the interval between his election and his inauguration, to evade contacts with the retiring President, and refuse to join him in any reassuring acts or statements. It is a hard thing to say, but on the record it looks as if his purpose was to make things look as bad as possible, so that he could work a Transformation Scene. . . .

Whatever may have been the President-elect's motives there can be no question but that discussion of campaign issues had made the public apprehensive over the possibilities of inflation and devaluation of the currency. To quiet this growing public concern during the campaign, candidate Roosevelt requested Senator Carter Glass of Virginia, a man of unquestioned probity who held conservative monetary views, to reassure the country about the soundness of the Democratic position on these questions. This Senator Glass attempted to do. A few days later, on November 4, four days before election, Governor Roosevelt said in a speech:

> One of the most commonly repeated misrepresentations by the Republican speakers, including the President, has been the claim that the Democratic position with regard to money has not been made sufficiently clear. The President is seeing visions of rubber dollars. But that is only a part of his campaign of fear. I am not going to characterize these statements. I merely present the facts.
>
> The Democratic platform specifically declares, "we advocate a sound currency to be preserved at all hazards." That, I take it, is plain English.
>
> In discussing this platform on July 30, I said, "Sound money is an international necessity; not a domestic consideration for one nation alone." In other words, I want to see sound money in all the world.
>
> Far up in the Northwest at Butte I repeated the pledge of the platform, saying "sound money must be maintained at all regards."
>
> In Seattle I reaffirmed my attitude on this question. The thing has been said, therefore, in plain English three times in my speeches. It is stated without qualification in the platform and I have announced my unqualified acceptance of that platform in every plank.

This statement, at that time, should have quieted public apprehension about his position on the questions of inflation and devaluation. It failed to do so because, partly through grapevine, partly through hints in the press and partly through leaks of the President-elect's confreres the word began to spread that inflation and devaluation were on the way.

That the grapevine was an especially potent force in destroying public confidence in stock values is illustrated by the advice given to friends of mine in the banking world. They were confidentially advised by some associates of the President-elect to dump all of their securities, help snowball the depression and depress the market and thereby enable the new administration to start from the bottom. If this were to be done then financial conditions would have to improve, since they could not get worse, and everyone who followed this course could make a real killing.

Effectively supporting the demoralizing effect on the stock market of such advice were the public comments on inflation and devaluation which were being made at frequent intervals by Senator Wheeler of Montana, Connally of Texas, Thomas of Oklahoma, Professor George L. Warren of Cornell University and a dozen or so Democratic congressmen.

By January 23, the public had become jittery on the subject. On that date Alexander Dana Noyes, financial editor of the *New York Times,* urged upon President-elect Roosevelt the necessity of his reassuring the public that he would not tinker with the currency.

> It is probable enough that the present spirit of hesitancy, not only in financial markets but in general trade is more or less influenced by lack of such reassurance. . . .
>
> In numerous older similar occasions doubt and mistrust prevailed with exceedingly bad effect on financial sentiment, until the President-elect took matters into his own hands and publicly avowed his purposes. This was notably true in the pre-inauguration period of 1885 and 1893, at both of which junctures the maintenance of gold payments was being discussed uneasily and at both of which Mr. Cleveland stated so positively and so courageously his own views of the general problem as to remove at once all apprehension.

On February 13, when no such reassurances had been made by the President-elect, Mr. Noyes returned to the subject with the following remarks:

> However ill-grounded may be the fear of dangerous experiment with the currency, the mere fact that such things are publicly talked about by their promoters has necessarily thrown a shadow over financial confidence at a time when mental influences are of paramount importance and when confidence is needed urgently. The Federal Reserve gold holdings . . . never [were] equaled in its history except one period of a few months.

In the meantime Senator Elmer Thomas of Oklahoma stated on the floor of the Senate, on January 30, 1933:

> . . . inasmuch as apparently the responsible leader of the United States, soon to be, is now convinced that something must be done to cheapen the dollar, I desire to make plain, if I may, my position upon this question.
>
> Mr. President, I am in favor of cheapening the buying power of the American dollar. If this can be done, to the extent that the dollar is cheapened to the same extent will commodity prices be increased.

Speaking before a Senate Committee on February 14, Bernard M. Baruch said that he regarded

> . . . the condition of this country the most serious in its history . . . inflation . . . is the road to ruin. . . . The mere talk of inflation retards business. If you start talking about that [devaluation] you would not have a nickel's worth of gold in the Reserve System day after tomorrow.

During the period while these doubts and fears were paralyzing commerce and industry, weakening or closing banks, starting anew in a frenzied, panicky way dollar flight and currency hoarding, the President-elect was on Vincent Astor's yacht taking a vacation.

Exports of gold reached $114,000,000 during the first two weeks of February and in the week ending February 11, domestic hoarding had jumped to $149,000,000. The banks in Michigan were in such bad condition by now that the governor of that state declared a bank holiday on February 14.

President Vainly Seeks Co-operation of President-elect

On February 17, despite his earlier rebuffs at attempted co-operation with the President-elect, President Hoover again addressed him. In this letter he said:

> A most critical situation has arisen in the country of which I feel it is my duty to advise you confidentially. I am therefore taking this course of writing you myself and sending it to you through the Secret Service for your hand direct as obviously its misplacement would only feed the fire and increase the dangers.

The major difficulty is the state of the public mind, for there is a steadily degenerating confidence in the future which has reached the height of general alarm. I am convinced that a very early statement by you upon two or three policies of your Administration would serve greatly to restore confidence and cause a resumption of the march of recovery.

The large part which fear and apprehension play in the situation can well be demonstrated by repeated experience in the past few years and the tremendous lift which has come at times by the removal of fear can be easily demonstrated.

. . . I therefore return to my suggestion at the beginning as to the desirability of clarifying the public mind on certain essentials which will give renewed confidence. It is obvious that as you will shortly be in a position to make whatever policies you wish effective, you are the only one who can give these assurances. Both the nature of the cause of public alarm and experience give such an action the prospect of success in turning the tide. I do not refer to action on all the causes of alarm, but it would steady the country greatly if there could be prompt assurance that there will be no tampering or inflation of the currency; that the budget will be unquestionably balanced, even if further taxation is necessary; that the Government credit will be maintained by refusal to exhaust it in the issue of securities. The course you have adopted in inquiring into the problems of world stabilization are already known and helpful. It would be of further help if the leaders could be advised to cease publication of RFC business.

I am taking the liberty of addressing you because both in my anxiety over the situation and my confidence from four years of experience that such tides as are now running can be moderated and the processes of regeneration which are always running can be released.

Incidentally, I will welcome the announcement of the new Secretary of the Treasury, as that would enable us to direct activities to one point of action and communication with your good self.

On March 1, President-elect's answer reached the White House. He wrote:

Dear Mr. President:

I am dismayed to find that the inclosed which I wrote in New York a week ago did not go to you, through an assumption by my secretary that it was only a draft of a letter.

Now I have yours of yesterday and can only tell you that I appreciate your fine spirit of co-operation and that I am in constant touch with the situation through Mr. Woodin, who is conferring with Ogden and with various people in N. Y. I am inclined to agree that a very early special session will be necessary—and by tonight or tomorrow I hope to settle on a definite time—I will let you know—you doubtless know of the proposal to give authority to the Treasury to deposit funds directly in any bank.

I get to Washington late tomorrow night and will look forward to seeing you on Friday.

Sincerely yours,
(Signed) Franklin D. Roosevelt

The President,
The White House

(Inclosure)

Dear Mr. President:

I am equally concerned with you in regard to the gravity of the present banking situation—but my thought is that it is so very deep-seated that the fire is bound to spread in spite of anything that is done by way of mere statements. The real trouble is that on present values very few financial institutions anywhere in the country are actually able to pay off their deposits in full, and the knowledge of this fact is widely held. Bankers with the narrower viewpoint have urged me to make a general statement, but even they seriously doubt if it would have a definite effect.

I had hoped to have Senator Glass' acceptance of the Treasury post—but he has definitely said no this afternoon—I am asking Mr. Woodin tomorrow—if he accepts I propose to announce it tomorrow together with Senator Hull for the State Department. These announcements may have some effect on the banking situation, but frankly I doubt if anything short of a fairly general withdrawal of deposits can be prevented now.

In any event, Mr. Woodin, if he accepts, will get into immediate touch with Mills and the bankers.

Very sincerely yours,
(Signed) Franklin D. Roosevelt

Fuel was added to the fire by reports published previous to President Hoover's receipt of Governor Roosevelt's letter which stated that Senator Glass, after an interview with the President-elect, had declined to accept the post of Secretary of the Treasury in the new cabinet. Uneasy widespread speculation held that he had declined either because he had learned of Governor Roosevelt's intention to go off the gold standard or that he had been unable to secure satisfactory assurances that he would not. This news sent new waves of panic through the nation.

The deterioration of the nation's economy was rapid from this point on. Upon becoming President Mr. Roosevelt declared a bank holiday and then within a few days reopened the nation's banks although they had received no additional essential assets during the closed period.

The record shows that banks which were reopened after the Roosevelt bank holiday held 92 per cent of the nation's deposits. This brings the record into a head-on clash with his letter of March 1 to President Hoover in which he said: *"The real trouble is that on present values very few financial institutions anywhere in the country are actually able to pay off their depositors."* (Italics author's.)

President Hoover on February 25, wrote to a friend as follows:

> Professor Tugwell, adviser to Franklin D. Roosevelt, had lunch with me. He said they were fully aware of the bank situation and that it would undoubtedly collapse in a few days, which would place the responsibility in the lap of President Hoover. He said, "We should worry about anything except rehabilitating the country after March 4th. Then there would be several moves; first, an embargo on exportation of yellow chips; second, suspension of specie payments; third, reflation if necessary, after one and two, and after that arrangements would be made for the so-called business men's committee of 60 prominent manufacturers who have been invited to spend a half day with Mr. Woodin on Tuesday in an attempt to again support the business interests for a program."
>
> When I consider this statement of Professor Tugwell's in connection with the recommendations we have made to the incoming administration, I can say emphatically that he breathes with in-

famous politics devoid of every atom of patriotism. Mr. Tugwell would project millions of people into hideous losses for a Roman holiday.

Through his Secretary of the Treasury Ogden Mills, via William Woodin, the President-elect's designated Secretary of the Treasury, President Hoover had offered to co-operate in any way that would help to relieve the situation but Mr. Woodin stated that his "instructions" were not to agree to anything.

Thus the stage was set for the Roman holiday.

The Democratic-Independent Springfield, Ohio, *Sun,* published by James M. Cox, Democratic party presidential nominee in 1920, on August 10, 1949, made an editorial appraisal of Mr. Hoover in which it said:

> . . . He is not a complicated personality, but rather a personality of monolithic simplicity. With no reflection on anyone, it might be said that whenever and wherever Herbert Hoover has mystified people or has been misunderstood by them, nearly always it has been because he is an extremely plain man living in an extremely fancy age. A plain man in the Presidency, of all places, poses especially poignant questions. . . .
>
> Several of the basic reforms Americans have come to associate with the New Deal were established or foreshadowed in legislation of the much-derided "Hoover era." Let's look at the record, as Herbert Hoover's great adversary, the late Alfred E. Smith, used to say. On Mr. Hoover's initiative, a GOP Congress enacted in 1929 the first agricultural marketing act. He was responsible for the Reconstruction Finance Corporation, sometimes erroneously attributed to FDR—as was another Hoover creation, the Federal Home Loan Bank Board. In 1932, safeguards to organized labor in the Clayton Antitrust Act of 1914 were reinforced by legislation, prohibiting injunctions against unions and affirming the technique of collective bargaining. This law, sponsored by GOP Senator George W. Norris and GOP Congressman Fiorello La Guardia, was signed by GOP President Hoover. Of the general period climaxed by Mr. Hoover's Presidency, Charles A. and Mary R. Beard note in their "Basic History of the United States" that "the so-called age of re-

action and disillusionment was in many respects an age of progress, not of retreat."

He is, in short, a very plain man; a bit stodgy, somewhat too conservative for his times; given to fundamental principles and abstract expression rather than to quick-witted extemporization and easy affability. But put him in an appointive rather than an elective job, give him work to do of the sort that can benefit everybody, and Herbert Hoover shows up at his best. As Americans have begun to realize on this occasion of his 75th birthday, Herbert Hoover at his best is an authentically great American.

PART FIVE

EX-PRESIDENT 1933–1949

CHAPTER ONE

Resting, Visiting, Watching and Thinking

In accordance with the custom of retiring Presidents, Mr. Hoover left Washington a few hours after his successor took the oath of office. He went to New York City and remained for several weeks before starting for his home in California. He sought the rest his body needed in overcoming his months of day and night nerve-wracking strains. While there he devoted some time to putting his philanthropic interests in order, visiting old friends and watching developments in Washington.

He left Washington neglected, exhausted and disappointed but not embittered. His sturdy philosophy carried him over the shoals of political caprice.

One commentator, in writing about the speech Mr. Hoover delivered at the Gridiron Club dinner in Washington shortly after the 1932 elections, stated that he gave "a beautifully phrased tribute to the spirit and institutions of [his] country . . . of high purpose and deep humility."

In keeping with his life record of public service he would have responded to any call for information or service which his successor might have made.

None ever came. In fact it was not until more than thirteen years had come and gone that a White House occupant ever either communicated with him or asked for his help in any form.

Once, when asked by General Julius Klein what he was doing in the war, Mr. Hoover replied: "It appears that President Roosevelt has no place for me in this war." General Klein then wanted to know whether or not Mr. Hoover would serve if invited to do so by President Roosevelt. Mr. Hoover answered: "I would do anything that

I am asked to do to help my country and to help heal the wounds inflicted on the world by this horrible war."

Later in Washington General Klein reported his conversations with Mr. Hoover to Undersecretary of War Robert P. Patterson, and to David K. Niles, confidential assistant to the President who, said General Klein, "supported the idea enthusiastically." The answer, from a higher authority, however, was *no*.

On October 17, 1949, the New York *World-Telegram* stated in an editorial note:

> At long last Herbert Hoover has been extended the courtesy of an invitation to the annual Army-Navy football game. And our only living ex-President has accepted. It has been the custom to issue special invitations to former Presidents. But Franklin Roosevelt ignored the custom. So has Harry Truman.
>
> This year, Maj. Gen. Bryant E. Moore, commandant of the Military Academy, invited Mr. Hoover to the game. We're glad he did. It's nice to see this merited courtesy revived after having been discarded for 16 years by Democratic administrations.

Men are strange animals.

In his recently published book, *27 Masters of Politics* (Funk and Wagnalls Co., New York, 1949), Raymond Moley, who knows whereof he speaks, in writing of this seemingly inexplicable situation says:

> . . . It was decreed in the stubborn mind of the man who succeeded him that Hoover should never officially be called by the nation to service befitting his talents. It was a grievous waste, compounded in later years when war magnified manyfold the reappearance of so many of the problems of the first World War. This studied neglect has often been noted and, again, I must disagree with those who attribute Roosevelt's neglect entirely to ungenerous and vindictive caprice. It was, I believe, the result of political prudence, for Roosevelt entertained a view that only Hoover among the notables of the Republican Party possessed the massive convictions and intelligence to provide an alternative to the New Deal.

Roosevelt actually believed that Hoover might well emerge once more as the leader and the candidate of his party. . . .

That fear of a Hoover renaissance surely had a part in the persistence with which the Democratic party under its skilful master perpetuated the myth that Hoover and Hoover alone was the architect of the depression and the impotent pilot of a nation in a great storm. Other lesser Republicans—like Stimson and Knox—who had been no less critical of Roosevelt than Hoover, were granted full political absolution. But Hoover was the stone rejected until advancing age had its way with his availability and a more generous soul inhabited the White House. . . .

In the early spring of 1933, Mr. Hoover left New York City for California. There, and in the mountains and valleys of the Far West and the great plains of the Middle West, he sought in long motor trips to renew his spiritual resources and revitalize his physical vigor. Usually one or more old and close friends accompanied him on these trips. They fished in fishing season; at other times they visited other old friends here and there or talked with men and women in all walks of life about their interests and problems, about citizenship and the state of the nation or what have you. (An article by Mr. Hoover on fishing and philosophy is reprinted in Appendix XVIII.)

A Close-up Picture of a Hoover Fishing Trip

O. Glenn Saxon added the following incidents about his fishing trip with Mr. Hoover which was referred to in an earlier chapter.

According to Dr. Saxon's account, they were on a trout stream practically every day—except Sundays—at 6 A.M., where they would fish until lunch time, then eat a picnic lunch, and during the afternoon drive two hundred miles or so to another stream for some more fishing until sundown.

An interesting incident of the trip occurred about noon one day as they were driving toward Yellowstone Park with Mr. Hoover at the wheel. They came to a crossroad in the middle of nowhere and saw standing there alone a stern-faced and determined-looking woman of about forty-five. She had nothing but a small weekend case in her hand. She signaled for a lift. "The Chief," said Saxon, "looked at me. I grinned and shrugged my shoulders. He slowed down and asked the lady where she was going. She replied 'Yellowstone Park' and got into the rear seat. He then asked her what she was doing on the road and she replied that she was a member of the Big Sisters League and that she worked out of Los Angeles, saving 'fallen souls' in tourist camps. In answer to his question as to the gospel she preached she said it was a short one—'First, Soup; second, Soap; and third, Salvation.' Whereupon he asked her how her activities were financed. She said, 'The Lord always provides.'

"We reached the park and proceeded for several miles until we came to a tourist camp and let the lady out. When she stepped from the car, the Chief asked if she were short of funds. She shook her head, thanked him for the ride, and said, 'The Lord always provides.' He then slipped a bill into her hand and said, 'This will help you to buy some soup and soap.' She took it, looked at it carefully as if she thought it was a counterfeit, handed it back saying, 'Don't you have any hard money?' Without a word, Mr. Hoover reached into his pocket and gave her all he had—about three dollars. As we drove away he turned to me and said, 'Glenn, she must be one of the few in the country who still believes in sound money.'"

A few days later, as they headed over the Divide into Idaho, they reached a cluster of cabins near a roaring trout stream late in the evening and decided to spend the night there. Dr. Saxon went into the central cottage to register himself and "J. B. Smith" of Palo Alto and was told by the proprietress-owner that she had only two cots left which were upstairs in the central building. Saxon said they would be okay and made arrangements for himself and Mr. "Smith" to get a six o'clock breakfast which she agreed to serve in her kitchen.

The next morning the two of them were there on time and so was she. As the two men entered the kitchen the proprietress was at the stove with her back to them and told them to sit down at the table, Mr. Hoover facing her and Saxon at one side. When she turned to place the food on the table she got her first look at Mr. Hoover. She said to Saxon, "Your friend looks very much like ex-President

Hoover." He replied, "Yes, he does, doesn't he!" and tried to keep a straight face. She poured coffee, took another look at Mr. Hoover, and jumped to her feet saying, "Why, you *are* Mr. Hoover."

When she had calmed down she proudly told her guests that her two daughters were students at Stanford.

When the conversation turned to trout fishing she opened a table drawer and pulled out a book full of trout flies. She had tied them, for she was a fly fisherman who tied her own. Then she got out a map and marked spots on the nearby stream where the rainbows would run to five pounds. Saxon tells how their hostess "shyly selected several of her flies and hesitatingly offered some of each kind to both of us. Suddenly she stopped short and said with a scorn such as only a fly fisherman has for those who bait their hooks with worms, 'I hope that you don't use worms like President Coolidge.' He took all the flies and shook his head and said with a poker face, 'No, I never stoop to such lowdown tactics, but this fellow Saxon, here, does—and don't give any of your flies to him—he wouldn't appreciate them.' "

Mr. Hoover Keeps His Counsel and Bides His Time

During the period of Mr. Hoover's travels, fishing and visiting he refrained from all speech making that concerned the current political situation. Unlike his opponents, who had organized and launched the "Smear Hoover" project a few months after he became President for the purpose of hampering and ultimately defeating him, he believed that his successor should be given every fair opportunity to work out his program.

All during these many months, however, he was following closely and appraising carefully what was going on in Washington and the world. Confidential information on all kinds of projects, subjects and problems flowed to him from many sources. I have always been amazed at the amount of secret "top drawer" information that has been constantly sent to the ex-presidents I have known. It comes from all over the world and most of those who supply it know what they are talking about. Thus through the newspapers and magazines, through such sources of information above mentioned and from the many callers who came to his home he was kept fully conversant with the current of affairs. And he usually knew what was going to happen or was likely to happen before it took place. As he watched he saw "the things he had given his life to broken."

For more than two years, however, he refrained from making any public comment.

How difficult it must have been for him to remain silent at times. One of these occasions was when, for no acceptable reason ever yet offered, President Roosevelt wrecked the carefully planned London Economic Conference in which sixty-six nations were participating.

President Roosevelt "Bomb-shells" London Economic Conference

Many governments had co-operated with the Hoover Administration in calling and planning for the London Economic Conference of 1933 at which policies were to be formulated, programs created and agreements sought which would serve as stabilizing and supporting forces in hastening world economic recovery then under way and to help maintain world peace.

Recognizing the tremendous potentialities of this conference as well as the vital necessity for the United States to prepare an adequate program without delay, President Hoover, after his defeat in November, repeatedly but vainly tried to enlist the President-elect's co-operation in advancing our preparation for participation in it. Among other proposals, President Hoover offered to appoint a Governor Roosevelt-selected delegation in an effort to provide for continuity of effort on our part. The President-elect declined to co-operate with Hoover. A few months later, in the summer of 1933, President Roosevelt, with his "bomb-shell" message to the just convened conference brought to a tragic end the efforts to advance world recovery and aid peace sought by the delegates of sixty-six nations.

Any reader who doubts the accuracy or fairness of the sub-head above is referred to pages 246 to 269, inclusive, of Volume I of the *Memoirs of Cordell Hull,* published in 1948 by Macmillan. Mr. Hull was Secretary of State in 1933 and chairman of the American delegation to the conference.

Mr. Hull states in his memoirs that when the American delegation sailed for London on May 31, 1933, he carried with him evidences of "approaching trouble." The trouble he spoke of flowed from the policies of two new government agencies, the NRA (National Recovery Administration) and the AAA (Agricultural Adjustment Administration). The success of these two agencies required import embargoes and higher tariffs, two points which conflicted with the objectives of the London Economic Conference, reduction of tariffs and trade barriers.

Mr. Hull also points out that preparations for the conference were delayed as a result of the Roosevelt administration's move, previous to the London Conference, of inviting eleven nations to send representatives to Washington to discuss economic questions. The talks, Mr. Hull states, were "most unfruitful." This was natural since programs and policies for international economic conferences cannot be improvised. These talks served also to limit the range of subjects with which the American delegation could deal at London.

President Roosevelt's shifts in policy concerning the conference and his inability or failure, as he stated in a cable to Mr. Hull, to secure legislation authorizing "tariff reductions and removal of trade barriers" as a result of "eleventh-hour rows in Congress over domestic problems" created a condition of "indescribable confusion."

Mr. Hull states that he left for London "with the highest hopes" but returned home "with empty hands."

The conference was thrown into an "uproar" by the receipt of President Roosevelt's message, the effect of which was to rule currency stabilization from the agenda. British Prime Minister MacDonald responded immediately with the preparation of a resolution, which he said would "hang around the President's neck the sole responsibility for wrecking the conference." Although the resolution was not presented, the conference, after three weeks of "desultory conversations," recessed indefinitely on July 27.

Mr. Hull expresses the belief in his memoirs that the collapse of the London Economic Conference had two tragic results: first, that it retarded the economic recovery of all nations and second, that it gave the dictator nations of Germany, Italy and Japan the conviction that they could proceed to rearm in comparative safety and also to build "their self-sufficiency walls in preparation for war."

The collapse of the Conference in Mr. Hull's opinion was the last real opportunity to "check these movements toward conflict."

Mr. Hoover watched the enactment of this cosmic tragedy, but he could do nothing to avert it.

Sees "Bureaus Piled on Bureaus"

He looked on with consternation as his successor, who in the 1932 campaign had charged the Hoover administration with having attempted "too many functions" and of "piling bureaus on bureaus, commissions on commissions," created nearly 5000 new agencies, commissions, bureaus and committees in less than two years' time. He saw that these new government bodies were creating more jobs, and that the federal payroll soon jumped from the 565,000 figure at which it stood on March 4, 1933, to 830,000 (whereas the Hoover administration had reduced the number by 10,000) and that the vast majority of these new job holders had not been selected under the rules of the merit system of the Civil Service Commission. (In 1949 there are 2,100,000 federal jobholders.)

He was troubled also when he recalled his opponent's charge that the Hoover administration was "the greatest spending administration in history" and that its "extravagance" was "appalling" whereas government spending would soon be increased from about three billion to more than four billion dollars annually instead of decreased by one billion dollars annually as he (Roosevelt) had promised to do if elected. And as he thought of these promises he recalled Theodore Roosevelt's statement that "a broken promise is bad enough in private life. It is worse in the field of politics. No man is worth his salt in public life who makes on the stump a pledge which he does not keep after election."

He saw bureaucracy grow and feed on itself, to struggle always for self-perpetuation, expansion and more power, as it helped to win elections. He saw it shift the administration of relief from local to state committees to its centralized control in Washington which he believed to be the negation of the free American spirit.

His later speeches indicated he was troubled by the negation of the free American spirit. This he feared would inevitably follow the centralization of government, growth of bureaucracy, corruption of the electorate with relief funds, and the loss of initiative through regimentation and weakening of the people's spiritual and moral purpose.

True liberty, he believed, meant liberty for the individual which rested upon the advancement of political morals; that a people corrupted by their government "cannot remain a free people."

Roosevelt's Tragic Air Mail Action

During the rest of 1933, all of 1934 and most of 1935, Mr. Hoover followed with increasing irritation and indignation: (a) President Roosevelt's repudiation of his campaign promises and continued violation of the Democratic party's 1932 platform pledges; (b) the Roosevelt administration's repeated charges of "graft, profiteering, collusion and lawlessness" in connection with the Hoover administration's air mail contracts. But he gave no public expression of either his irritation or indignation. He waited for time and the courts to produce support of the Roosevelt administration's sweeping charges of wrong-doing in the Hoover administration air mail contracts.

Time has completely disproved them. The case never reached the courts because of the Roosevelt administration's inability to find the slightest shred of evidence to support its ballyhooed claims of "collusion and graft." There is no evidence on record to show that the government has prosecuted a single one of the individuals or concerns it indicted in the newspapers and over the radio as having been guilty of "graft, profiteering, collusion and lawlessness." The public has never learned whether the Black Committee "of high-handed and invidious memory" convinced President Roosevelt it could find conclusive evidence to support its headline charges. It seems impossible to believe that he would have issued an order in his postmaster-general's name which (a) cancelled the Hoover administration's air mail contracts and (b) ordered the army air pilots to fly the mail.

Aviation experts, including Colonel Lindbergh, immediately pointed out that the army air pilots were unqualified to fly the mails because this hazardous business called for special training. They were howled down, and the army pilots took over under orders from their Commander in Chief, President Roosevelt. These orders very soon proved to have been death sentences for twelve of them. As crash-after-crash and the tragic death-after-death of pilots piled up, the aghast public all over the nation broke into a storm of protest over this uncalled-for waste of human life. President Roosevelt stilled this protest by issuing a new order calling for new contracts with the aviation companies whose contracts had been cancelled by his first order.

Following the issuance of and withdrawals of President Roosevelt's different orders, a Senate investigating committee, with the then Senator and now Associate Justice of the Supreme Court Hugo R. Black as prosecutor, searched the government files, interrogated a horde of witnesses, filled newspaper columns and air waves with innuendoes and intimations of the mountains of "graft" and "profiteering" that would be forthcoming. In the end the Black Committee was unable to produce a molehill of fact to support its innuendoes and intimations. All that it discovered was a brick under this Hoover hat that they had kicked so hard.

This brick was politically astute and incorruptible Walter F. Brown, Hoover's Postmaster-General. He quickly demonstrated to the Black Committee that he was a fighter by instinct and training and a resourceful political strategist.

Once during the course of the Black Committee hearings when intimations were whispered everywhere that conclusive proof of Brown's perfidy would be produced, I telephoned him and said: "I just wanted to tell you, Walter, that I love you and believe in you as much as I always have." He replied, "Why don't you come down for lunch and tell me that to my face. I'm pretty lonely these days."

During our visit I asked, "Why did you peach on Farley? That's the only thing I don't understand." He answered:

> I had to get Farley on the stand because I knew he could not say under oath that I had done a single thing that was wrong. Although he was the only man who knew everything there was to know about the air mail contracts Senator Black had failed to call him as a witness. I had to use subterfuge to make Black subpoena him. The best way seemed to be that of making the Senator mad at Farley. I did this by innocently remarking on the stand that Farley had called Black a "publicity hound." Black flared up at that and issued the Farley subpoena right then. (From author's memory.)

A few years after he left public service Mr. Farley publicly stated that he had protested the use of his name in issuing the cancellation order without his consent.

Smearing Continues—Broken Campaign Planks Litter the Nation's Course

Mr. Hoover, as a private citizen, remained silent. The smear campaign against him continued. He followed the slow moving re-employment program and its barely perceptible rise of only 5 per cent during a five-year period at a "pump-priming" expenditure of more than ten billion dollars.

The Roosevelt Administration in addition to the initiation and projection of a great number and variety of its own proposals, also carried out Mr. Hoover's long and earnestly advocated program for reforming the nation's banking system which a Democratic Congress had refused to approve.

Mr. Hoover had sought to hobble the Stock Exchange while President and had earnestly urged that such action be taken for a period of three years but the Democratic Congress refused to support him. They did, however, support his proposals when they were advocated by his successor. The Roosevelt Administration carried forward and enlarged the Hoover Administration's enormous government construction work program which the Hoover Administration already had well under way in 1933. Its expansion of the highway and public school building programs greatly improved the nation's highway system and gave it many vitally needed school buildings.

These and many other Roosevelt Administration programs and projects also were "noble in motive and lofty in purpose." Mr. Hoover, I feel sure, must have approved the motives which prompted them as did many of his old supporters. But they were made morally indignant when they saw political corruption raise its ugly head and with evidence abounding became convinced that a few men with great power were determined "to tax and tax and spend and spend" because, in their conceit, they believed themselves to be wiser than all of the people.

Political corruption was aided and abetted, and supported with intellectual dishonesty. They also watched with consternation the administrative confusion which was created in part by President Roosevelt's practice, as stated by a member of his official family: "The boss," he said, "either appoints one man to do four jobs or four men to do one. Often he does both."

Mr. Hoover saw his successor ignore his campaign promises to maintain the gold standard and next devalue the dollar on the advice of a man whose most serious claim to public recognition rested on his having discovered that hens could be fooled into laying more eggs by keeping electric lights turned on in the chicken house. This expert's other "discovery" was that the people could be fooled into believing they would have more money if the dollar were devalued. When this was done it also was applauded by the public.

Senator Carter Glass had stated on the Senate floor of the proposal, "To me it means dishonor; in my conception it is immoral."

From his newspaper reading and other sources of information as well as from his travels around the country, Mr. Hoover found existing evidence of the evils which he had foreseen that are inherent in direct federal government relief. Everywhere he found that federal government relief cost far more than would community-directed relief. Evidence abounded also that federal relief as it was being conducted was corrupting the electorate—an unsurpassable evil in a free government. Almost equally as bad for the perpetuation of a democratic form of government, it was being used as the means of an administration to perpetuate itself in office.

"More Than a Contest Between Two Political Parties"

The sharp turn which the Roosevelt administration had taken from the American tradition—as Hoover believed and had tried to interpret it to be—made his statement in his Madison Square Garden speech of October 31, 1932 (see Appendix XIX) sound ominously prophetic. In it he had expressed his conviction that "this contest," referring to the 1932 presidential campaign, "is more than a contest between two men. It is more than a contest between two (political) parties. It is a contest between two philosophies of government."

The more he saw and heard, the more he realized that a new concept of government was being introduced. He was troubled by this threat to our system of government, the product of our race and experience, which had enabled us to build a nation to heights which had never before been reached by any nation in the world's history.

He believed with all his heart that the hard core of America's greatness had been achieved through ordered liberty and freedom and equal opportunity to the individual. He believed that this concept was what had helped the individual to spur the march of our progress. Coupled with the co-operation of free men it had kept America young and her people hopeful; and made her the envy of the world.

As he watched from the sidelines he saw the concept of the importance of the individual cast aside and replaced by the concept of government as the *be-all* and *end-all* of man's existence.

During this period of watching, waiting, visiting and thinking—the first such period in his adult life when he was free of personal, business or public duties and demands—he had time and opportunity to relax and to make an appraisal of himself, of his methods and his principles. As time passed his older friends could see that he had begun to mellow, to be more his old whimsical, gentle and, in a sense, sweet-natured self. Right was still right to him and wrong-doing must be challenged. But with it all there was evident in him a change for the better in his relations with men and women, which when carried forward meant his relations with the public. This change in his outlook and actions was of marked importance because, as our political system works, his administration had been weak in its relations with the public.

A Quaker Moved by the Spirit

Now, after nearly two years of semi-leisure, during which he had been able to think the nation's problems through, Mr. Hoover, after the manner of his fellow Quakers, felt a concern to follow the promptings of his heart and give expression to his convictions.

He knew what he believed; he knew why he believed it; he was sure about the source of his faith. Also, after the manner of his fellow Quakers, no odds could deter him when confronted with a righteous cause. Undaunted, he went forth to preach, according to his light, the gospel of the place of government in the life of an individual, the place of the individual in his relations with other individuals and government and the place of the individual in God's unfolding purpose for the universe. But for several years he was a lone voice crying in the wilderness.

Some of the speeches he delivered during the years following his departure from the White House rank with the greatest that ever have been delivered. One man, after listening to one of Mr. Hoover's best speeches, said: "To me he sounds like God talking."

Through these speeches Mr. Hoover slowly but gradually built up an understanding, believing and finally an ardent audience. During the intervening years from 1933 to 1949, Mr. Hoover made more than forty major addresses and most of them were the greatest of his career. Excerpts from some of these addresses appear in the Appendix. A few are given in full, one of which is his Commencement Day Address (Appendix XX) at Haverford College in June, 1941, in which Hoover the scientist spoke, and another is his seventy-fourth birthday address (Appendix V) delivered at West Branch, Iowa, the village of his birth, in August, 1948, in which Hoover the philosopher and statesman spoke.

In addition to his addresses, he wrote several magazine articles, two books and issued a large number of press releases. Although his treatment of the subject varied, the heart of his message varied extremely little. It was a plea for a resurgence of the spirit of justice and ordered liberty. It was an exposition of the need for a clearer appreciation of the indispensable place which moral and spiritual values occupy in the lives of men. It expressed his conviction that man's destiny was fixed by a higher power.

CHAPTER TWO

Correcting the Record and Expressing His Faith

Mr. Hoover's first formal public utterance after he left the White House on March 4, 1933, was made in a speech he delivered at Sacramento, California on March 22, 1935. In it he stated his belief that the American people

> . . . have directly before them the issue of perfecting our system of orderly individual liberty under constitutionally conducted government or of rejecting it in favor of the newly created system of regimentation and bureaucratic domination in which men and women are not masters of government but are pawns or dependents of a centralized and potentially self-perpetuating government.

Two months later in answer to a press request that he make a statement on the ill-fated NRA, he said in part:

> The whole concept of the NRA is rooted in a regimented "economy of scarcity"—an idea that increased costs, restricted production and hampered enterprise will enrich a nation . . . the only substitute for an action that rests on definite and proved economic error is to abandon it.

On June 16, 1935 he told the graduating class of Stanford University, that "The first of social securities is freedom—freedom of men to speak, to direct their energies, to develop their own talents and to be rewarded for their effort." Other excerpts from this notable address appear in Appendix XXI. September 17, 1935, found him in San Diego, California, making an address on the Bill of Rights in which he admitted that "many, [men] in honest belief hold that we cannot longer accommodate the growth of science, technology and mechanical power to the Bill of Rights and our form of government. With that I do not agree."

Later that same year, December 16, at St. Louis, Missouri, Mr. Hoover took his gloves off for the first time. In this speech he challenged the accuracy of a statement President Roosevelt had made a short time before that "The mechanics of civilization came to a dead stop on March 3, 1933." Mr. Hoover supported his challenge with facts, force and logic. He also contrasted his own administration's relief services, costs and results with those of his successor. (See Appendix XIII.)

In another St. Louis speech (see Appendix XXIII) Mr. Hoover stated that the cost of unemployment relief during the last year of his administration was "about $1,100,000,000" and that the overhead cost to the federal government was "not over $250,000" and the total number of its employees to administer this relief "was less than 200." He added that American Federation of Labor average monthly figures showed that there were 11,600,000 unemployed during the last year of his administration whereas they showed an average of 11,100,000 as of the end of October 1935; or about a 5 per cent decrease in the relief load.

He then added:

> Now let us note the increase in relief cost. However, the marvelous migratory habits of these relief funds from one place in the alphabet to another make them difficult hunting. But judging from Treasury and other statements the expenditures on all relief alphabets in the year ending last October for federal, state, and local were over $3,500,000,000. This also includes Federal Public Works over normal, but does not include relief to agriculture. There were over 140,000 officials on the federal payroll, not including the people on relief. The salaries of these officials alone must come to about $300,000,000 a year. It is easy to detect another $200,000,000 in pencils, typewriters, offices, automobiles, Pullman fares, etc., not to mention press releases. That is an overhead of four or five hundred million per annum. Some increase in relief was necessary, but an increase of 300 per cent in costs in the face of a 5 per cent decrease in unemployment load is significant. And the overhead amounts to nearly one-half the whole cost of relief three years ago . . .

In time he discussed the use of relief funds by the federal government to influence elections, a fact known which was denounced by those who had not lost their faculty of indignation over public wrongdoing. In one speech Mr. Hoover stated that "the hideous morals of these actions in a free republic were denounced by a few Democratic senators whose morals rise above elections" and added:

> Democratic Senator Hatch proposed a law in the Senate designed to stop relief officials from using relief for vote-getting purposes. The Senator said, "Those who believe that out in the counties and in the cities and in the precincts this instrumentality which we have set up is not being used for political purposes are more credulous than I am."
>
> However, Senator Barkley, President Roosevelt's selected leader of the Senate, led the opposition to Senator Hatch's motion. The motion was defeated by President Roosevelt's rubber-stamp followers in the Senate.
>
> Would this law have been defeated if President Roosevelt had breathed one whisper of approval for it? Or better, if he had expressed one word of indignation at the action of his supporters in the Senate? Instead, Mr. Roosevelt journeyed to Kentucky to endorse the re-election of Senator Barkley.
>
> And this sample in Kentucky could not be unknown to Mr. Roosevelt. Some months ago the Democratic Scripps-Howard papers courageously exposed the use of the WPA in Kentucky "as a grand political racket in which the taxpayer is the victim." Harry Hopkins as usual denounced the reporter as untruthful. Later on, even the Senate Committee, after investigation, had to stigmatize this stench. They said, "These facts should arouse the conscience of the country. They imperil the right of the people to a free and unpolluted ballot." I notice it was the conscience of the country that they summoned. (From "Morals in Government," an address before the Joint Republican Organizations, Kansas City, Missouri, September 28, 1938.)

In an earlier speech, one which he delivered at Philadelphia on May 14, 1936, Mr. Hoover stressed the "gigantic question of morals," which was involved in the New Deal relief spoils system. After quoting a statement by Theodore Roosevelt, who held that the man who debauches our public life "by the corrupt use of offices as spoils" is our greatest foe, Mr. Hoover said:

> Recently I had opportunity to observe comparative morals in the spoils systems by a contrast between Tammany Hall and the New Deal. In a Tammany-dominated borough in New York in early 1933 before the New Deal, there were about 11,000 persons on relief. Tammany had appointed about 270 additional officials under their particular spoils system to manage the relief at a cost of under $30,000 a month for the officials. This job was taken away from wicked Tammany influence and directly administered by the New Deal. At a recent date there were in the same borough 2,000 Federal officials appointed under the New Deal spoils system at a cost of $300,000 per month for salaries to manage 16,000 persons on relief. Tammany may learn something new in the spoils system. It was only 10 per cent efficient. And the same thing is going on all over the country and you know it.
>
> Can the American people be bought with their own money? *

Again in speaking of the moral corruption which was created by these huge expenditures of public funds he asked:

> Do you wonder that our own people lose faith in honesty? Do they not lose faith in Democracy? Does it not disintegrate the moral standards of our people?

One wholly new threat to our heretofore free, classless life which stirred Mr. Hoover was that of the "moral aspects of stirring ill will, conflict and hate." Speaking on the subject of "Morals in Government" as it related to class conflict, he said:

> Class hate is the rock upon which every republic has been wrecked. And this is the most classless nation yet born. And hate is preached from the White House for the first time. I shall not go further into it than to say it has set worker against employer, employer against worker, worker against worker. And I give you a statistic of only

* "The Obligation of the Republican Party to the American People," address before Republican Women of Pennsylvania, Philadelphia, Pa. May 14, 1936.

one of its consequences. In the three years of depression stress before the New Deal, the man days lost by strikes and lock-outs averaged five million per year. In the five years of the New Deal, they have averaged eighteen million per year. That is an increase of 350 per cent. Is that building good-will and co-operation? *

The great Roosevelt (Theodore) in his lecture, "Citizenship in a Republic," which he delivered at the Sorbonne in Paris on April 23, 1910, expressed a somewhat similar view about the evils of class hatred and the malign influence of men who fomented it where he said:

> . . . The gravest wrong upon his country is inflicted by that man, whatever his station, who seeks to make his countrymen divide primarily on the line that separates class from class, occupation from occupation, men of more wealth from men of less wealth, instead of remembering that the only safe standard is that which judges each man on his worth as a man, whether he be rich or poor, without regard to his profession or to his station in life . . .

In Mr. Hoover's speech on "Morals in Government" he further expressed the belief that if

> . . . the standards of honor, sincerity, and truth in public life are to differ from those we learned at our mother's knee then this Republic is lost. It is the moral slide more even than the economic degeneration that in the last twenty years has carried nation after nation over the precipice to dictatorship.

He was, he said, "Proud to carry the banner of free men." He believed in the American system of free enterprise "not because it is a property system or a profit system . . . but because it is inseparable from intellectual and spiritual liberty . . . it is the only road to higher standards of living . . . it is the only system under which morals and self-respect of men can survive." He believed in the American system of liberty "from a thousand experiences." He stated further:

> I believe that upon its foundation is the one hope of the common man. It has faults. But it contains the only real ferment of progress.

* "Morals in Government," address before Joint Republican Organizations, Kansas City, Missouri, Sept. 28, 1938.

> There are other systems of Liberty. But at the heart of our American System is embedded a great ideal unique in the world. That is the ideal that there shall be an opportunity in life, and equal opportunity, for every boy and girl, every man and woman. It holds that they have the chance to rise to any position to which their character and ability may entitle them.

In the same speech he challenged the attitude of those

> . . . who scoff at individual liberty as of no consequence to the poor or unemployed. Yet it is alone through the creative impulses of free and confident spirits that redemption of their suffering must come. It is through them alone that social security can be attained. Our job is not to pull down the great majority but to pull up those who lag behind.*

Again and again he called upon the government and the people to be honest. "Integrity," he once said, "lives not alone in the pocketbook. It lives also in the mind." The first objective of government he held was "to re-establish morals, to give the nation leadership in moral regeneration as the road to national security." Moral standards he held can more easily check greed and hate than can policemen. "There is," he said, "no double-standard of morals, one in public and one in private." How similar his position on this is to the one his fellow Quakers hold on oath taking! But, he held, and here the indomitable faith of the man speaks, "there are lights upon the horizon. There is a moral purpose in the universe."

In speech after speech he defined his hopes and his visions for his country.

"What," he asked in one speech, "do we want as a minimum standard of living for all the people?" (See Appendix XXII.)

In speech after speech he spelled out for his audience his interpretation of what liberty meant to men in all walks and positions in life. In other speeches, as a student of their tactics and techniques, he sought to describe methods which men greedy for power had used to dethrone liberty and establish themselves as dictators.

---

* "The Choice for Youth," address before Young Republican League of Colorado, March 7, 1936.

The would-be dictator, he said, launched his program by first ascribing the "tragic miseries of the times, not to the great war, where it belongs, but to some party or class." That done they proceeded to make wonderful promises and at the same time they "demanded violent action against human ills that are only slowly curable." These points made the would-be dictators ready to launch the nub of their program. This they did by insisting that:

> . . . sporadic wickedness in high places had permeated the whole system of liberty. They shouted new destructive slogans and phases day by day to inflame the people. They implanted unreasoning hates in the souls of men. They first grasped at power through elections which Liberty provided. Then began the 'must emergency instruments of power,' 'to save the nation.' The first demands were powers of dictation over industry and agriculture and finance and labor. Legislatures were reduced to rubber stamps. Honest debate was shut off in the halls of deliberation. A powerful government propaganda was put on the taxpayers' bill, that hates and suspicions could be further inflamed. And all of these men insisted that civilization had begun all over again when they came into power.
>
> In the final stages of European degeneration Liberty died from the waters of her own well. That was when the waters of free speech were poisoned by untruth. Then have followed the last steps to dictatorship, with suppression of freedom of speech, freedom of worship, of the courts, and all other freedoms. Men were goose-stepped in a march back to the Middle Ages . . .*

In another speech on the subject of liberty he stated that he had

> . . . spent years in public service in many countries during this most fateful period of human history. I saw as few men in the backwash of war upon the common man of these countries. I saw at first hand revolution creeping in under promises of relief from the agonies of war destruction. I have seen the insidious destruction of liberty by propaganda. I have seen suffering humanity sacrifice that liberty, the greatest of all human achievements, for an illusion of

* "The Choice for Youth," address before Young Republican League of Colorado, March 7, 1936.

security. The farmers of Russia supported the Bolsheviki against the new-born Democracy on the promise of the land. Today they have the choice of Siberia or the collectivist farms. I have seen freedom, the most priceless heritage, torn from children that this generation might escape its responsibilities. I wish to say to you unhesitatingly that our country has been following step by step the road through which these millions of people in foreign countries lost their liberties . . .*

In those of his speeches which Mr. Hoover delivered to Republican party audiences he repeatedly tried to outline a program of constructive action based on high, patriotic purpose for the nation. He unquestionably was the most able, fully qualified man the party had for a standard bearer in 1936. The public generally believed that he was a receptive candidate for the nomination that year.

Whatever the case may be this much seems certain to me: Had the Republican party nominated him in 1936 it thereby might have saved its soul.

Aside from the speech Mr. Hoover delivered (see Appendix XXV), the convention's proceedings were commonplace. Mr. Hoover's message moved the audience profoundly. When he finished speaking the assembled delegates broke into round after round of applause and cheers which gained strength, as they swept along. State standards fell into line and the marching began. I was standing on the convention floor at the time and watching the swift growth of a stampede. A Southern delegate, one of the most able of the Republican party leaders came to me in the height of the frenzied outburst and asked, "What's it mean, Mr. Dave?" I replied, "I think these people are trying to tell Mr. Hoover that they are ashamed of the way they doubted him and deserted him and that now they know him to be their party's and the nation's finest and greatest man and are trying to convince him that their hearts are with him." He replied, "I think it means that they're going to nominate him!"

---

* "Further Explorations of the New Deal," address before Meeting of Republicans Sponsored by Nebraska Republican State Committee, Lincoln, Nebraska, Jan. 16, 1936.

He was wrong.

It was not in the cards. That the Republican party was not in a heroic mood at that time is indicated by the fact that after continued efforts to restore order the presiding officer in an enforced comparative lull stated that Mr. Hoover already had left the convention hall to catch a train for New York. He was then resting in a nearby room.

Thus is history colored by untruths. Thus, except for Mr. Hoover's inspiring speech, an otherwise drab convention went about its business of nominating for its standard bearer a man with an admitted preference for courthouse politics.

Some notes I made following the 1936 November election show that in early July Mr. Hoover wrote John D. M. Hamilton, chairman of the Republican National Committee and stated in substance: "I am completely at your disposal for any service which you think I can render."

The information concerning the reception of the follow-up of Mr. Hoover's offer came to me directly from three sources, Messrs. Hoover, Hamilton and Landon and is as follows:

Mr. Hamilton, in reply to that letter, told Mr. Hoover that they very much wanted his help in the campaign. To this Mr. Hoover replied that he would be glad to do everything he could provided Governor Landon, the candidate, invited him to do so. He wanted, he said, to be certain that Governor Landon really wanted him.

Mr. Hamilton thereupon asked Mr. Hoover what he wished Governor Landon to say in the invitation. Mr. Hoover replied that the Governor need not write more than three or four lines, merely an invitation to him to participate in the campaign and to sign his name to the letter.

Somewhat later Mr. Hamilton telephoned Mr. Hoover to inquire whether or not it would be agreeable to him if Governor Landon extended his invitation over the telephone. Mr. Hoover agreed to this arrangement.

The next word Mr. Hoover had on the subject came to him when he reached the Glendale, California, railroad station one evening where he was to take a train to his home in Palo Alto. The station agent told Mr. Hoover that Topeka, Kansas, was calling him. Mr. Hoover told the agent that since the train was due to leave in ten minutes he preferred to complete the call from his home the following morning.

It may be of interest to tell here the manner in which Mr. Hoover was located at the railroad station by the long distance telephone operator. As I remember, the story as he told it to me was to the effect that there was a long distance telephone operator in San Francisco who took great pleasure in completing long distance calls for him. She would use her judgment on what calls she considered important. When one came in that she thought was important she would learn where he was or the route he had taken. If he were traveling by car she would notify filling station attendants along the route he was taking and ask them to flag him and to call her. At other times she sent messengers fifty or seventy-five miles into the mountains where he was fishing and asked him to come out to answer one of his calls.

Upon reaching Palo Alto the next morning Mr. Hoover completed the telephone call during which Governor Landon extended a cordial invitation to him to take part in the campaign by making eight or ten speeches. Mr. Hoover replied that this would be impossible since he wrote his own speeches and he required two or three weeks to whip each one into shape. Governor Landon then pressed him to make all of the speeches he could and in addition requested him to make Chicago his headquarters so that he might be available to advise the staff on the strategy of the campaign.

This Mr. Hoover agreed to do and late that afternoon he left for Chicago. In taking the Overland Limited at Oakland an Associated Press reporter asked him if he were going to take part in the campaign. He replied that he was. The reporter then asked him if he had heard from Governor Landon. Mr. Hoover replied that he had. The reporter next asked what Governor Landon had said. Mr. Hoover replied, "You will have to ask Mr. Landon that. I am not quoting him other than to tell you that he asked me to devote all my time to the campaign. I am doing so."

The next morning at Elko, Nevada, another Associated Press reporter looked up Mr. Hoover on the train and showed him an Associated Press dispatch from Topeka in which a member of Governor Landon's secretarial staff denied that Governor Landon had talked with Mr. Hoover. The reporter asked for Mr. Hoover's comment.

He said in substance: "I will not give you a statement for publication here. I request, however, that you send the Associated Press correspondent in Topeka the following message: 'When Mr. Hoover was shown the Associated Press dispatch in which a member of Governor Landon's secretarial staff denied Mr. Hoover's statement from Oakland that the Governor had talked with him, Mr. Hoover said: "This is the first time anyone has ever dared to challenge the integrity of a statement I made. I will not make a statement for publication at this time but if this denial is persisted in by members of Landon's staff I will be prepared at Ogden, Utah, upon arrival of this train at that place to have published the complete stenographic notes of my conversation yesterday morning with Governor Landon which were taken down by my secretary on the extension telephone."'"

A flock of newspaper men met him at Ogden but there was nothing for him to say since the Governor's staff had corrected that mistake.

Mr. Hoover continued his journey to Chicago as Governor Landon had requested and upon arrival there found the headquarters cool toward him. The headquarters also delayed making arrangements for any Hoover speeches. According to them they found it extremely difficult to work out a satisfactory schedule. They also indicated that local party officials were reluctant to arrange meetings for him. After a few such rebuffs Mr. Hoover arranged for his own speeches and broadcasting and operated throughout the campaign entirely as an independent unit.

Raymond Moley expresses his belief in his recently published book *Twenty-Seven Masters of Politics* that:

> The concentration of Democratic policy against Hoover succeeded even beyond the expectations of its progenitors. For the Republican party itself caught the malicious infection. Candidates Wendell

Willkie and Thomas E. Dewey skirted the Hoover issue with conspicuous but wasted caution. Both of these more recent candidates, by studied omission, implied that their Republican party began some time after 1933. The veil with which they covered the past was an insubstantial thing. Democrats seeing that past stark and unprotected, made it the center of their attack. Undefended by Republicans, the Hoover history as it was learned by millions of new voters was exactly what Democratic bias and vindictiveness wanted it to be. And this distortion proved in large measure to be the decisive factor in five successive Republican defeats.

In his newspaper column of August 18, 1949, Raymond Moley, in writing of the 1936 campaign, stated:

> The Democrats succeeded so well in this campaign of tarnishing the Hoover record that the infection spread to Republican leaders and candidates. Willkie and Dewey by studied effort sought to shroud the Hoover achievements and to create the impression that the Republican party they were leading had its origins some time after 1933. This was futile, of course. The Democrats were thus free to attack the Republican past, which was left starkly undefended.

One of the most notable addresses was before the Republican National Convention in Philadelphia, June 22, 1948. It is presented in full in Appendix XXVI. Another important recent address was delivered on the occasion of the celebration of his seventy-fifth birthday, August 10, 1949. This, too, is presented in full in Appendix XXV. An indication of the sense of duty and responsibility which motivates Mr. Hoover's actions is contained in his remark to me at a small dinner party that evening, shortly after the speaking exercises.

"A birthday party," he said, "certainly isn't any place to make an economic speech." Then the Quaker sense of duty came out and he added, "But with a four-network hook-up and millions of listeners I felt that I had to give the people something worthwhile."

CHAPTER THREE

Hoover Institute and Library on War, Revolution and Peace

One project that holds tremendous potential significance and has claimed a considerable portion of Mr. Hoover's thoughts, time and effort during recent years is the Hoover Institute and Library on War, Revolution and Peace.

The idea grew out of the "ineradicable vividness" his mind held of "the colossal error of war as an instrument of national policy," the "futility of war as a solvent of great human problems" and the "fearful toll that war takes of the generations succeeding the one which fought the battles." He first glimpsed it while making a crossing over the mine-strewn North Sea, during World War I, a crossing so full of hazards that the boat stewards collected cash for their services upon performing them as a result of their having suffered heavy financial losses when passengers who had signed chits had been lost with the boats that had been torpedoed.

Having had time on these crossings to weigh the waste and horror of war his constructive mind began to consider ways to eliminate the causes of war. The idea for an Institute and War Library which would serve this purpose gradually took form in his mind. When he decided what to do he took steps to carry out the plan. The Hoover Institute and Library stands today as the realization of his peace dream, which rests on his "profound conviction that the very first of all the problems pressing upon the human race is the problem of prevention of future wars."

His thinking on the subject was pointed up, he has stated, by his having read:

> Some remarks by President Andrew D. White of Cornell on the difficulty he experienced in the study of the French Revolution be-

cause of the disappearance of contemporaneous documents and fugitive literature. The position I held at that time required regular visits to several belligerent countries. It seemed to me to offer a unique opportunity to collect and preserve such records. I therefore established centers for such collections in each country and enlisted the aid of others who believed in the importance of this work. After the Armistice I was able to have these records sent from the various countries to Stanford University.

On my return to the United States to participate in the war administration, I was able to expand further these collections on the American side and to secure material from the many agencies of the Allied governments . . .

Soon after the war I became impressed with the fact that the most important aspect of the century was perhaps not the war so much as the consequences of the war, that is, the social, economic, and political currents which had sprung from it. The rise of democracy in Europe after the war and its collapse into Communism, Fascism, and National Socialism have contributed to make one of the greatest human crises in history. Therefore, instead of limiting the new Library to purely war material, I determined that the work of collecting should be continued and should be directed especially to securing records of these movements. In the building up of these collections the Library has had the co-operation of many governments and a great many individuals, and it now bids fair to possess one of the largest collections on Communism, Fascism, and National Socialism outside of the countries in which those movements originated . . .

I am confident we have established an institution of primary value to the American people. This period of world-wide experimentation in social, economic, and political institutions will be of importance for a thousand years to come. The work of collection will not be complete until these social and economic currents have run their course and have reached again some common elements of stability.*

---

* *Special Collections in the Hoover Library on War, Revolution and Peace,* by Nina Almond and H. H. Fisher, published by Stanford University, California, 1940. Above from Foreword by Herbert Hoover.

Some of his Quakerism is found in his statement that he looked upon war as "a supreme human problem." The crushing burdens of debt it created were bad enough, as also were its destruction of property and the disorganizations and dislocations of economic life which followed in war's wake, but over and above those catastrophes he saw "the loss of the glorious young manhood of the world who, but for war's slaughter, would lead the bright columns of human hope and human idealism and human progress to levels far above the past." In an address he delivered at Salt Lake City, Utah on November 7, 1932, he said:

> . . . wars in terms of women, widowed or unwed, with fond hopes blasted, of homes and children . . . born into lives foredoomed to ignorance and toil that dwarfs both the mind and the spirit . . . its fatal poison subtly invading the moral ideals of the people, bringing grossness and cynicism where should grow the fine flower of idealism.

In all of his official and unofficial acts he had sought, he said, to upbuild "the spirit of peace in the world and the maintenance of peace among nations."

Mr. Hoover's long-nurtured convictions about peace, his first hand experiences and observations about war's horror, the waste and futility of war which he had gained as a humanitarian and a public official together combined to challenge his thinking as a scientist and man of business.

He met this challenge during World War I by beginning to collect printed and manuscript materials which shed light on the important political, social, economic and ideological events of this century and founded the War Library as a part of Stanford University. His position as chairman of the Belgian Relief Commission and later of the American Relief Administration facilitated this collection. His more recent leadership in humanitarian work, his position as Secretary of Commerce and as President enabled Mr. Hoover and his friends to locate and acquire for the War Library gifts of irreplaceable material from governments, associations and individuals which would cost a larger sum to replace (if it could be done) than the $3,450,000 in cash which Mr. Hoover and his friends and institutions have contributed to the project.

The Library collections are housed in the Hoover Tower and War Library building which was dedicated in 1941. The two-hundred-eighty-five-foot Tower has fourteen levels which contain books, periodicals and manuscripts, and twenty-two cubicles for research workers on one floor. Newspaper and map collections are in the basement. The material which crowds the Library's shelves is devoted primarily to international relations which bear upon peace. It embraces the largest collection in the world on the Communist, Fascist, Nazi, and Socialist Revolutions, their underground operations and also the operations of both world wars. Many public figures of our century have deposited confidential documents to be opened after a stipulated period.

Included in the Hoover War Library are a priceless collection of millions of items on war, revolution and peace in eighty-nine different languages. Large numbers of scholars, students and researchers may find there:

1. Fifty thousand volumes of official publications of some sixty nations;
2. One hundred thousand books and pamphlets from all parts of the world;
3. Three thousand newspaper titles in more than thirty languages;
4. Fifteen thousand periodicals in some thirty-five languages from forty-five countries;
5. Publications of more than five thousand political parties, special interest groups, and learned societies; many thousands of letters and significant collections of posters, maps, charts, films, recordings, currencies, photographs and medals.

In his speech at the celebration of Mr. Hoover's seventy-fifth birthday, Dr. J. E. Wallace Sterling, President of Stanford University, in speaking of the Hoover Institute and Library said that:

> The Library began as a collection of contemporary materials on the first world war. The enterprise was motivated by the conviction that the evil of war could not be reduced or eliminated without study and understanding of its causes. The war collection has grown

in the past 30 years into the great Library of today. If its records could now speak, they would do so in thirty-five languages and they would say "We embody the essential history of the first half of the twentieth century. It behooves man to unlock our secrets and learn the lessons we have to teach."

As the Library has grown in size, so the conviction that inspired its founding has grown in strength, tempered and toughened by hard experience. This conviction holds, as I have already suggested, that prime and necessary values derive from honest inquiry. For centuries the scientific method of inquiry has been successfully used to penetrate mysteries of the physical universe and to wrest from Mother Earth amazing power and treasure. The same sort of attack on social problems is, comparatively, in its infancy and needs urgently to be placed under forced growth. Speculation as to what may or may not be so, grows quickly and in shallow ground, but it bears poor fruit. Investigation on the other hand requires more labor, and superior husbandry, but its yield can be rich and wholesome. The Hoover Library was founded and brought to its present high station in order that society might benefit from its resources through the work that is carried on within its mighty tower to advance the cause of peace. An enumeration of its achievements to date would be overlong here. But I would point out that in addition to continuing research activities, it offers also a growing program of instruction, and, as you might expect, the fact that such instruction is given here is of great consequence in the eyes of the Library's founder.

Many facets of character distinguish Herbert Hoover. Of these I presume to mention only two of the most outstanding: One is his great desire to get the facts bearing on a situation. This was manifest during his presidency by his creation of the Committee on Social Trends; and more recently by his work in the reorganization of the Executive Branch of the Federal Government, and it is manifest at least as convincingly in the Library which he has founded, generously supported and continuously inspired. The other facet is his great love for and his abiding faith in his fellow man. To this his whole life is magnificent testimony. In this Library and Institute which proudly bear his name, these two characteristics find harmonious expression. Here are the facts, and the intent to use them for the advancement of knowledge toward the betterment of mankind.

The Institute is a dynamic teaching institution which offers the opportunity for young postgraduate students to prepare themselves for governmental or private service in international affairs. It conducts research in many directions, and twenty-four volumes of important material have been published under the Library's imprint.

The Institute has carried on special programs financed by the Army, the Navy, the Belgian-American Educational Foundation, the Carnegie Corporation, the David Starr Jordan Fund, the Rosenberg Fund, and the Rockefeller Foundation. During and after World War II, the Institute, at the request of the Army and Navy, conducted a Civil Affairs Training School, a Civil Communications Intelligence School, and a School of Naval Administration.

Mr. Hoover's own definition of the Institute's and Library's purpose is: "to promote peace. Its records stand as a challenge to those who promote war. They should attract those who search for peace."

Many hundreds of Mr. Hoover's friends sent him a birthday present in the form of a contribution to help finance this project which is closest to his heart. In acknowledging his deep appreciation of these contributions which aggregated approximately $165,000, Mr. Hoover said at the beginning of his speech:

> My first duty is to acknowledge your generous reception and these most generous gifts to the Library.
>
> It is now thirty-four years since this Library on War, Revolution and Peace was founded. Over these years friends of the Library have contributed over $3,450,000 toward its support. And of priceless value have been the millions of documents and materials furnished freely by hundreds of individuals and three-score governments.
>
> This institution is not a dead storage. It is a living thing which over the years will correct a vast amount of error in the history of these troubled times. It will also teach the stern lessons of how nations may avoid war and revolution.
>
> Not being a government institution, it has never received a dime from government sources, and its scholars therefore can be as free

as the Sierra winds in its use and in the expression of objective truth. . . . (See Appendix XXVII.)

Since reason, based on accurate information and applied with understanding, never yet has failed man it is possible that this Institute and War Library which Mr. Hoover conceived and has helped so effectively to develop in time yet may prove to have been the greatest of all of his many important contributions to mankind. Its potentialities lie in its unique scientific approach to the cause of war and the ways to secure peace. If realized they will help end the scourge of war. This, however, it may not be able to do unless it is possible to secure an additional sum of $2,500,000 with which to bring the Institute and Library to their highest degree of usefulness and to make their work in the future secure.

Mr. Hoover looks upon the effort to secure additional funds for the Institute as one of his most important future tasks.

CHAPTER FOUR

Boys' Clubs, Relief and Food Leadership

Having worked hard all his life and loved it, Mr. Hoover could not completely relax, sit back and take it easy.

Between his speeches and his writings, visiting old friends, fishing, conferring with an endless stream of callers, conferring with Republican party leaders, he was for a period trustee of the New York Life Insurance Company, became a leader in Boys' Club affairs, conducted relief activities and rendered his alma mater, Stanford University, uniquely important services. In 1938 he revisited Europe for the purpose of making a first-hand study of conditions and to gain impressions and information on social, political and economic trends on that continent.

Mention of his service as trustee of the New York Life Insurance Company brings to mind a pleasant human story. It was told me by the late George Cortelyou, who then was chairman of the insurance company's committee responsible for discovering and recommending men for membership on the board. In this capacity he suggested to Mr. Buckner, then the company's president, that Mr. Hoover would make a fine addition. Mr. Buckner agreed, but pointed out that since Mr. Hoover's 1928 opponent, Al Smith, was a member of the board, it was possible that Mr. Smith might not approve such action. Mr. Cortelyou told Governor Smith what he had in mind, and the great Al heartily replied without hesitation, "Of course I'm for it. I'm regular. I'm organization. If you'd like me to nominate Hoover for the place I'll be glad to do it."

Belgian–American Foundation

One activity which has claimed Mr. Hoover's special interest since the end of World War I to the present date is concerned with the exchange of students between Belgium and the United States.

On August 28, 1919, Mr. Hoover, in writing to M. Delacroix, Prime Minister of the Belgian government, called attention to that government's formal approval (along with that of other concerned governments) of a method for settling the accounts of the Commission for Relief in Belgium. One sentence in this memorandum had stipulated that "Such balances will be appropriated or invested for the benefit of the population in Belgium and Northern France as shall be determined by the commission."

Mr. Hoover then proposed that a portion of the commission's balance be used for "the creation of a foundation, the income from which shall be applied in principle to enable the children of families who have not the means to otherwise secure such an education, to obtain it. This may be accomplished by gifts, scholarships or otherwise to obtain this general principle. I would propose that this foundation should be vested in a board of half each of Belgian and American trustees, the American trustees to be selected by the Directors of the Commission for Relief in Belgium. Some minor proportion of this fund, as the trustees may consider advisable, could well be applied to the extension of such education as will look toward the protection of child life."

Many years later, in response to a request from Senator J. William Fulbright for his views on the purpose of S. 1636 (later known as the Fulbright law) which sought to provide intellectual exchanges between the United States and other countries, Mr. Hoover stated:

> In 1920, as a disposal of part of the funds from liquidation of supplies, etc. from the Belgian Relief Commission, I established the Belgian–American Educational Foundation, the purpose of which was exactly what you propose. In its twenty-five years, more than 700 individuals (477 Belgians and 225 Americans) were "exchanged" during the period between World War I and World War II. Several important results have followed. At the outbreak of World War II nearly one-quarter of the teaching and research faculty of the Belgian Universities had been graduate students in American universities. One prime minister and six cabinet members have likewise done graduate work in American universities. Numbers of American and Belgian professors and specialists have been ex-

changed between our American and Belgian universities. I doubt whether there is a country in Europe where the ideals and purposes of the American people are so well understood and so respected as they are in Belgium. And although Belgium is a small country, there is a much greater understanding of it and respect for it in the United States than for some larger and more powerful states. I enclose a recent report on the Belgian-American Educational Foundation.

In a later letter to Senator Fulbright, Mr. Hoover stated that in its operations the Belgian-American Foundation "has carried on intellectual exchanges in various ways between Belgium and the United States. Our main interest has been in advanced and graduate fellowships. We have brought over 750 Belgian professors, students and scientists to this country and sent 230 Americans to Belgium. Most of the Belgians who studied or traveled in this country are in teaching and public service. There have been and are now former fellows in the Belgian Cabinet and in other official posts."

Finnish Relief and the Small Democracies Crusade

In response to an appeal for help which high officials of the Government of Finland made to him in December, 1939, following Russia's attack on their country, Mr. Hoover organized and directed the first effort to relieve distress abroad that had been conducted on a national scale following the outbreak of World War II.

Finnish authorities in seeking to enlist his help had stated that an announcement of such an effort from those in whom their people had so long a confidence would greatly strengthen the morale of the civil population who were suffering bitterly from barbarous air-attacks. The Finns were under the necessity of mobilizing their utmost manpower to save their freedom. Since their bread winners were at the front and their economic life disrupted there consequently was great destitution and suffering in the civil population.

Mr. Hoover and his associates raised approximately six million dollars to aid the people of gallant Finland.

In August 1940, leaders of the five little democracies of Belgium, central Poland, Finland, Holland and Norway asked Mr. Hoover to raise his voice in their behalf. They stated that without receipt of food supplies their peoples would be devastated by famine and pestilence during the coming winter. They did not appeal for charity. Each of the countries had a quantity of liquid resources outside its own borders with which they would be able to pay for the necessary supplies. They also had the ships for transporting it.

The crux of their problem was identical with the one Mr. Hoover faced in the Belgian Relief Commission project in 1917. Here again the Allies insisted that the Germans should feed these victims; the Germans insisted that it was not their responsibility. Mr. Hoover sought only two concessions: (a) that the Allies lift their blockade sufficiently to permit food ships to pass; (b) the Germans give guaranties not to appropriate these food supplies.

Holding that "American public opinion and American moral leadership have responsibilities" he made his plea because, as he said:

> . . . I cannot forget the faces of the hungry, despaired, and terrorized women and little children, who are the real victims of modern war. I cannot forget the unending blight cast upon the world by the sacrifice of the flower of every race not only in the trenches but in the cradle. All that was dreadful in the last war beyond any words of mine. But it is far worse and there is far more of it in this war. It is not alone the vast increase in air power. But there is an increase in its ruthlessness and brutality. And while in the last war only one little democracy was invaded, today there are all these others. . . .
>
> There are things in this world that are not silenced by ideological argument or armchair strategists or declamation as to who is responsible. They are not to be settled that way because of the teachings of Christ which have resounded down these two thousand years. That teaching gave to mankind a new vision and part of that vision was mercy and compassion. The greatest Teacher of mankind did not argue and debate over the ideology and the sins of the two thieves. And he thundered scorn at the priest and the Levite who passed by.

Mr. Hoover carried on a gallant but losing three-years' fight for the starving people of the small democracies. He failed because the administration in Washington was hostile to his proposal.

Food Leadership in World War II

During the war the Roosevelt administration made no use of Mr. Hoover's qualifications as the world's first authority on food production and distribution.

Mr. Hoover, a private citizen, without portfolio or official encouragement, gave America its only really able leadership in the all-important food field in World War II. By means of radio and other public speeches and by interviews and articles he pointed out the weaknesses of the administration's mistaken and misguided farm policy which had created shortages in fats, oils, oleomargarine, cotton seed and dairy products. He offered constructive suggestions about how to solve its problems. His leadership crystallized public opinion so effectively that it, in turn, forced administration officials to correct their mistakes.

In his speech delivered at the Midwest Governors' Conference at Des Moines, March 15, 1943, he discussed some of the weaknesses on the home front, and then added:

> One of these weaknesses is in the food sector. And, indeed of the different sectors of the home front, food is the greatest. It stands next to the military effort in importance. Food serves on both the home and the foreign fronts. We have not only the job of feeding ourselves, but also our Allies. And if we would have peace after the war instead of the anarchy of starving Europe, we must be prepared to meet that also. Therefore our food production must be strengthened for a huge and a long sustained effort.

CHAPTER FIVE

World Food Mission in 1946

In February, 1946, soon after Mr. Hoover gave public support to President Truman's appeal to the world to save food, the President requested Mr. Hoover and Secretary of Agriculture Clinton Anderson to prepare and recommend a comprehensive program designed to alleviate world famine conditions.

This was the first request of any nature, for either information, advice or service, made by an occupant of the White House since March 4, 1933.

The then seventy-two-year-old Hoover, who holds that "saving of human life is a moral and spiritual duty" accepted without hesitation President Truman's call to duty. Before he started on this arduous mission of mercy Mr. Hoover gathered and analyzed all available data about the world's food needs and sources as follows: (a) The caring for the basic food needs of 800,000,000 undernourished men, women and children; (b) the amount and sources of minimum food supplies; (c) consideration of these 800,000,000 people as the basis of civilization's future.

When he began this trip of fifty-seven days of hard travel and harder work which called for many hours of fifty-seven nights, Mr. Hoover stated that its purpose was "to study means and methods of making the available food supplies in the world, save the maximum number of lives and present the situation as clearly as we can to President Truman and to the American people together with such advice as we can give."

Mr. Hoover and his volunteer staff, formerly members of the post-World War I relief and rehabilitation activities, visited and surveyed food needs and sources in twenty-five countries and examined those of five other countries. They traveled more than 50,000 miles in a U. S.

Army Transport Service C-54 airplane. They took with them the studies which had been prepared by the Combined Food Boards in Washington in March, 1946. These studies, based on statements of the deficit nations, placed the total requirements of cereals at 26,000,000 tons. Available supplies were estimated at 15,000,000 tons, leaving a world food supply shortage of 11,000,000 tons, or nearly 43 per cent of the total need. That gap could mean famine and death to millions.

The Hoover mission's members, upon arrival in a new capital, used the detailed information which had been compiled for them by various American government agencies. The data supplied by agricultural agents and army specialists were particularly useful as also was that provided by relief organizations. Government officials in the countries visited, usually the food minister, the minister of agriculture and the transportation officials, supplemented this information. Mr. Hoover gave each member of the mission his own assignment in the collection of data. Maurice Pate, for example, now the director of the International Emergency Children's Fund, inquired into the special needs of children.

Mr. Hoover and Dr. Dennis FitzGerald of the Department of Agriculture, who was the Secretary of the Combined Food Boards which controlled supplies during and after the war, secured the information regarding needs and possible available imports of supplies. Perrin Galpin, president of the Belgian-American Educational Foundation, and a member of the mission, is authority for the information that Mr. Hoover wore out 127 pencils on the trip.

Never before in history had a mission of experts visited so many countries to seek solutions to a single problem—food. Everywhere they used the same scale of values to determine how best to meet the acute immediate problem.

They gained the information to frame their expert judgment on the food problems by personal contact and intimate discussions with officials and others on the spot. Mr. Hoover's years of experience enabled him and his associates to appraise a situation quickly and accurately and to suggest action to meet the immediate emergency.

By radio from Cairo to a U. S. network, Mr. Hoover reported on conditions and needs in the European countries that he had just visited. His estimates were that a minimum of 11,000,000 tons of cereals would be needed to provide a 1500 daily calorie ration to the consumer. In addition, as much fats as could be secured for Europe and Asia would also be needed. About 6,000,000 tons of cereals were available to meet this need in normal commercial supplies. Mr. Hoover next directed his appeal to the food surplus countries—and he visited all of them except Russia and Australia. These were: Canada, the United States, Great Britain (which had extra food enroute), the Argentine and Siam. Mr. Hoover also made practical suggestions on how to close the gap during the four-month crisis until the harvest of 1946.

The estimated gap, he stated, could be partly closed by reducing the food imports needed on a calculated scale; by reducing consumption in producing countries; by transfers of supplies inside some countries (such as India); by loans of some cereals and by substitution of other cereals for rice and wheat. At the end of the tour when he made his final report, the gap between need and supply was estimated at 3,600,000 tons instead of the 11,000,000 tons which it had been when he started the trip.

This reduction of 7,400,000 tons from the earlier estimated food needs was made possible by Mr. Hoover's (a) personal appeals to the heads of governments and (b) by his suggestions as to improved methods. He saw many troubling situations and bad methods but he said "criticism can wait for history." Now, as he saw it, the job was that of saving millions from starvation. "The vital need," he added, "is unity and co-operation *now,* so that we may master the crisis." He won that co-operation.

Enduring peace was his dream and his goal. On his Food Mission trip his path crossed that of Dr. Ernest L. Klein and Ambassador Edwin W. Pauley in Honolulu. Dr. Klein has stated that Mr. Hoover urged that reparations be considered not as punishment, not as a desire to weaken our late enemies and strengthen ourselves, but as a means of distributing wealth and productive capacity in a way that would insure an orderly world economy that in turn would exert a powerful influence for peace. While the United States did not attempt to profit from the defeat of our enemies, we did fail to insist that our allies be equally magnanimous, and the world will rue the day that Mr. Hoover's policy of working for peace, first, last, and always did not prevail.

Everywhere he stressed the problem of children both because he believed they were most in need of enough food and because he believed help to children to be the most needed reconstruction effort in the world.

Mr. Hoover closed his report with a statement he had invariably made to the heads of the governments he visited:

> To succeed is far more than a necessity to economic reconstruction of the world. It is far more than the path to order and peace. It marks the return of the lamp of compassion to the Earth. And that is a part of the moral and spiritual reconstruction of the world.

One by-product of the Hoover Food Mission, and an important one, was that the presence of a former President of the United States served in many countries to bring together highly antagonistic elements on the single issue of food. This was the case in Bombay. It also was the case in Germany where the presidents of the German States in the American zone of occupation met with Mr. Hoover and American military government officials. This was the first official recognition that had been given the defeated Germans.

Upon conclusion of his trip to the food deficient nations, President Truman requested Mr. Hoover to visit the food exporting countries of South America, particularly the Argentine.

He and his mission staff visited the following countries in the two trips in the order given and between the dates mentioned.

Trip from March 17—May 12, 1946

Newfoundland
Azores
France
Italy
Switzerland
France (again)
Czechoslovakia
Poland
Finland
Sweden
Norway
England

Trip from March 17—May 12, 1946 (continued)

Belgium
Holland
Denmark
Germany
Austria
Yugoslavia
Greece
Egypt
Iraq
India
Siam
Philippines
China
Korea
Japan
Hawaii
U.S.A.

Total—28

Trip from May 25—June 19, 1946

Mexico
Panama
Colombia
Ecuador
Peru
Chile
Argentina
Uruguay
Brazil
Venezuela
Cuba
U.S.A.

At long last, after thirteen years, the world through President Truman had called the "old family doctor" and the most able living diagnostician from a retirement which political leaders had forced on him, and asked him to treat the world's grave illness. Threat of death from starvation overcame political prejudices. It could be met only with the services of recognized experts. Hundreds of millions of hungry people are now alive and able to give thanks that the experienced, expert, humanitarian Herbert Hoover was able to help them in their grave need.

CHAPTER SIX

Hoover Commission on Government Reorganization

The time lag in a democracy between the original presentation of a sound proposal and official acceptance of it is well illustrated by the unanimous action of the Congress in the summer of 1947 in approving the Lodge-Brown act providing for the reorganization of the executive branch of the federal government.

As President, Mr. Hoover repeatedly asked the Congress for such authority but the then Democratic majority for unadmirable political reasons just as repeatedly denied him this authority.

In 1947 the Congress called him back into the public service. In doing so they gave him a job which by experience he was better fitted than any living man to undertake.

What Congress asked him to undertake as stated in the directive which the enabling legislation was:

> It is hereby declared to be the policy of Congress to promote economy, efficiency, and improved service in the transaction of the public business in the departments, bureaus, agencies, boards, commissions, offices, independent establishments, and instrumentalities of the executive branch of the Government by
>
> 1. Limiting expenditures to the lowest amount consistent with the efficient performance of essential services, activities and functions;
> 2. Eliminating duplication and overlapping of services, activities, and functions;
> 3. Consolidating services, activities, and functions of a similar nature;
> 4. Abolishing services, activities, and functions not necessary to the efficient conduct of Government;
> 5. Defining and limiting executive functions, services and activities.

The first meeting of the commission was held at the White House. President Truman met with it for a few minutes, gave it his blessing, and although acting without authority, suggested that Mr. Hoover and Mr. Acheson would make appropriate chairman and vice chairman, respectively, of the commission. After President Truman had left the meeting the commission unanimously acted upon his suggestions.

Mr. Hoover was nearly seventy-three years old when he agreed to undertake this assignment in July, 1947 with the statement that it was to be his last public "office" but that he hoped to serve the public in one way or another for some time to come.

The first test of Mr. Hoover's resolution not again to hold public office came in the summer of 1949 in the form of Governor Thomas E. Dewey's offer to appoint him United States Senator from New York to fill the place made vacant by Senator Wagner's resignation. Mr. Hoover declined Governor Dewey's offer of appointment.

Whatever his other reasons may have been for declining, an important one was that he had not finished his job of reorganizing the federal government begun in 1947.

Now, more than two years later and at the age of seventy-five, Mr. Hoover sees daylight ahead. During this time he has carried forward this comprehensive program with the helpful co-operation of the twelve-man bipartisan commission, and the assistance of three hundred or more of the nation's foremost experts in various fields of government activity.

Congress appropriated $2,000,000 for the Commission's expenses, much of which has been spent for travel, secretarial services and printing expenses. A few of the twelve members of the commission, with limited means, received per diem compensation for their services in addition to their expenses. Other members, including Mr. Hoover, who could afford to do so, received no compensation. The commission's recommendations are based on the most exhaustive, comprehensive and able survey ever made of our governmental machinery. If Congress accepts and puts into effect the commission's recommendations, it can, by eliminating waste, duplication and overlapping services, reduce the cost of the executive branch of our federal government by more than three billion dollars per year. When translated into individuals this means that the government would leave $21.44 more in the pocket of each of the men, women, teen-agers and babies in the country.

Magnitude of the Task

The magnitude and complexity of the commission's task is illustrated by the fact that today there are 1812 federal government agencies. Twenty years ago there were 362 such agencies. Today these 1812 agencies are staffed by 2,100,000 job holders. Some of them were created to meet a temporary emergency but live on and thrive after the emergency has become history. Some of them were created at the demand of pressure groups; some because someone with power thought that their creation was a good idea and others for less understandable reasons. Bureaucrats, like the brook, go on forever.

Few of the heads of the overlapping agencies dare permit the curtailment of its activities. If he did so, his staff would lose their jobs.

In 1945, Comptroller-General Lindsay Warren pointed out in hearings before Congress that seventy-five bureaus, divisions, and agencies had important connections with the field of transportation. In more recent hearings before the House of Representatives he stressed the fact that three separate federal agencies examine insured banks. For good measure, Mr. Warren added:

"I say the present setup is a hodgepodge and crazy quilt of duplications, overlappings, inefficiencies, and inconsistencies with their attendant extravagance. It is probably an ideal system for the tax-eaters and those who wish to keep themselves perpetually attached to the public teat, but it is bad for those who have to pay the bill."

No one should discount the importance of the commission's recommendations which, if adopted, will cut the cost of the federal government nearly four billion dollars annually. But their adaption also will help bring some order out of chaos in Washington and thereby make our bungling bureaucracy more efficient and responsive.

This point is emphasized by a general indictment which accompanied the first of the commission's nineteen reports to the Congress which stated:

"Definite authority at the top, a clear line of authority from top to bottom, and adequate staff aids to the exercise of authority do not exist. Authority is diffused, lines of authority are confused, staff services are insufficient. Consequently, responsibility and accountability are impaired."

In an address delivered on December 12, 1949, Mr. Hoover, in speaking of the commission's recommendations, stated that the movement to encourage their adoption "has become a crusade for the intelligent reduction of the expense of government. It is a crusade to clear the track for competency. It is a non-partisan crusade. It is a job for citizenship rather than partisanship."

He added that there were four reasons why the crusade in responsible citizenship which had grown out of the commission's recommendations had "wider implications than specific reforms."

The first of these implications "relates to our fiscal and economic survival." The second was that "millions of Americans are receiving a lesson in the fundamentals and methods of good government." The third, he said, "in a larger sense," is "to make democracy work" and added, "There is today much apprehension lest the American experiment will fail. We have need to re-establish faith that the whole of the preamble to the Declaration of Independence and the Gettysburg Address are still related to government. If the republic is not to be overwhelmed, the people must have such methods and systems as will enable good officials to give them good government.

"Success in our crusade will help bring faith instead of cynicism and disillusionment."

His final point was that the success of this "crusade to reduce cost of government is a necessary condition to winning the cold war. We are fighting this war at frightful cost. The way to win that war is to reduce our wastes, give competence a chance, and defer some government ventures. By these reforms and these self-denials, we can help disappoint Mr. Stalin."

In conclusion, he warned, "We must conserve our strength and stop wasting our heritage if we are to survive as a free people."

According to a speech made at the New York *Herald Tribune* Forum on October 25, 1949, Arthur S. Flemming, formerly a United States Civil Service Commissioner and a member of the Hoover Commission and now President of Ohio Wesleyan University, asked:

> What did the twelve members of this bipartisan commission have in mind when they unanimously agreed to such an indictment? Well, for one thing we had in mind situations where a bureau is located, let us say, in Department X, but where the head of Department X has very little, if any, control over the operations of the bureau.
>
> And it was because we knew as a commission that this and other similar situations do exist that we said to the Congress—'to remedy this situation is the first and essential step in the search for efficiency and economy in the executive branch of the federal government.'
>
> And that brings us to the theme to which I have referred. In all of our reports we have, in effect, said this:
>
> First, it is imperative to fix responsibility in a clean-cut manner for the various duties and responsibilities which are assigned to the executive branch of the government.
>
> Second, it is imperative to give persons to whom responsibilities are assigned sufficient authority to act so that they can carry on their work in an efficient and effective manner.
>
> Third, it is imperative to establish controls which will insure that those who have authority to act, act within a framework of standards set by the Congress and by the President of the United States.

Mr. Flemming also discussed the commission's findings and recommendations regarding the nation's water resources by quoting one paragraph of the report of this task force which said:

"Under conflicting laws, rival federal agencies compete for the taxpayer's money in what often appears to be premature and unsound river-development projects duplicating each other's survey and bidding against each other for local support at national expense."

Mr. Flemming pointed out that the competition for the taxpayer's dollar between, for example, the Bureau of Reclamation of the Department of the Interior and the Army Corps of Engineers is indefensible. It results in a waste of money as well as in a failure to develop plans which, for example, take into consideration irrigation needs as well as flood-control needs, or flood-control needs as well as irrigation needs.

And all of this is taking place in an area where present plans call for spending in excess of $50,000,000,000 in the year just ahead.

"A majority of our commission recommended therefore," Mr. Flemming stated, "that the activities of the Bureau of Reclamation and the Army Engineers in this area should be telescoped and that the Secretary of the Interior should be made responsible for the entire operation. His plans would be checked by a board of impartial analysis and review to be located in the office of the President."

In continuing Mr. Flemming pointed out that the commission found competition and duplication between the Bureau of Reclamation of the Department of the Interior, the Forest Service of the Department of Agriculture, and the Soil Conservation Service of the same department.

The commission recommended that responsibility for land-management activities be fixed in one department; namely, the Department of Agriculture, and that the Secretary of Agriculture should be given adequate authority to act.

In his examination and discussion of the field of public health and medicine Mr. Flemming stated that the administration of federal hospitals is divided between the Army, the Navy, the United States Public Health Service, and the Veterans Administration. As a result, we often go ahead and construct new hospitals without first of all determining whether or not we can use some of our existing facilities. On June 30, 1948, there were 155,000 patients in government hospitals having a capacity of 255,000.

He added, "We have recommended the creation of a united medical administration which, among other things, would administer all of our federal hospitals in this country. This administration should be under the direction of an administrator who would see to it that existing facilities, both public and private, are used and who would also have responsibility for developing plans for new hospitals on something other than a hit-or-miss basis."

Wasteful procedures—which means waste of money that comes from the taxpayer's pocket—in the federal Medical Service, as brought out by the commission's study serves to illustrate conditions which exist throughout the federal government structure.

The medical task force found that in 1948, more than forty-four federal agencies spent about one and one-quarter billion dollars for health and medical services, and in 1949, the Veterans Administration *alone* spent as much as all these federal agencies did in 1948. The task force points out that the federal government now assumes a varying degree of care for some twenty-four million persons—about one-sixth of the population; and the Veterans Administration alone will require three hundred thousand beds to meet its needs in 1980, all without any central plan.

Summarizing the results of their detailed studies of federal hospital facilities in several areas, the task force revealed that in the New York City area, for example, four Army and Air Force hospitals could be closed, under a unified hospital plan, reducing the requirements for medical officers by 80 per cent, yet at the same time providing a higher standard of services. It also pointed out that several federal agencies are planning to build hospitals in this area to cost $100,-000,000. This means a doubling of the permanent plant when there is no evidence that such additional beds are needed.

Its investigation of the federal hospital construction program revealed that, in the Veterans Administration alone, proposed new facilities will cost more than $1,100,000,000. Cost estimates range from $20,000 a bed to as high as $51,000 per bed, depending on the size and location, while the average total cost of construction per hospital bed for private hospitals is about $16,000.

Such waste is almost beyond imagination but it exists.

Dr. Robert L. Johnson, President of Temple University and National Chairman of the Citizens' Committee for Reorganization of the Government Executive Branch, has publicly stated that:

"Legislation embracing fully 20 per cent of the commission's recommendations has already been enacted. Conservatively, savings of one and one-half billions a year in the operating costs of government can be realized as this legislation is put into effect.

"Basic laws have been passed in four areas:

"One—to renew the President's authority to submit 'plans' to Congress for the realignment and regrouping of agencies. (In the session just ended President Truman presented seven such plans, of which six were accepted.)

"Two—to consolidate and simplify the purchasing, inventory control, records management, and other so-called 'housekeeping' functions of government.

"Three—to strengthen unification and economy in the management of the Armed Services.

"Four—to provide for partial reorganization of the State Department."

Mr. Johnson adds that:

"It is not too much to hope that the next session of Congress may see action on as much as 60 per cent of the remaining recommendations. These can bring additional operating economies of at least two billion dollars a year. The historic odds considered, I think any advocate of reorganization would cheerfully have sold his soul in April for a solid promise that he would be able to say in October the things I have just told you."

Whether or not the public yet recognizes the grave danger inherent in Big Government, that danger does exist because vastness and complexity of Big Government are becoming increasingly threatening to our free institutions. Whether or not the size of government can be streamlined in this day and age of the kind of public thinking which dominates the nation cannot be here answered. But a majority of the "twelve tough-minded individuals of different political and ideological views" were able to reach agreement on all but one or two points of their far-reaching assignment. They were all agreed on the point that government should be made as efficient as man is capable of making it.

In an early statement Mr. Hoover held that the commission's

. . . field of inquiry not only concerns every citizen, it concerns the very strength and vitality of democracy itself. The success of this mission may well set the pattern for future joint participation by private citizens and government representatives on matters affecting national welfare.

Indicative of the extent and comprehensive nature of the work of the Commission is the enumeration of its task forces:

1. Office of the President and its relation to the department and agencies
2. Post Office Department
3. Procurement Functions of Civilian Departments
4. Transportation and Communications Functions
5. Veterans' Affairs
6. Public Welfare Functions
7. Fiscal, Budgeting, and Accounting Functions
8. Federal-State Administrative Relationships
9. Public Works Functions
10. Federal Field Offices
11. Revolving Funds and business enterprises of the Government other than leading agencies
12. Lending Agencies
13. Federal Personnel Management
14. Foreign Affairs
15. Natural Resources
16. Regulatory Agencies
17. Agricultural Activities
18. Medical Services
19. Indian Affairs
20. Government Statistic Services
21. Records Management
22. National Security Organization

These task forces, working for periods of ten to fourteen months with the full co-operation of government agencies, have produced the most comprehensive body of research in the history of government. The end result is a panoramic picture of the world's largest business, that of our federal government today. Not all the task force recommendations agreed on secondary questions in areas where their researchers converged. One of the commission's problems has been the resolving of its differences into a unified pattern of government.

The research work of the task forces for the most part was completed by the end of October, 1948. It placed the mass of uncoordinated data on the desk of the commission, which undertook the job of analyzing and formulating reports to the Eighty-first Congress which would embody intelligent recommendations for modernizing the executive branch of the government.

Some Of Its Recommendations

The Commission has drafted nineteen topical reports which present their findings and recommendations. These were released to Congress and to the public during the months of February and March, 1949. Recommendations of the task force include the establishment of a National Bureau of Health within the Cabinet Department embracing health, education and security. The bureau would administer all general hospitals of the Armed Services and most station hospitals except those at outlying posts; the medical functions of the Veterans Administration; and the hospitals of the Public Health Service. Further, it urged the integration of the federal hospitalization system and non-federal hospitals to secure greater efficiency and service, and better to utilize the professional medical manpower.

One other illustration which helps project the nature and complexity of the Commission's work as well as the scope and potential taxpayer benefits which it holds, is that which deals in the field of government housekeeping activities—supply, records, management and operation and maintenance of public buildings.

It found that due to outmoded regulations and the lack of any central body to coordinate Government purchasing, about one-half of the three million purchase orders issued annually by civilian agencies are for ten dollars or less and the "paperwork" on each of these transactions exceeds the cost of the items purchased.

Similar inefficiencies existed with respect to storage and issuance procedures. For example, there are seventy-two different activities of the Government which operate storage facilities in the Washington metropolitan area alone. In addition 42 per cent of the Washington stores' inventories are for the benefit of field stations. The obvious conclusion is that this stock could have been shipped direct to field stations, saving unnecessary transportation and warehousing costs.

A study of stock facilities of ten civilian agencies by the Office of the Budget showed that excess stocks average about 72 per cent of total stock inventories. A contributing factor to this condition is the agency practice of investing appropriation balances in inventories and supplies to avoid returning such funds to the treasury at the end of a fiscal year.

As to records management, the commission disclosed that the federal records now in existence would fill approximately six buildings each the size of the Pentagon. The commission believes that by destroying duplicating records and by establishing a central records center approximately 50 per cent of the total records of the average government agency can be eliminated.

The commission recommended that the responsibility for the activities of supply, records management, and operation of public buildings be placed in a new Office of General Services under a director appointed by the President. This agency, by simplifying and coordinating procedures, could save $250,000,000 annually in supply purchases, and could reduce inventories by $2,500,000,000. Taxpayers should like this.

Congress, by passing the General Service Act in the summer of 1949, made these recommendations law and by so doing put into process the machinery which eventually will save the taxpayers $250,000,000 per year. The adoption by Congress of the Tydings bill on August 3, cut the annual federal government costs still further.

To date, mid-December 1949, twenty per cent of the commission's recommendations have been made effective and have resulted in potential economies of more than one billion dollars annually.

This saving makes an excellent dividend on the commission's total taxpayer investment of less than $2,000,000 in the commission's cost.

Adoption of Report Could Revitalize Constitution

If and when the commission's recommendations are adopted time may demonstrate that its major contribution, greater even than the billions of dollars it will annually save the taxpayers, will be that of having revitalized our Constitution through having made government more efficient and responsive.

The timeliness of its study and proposals is emphasized by the fact that today large numbers of confused men throughout the world are giving credence to the specious belief that democratic government is synonymous with inefficiency and waste: that totalitarian government holds a monopoly on efficient public service.

Anticipating that some individuals might hold that it would be dangerous to give some officials the amount of authority it recommended the Hoover Commission stated in its first report the belief that:

"An energetic and unified executive is not a threat to free and responsible government. Strength and unity in an executive make clear who is responsible for faults in administration and thus enable the legislature better to enforce accountability to the people."

No one knows to what extent Congress, either for political reasons, pressure-group or vested-interest demands; for selfish reasons (the big vested interest in this situation is that of the bureaucrats whose positions may be in jeopardy and if lost would be forced to find jobs and work for a living) will emasculate the Hoover Commission's recommendations.

Dr. Robert L. Johnson of the Citizens' Committee has stated that:

"Reorganization faces many obstacles mechanical, procedural, and human and of these the greatest is human. Resistance to change is not a monopoly of government. It is natural to defend what you're doing. This results, however, in what might be called the 'Yes But' psychology of government. 'Yes,' says this department head or that agency chief, 'I believe heartily in reorganization . . . BUT reorganize the other fellow not me.' This, in turn, results in pressures on Congress for exemptions here and exceptions there in reorganization laws. These are what Mr. Hoover has termed the little 'grasshopper bites' which have doomed one reorganization plan after another."

The Hoover Commission's part of the job is done. In its final report it demonstrated that it practiced as well as preached economy by returning $31,000 of its appropriations to the United States Treasury.

The issue is now up to the people who foot the government's bill. The commission's report will long stand as the most able, understanding and comprehensive study and program ever made which is designed to enable free men to remain free and at the same time to be able to afford such services of government as an enlightened social conscience demands. If the people organize and act they can insure the adoption of nearly all, if not all of the recommendations of the Hoover Commission.

The only two American studies comparable to it in penetrating understanding, comprehensiveness and fruitful suggestions were both initiated, sponsored and guided by Mr. Hoover.

The first of these was made by the committee on Recent Economic Changes which was begun in January, 1928, and completed February, 1929. Its purpose was to make an analysis of postwar development in American economic life, particularly those developments since the recovery from the depression of 1920–1921.

The committee was directed to make a critical appraisal of the factors of stability and instability; in other words, to observe and describe the American Economy as a whole, suggesting rather than developing recommendations.

In its later deliberations the chairman, Herbert Hoover, was unable to take part and A. W. Shaw served as acting chairman.

The basic investigations for the Committee on Recent Economic Changes, like those for the Committee on Business Cycle and Unemployment, were made under the auspices of the National Bureau of Economic Research, Inc., with the assistance of an unprecedented number of governmental and private agencies.

In writing of this committee's field of endeavor, Dr. Frederick A. Mills pointed out that:

> Prices and price relationships almost completely dominate the economic life of the nation. Fundamental to human welfare as are the activities of production, distribution and consumption of goods, it is prices as a medium of control which, in their ceaseless changes and readjustments, stimulate or retard the very processes by which

our industrial and commercial life is carried on, and govern the direction of human effort.

The second major study that Mr. Hoover initiated, sponsored and guided was that made by the Committee on Recent Social Trends and Developments which he created when President.

CHAPTER SEVEN

Summation

An Appraisal of the Man

Mr. Hoover is a man of many paradoxes.

Warm humanitarian impulses arouse him but only hard relentless facts, in hand and appraised, can move him to act.

Public sentiment in the raw as expressed in the ballot box and in the hearts of the people quickly catches his interest but it does not convert him to a cause. His conversion comes only after he has assembled and appraised all pertinent facts and conceives a way to weld the people's aspirations with administrative action.

The late William Allen White made the foregoing and some of the following points in an article he wrote in 1933 about Mr. Hoover for the *Saturday Evening Post.*

Mr. Hoover's business administrative experience caused him to consider the White House as primarily an administrative office, whereas in reality it has become the source of democratic leadership. The presidency, first of all, has become an evangelist's pulpit. Over the decades and the generations the presidency has grown into the nation's headquarters for making public sentiment, and after making it to channel it through Congress.

Thus the President's chief job, rightly or wrongly, has become that of leading the American people—all one hundred and fifty million of us, rich and poor, intelligent and dumb, kindly or vicious.

President Hoover's executive training, his lack of histrionic ability, his Quaker inhibitions which caused him to walk kindly, but seriously, about his duties, his Quaker dourness which disconcerted gay spirits that constantly have to be heartened, and his principles which prompted him to treat Congress as an important branch of the government instead of a collection of an above-the-average lot of

Americans whose chief interest was to be returned to Washington every two or six years; combined to create many of his Presidential problems.

Neither the genuineness of his humility and sincerity, nor his utter simplicity and self-abnegation (which are the core of strength in any man) were able to charm the members of Congress. And his certain, deep integrity made it impossible for him to glad-hand them. Lacking long political experience he had never learned the basic lesson which deals with political success; namely "God is always good and men are apt to be careless, so smile and forget their waywardness."

Public applause and approval, and especially that of their fellow partisans also served to stimulate many of Mr. Hoover's predecessors to yield to public demands on issues. Mr. Hoover also liked these intangibles which are political realities, but not the meat and bread of his life as they were to those of his predecessors whose political education was gained from caucuses and conventions, the stump and the legislatures.

Although as sensitively aware of the popular will as most of his predecessors in the presidency, he was far slower than the great majority of them in being moved quickly in response to popular demand. As a man he saw visions and dreamed splendid social, political and economic dreams. He understood and had sympathy with the people's aspirations, but as a scientist he could not bring himself to go all out for them until he had determined what it would cost in the stresses and strains of democratic action.

Mr. Hoover's cautious, scientific method of treating public problems and policies caused people to believe that he was primarily interested in preserving the *status quo*: actually what motivated him were his unchanged and unchangeable purpose in preserving the middle class American, social, political and economic institutions.

This middle class ideal, for that is what it was, had grown out of three hundred years of experience on this continent and flowered into a social order which, in addition to the unique culture it produced, provided an approximation of justice for men in every station of life.

The American middle class, which produced Mr. Hoover, has created most of the nation's wealth, done a large share of its work and nearly all of its praying. In the past it has formulated the policies and administered the laws of the government and it has supported our charities in season and out. This American middle class, a fluid body with vast numbers of new recruits constantly entering its ranks from the bottom and with a few of its members moving into the upper class each generation, roughly comprised, until present decades, 85 per cent of the population.

In all his essential aspects Mr. Hoover was a middle class President who strove to perpetuate middle class ideals. He distrusted the masses and he scorned the idle rich. He was a worker and a driver who had little regard for the more subtle social amenities. He likes plain men. And he is fond of fishing. In 1947, Dick Goodman wrote that as a fisherman Mr. Hoover "thrills to the outdoors like a poet. It isn't the fishing alone, it's the whole, clean wonderful beauty of the outdoors combined, which he loves."

As an administrator and an executive he seemed not to realize how much counsel and guidance the people needed in the form of radio addresses and speeches from their leaders when they were in the gloom of distress. His interest in facts and the application of them had a tendency to cause him to give secondary consideration to his position as a leader. Because a segment of the public could not sense this, they lost confidence in him.

Business-wise, Mr. Hoover's approach to such problems was a sound one, since in business three out of five moves must succeed. But political-wise, in a democracy and especially with the kind of a going concern our federal government is, the people have come to expect their President to make five moves out of a possible five and are satisfied if only two of these moves succeed. But Mr. Hoover was too conscientious to make concrete promises until he knew what he could do. He was a courageous leader. But as President he never assumed heroic roles and by eschewing them he was unable to rouse the public to high acclaim of his deeds.

Viewed objectively the Hoover way is far superior to that of the people. But, and here's the rub, the Hoover way shattered itself against the imponderable of the people's political habits. And habits, especially political habits, are so tough-fibered and durable that they cannot be easily or quickly changed. This was doubly true during the period of depression distress.

In a paragraph which appraised Mr. Hoover as a politician Arch Shaw wrote:

> The process of politics in the sense that so many Americans envisage the word suggests opportunism, intrigue, insincerity and the use of patronage which lead by devious paths into intellectual dishonesty. In that sense he was not a politician. In the sense of being a man alert to political currents and the needs and tendencies of his time, of steadfastness to principle and of inspirational leadership, he always has been.

Some others of our Presidents who came to their high office from the stump and the hustings, from caucuses and conventions, developed certain qualities which served them well in the White House. Their experiences had toughened their hides and thereby made them largely immune to criticism. Because Mr. Hoover had missed these political hide-toughening experiences of those of his predecessors who have moved from the court house to the White House, he was troubled by his opponent's attacks.

His politically trained predecessors also gained from their political experiences the Indian's rare sixth sense of caution—the ability to sense trouble before others around them are aware of it.

Other Presidents whose training enabled them to ignore attacks and yet develop a peculiar political sensitivity which enabled them to sense the approach of danger, acted quickly in response to public demand. They often mistook the voice of the people for the voice of God. They acted quickly in response to that voice.

Politically Trained Presidents Tried to Rule Congress

Those who reached the presidency through politics seemed to believe that public approval and applause gave them a charter for congressional leadership, the Constitution to the contrary and notwithstanding. This was natural because their training and experience had fixed their eyes on men and measures, on political parties and their factions. They inevitably thought in terms of this law or that measure as the means to the end. As a result they almost habitually considered first political techniques when looking for their answers to problems. This in turn inclined them to give less consideration to administrative phases of the proposed law. Frequently schooled by this type of presidential action the people, on their part, demonstrated a growing tendency to believe that it was true political leadership.

Mr. Hoover, while equally responsive with his predecessors to the people's aspirations, weighed every proposal in terms of the ultimate administration of the proposed new law. The implied social justice of the proposed measure could not alone induce him to act. He acted only after he had determined in legislative terms exactly how that policy might be best applied. Few of his predecessors had more than passing interest in the administrative side of governmental operation whereas Mr. Hoover's concern was to make the new policy a realizable ideal.

Thus we have another paradox. Hoover the cautious administrator who was also a man who dreamed dreams and saw visions of an exact realizable ideal of social, political or economic organization. He could not have been a St. John crying in the wilderness, nor a vocal St. Paul. His silence was his salvation as a man of integrity but it was his evil influence politically.

An examination of Mr. Hoover's record shows that his abiding belief, deeper than any other conviction he held, is that an ideal is only realizable if it can be concretely worked out in a definite administrative way. He shrunk from "government in business" not because it is not a noble theory but because he is convinced that it won't work in its contacts with the individual person; because of state socialism's lack, in the hearts and habits and traditions of our people, the material for any political tool which will guarantee honest and effective administration of such an utopian scheme.

As a corollary to his belief that an ideal is realizable only if it can be concretely worked out, he believed wholeheartedly in the free enterprise system because of its demonstrated ability to help the individual grow in strength and purpose.

His heart was quick in sensing and sympathizing with the yearnings of the people. It responded to the justice of much that they wanted but his mind forced him to be cautious, to be sure that a method could be found by which their yearnings could be satisfied without hurting them more than helping them.

These qualities and traits of his and the lack of the fire of the prophet in his voice and manner helped to cause the people to misjudge him because emotion is quicker than reason, feeling is faster than logic, information outruns wisdom.

He sought the "abolition of economic and intellectual poverty." He had "undaunted faith in those mighty spiritual and intellectual forces . . . the true glory of our people." Again he said: "The social order does not rest upon orderly economic freedom alone. It rests even more upon the ideals and character of a people. Governments must express those ideals in frugality, in justice, in courage, in decency, and in regard for the less fortunate, and, above all, in honor. Nations die when these weaken, no matter what their material prosperity."

That is a mystic speaking, who considers "the forces of righteousness and wisdom" as a material part of our material life. Again he spoke of "our American conception of mutuality of interest in our daily work."

There again is a Hoover paradox. The scientist and engineer who deals with intangibles as frankly as a chemist deals with an unknown reagent which produces calculable results.

He was not a believer in perfection, nor paradoxically, was he "blind to the errors and crudities of our civilization and human nature." At the same time he remained "confident of our ability to cure them."

In one speech he said that "of course our political and social system does not work perfectly" and added, "the human race is not perfect" but he always sought sincerely to make our political and social system work better. Once he said something like this: "Wisdom consists in knowing what to do next, rather than in debates on perfection."

Again he said, "I cannot conceive of a wholesome social order or a sound economic system that does not have its roots in religious faith. Materialism cannot seriously and finally engage the loyalties of men. . . . We are not dedicated to the pursuit of material things but to the pursuit of a richer life for the individual."

Another Hoover paradox is that he thinks like a pessimist but acts like an optimist. Recently in a private conversation he remarked that when one looked down every man-made alley, whether social, political or economic, one saw a precipice ahead and then added, "But I don't believe we'll reach it."

Lloyd George once remarked that Mr. Hoover had many excellent qualities and added, "But tact is not one of them." Actually, he can be one of the most charming and tactful of men.

Many men have remarked in recent years that Mr. Hoover has mellowed. He has not changed. Instead, in recent years, he has had time to be to large numbers of men what he has always been to his close friends—gentle, mellow, kindly, whimsical and witty.

Were it not for the world depression Mr. Hoover undoubtedly could have created and established a new concept of the place of government in the lives of the people, and would have introduced methods and procedures with the twin purpose of guiding and protecting men in their material lives and of lifting their eyes and fixing their purpose to the realization of those ideals which set man apart from the lower animals.

An Estimate of His Service

In his successful professional life, in his role as director of the greatest humanitarian undertakings in history, in his services as Secretary of Commerce and as President, in his private citizen activities as a leader of the moral, spiritual and intellectual forces of the nation and the world, as Chairman of the Reorganization Commission and in his personal relationships, Mr. Hoover has advocated earnestly and worked tirelessly to strengthen the principles of liberty. These he has defined as "an endowment from the Creator of every individual man and woman upon which no power, whether economic or political, can encroach and that not even the government can deny—that man is the master of the state, not the servant; that the sole purpose of government is to nurture and assure these liberties."

Although he has never so stated it, Mr. Hoover's words and works indicate that he starts from the premise that social progress is limited to the productive capacity of a nation's economic system; that the fight for human rights and individual liberties ever and always has been joined to that of the control of public expenditures.

In his seventy-fifth birthday address entitled "Think of the Next Generation," he outlined his beliefs about the ultimate effect the present rate of government spending will have upon the life of the people and the nation by saying:

> . . . During the past two years I have added somewhat to my previous knowledge of the currents of government in this Republic. Beyond the immediate problems of efficient organization of the federal departments, there arise from these investigations some grave questions as to our whole future as a nation.
>
> . . . Our thinking must square against some lessons of history, some principles of government and morals if we would preserve the rights and dignity of men to which this nation is dedicated.
>
> . . . We must wish to maintain a dynamic progressive people. No nation can remain static and survive. But dynamic progress is not made with dynamite. And that dynamite today is the geometrical increase of spending by our governments—federal, state and local.
>
> Perhaps I can visualize what this growth has been. Twenty years ago, all varieties of government, omitting federal debt service, cost the average family less than $200 annually. Today, also omitting debt service, it costs an average family about $1300 annually.
>
> One end result of the actual and proposed spendings and taxes to meet them is that the government becomes the major source of credit and capital to the economic system. At best the small businessman is starved in the capital he can find. Venture capital to develop new ideas tends to become confined to the large corporations and they grow bigger. Governments do not develop gadgets of improved living.
>
> Another end result is to expose all our independent colleges and other privately supported institutions to the risk of becoming de-

pendent upon the state. Then through politics we will undermine their independence which gives stimulus to government-supported institutions.

No nation grows stronger by subtraction.

Along this road of spending, the government either takes over, which is socialism; or dictates institutional and economic life, which is fascism.

Most Americans do not believe in these compromises with collectivism. But they do not realize that through governmental spending and taxes, our nation is blissfully driving down the back road to it at top speed.

In the end these solutions of national problems by spending are always the same—power, more power, more centralization in the hands of the state.

We have not had a great socialization of property, but we are on the last mile to collectivism through government collection and spending of the savings of the people.

The centuries-long struggle in England was for a system of government which would combine "freedom with efficiency and local rights with national union." All of our institutions rest on that rock. Local rights, and responsibilities too, are still vital to free men. And national union can be strong only when it is properly dovetailed with local rights.

Mr. Hoover said in concluding his seventy-fifth birthday address:

> A splendid storehouse of integrity and freedom has been bequeathed to us by our forefathers. In this day of confusion, of peril to liberty, our high duty is to see that this storehouse is not robbed of its contents.
>
> We dare not see the birthright of posterity to individual independence, initiative and freedom of choice bartered for a mess of a collectivist system.
>
> My word to you, my fellow-citizens on this seventy-fifth birthday is this: The Founding Fathers dedicated the structure of our government 'to secure the blessings of liberty to ourselves and our posterity.' We of this generation inherited this precious blessing. Yet as spendthrifts we are on our way to rob posterity of its inheritance.

> The American people have solved many great crises in national life. The qualities of self-restraint, of integrity, of conscience and courage still live in our people. It is not too late to summon these qualities.

Ours are cataclysmic days. The genii brought forth by our physical scientists from the test tubes and laboratories have created a new earth. Their discoveries have stimulated a disbelief in man's long-held conception of heaven where principles were all-important and all-enduring.

Today's demands for human security as well as the needs for adaptation of our political and economic machinery to meet new situations; the rules for governing group action and of individual living belong to the field of inexact social sciences. Their development has lagged far behind that of the exact physical sciences.

Time, trial-by-fire and debate will determine the ultimate outcome; whether mankind, in its frantic search for immediate security—food and shelter and clothing always are more pressing in their demands than are the seemingly distant but ever-close imponderables of liberty and freedom—will give up its liberties to gain immediate security and by so doing eventually also lose that security.

Whether or not the principles of liberty and freedom—the most persistent trait in the wildest animal ever born—will survive, will be known only when tomorrow's history pages have been written and read. Only then will it be possible to learn whether or not today's and tomorrow's generations have heard and weighed Mr. Hoover's words and clung to, advanced and strengthened the principles of liberty which, with words and actions, he has so ably interpreted.

It may be that we of this generation are unworthy to hold the sacred rights and privileges on which our government was founded and which made America the hope of the world. It may be that, as in the past, man must grovel under dictators every so often. It may be that the blood of martyrs alone can purify the stream of civilization.

Inadequate though we yet may prove to be in this crisis that threatens our free institutions, we cannot destroy man's insatiable desire and sure instinct for them. The leaders of another day and another generation are as sure to follow us and recreate a government of laws which place the individual ahead of the state as the stars and the sun are to keep on shining. When this happens Herbert Hoover's speeches and writings between 1933 and 1949 may well serve as the source of the inspiration of such men.

Sometime again, should we now destroy our liberties for the illusion of security, a stronger better generation will regain them. The march of the race is forward. Except in its weak, weary or confused moments the race seeks ever higher, finer social goals and strives to establish and perpetuate free government—the only types that nurture the golden hopes of men.

The heart and purpose of the Quaker message is for its members to be tolerant of others, to be rigidly honest and uniformly kind and to render unselfish service to all mankind in the belief that in God's good time Divine law and human law may be made one.

If Herbert Hoover's words and works are judged by this standard he is a good Quaker.

APPENDIX

I

Newspaper Editors Evaluate Herbert Hoover

Despite their penetration and wisdom, their clarity and readability, the best of our newspaper editorials pass as completely out of the lives of the people as do the leaves of the forest. This is unfortunate because many of them should have a permanent place in our national literature. Since that seems possible only in rare instances, I am attempting in the following pages to preserve within the covers of this book a few of the more significant editorial expressions which were printed in connection with Mr. Hoover's seventy-fifth birthday during the second week of August, 1949.

Editorial Birthday Greetings

The editorially expressed birthday greetings were general and generous.

It was the belief of the Augusta, Georgia, *Chronicle* that: ". . . People are just beginning to recognize the solid virtue of this man who is so typically American. Herbert Hoover, influenced by the Quaker faith to which he adhered, never developed the capacity to hate those who criticized and reviled him. He hated only those things which he conceived to be wrong, and when he was stirred to anger on this score he was always righteously indignant. . . ."

A writer in the Fairfield, Iowa, *Ledger* stated that: "A staunch Democrat told me recently that he regarded Hoover as one of the greatest men in American history, and I think it's high time all prejudices be buried and credit be given to whom credit is due. . . ."

The Long Beach, Calif., *Press-Telegram* pointed out that: "There is a man whose name has been vilified but whose countrymen have now come to love and respect him as indisputably our most distinguished private citizen. That man is Herbert Hoover." The Elkhart, Indiana, *Truth* believed that: "More men like Hoover will be needed in the high councils of all governments if moral progress is to catch up with scientific progress in time to save us."

In extending birthday felicitations to Mr. Hoover, the Elgin, Illinois, *Courier-News* expressed the opinion that: ". . . the finest birthday tribute of all—the one real expression which Mr. Hoover, personally, would most appreciate—would be the genuine public awakening to and an acceptance of the principles of the Hoover Commission recommendations for governmental streamlining and administrative economy."

The Wichita Falls, Texas, *Times* held that the people today "are inclined to look upon his career as a whole and to recognize the great usefulness of which it has partaken." And in the opinion of the Marietta, Georgia, *Daily Journal* Mr. Hoover "once again stands in high regard. We hope he so continues for many more happy birthdays." The El Paso *Times* continues to believe that Mr. Hoover "was wrong in 1930–1931. . . . But this newspaper believes that Mr. Hoover is just about right today. . . ."

The Charlotte, North Carolina, *Observer* stated that: ". . . As he receives the cordial greetings of multitudes of his countrymen on his birthday anniversary today, he can enjoy the assurance that his place in history as one of the really great American statesmen has been made secure and that he has the high esteem and full confidence of the people." After stating that "The sunshine of the nation's gratitude is in his afternoon," the Cincinnati *Times Star* added: "It will be fruitful, and may it be long! . . . Full and fair the sunlight falls on Herbert Hoover. The people of the Shadow, his detractors? They have passed 'in a desperate disarray over the hills and far away.'"

In the opinion of the Stillwater, Okla., *News-Press* Mr. Hoover "is an outstanding American citizen. May his kind increase and prosper."

In the recognition of Mr. Hoover's birthday, the Pittsburgh *Sun Telegraph* stated that it was highly fitting for the American people to "acknowledge the high stature of Herbert Hoover, his contributions to the public welfare, and his personal virtues of integrity and constancy in the face of unjust and undeserved belittlement and criticism," while the Astoria, Oregon, *Astorian Budget* held that: "It is an honor long-delayed, but well deserved."

Despite the fact that Mr. Hoover had never tried to regain his lost public esteem, he has done so, in the belief of the Chattanooga *News-Free Press* "because the American people have slowly become aware of his great worth and of the magnitude of the injustice that was done him." And the Nashville *Banner,* in speaking of birthday messages to Mr. Hoover, said: "He is honored, in truth, not so much as a former President, but as a great American." The Fergus Falls, Minn., *Daily Journal* held that "the American people are showing a somewhat belated sense of justice in honoring a man who has been viciously and savagely maligned during most of his career."

The Saratoga Springs *Saratogian* held that: "Really great men are few, men of moral courage and integrity in our highest offices. Mr. Hoover, who was honored yesterday on his seventy-fifth birthday, was a conspicuous example of one such. They cannot be too greatly honored." Touching on the same point, the King Ferry, New York, *Tribune* said that: "It is fitting that all America should pay homage to this great man—and do it in the day in which he lived. All that goes for true democracy; for integrity and honesty; for putting America and her ideals above that of selfishness; for putting the welfare of the nation, both present and future, ahead of political aspirations can be summed up in one word—Hoover." One reason for the high esteem in which Mr. Hoover is held today, in the opinion of the Albany, N. Y., *Knickerbocker News* is that: "He is a symbol of an era of construction that is passing. . . . He is one stalwart figure on a stage cluttered with midgets."

Stating that Mr. Hoover has lived a life of "superb usefulness," the New York *Herald Tribune* pointed out further that "like only one or two other statesmen in our history he has been able to go from service to service, making the Presidency only one step in a career which reaches its climax in the total and cumulative record of work done, good causes unselfishly pursued and arduous responsibilities carried through to the end. If ever a man were entitled to feel the deepest kind of satisfaction and content, it is Mr. Hoover at this milestone." Because of his record of service, the Sarasota, Florida, *Herald Tribune* stated that "Mr. Hoover now dominates that respected group of non-political advisers we refer to as 'the elder statesmen.' Whether Democrat or Republican, today's American, with respect and sincerity, wishes Herbert Hoover a happy birthday." In the opinion of the Clay Center, Kansas, *Dispatch,* "The most sincere tribute being paid Hoover, as he reaches his three-quarters of a century milestone, is that every day more and more voters come to regret that they did not vote for his re-election to the Presidency in 1932. . . . Time tests a man's abilities and Hoover's reputation is standing that test of the years." And the New York *Daily News* held that "Mr. Hoover has come to be one of the most respected and admired Americans that ever lived. . . . His career reminds us more than anything else of the lines from Rudyard Kipling's 'If,' about how 'if you can trust yourself when all men doubt you but make allowance for their doubting too . . . watch the things you gave your life to, broken, and stoop and build 'em up with worn-out tools.'" The Owensboro, Ky., *Inquirer* stated that: "At the beginning of his seventy-sixth year, Herbert Hoover is growing in strength among his fellow Americans, and to him they turn more often when words of wisdom are needed."

The editor of the Shreveport, La., *Journal* stated that: "It is most befitting that this American citizen be honored on his birthday with special recognition of his inestimable worth to the nation and its people. The honor is one of unmistakable merit. His birthday greetings, to which the *Journal* takes pride in participating, reflect the widespread esteem in which Mr. Hoover is held by his fellow countrymen."

The tendency of justice to move forward with laggard steps prompted the editor of the Louisville, Ky., *Courier-Journal* to point out:

> . . . Too seldom in this troubled and imperfect world does the right prevail or do we live to see justice done. Particularly is this

true in the case of our public men. Regularly, the cheap and flashy triumph over the solid and sincere. Far too infrequently does retribution overtake the selfish and shoddy, and usually appreciation comes too late to the truly great. The present high position of Mr. Hoover, indisputably our most distinguished private citizen, along with the great esteem and appreciation in which, regardless of party or class, he is held by the American people generally, is a thrilling demonstration that occasionally the right really does prevail and this appreciation comes before it is too late. . . .

Unscathed, he has survived a prolonged attack of almost incredible scurrility. As his seventy-fifth birthday approaches, out in his Palo Alto (Cal.) home, serene, philosophical, untouched by hate or malice, physically and mentally fit, beloved by thousands of personal friends all over the country, respected and admired by the people generally, Mr. Hoover is today a larger and finer national figure than ever he has been in all his long and eventful career. One way or another the anti-Hoover liars and slanderers have been silenced. The groups of detractors who still keep it up are discredited and ineffectual. Some few are ashamed. At last the right has prevailed. It was long overdue.

In the opinion of the Portland, Maine, *Press Herald* Mr. Hoover today is at the crest of his popularity, and adds: "He made mistakes during his White House tenure, as do all Presidents, but no one can question his highmindedness and devotion to public service."

Speaking of the Hoover birthday celebration, the Baltimore *Sun* spoke of it as "a proper demonstration by his admirers of the esteem in which he is held by his countrymen."

The Salisbury, Md., *Times* stated that "Millions of his countrymen honor Herbert Hoover on his seventy-fifth birthday. There is no thought of politics now. There is only the thought that the United States is privileged to show its respect and love for a great American who has shown his respect and love for America." While the *Christian Science Monitor* held that: "Not often has there been so widespread and spontaneous a desire to honor such a man during his lifetime." In the opinion of the New Bedford, Mass., *Standard-Times,* "Today no American is held in higher regard. . . . Most of his life has been devoted to good deeds and his seventy-fifth birthday finds him firmly established in the esteem of his fellow countrymen." And the Chicago *News* pointed out that: "Few men have in their lifetime undergone such profound fluctuations in public esteem as Mr. Hoover. He has maintained his dignity and composure in victory and defeat. In perspective, it can be seen that his public service was all of a piece—patriotic, sincere, humanitarian, and staunchly built on unshakable moral principle."

The changed public attitude toward Mr. Hoover during the past sixteen years was not strange to the Salt Lake City, Utah, *Deseret News* because:

> . . . Few men, if any, in modern times have done more than he for the lasting benefit of his country and of the world. And yet few public servants, if any, since Lincoln, have been so cunningly and consistently maligned, or have had their administrative policies so purposefully and unfairly misconstrued than happened in his case.

In writing on the same subject the Richmond, Va., *Times Dispatch* stated that "during the intervening sixteen years his fame has grown steadily, until he is generally considered by members of both major parties to be one of our abler Presidents. Mr. Hoover's public service has been extraordinary, and he has rendered it gladly."

The New York *Sun* interpreted the ups and downs and ups again of Mr. Hoover's career by stating:

> . . . From this peak of achievement he was plunged into a morass of misrepresentation and vilification which would have broken the heart of anyone less valiant. He was blamed for the operation of economic forces which no man, no set of men, could control. But when abuse was at its highest, Herbert Hoover was at his serenest. And now time is working a revenge for him—the only kind of revenge which a man of his Quaker upbringing could accept. Today he enjoys the confidence and esteem of all men of good faith, regardless of creed or party . . . on this birthday, he is receiving floods of congratulatory messages.
>
> Happy birthday, Mr. Hoover!

The "Smear Hoover" Campaign

One subject that the great majority of editorial writers discussed, and almost unanimously condemned was that of the vindictive character assassination attacks which were directed at him.

These were deplored without exception by the editors of the nation's newspapers during the week of August 8, 1949.

Collier's Weekly, in its "Happy Birthday, Well Deserved" editorial stated:

> . . . Like all Presidents, Mr. Hoover made his mistakes. But for years his political opponents unjustly held him responsible for the depression of the thirties. His distinguished career of public service was forgotten in a storm of insult and criticism. A lesser man of lesser faith might well have grown bitter. He might have retired to a life of prosperous idleness which Mr. Hoover could always have had and which he always scorned. . . .

The Savannah, Georgia, *Press* held that Mr. Hoover "who has emerged with increased stature from the smears dumped upon him for the purpose of political assassination by his opponents in the 1932 presidential election, has performed another service for freedom-loving Americans in the forthrightness of his seventy-fifth birthday message."

The Dallas, Texas, *News*, after stating that the nation had not before realized what a good fellow Mr. Hoover was, added that his presidential character had been "assassinated with malice aforethought largely by the astute late Charles Michelson. His personal and political integrity were unassailable. He viewed his office as a trust to be held beyond the reach of either personal or political chicanery. It is a striking commentary on his character that the only recourse his political enemies had was to create for him personal responsibility for a national depression." It was also the Little Rock, Ark., *Democrat*'s comment that: "Mr. Hoover's character was brutally assassinated by Charles Michelson, perhaps the most potent press agent—he was that and nothing more—the Democratic party ever had. And Mr. Hoover was an easy target for he became President almost entirely without a political background. . . . Herbert Hoover was too naive . . . but he has been forgiving . . . he has not sulked in his tent . . . he richly deserves the tributes being paid him."

In touching on the same point the Bridgeport, Conn., *Telegram* stated that: "When the United States was caught, as were all other nations, in the grip of the last bitter economic depression . . . he [Hoover] became the object of smears unprecedented in our history. . . . During the years that passed Mr. Hoover never changed . . . his popularity has swung back to a high point after hitting an all time political low."

The Denver *Rocky Mountain News* offered its answer as to the why of Mr. Hoover's persecution after first stating: "Some people are wondering why Herbert Hoover is today . . . one of the most revered Americans, possibly the most revered. The answer is quite simple. Hoover was the victim of Hegelian Dialectic."

For its part the Oakland, Calif., *Post Enquirer* held that: ". . . It can already be assumed that the name of Herbert Hoover will be recorded with special luster . . . redeemed from the unjust and undeserved blame that petty, parochial politics attached to his courageous, dignified and fundamentally sound efforts to direct the country during his Presidential regime."

In explaining why Americans who dislike Mr. Hoover are hard put to understand the why of Mr. Hoover's popularity today, the East Liverpool, Ohio, *Review* states the answer to be that they "were taught to hate him. There was a deliberate purpose behind the teaching. It was a discredit to the principles of the United States. . . ."

Stating that he had lived down, as though they never touched him, the lies and slanders that were manufactured against him for selfish political ends the Columbus, Ohio, *Dispatch* adds: "Through it all he kept, as even now he keeps, his serenity, his faith in the everlasting righteousness of justice and fair play. Never once has he permitted himself the cheap luxury of striking back with the dirty sticks that were used first to smite him. Not once has he ever stooped to recrimination, to mud-slinging or to chicanery, to 'get even' with those who hurt him. . . ."

It is the opinion of the Lansing, Mich., *State Journal:* ". . . Time and unemotional judgment of history have been kind to Mr. Hoover. Today, less than twenty years after the great depression that made the Hoover name anathema to millions of Americans, history has already begun to rectify the errors of judgment that were made of Mr. Hoover in the heat of a great economic and social upheaval. Those millions are already sorry for being taken in by the politicians whose tirades made Mr. Hoover the whipping boy of the depression. . . ." And the Paducah, Ky., *Sun-Democrat* points out: ". . . We know the adage about giving a bad name to a dog. The 1930 depression gave Mr. Hoover a bad name, unjustly, and there are still many partisans—they are nothing else—who can not realize that he was not chargeable with that situation. . . ." Another Democratic paper, the Fredonia, N. Y., *Censor* began its Hoover editorial by saying:

> . . . It may seem incongruous that a newspaper of Democratic leanings should offer such a suggestion in honor of an elder statesman of the opposite political bent, but a closer glance reveals it to be genuine and proper. . . .
>
> Mr. Hoover was unjustly the major political victim of the depression, a fact deplored even by those who were triumphant in his defeat, but he has never permitted it to embitter him nor to color his acts. . . .
>
> The *Censor* is glad to wish Mr. Hoover a happy birthday, and many more of them. He is a great American who has become greater with the years.

Florida's Miami *Herald* expressed the belief that:

> What is exceptionally singular is that he has come through the fires of misunderstanding and unwarranted belittlement by an unthinking and confused time to command the grateful praise of this people which he has served faithfully and with steadfast courage during thirty years of public life. . . .
>
> Honesty compels the admission that the American people humiliated their ex-President. Hoover accepted the situation with dignity. He was confident that time would vindicate him. It has. What is particularly gratifying on his seventy-fifth birthday is that he has lived to see that vindication. . . .

Holding that the case of Mr. Hoover is unique in the Presidential history of the United States, the Grass Valley, Calif., *Morning Union* adds: "He was . . . an unpopular President to the point of crucifixion but during his sixteen years as ex-President he has become the most popular and listened-to retired President perhaps since Washington. . . . His position today as an elder statesman is completely divested of the rancor which was once showered on him." And the Visalia, Calif., *Times Delta* tells how "cast aside, berated and vilified Herbert Hoover was far from a broken man when he was defeated for the Presidency. . . . [He] didn't make a comeback. He was here all the time, but everybody didn't know it and appreciate it."

In Springfield, Mass., at least, if the *Morning Union* of that city is correct, the opinion is held that "Only a few members of the irresponsible fringe any longer hold him to blame for events for which he is blameless. He is acclaimed as one of our first citizens. May he be spared for many years of further work for humanity." The Birmingham, Ala., *News* states that in the years 1930 to 1932 Mr. Hoover "caught much of the blame for the depression in spite of the fact that he worked unceasingly to combat it." The Mobile, Ala., *Press* described Mr. Hoover as "one of the most abused men ever to serve their nation with distinction . . . he has never been more popular than he is today."

The editor of the Escondido, Calif., *Times-Advocate* expressed the thought which ran through many editorial columns when he said: "Few men have done so much for their country . . . [and] at the same time been subjected to the bitter criticism. . . ."

Another widely expressed thought was stated as follows by the Los Angeles *Times* when it said: ". . . It is a tribute to Mr. Hoover that the abuse he received upon stepping down from the Presidency did not leave him an embittered old man. It is a tribute to the good sense of the American people that the unprecedented campaign of calumny sparked by his successor in office did not fool them forever. . . ."

The Indianapolis, Indiana, *Star* was glad "that Mr. Hoover now knows that those who once scorned him have come to understand and to love him, that those who once blamed him unjustly now praise him unanimously. Happy birthday, Mr. Hoover, and God bless you, sir."

The San Francisco *Call Bulletin* held that: "Happily for Mr. Hoover and fortunately for the nation, the biased criticisms of partisan politics to which he has been subjected have now subsided. The man is beginning to emerge in his true stature and to receive public recognition for his true worth—a splendid example of a good American citizen, whose whole life and career have been fully in accord with the best traditions of our country."

Across the Bay, the Oakland *Post Enquirer* stated that: "It is highly fitting that on his birthday, the American people acknowledge the high stature of Herbert Hoover, his contributions to the public welfare, and his personal virtues of integrity and constancy in the face of unjust and undeserved belittlement and criticism."

From Southern California the Los Angeles *Mirror* pointed out that Mr. Hoover "was paid some long overdue honors at his birthday celebration. The American people have come to know that here is a great, self-effacing, selfless patriot."

The *World-Herald* of Omaha, Nebraska, called Mr. Hoover "An elder statesman [who] is held in warm affection by the American people and is recognized as one of the great Americans of modern times. We join with millions of others in saluting him, and we wish him many more years of service for the people of the Country he loves."

The *Oregonian* at Portland, Oregon, stated:

> . . . Time was when Herbert Hoover was thought cold, but in this also time has shown us the error. What was so casually and unfairly believed to be chilliness of spirit now is seen to have been something of shyness and something of dignity, alike native to the man's character. When it is considered also that he could not feign camaraderie, which so often is a political art, it is not to be wondered that the people his generous heart so truly wanted to serve, with patriot devotion, flippantly and callously misjudged him. They were blinded by the disasters of the period. They requited his fidelity by naming him scapegoat. Now they know that they were

wrong, as their attitude toward him bears witness. And, too, there's no gainsaying the fact that the years have mellowed his dignity, which never was truly austere, and that he has mastered in great part his shyness. Against the background of the present Herbert Hoover looms as an amiable and devoted giant. We can think of none to compare with him except perhaps Winston Churchill.

Herbert Hoover has given more than thirty years of his life to America, in one way or another. Never a moment of these, we dare say, was spent save in utter sincerity and unselfishness. He has made the United States of America his career as few men have done. Now in the autumnal years his countrymen regard him with admiration and fondness, and it no longer matters that once they would have none of him. This is victory, isn't it? . . .

The Battle Creek, Mich., *Enquirer News* stated that: ". . . Truly, long life has added luster to a brilliance of character which stands out all the more by contrast with the kind of politics with which he never would cheapen himself." To the editor of the Columbus, Ohio, *Dispatch* it seemed that: ". . . The universality of good feeling toward Mr. Hoover today . . . has happened undoubtedly because the New Deal smear against him was in the first place not only unfair but untrue. It couldn't stick. Mr. Hoover never in all his long private and public careers ever approached in likeness the vicious untrue picture painted of him by the Charlie Michelsons and others who combined in a political alliance to defeat him in 1932. . . ."

The Philadelphia *Bulletin* pointed out that: "Mr. Hoover's Presidency was a ceaseless struggle with the burdens imposed by a depression made inevitable long before he entered the White House. The nation's suffering had brought on him an undeserved unpopularity. But he had in him inner resources of mind and soul to meet and triumph over thoughtless carping and undeserved blame. At seventy-five he stands universally honored as Elder Statesman and Counselor of the Republic."

After noting that "Mr. Hoover's popularity has swung from highest to lowest and back again," the Boston, Mass., *Herald* stated that: "Historians still differ about his effectiveness as a President in a time of economic crisis. But his honor and great capacity as a public servant have never suffered the slightest question. And now in the maturity of his years he is enjoying the just reward of service, which is the fond regard of his countrymen. . . ."

It was the belief of the Glens Falls, N. Y., *Times* that "To understand and appreciate him the people had to understand and appreciate sincerity, modesty, and the serious consideration of public questions, with greater regard to their merits and their final effect on the public welfare, than to the ballot box. . . ."

Mr. Hoover as a Politician

A large number of the Hoover newspaper birthday editorials either mentioned or else emphasized the belief of the writers that Mr. Hoover possessed few if any political arts such as have been perfected in our rough and tumble school of politics.

"Politically," says the Dallas, Texas, *News,* "the naive, the frank, honest Quaker boy can not understand how some will do anything in first-ward fashion to get elected, then turn around and caress and applaud the attacked. In the Hoover rules, you don't pole-ax a man one month and halo him the next. . . .

"Sixteen years ago he left Washington the day Franklin Roosevelt was inaugurated. He offered his services in the crisis for whatever use they might be. No call came. One finally did—about thirteen years later. Mr. Truman enlisted his help to relieve the world's food troubles and dislocations as a result of the war . . ."

"His sin," according to the Albany, N. Y., *Knickerbocker News,* "was that he was not also a great politician. Essentially a man of reason and intellect, he was not an emotional leader capable of inflaming the minds of others. . . ." Nor has he "been without defect" in the opinion of the Kalamazoo, Mich., *Gazette.* "He was not a politician. He could not practice the art or the tricks of getting along with Congress. He has been, except in recent years, an uninspiring public speaker. . . ." The Parsons, Kansas, *Sun* held that: ". . . During his years in the White House, Mr. Hoover was an inept politician. He was succeeded by a master politician and the contrast was that of day and night. Fortunately, the Hoover qualities . . . have had an opportunity to make themselves felt in the latter years. . . ." Nor was he, according to the Detroit *News,* "a match for the ready weeper. He was never a politician in the sense that politics is the Great Game. His entrance into public life was on the level of statesmanship, and had he been willing he still would have been a poor hand at operating on any lower plane. . . . Character, in the long run, counts for everything. If Mr. Hoover is fortunate now, it is in having survived into a time when the process has begun to work in his favor. Not all his well-wishers are gathering in Palo Alto. Attending in spirit at least are millions more, including many only gradually converted to recognition of his true worth."

Again and again in newspapers over the country Mr. Hoover's lack of political flair was commented upon. The Jacksonville, Florida, *Journal* pointed out that: ". . . Although he is strictly not a politician, Herbert Hoover is a splendid American. And his countrymen wish him well on his seventy-fifth birthday." Holding that "most Americans regard Mr. Hoover as the greatest living American," the Lake Worth, Florida, *Leader* adds that: ". . . In these sunset years he is more highly esteemed and appreciated than ever before. His political ineptitude did much to discredit him during his years as President. Nor could he seem to extricate himself from administrative ramifications. But now he is appreciated for his strength of character and perspective. We recognize him now as one of the great stalwarts of America. . . ." The Racine, Wisconsin, *Journal Times* believed that: "History will picture Herbert Hoover as a poor politician, perhaps, but a distinguished statesman who gave a lot, unselfishly, to his country and the world at large. None of the 'wolves' who howled so loudly at his heels has done a fraction as much."

The Portchester, N. Y., *Item*'s explanation of the reason for Mr. Hoover's political difficulties said: ". . . That, indeed, he is—an honorable gentleman, one perhaps not fitted by nature for the rough-and-tumble hurly-burly of partisan politics, because he would not make tongue-in-the-cheek promises, because he would not sway with political winds, because he would not align class against class for political expediency—but nevertheless one of our greatest citizens and one whom history undoubtedly will recognize as one of our greatest Presidents. . . ." The editor of the St. Petersburg, Florida, *Independent* believed that: ". . . he must be partisan indeed who would not admit that our only living ex-President has behind him one of the most useful careers in modern world history. . . . No President has ever labored harder than he did on the job. . . . No politician, he further failed to carry the ball to the public, to dramatize and to reassure, at a time when the public relations approach was of unique importance. . . ."

Editors Interpret Mr. Hoover's Greatness

One of the most interesting phases of these many Hoover birthday editorials was their appraisal of Mr. Hoover as a great man.

The New York *Journal of Commerce* spoke of him as "the symbol of the American way of life at its best." And the Decatur, Illinois, *Review* held that: ". . . His many articles on peace established him as a foremost proponent of world peace. His well prepared documents on American life came out of experience such as few men have enjoyed. . . ." To the La Porte, Indiana, *Herald-Argus* it seems that "as a humanitarian he made his deepest dent on the world" and that "To many persons in lands beyond the seas Herbert Hoover's name is still synonymous with a benevolent America which gave from its abundance to unfortunate populations." The Savannah, Georgia, *Press* stated that: "The truth about the greatness of this American is now well emerged from the smear campaign launched against him in politics in the thirties."

"In the years after his defeat" the Texarkana *News* stated, "Hoover probably was one of the most severely maligned chief executives in U. S. history. . . . But what has happened in the meantime? Did his humiliation . . . scar him deeply? . . . The jobs he has since held . . . are proof of his courage in rising above crushing defeat . . . of a genuine desire for public service beyond any normal call of duty."

It was the belief of the Crestion, Iowa, *News Advertiser* that "in the twilight of his career, he again stands forth as a great American statesman, conscientious in his desire to serve, respected for his good judgment and ability, admired for his continued faith in his fellow citizens." In the Macon, Georgia, *Telegraph* the statement was made that: "This newspaper does not hesitate to say that former President Hoover is today one of the greatest living Americans. . . ." While the Cedar Rapids, Iowa, *Gazette* held that: "He can look back today on a record of noteworthy achievement such as few statesmen in the history of the republic ever have achieved. . . ."

The change in the public's attitude toward Mr. Hoover is due, according to the Cincinnati, Ohio, *Enquirer,* to the fact that "it is abundantly evident that Mr. Hoover is one of the world's top experts in statecraft, a man of great vision and a public servant of tremendous capacity and ability." Although he was defeated for re-election in 1932, the Columbia, S. C., *State* holds that he "has risen steadily in the esteem of the nation, and stands now in such high regard that all sting of failure to be named for a second term should be more than offset. . . ." To the Brooklyn *Eagle* Mr. Hoover "is one of America's truly great men. He has devoted many years of his life to patriotic public service. We are all deeply indebted to him. On this happy occasion we feel that Americans, regardless of party, hold our only living ex-President in admiration and, indeed, affection and will wish him health and happiness for many years to come."

The Portland, Maine, *Press Herald* believes that "Hoover's words and deeds have elevated him to a position among Great Americans." And the Detroit *Free Press* in acclaiming Mr. Hoover "as a truly great American" added: "He was bigger than personal ambitions, bigger than party politics, bigger than immediate history because from the depths of his soul he knew that truth would prevail. In the darkest hour of his personal political tragedy and the darkest hour of this Nation he never faltered in his faith in his fellow mortals, in the America of his dreams as a free man, in his trust in God."

After stating that the people are revising their earlier estimate of Mr. Hoover, the Lawrence, Mass., *Tribune* attributes the reasons for this action to the fact that: "They are wondering if it probably isn't true that he puts his country's interests before his own and believes most sincerely in the institutions which have made possible his own great personal success." The Port Huron, Mich., *Times-Herald* calls him "a great public figure who commands respect throughout the world." This was similar to the opinion of the editor of the *Apollo-Journal* of Belvidere, N. J., who stated "that Mr. Hoover is certainly one of the greatest living Americans, and one has but to look at his record to establish that fact."

Mr. Hoover's "genius for constructive accomplishment" prompted the Tampa, Florida, *Times* editor to add that he "has adhered to strong principles born of hardship and experience during his life that made him capable of overriding defeatism and kept him ready to serve his country again and again. His service has earned him a place of esteem in the annals of the Nation and although his prominence in public life came out of a political party, his life achievements transcend party lines."

The Watsonville, Calif., *Register-Pajaronian* wrote that: "Most of us have come to realize, in the cool perspective that time brings, the excellent qualities of this man. We know that he lacked political color and that he made his mistakes, yet we know that he stands today as one of the great men of our country." And the editor of the Chico, Calif., *Record* believes that "Mr. Hoover still stands back up there at the fork, pointing down the main road. By looking back at him we can see which way we have moved, and how far." While holding that no one supposes Mr. Hoover to be a perfect man, the Los Angeles, Calif., *Times* states: "But with each passing year it becomes more apparent that he is a big man." Mr. Hoover's "own quiet dignity" has, in the opinion of the Waterbury, Conn., *American,* helped to cause the public to make a reappraisal of him.

The Meriden, Conn., *Record* holds that "We now know that he was as great a statesman when he was President as he is today. We were the ones who couldn't take it. We wanted our bitter pill sugar-coated. We wanted pretty promises to camouflage ugly reality when Mr. Hoover couldn't give us what we wanted. It wasn't his way. Today . . . we can tell him he is a bigger man made of sterner stuff than the rest of us." It was his character and faith that did not fail, which enabled him to "keep on keeping on" in the opinion of the Framingham, Mass., *News* which today has him "trusted and honored by his fellow countrymen—unquestionably once one of the most defamed yet now the most illustrious of America's private citizens in our time."

It was Mr. Hoover's "devotion to principle" which, in the judgment of the Spokane, Wash., *Spokesman Review,* "has proved to be a stronger force than those forces with which he was in conflict. Time has confirmed the greatness of his character and the homage that he will receive on his anniversary will show that that greatness is widely recognized." The Casper, Wyoming, *Tribune Herald* adds that "time has proved him to be a great American citizen." The Springfield, Ohio, *Sun* referred to Mr. Hoover as "an authentically great American."

Mr. Hoover's "Selfless Service" Widely Noted

One of the many facets of Mr. Hoover's character which has been reflected in the interests and activities which have engaged his time and effort is that of service for others. With him it seemingly has been that *To live is to serve.* A great majority of the editorials about him made some mention of this marked characteristic of his.

The Denver *Post* believed that "Both as a statesman and as a man he has earned this regard by unselfish public service and impeccable conduct. He enjoys the admiration and respect now of many people who once hated and abused him."

To the editor of the Hartford, Conn., *Courant* Mr. Hoover "has always been what he is today, a fine unselfish public citizen, devoted to the welfare of his country and to the world."

The Syracuse, N. Y., *Post Standard* believed that "Hoover is a great man and has served his nation and the world without thought of self. If any man deserves honor on his birthday, he is the one." The Miami Beach, Florida, *Sun* held that on domestic policies "few will disagree that he is a great humanitarian who has rendered outstanding service not only to America but also to the world at large." And to the Burlington, Iowa, *Gazette* Mr. Hoover's "has been an abundant life of notable public service in many fields of endeavor." The South Bend,

Indiana, *Tribune* held that because "he has served so selflessly and with such efficiency in various ways in the public service zone that . . . in itself commands recognition for the accolade of greatness." To the Elyria, Ohio, *Chronicle Telegram* Mr. Hoover's "career of public service has been a long and distinguished one . . ."

The Marshfield, Oregon, *Coos Bay Times* "which has often taken issue with his thinking but never with his motives or great heart" after wishing Mr. Hoover the very best of anniversaries added "and the satisfaction which must be his for having given so greatly to the growth of his country."

The Sunbury, Penn., *Item* held that Mr. Hoover's "fellow Americans are everlastingly indebted to him and as might have been expected, have discovered for themselves the validity of that obligation." To the Macon, Georgia, *News* "Best of all" was the fact that Mr. Hoover "has demonstrated what an ex-President can do if he is determined to be useful and not to be thrown into the discard." The Columbus, Ohio, *State Journal* after stating that Mr. Hoover "was above politics" added: "The country is fortunate in still having him to call upon, it is grateful for his services and his wisdom, and it rejoices in his anniversary." The Troy, N. Y., *Morning Record* held that Mr. Hoover "is essentially the same Hoover with a heart warm with humanity that gained expression in his concern for starving Europe whose savior in those bitter World War I days he became. He is the same Hoover, conscientious, patriotic, honest and with a stern sense of responsibility toward the country of which he is a proud citizen. Never a politician . . . he has demonstrated beyond question that he is a statesman of the highest order, and a man of penetrating vision." The Detroit *Free Press* believed that "As long as this rugged American walks and talks among us, he will serve as a symbol and an exemplar."

To the editor of the San Francisco *Chronicle* it seemed that "thoughtful men everywhere, caught up in the great, tearing tensions of a world divided against itself, have recognized in this man a symbol of their own deepest hopes and beliefs, and strivings for a better life. For this kind of man, history has always reserved a place of eminence." The *Chronicle* also stated: "Life has remained earnest for him and a profound sense of responsibility has been his enduring monument, but he has also remained warmly human. If this quality was not generally grasped by the public until his later years, it was perhaps because of his inherent reserve—and his credo that his job was more important than himself. He thus has violated a basic politicians' maxim but he has never reached for political favor."

Hoover's Patriotism and Americanism Get Consideration

The nation's newspaper editors touched on or treated rather fully almost every one of Mr. Hoover's qualities. Two of these were his patriotism and his Americanism. These, they unanimously held, were above question. And because the public had now come to know and believe that to be the case it had looked upon him in a more favorable way.

Holding that Mr. Hoover's positions on public questions "may not always be popular" the Watertown, N. Y., *Times* believed, however, that they "are sincere" and that "His patriotism, the realization of his responsibility as our only ex-President and his high sense of public duty are distinguishing features of Herbert Hoover." Pointing out that "we who might lose hope found it again in the words of our elder statesman" the Redwood City, Calif., *Tribune* commended him for his deep faith in our institutions.

It was the belief of the Washington, D. C., *Post* that: "When Mr. Hoover was a cabinet officer and candidate for President much was made by his political enemies of the long absences from his country during his earlier career as an engineer. It was said that he had lost touch with the American genius, that he had become in a sense denationalized. Yet, both in his qualities and in his limitations, he has shown himself the most characteristic American of his generation, deeply devoted to all the native pieties. This has been reflected in his extroverted energies, in the essentially pragmatic character of his mind, his implicit faith in progress and in the power of technology to solve the age-old problems of human poverty and suffering." The Danbury, Conn., *News-Times* looked upon him as "an outstanding example of the kind of citizen who has a strong faith in the soundness of our country and who believes in the brightness of its future based upon the traditions that made it great." Stating that Mr. Hoover has remained "a man of great faith in times of adversity" the New Haven, Conn., *Register* added that he had "displayed an amazing constancy in these days of national inconstancy and bewilderment, an unswerving respect for our traditions of the past and an abiding confidence that our national future will measure to our democratic standards."

It seemed to the Griffin, Georgia, *News* that "as the years are passing people are beginning to evaluate Hoover for his true worth. His devotion to his nation is unquestioned. And in this day and time when so many people owe first allegiance to some 'ism,' his devotion stands out." To the Richmond, Virginia, *Times Dispatch* Mr. Hoover "loved his native land so well that he was able to summon the moral courage and inspirational powers of patriotism to save his country from the follies of parliamentary bungling." And the *Mesabi Daily News* of Virginia, Minn., held that: "Mr. Hoover's only concern is for the perpetuation in America of a government which shall be the servant of the average citizen, not his master and oppressor. Today's imposition upon the populace of this bureaucratic barnacle is a threat to constitutional government." The Los Angeles *Herald-Express* stated that: "Through all of his activities, in private and public life, Mr. Hoover has manifested an unshaken faith in the American ideal—the value of freedom to the individual, the enduring worth of good and honest government."

Quaker Traits and Integrity Stressed

One of the most interesting phases of the editorial comment about Mr. Hoover to me, a Quaker born and reared individual, was that of the large number of editors who found in his words and actions, his conduct and his outlook traces of the influence which Quaker tenets and Quaker practices had had upon his life.

The Lewiston, Idaho, *Tribune* held that "public service has been a cornerstone of his life. A practicing Quaker, he follows the tenets of that faith in his everyday living." After speaking of his "deep devotion to the principles to which he clung" the Ventura, Calif., *Star-Free Press* added that "His rugged Quaker qualities of perseverance under pressure were not matched with imaginative political skill." It was, according to the Bristol, Conn., *Press* "Because of his Quaker background and deep sense of dignity he bore this ('abuse and calumny') without complaint." And the Abilene, Texas, *Morning Reporter-News* stated that: "He has mellowed and grown graceful and gracious, though never at any time did he display anything but a gentle Quaker nature. . . ." To the Faribault, Minn., *News* it seemed that "More than any other man of his generation, probably, Mr. Hoover has expressed and exemplified the high ideals of the American spirit. His life is a monument of service to others. Like his Quaker forebears, he has been a man of peace, a man dedicated to the high cause of making this a better world for his fellow men. There could be no finer destiny." It was the belief of the Olympia, Wash., *Olympian* that Mr. Hoover was able to face "severe criticism and even slander with a forbearance, patience and dignity which may have been a product of his Quaker training. As the years passed the stature of Mr. Hoover increased, and more and more persons began to realize that he possesses qualities found in few other Americans. In his public speeches he has appealed repeatedly for the support of our traditional system of government—which is unrivaled anywhere on earth. . . ." The Appleton, Wis., *Post Crescent* after pointing out that President Hoover always turned the other cheek when political vituperation struck him, added: "Perhaps it was the Quaker in him. Perhaps he realized that in the fullness of time he would tower like a gigantic mountain peak over the scrawny hills when comparisons were made . . ."

Recognizing that while the true inwardness of Quaker principles and Quaker ways may compare favorably with sweetness and light, the outward manifestation or, at least the popular interpretation of their outward manifestation does not always gain popular approval or meet the public's needs, the Detroit *News* stated that: ". . . The unostentatious, Quaker way of life, stoical and devoid of outward emotion, has lent him on such occasions as the 1932 crisis, an appearance of hardness, belied by earlier labors which had made his name synonymous through the world with compassion for all humanity."

The Kalamazoo, Mich., *Gazette* was of the opinion that "his shortcomings, either in official action or in personality, seem small indeed when compared with the rest of his long record or with the elements of goodness and greatness in his character. In him the Quaker virtues blend with the most modern and most efficient Americanism. A successful engineer and businessman, a superb organizer and administrator, a great humanitarian, a sound and progressive thinker, he is, withal, a man of warmth, kindness, transparent honesty, and gentle humor. . . ."

The Salinas, Calif., *Californian* held that: "The world has admired him as a fair, tolerant, modest, compassionate and kindly man with a penchant for performance of duty without explanation."

George Sokolsky devoted one of his widely read columns to a discussion of Mr. Hoover's qualities. In one part of it he said:

> I prefer to write of the man's growth in defeat. To me it is infinitely more interesting to note the true greatness of a man in adversity.
>
> In the bitter days of 1933, forsaken by many to whom he had given opportunity, smeared, attacked, defeated by a vast and potent machine set up for that purpose, betrayed by his own political party, he took it all with patience, forbearance and good will.
>
> I used to visit him nearly daily in those bleak years and never once did I hear him answer abuse with abuse. Somehow he maintained total objectivity.
>
> It is not that he has no anger; his moral indignation is fierce. It is rather, I think, that the Quakers do not expect too much of people. It is easier for them to forgive.

One of the earliest and best learned lessons Mr. Hoover was taught in Quaker homes concerned integrity. Integrity in word and in action. It is the cornerstone of any truly successful life and the keystone of the structure of lasting worthwhile human relations.

Many editors wrote of this quality of Mr. Hoover's. The Bellingham, Wash., *Herald* stated that: "Whether the tide of fortune has run with or against him, Mr. Hoover never has faltered, never compromised his principles or his integrity, never lost faith in the basic good of humanity. . . ."

Holding that the American public finally realized that there are qualities vastly more valuable to them than that of being a good politician the Steubenville, Ohio, *Herald-Star* stated that it "respected him for his flawless integrity. He did not change his mind from year to year to suit the shifting winds of opinion." And the Omaha, Nebraska, *Herald* believed that at long last the "people began to understand that Herbert Hoover was a man of profound conviction, of warmest sympathy, a man above rancor and spite and partisanship, a man of granite integrity and surpassing ability. . . ."

The Butte, Montana, *Standard* said: "Mr. Hoover has remained constant in his opinions, judgments and philosophies. Perhaps the fact that he has been guided solely by public responsibility and not by personal or political aspirations has been the key factor in his rise in stature. Paradoxically, this same set of circumstances contributed to his downfall. Seventeen years ago he refused to compromise personal integrity for political expediency."

To the Fitchburg, Mass., *Sentinel* it is evident that: "Now his name and his fame are shining symbols of honor in a period when dishonor is rampant in high places. His detractors, some dead and others living, are held in far lower esteem, if some of them are held in esteem at all."

William Allen White's old paper, the Emporia, Kansas, *Gazette,* expressed the belief that "The White House never had under its roof a man more honest, more conscientious than Herbert Hoover. It is good to see the American people realizing that they roughly mistreated him. His comeback is a fine example of poetic justice."

David Lawrence, the distinguished columnist, who has been an observer and interpreter of the national political scene ever since that long ago campaign in 1916, wrote in one of his columns:

> . . . One characteristic that will always be written on the pages of history as outstanding in the case of Herbert Hoover is his integrity and character.

Men can win public office, they can amass votes, they can make speeches lambasting their opponents, they can be great orators, and they can be bitter partisans—and the nation will not disapprove of any of these. But let a President lack anything in character or integrity, let him exercise bad taste and violate what is conceded to be public morals, and he will go down into oblivion.

Herbert Hoover's name will shine because his character is unblemished and his record as custodian of the people's funds and the people's interests stands untarnished through the years.

The Cherokee, Iowa, *Times* "above all else" congratulated Mr. Hoover "on his Christian ability to forgive and forget the injustice that was done him during the last three years he served as president." The Los Angeles *Herald-Express* commended Mr. Hoover for his "enormous strength of character and moral purpose and staunch integrity and an abiding faith in the opportunities of America" and added, "Through all of his activities . . . Mr. Hoover has manifested an unshaken faith in the American ideal—the value of freedom to the individual, the enduring worth of good and honest government."

The St. Joseph, Mich., *Herald Press* pointed out that "Destiny tapped Mr. Hoover for the presidency in 1929. He carried with him into the White House the great moral principles which constituted the fabric of his character." To the editor of the Benton Harbor, Mich., *News Palladium,* "Mr. Hoover's anchor throughout life's passage has been an unconquerable faith in his fellow men, in democracy and in those fundamental religious precepts that make love, hope and charity guiding ideals."

"This nation," stated the Tucson, Ariz., *Star,* "has come to realize Herbert Hoover's real integrity and his real value to humanity . . . a wise selfless leader whose advice is worth following." "People," held the Decatur, Ala., *Daily,* "no matter their political affiliation have come to respect former President Hoover for his Americanism . . . he has known all along what we have come to realize today: that the laws of supply and demand cannot be changed."

Mentioning another widely admired Christian trait, the Portland

Oregonian stated: "He is one of those rare spirits who, on being given the cup of bitterness, refused to be embittered."

To the New York *Times* it seemed that: "Greater perhaps than the abilities which have stood out in the various phases of the ex-President's long and useful life; greater than the engineering approach which has always sought a springboard of solid facts from which to proceed and an amazing clearness of thought in putting first things first, is the character of the man himself. In one era glorified, in another bitterly criticized, he has found the inward strength to follow a true course as he saw it. . . .

"Inevitably, Herbert Hoover has grown in the respect and affection of his countrymen. We join today in wishing him many more years of active and useful life."

Holding that the "nation and the world have already conceded that his immense stature rests upon foundations of such solid stuff that history must accept it without qualification" the San Francisco *Chronicle* expressed the belief that one reason Mr. Hoover has "acquired the tremendous new stature that is recognized in this country and throughout the world is that more and more people have come to realize that his relentless search for truth, his very humanitarianism are rooted in his profound faith in the quality and the individual dignity of man."

II

Congressional Record, appendix, page 363, June 21, 1917.

Hoover's achievements in mining parallels his subsequent record in all fields. One episode, however, should be related, as it displays the sterling integrity of character which has proved the principal formative factor in Hoover's success. Shortly after he allied himself with the London firm he discovered that owing to the dishonesty of a subordinate there had been an over-issue of the capital stock of one of the most successful mines managed by the firm. Exactly how many shares had been over-issued and sold he did not know, but it afterward transpired that $50,000 would have covered fully any legal or moral claim that could be brought against Hoover, as one of the partners, since his connection as such was recent. But Hoover did not stand on any such technicality. He was a full partner of the firm; its honor, he felt, was his personal honor and he insisted on paying his full quota. It cost him more than $500,000, which put an obvious crimp in his newly-acquired wealth; but it settled for once and all the sort of man he was.

Statement by the Chinese statesman, Tong Shao-yi, on Herbert Hoover's business activities in China.

I believe I am the only Chinese man now living, who was closely identified with the Chinese Engineering and Mining Company, which in 1878 obtained the concession from the Throne for opening the Kaiping coal mines. The company was founded by my uncle, Tong King-sing, and our family always has been among the largest shareholders.

Mr. Hoover's record in China was not only clean and honorable, but highly creditable and in many ways remarkable. Twice Mr. Hoover saved the Chinese Engineering and Mining Company for the Chinese shareholders. In the period immediately preceding his connection with the company, during the Boxer uprising, there is no accounting how many lives he saved. While following Mr. Hoover's career of international relief work through the long years that have passed since then, I have always felt that his first actual relief work began in China.

Mr. Hoover had come to China originally as an engineer for the Chinese Government. Following the flight of the Imperial Government to Sianfu during the Boxer Rebellion in 1900, Mr. Hoover was offered, and he accepted, the post of consulting engineer with the Chinese Engineering & Mining Company. The shareholders comprised four different groups, which having diverse interests did not always work harmoniously. One combined Chinese and German interests; then there were two separate British groups and a Belgian group. With the arrival of foreign troops to suppress the Boxer Rebellion, possession of the property became a bone of international contention. Properties of the company were seized and occupied by the troops of four foreign governments—Russia, Japan, Germany and Great Britain—although the company was Chinese.

It was Mr. Hoover's prompt action which saved the company for the Chinese and other shareholders at that critical time. He went to London and reorganized the company. Following the reorganization, the Chinese insisted that they be represented on the board and that Mr. Chang Yen-mao should continue as director general. Everybody concerned approved of this. It was so agreed in the form of a memorandum signed by both parties in February, 1901. Mr. Hoover was the one man in whom all the interested parties reposed confidence, and he was made the general manager. He was not in charge of the finances, each group having its own separate financial representative.

Later in the same year the Belgians obtained control of the company and Mr. Hoover severed all connection with it and returned to the United States.

Subsequently the Belgian group failed to abide by the terms of the memorandum. A suit was instituted in British courts in England against the old English company in 1905. Mr. Hoover was not a defendant to the suit, but was called as a witness. Largely on his testimony the validity of the memorandum was established and the Chinese complainants won their suit, whereupon Mr. Chang Yen-mao was reinstated as director general.

In the eighteen months during which Mr. Hoover was associated with our company as engineer and later as manager, he transformed our property from one that had been financially unsuccessful to a highly profitable enterprise, which has continued to pay handsomely ever since.

These are the facts as I recall them. My warmest admiration and respect for Mr. Hoover, however, are based on his humane and courageous conduct during the Boxer uprising. He and Dr. Tenney of the American Legation for twenty days, absolutely fearless in their humane mission, supplied the thousand odd Chinese refugees in the compounds of the Foreign Settlement and Bank of China with food and drink.

At a time, when my wife and one of my daughters were killed by stray shots, Mr. Hoover rushed to my house and at the risk of his life carried out a number of the dead and injured. Presently, when my house caught fire, Mr. Hoover braved the flames and saved the life of my fifth daughter, then four years old. [Later she became Mrs. Wellington Koo.]

Mr. Hoover took away from China far less than he had honestly earned. He left in China the high respect and esteem of all who knew him.

Statement (from a letter) by W. T. Turner, Chairman of the Board of Directors of the Chinese Engineering and Mining Company.

Referring to our interview today on the subject of Mr. Herbert C. Hoover's connection with the affairs of the Chinese Engineering & Mining Company Limited (which was formed in the year 1901) and with the litigation in the years 1905 and 1906 arising out of it at the instance of the late Chang Yen Mao, I repeat what I then stated, viz., that I have been intimately acquainted with these matters from their inception (having been a director of the original company and being chairman of the Board of Directors of the present company which was formed in 1912), and I am able to say that there is no ground for any suggestion that Mr. Hoover's conduct in relation to the matters in question has been other than of a perfectly honorable character.

Excerpt from letter received by Mr. Hoover from E. deCartier, former Ambassador from Belgium to the United States.

I have been astonished to hear mis-statements with regard to your connection with the Chinese Engineering & Mining Company, which operated in the Kaiping Mines during the period when I was Belgian *charge d'affaires* in China. As such, I looked after the very large Belgian interests in that enterprise and had personal knowledge of all the facts relating to the transfer of the property, some of which led subsequently to litigation in the English courts. Throughout your administration of the company's affairs, both as chief engineer and as director, you acted concededly for the best interest of all the stockholders,

Chinese, Belgian and English alike, with the highest sense of honor. The termination of the litigation was a complete vindication of your conduct and largely turned upon your testimony. The best proof of this lies in the fact that the Belgians interested in these properties were the very men who called upon you to come to the assistance of their country in its extremity.

III

Excerpts from statement by Herbert Hoover, as Secretary of Commerce, on elimination of waste in industry.

. . . Just as twenty years ago we undertook nation-wide conservation of our natural resources, so we must today even more vigorously sustain this campaign of better nation-wide utilization of our industrial resources and effort. More especially is this the case in view of the many complex forces which have arisen from the war, and particularly the difficulty of maintaining our situation as against the competition of a world of lower standards overseas.

The term "elimination of waste" is subject to some objection as carrying the implication of individual or wilful waste. In the sense used in these discussions elimination of waste refers wholly to those wastes which can be eliminated solely by co-operative action in the community. It does not refer to any single producer, for in the matters here discussed he is individually helpless to effect the remedy. Nor does the elimination of such wastes imply any lessening of fair competition or any infringement of the restraint of trade laws. In fact, the most casual investigation of the work in progress will show that its accomplishment establishes more healthy competition. It protects and preserves the small units in the business world. Its results are an asset alike to worker, farmer, consumer and business man.

It may be worth while repeating the major directions for national efforts as they were outlined by the department at the beginning of the undertaking:

1. Elimination of the waste imposed by inadequate railway transportation, by improved equipment and methods, and the establishment of better co-operation.

2. Vigorous utilization of our water resources for cheaper transportation of bulk commodities, flood control, reclamation, and power.

3. Enlarged electrification of the country for the saving of fuel and labor.

4. Reduction of the great waste of booms and slumps of the "business cycle" with their intermittent waves of unemployment and bankruptcy.

5. Reduction of waste in manufacture and distribution through the establishment of standards of quality, simplification of grades, dimensions, and performance in non-style articles of commerce; through the reduction of unnecessary varieties; through more uniform business documents such as specifications, bills of lading, warehouse receipts, etc.

6. Development of pure and applied scientific research as the foundation of genuine labor-saving devices, better processes, and sounder methods.

7. Development of co-operative marketing and better terminal facilities for agricultural products in order to reduce the waste in agricultural distribution.

8. Stimulation of commercial arbitration in order to eliminate the wastes of litigation.

9. Reduction of the waste arising from industrial strife between employers and employees.

IV

Excerpts from an address by Herbert Hoover, "Attitude on Morals in Government," Boston, Massachusetts, October 26, 1937.

Today as never before we are faced with moral questions in public life. We have had a New Deal in public honor. To indicate its significance let me ask you a few questions.

The first of these questions involves intellectual honesty in officials and in government.

Can your government broadcast half-truths and expect the citizen to tell the whole truth?

Do you think you can pollute thought with framed government propaganda and maintain honest thinking in the citizen?

Do you think government, which engages hundreds of paid publicity agents daily and hourly to eulogize its official acts, can hold the faith of the citizen in what his government says?

Is it honest or sportsmanlike to answer the argument, protest or appeal of the citizen by smearing him as the enemy of the people?

Do you believe all the official statements today?

Do you think you can let down intellectual honesty in high officials and hold up conscience in citizens?

And there are questions relating to public administration.

Does not the wholesale appointment of government officials by politics and not by merit mean a decadence in public morals? What is the morality of the recent return to the spoils system?

And there are questions involving commercial honesty.

Can your government repudiate the covenant of its bonds and expect citizens to hold to their obligations?

Can the government ruthlessly crush competition and hold the business man to fair play?

Can the Treasury deliberately manipulate the market in government bonds and expect the citizen not to do the same thing in stocks?

Is it moral for a government to collect hundreds of millions from the wages of workmen under the promise that they are kept in a fund for their security and then spend this fund on its current expenses and extravagances?

Is it moral to evade the Corrupt Practices Act by selling books to corporations for political funds?

And there are questions involving the sacredness of law.

What happens to the morals of a people when the federal government connives at lawlessness?

What of governors who obstruct the courts and refuse to maintain public order?

Or of workmen beaten and killed by police squads on one hand and beef squads on the other?

Do not all moral restraints disappear and the ugly spectres of vigilantes arise?

And there are the questions involving the building of character in men.

When the public purse is used to subsidize, threaten, or cajole the congressmen and the local communities, are you not corrupting the people?

When you direct the mind of the citizen to what he can abstract from the Treasury, are you building for self-reliance and stamina in the citizen?

And there are questions involving the spirit of a people.

Is it moral for high government officials to stir hate of group against group, of workman against workman?

Is not hate a moral poison to a nation more deadly than fear?

And there are questions involving the sacredness of the ballot.

What does the common expression "you cannot beat Santa Claus" mean in public morals?

Can democracy survive with more and more of its cities in the hands of corrupt political machines?

Do not a multitude of vicious rackets, of bribery, blackmail, coercion and crime flourish under the hands of these corrupt city governments? What does this do to the moral standards of citizens and the community?

Is the federal government not abetting these machines when it places enormous sums of public money directly and indirectly at their disposal—too often just prior to elections?

Can we hope for self-government when these city political machines regularly manipulate the vote? Does not this influence not alone municipal but state and federal elections?

Do you think you can maintain confidence in our institutions and continually pollute the ballot box?

A nation is great not through dams in its rivers or its ships on the sea or the deposits in its banks. It is great by the moral fiber and character of its citizens. Nations die when these weaken.

Is it not the duty of the Republican party to raise the banner of emancipation of the American people from this degradation, both national and local?

V

Excerpts from address by Herbert Hoover on his seventy-fourth birthday, West Branch, Iowa, August 10, 1948.

. . . I recount all this in order that, in Quaker terms, I can give my own testimony.

The meaning of our word "America" flows from one pure spring. The soul of our America is its freedom of mind and spirit in man. Here alone are the open windows through which pours the sunlight of the human spirit. Here alone is human dignity not a dream, but an accomplishment.

Perhaps another etching of another meaning of America lies in this community. It was largely settled by Quakers over ninety years ago. This small religious sect in England had declared that certain freedoms of man came from the Creator and not from the state 150 years before the Declaration of Independence. They spent much time in British stocks and jails for this first outburst of faith in the dignity of the individual man.

They first came in refuge to New England. But the Puritans cut off their ears by way of disapproval of their religious individualism. Then came the great refuge which William Penn secured for them. From New England and Pennsylvania some of the Ancestors of this community, before the Revolution, migrated first to Maryland, and after a generation, they moved to the Piedmont of North Carolina. Then early in the last century slavery began to encroach upon them. Most of that community—5,000 of them—organized a concerted trek to Ohio and Indiana.

This time they were seeking freedom from that great stain on human liberty. Again after a generation they hitched their covered wagons and settled on these prairies.

Everywhere along these treks there sprang up homes and farms. But more vital was the Meeting House with its deep roots in religious faith, its tolerance and devotion to liberty of the individual. And in these people there was the will to serve their community and their country. Even this village was a station on the underground through which Negroes were aided to the freedom of Canada. Sons of this community were in the then Red Cross of the Civil War. And despite their peace-loving faith, many of their sons were enrolled in the Union Army to battle for free men.

That imbedded individualism, that self-reliance, that sense of service, and above all those moral and spiritual foundations were not confined to the Quakers. They were but one atom in the mighty tide of these qualities of many larger religious bodies which make up the intangible of the word *American*.

At the time our ancestors were proclaiming that the Creator had endowed all mankind with rights of freedom as the child of God, with a free will, there was being proclaimed by Hegel and later by Karl Marx a satanic philosophy of agnosticism and that the rights of man came from the state. The greatness of America today comes from one philosophy, the despair of Europe from the other.

There are today fuzzy minded people in our country who would compromise in these fundamental concepts. They scoff at these tested qualities in men. They never have understood and never will understand what the word *America* means. They explain that these qualities were good while there was a continent to conquer, and a nation to build. They say that time has passed.

No doubt the land frontier has passed. But the frontiers of science are barely opening. This new land with all its high promise cannot and will not be conquered except by men inspired from the concepts of free spirit.

It is those moral and spiritual qualities in free men which fulfill the meaning of the word *American*. And with them will come centuries of further greatness to our country.

VI

Excerpts from Mr. Keynes' letter on Herbert Hoover's work in Paris.

. . . He imported into the councils of Paris, when he took part in them, precisely that atmosphere of reality, magnanimity, knowledge, and disinterestedness, which, if they had been found in other quarters also, would have given us the Good Peace.

The ungrateful governments of Europe owe much more to the statesmanship and insight of Mr. Hoover and his band of American workers than they have ever appreciated or ever will acknowledge. The American Relief Commission, and they only, saw the European position during those months in its true perspective and felt toward it as men should. It was their effort, their energy, and the American resources placed by the President at their disposal, often acting in the teeth of European obstruction, which not only saved an immense amount of human suffering, but averted a widespread breakdown of the European system.

VII
Riga Agreement

Agreement Between the American Relief Administration and the Russian Socialist Federative Soviet Republic

Whereas a famine condition exists in parts of Russia, and

Whereas Mr. Maxim Gorky, with the knowledge of the Russian Socialist Federative Soviet Republic, has appealed through Mr. Hoover to the American people for assistance to the starving and sick people, more particularly the children, of the famine-stricken parts of Russia, and

Whereas Mr. Hoover and the American people have read with great sympathy this appeal on the part of the Russian people in their distress and are desirous, solely for humanitarian reasons, of coming to their assistance, and

Whereas Mr. Hoover, in his reply to Mr. Gorky, has suggested that supplementary relief might be brought by the American Relief Administration to up to a million children in Russia.

Therefore, It is agreed between the American Relief Administration, an unofficial volunteer American charitable organization under the chairmanship of Mr. Herbert Hoover, hereinafter called the A.R.A., and the Russian Socialist Federative Soviet Republic, hereinafter called the Soviet Authorities,

That the A.R.A. will extend such assistance to the Russian people as is within its power, subject to the acceptance and fulfillment of the following conditions on the part of the Soviet Authorities who hereby declare that there is need of this assistance on the part of the A.R.A.

The Soviet Authorities agree:

FIRST: That the A.R.A. may bring into Russia such personnel as the A.R.A. finds necessary in the carrying out of its work and the Soviet Authorities guarantee them full liberty and protection while in Russia. Non-Americans and Americans who have been detained in Soviet Russia since 1917 will be admitted on approval by the Soviet authorities.

SECOND: That they will, on demand of the A.R.A., immediately extend all facilities for the entry into and exit from Russia of the personnel mentioned in (1) and while such personnel are in Russia the Soviet Authorities shall accord them full liberty to come and go and move about Russia on official business and shall provide them with all necessary papers, such as safe-conducts, laissez passer, et cetera, to facilitate their travel.

THIRD: That in securing Russian and other personnel the A.R.A. shall have complete freedom as to selection and the Soviet Authorities will, on request, assist the A.R.A. in securing same.

FOURTH: That on delivery of the A.R.A. of its relief supplies at the Russian ports of Petrograd, Murmansk, Archangel, Novorossisk, or other Russian ports as mutually agreed upon, or the nearest practicable available ports in adjacent countries, decision to lie with the A.R.A., the Soviet Authorities will bear all further costs such as discharge, handling, loading and transportation to interior base points in the areas where the A.R.A. may operate. Should demurrage or storage occur at above ports mutually agreed upon as satisfactory, such demurrage and storage is for the account of the Soviet Authorities. For purposes of this agreement the ports of Riga, Reval, Libau, Hango and Helsingfors are also considered satisfactory ports. Notice of at least five days will be given to Soviet representatives at respective ports in case the Soviet Authorities are expected to take c.i.f. delivery.

FIFTH: That they will at their own expense supply the necessary storage at interior base points mentioned in paragraph (4) and handling and transportation from same to all such other interior points as the A.R.A. may designate.

SIXTH: That in all above storage and movement of relief supplies they will give the A.R.A. the same priority over all other traffic as the Soviet Authorities give their own relief supplies, and on demand of the A.R.A. will furnish adequate guards and convoys.

SEVENTH: That they will give free import re-export and guarantee freedom from requisition to all A.R.A. supplies of whatever nature. The A.R.A. will repay the Soviet Authorities for expenses incurred by them on re-exported supplies.

EIGHTH: That the relief supplies are intended for children and the sick, as designated by the A.R.A. in accordance with paragraph (24), and remain the property of the A.R.A. until actually consumed by these children and the sick, and are to be distributed in the name of the A.R.A.

NINTH: That no individual receiving A.R.A. rations shall be deprived of such local supplies as are given to the rest of the population.

TENTH: That they will guarantee and take every step to insure that relief supplies belonging to the A.R.A. will not go to the general adult population nor to the Army, Navy or Government employees but only to such persons as designated in paragraphs (8) and (24).

ELEVENTH: That Soviet Authorities undertake to reimburse the A.R.A. in dollars at c.i.f. cost or replace in kind any misused relief supplies.

TWELFTH: That the A.R.A. shall be allowed to set up the necessary organizations for carrying out its relief work free from governmental or other interference. The Central and Local Soviet Authorities have the right of representation thereon.

THIRTEENTH: That the Soviet Authorities will provide:

A. The necessary premises for kitchens, dispensaries and, in as far as possible, hospitals.

B. The necessary fuel and, when available, cooking, distributing and feeding equipment for the same.

C. The total cost of local relief administration, food preparation, distribution, etc., themselves or in conjunction with local authorities. Mode of payment to be arranged at later date.

D. On demand of the A.R.A., such local medical personnel and assistance, satisfactory to the A.R.A., as are needed to efficiently administer its relief.

E. Without cost railway, motor, water, or other transportation for movement of relief supplies and of such personnel as may be necessary to efficiently control relief operations. The Soviet Authorities will for the duration of the A.R.A. operations assign to the A.R.A., for the sole use of its personnel, and transport free of cost, such railway carriages as the A.R.A. may reasonably request.

FOURTEENTH: In localities where the A.R.A. may be operating and where epidemics are raging, the A.R.A. shall be empowered by the Soviet Authorities to take such steps as may be necessary towards the improvement of sanitary conditions, protection of water supply, etc.

FIFTEENTH: That they will supply free of charge the necessary offices, garages, store-rooms, etc., for the transaction of the A.R.A. business and, when available, heat, light and water for same. Further that they will place at the disposal of the A.R.A. adequate residential quarters for the A.R.A. personnel in all localities where the A.R.A. may be operating. All such above premises to be free from seizure and requisition. Examination of above premises will not be made except with the knowledge and in presence of the chief of the A.R.A. operations in Russia or his representative and except in case of flagrant delit when examiner will be held responsible in case examination unwarranted.

SIXTEENTH: That they will give to the A.R.A. complete freedom and priority without cost in the use of existing radio, telegraph, telephone, cable, post, and couriers in Russia and will provide the A.R.A., when available and subject to the consent of competent authorities, with private telegraph and telephone wires and maintenance free of cost.

SEVENTEENTH: To accord the A.R.A. and its American representatives and its couriers the customary diplomatic privileges as to passing the frontiers.

EIGHTEENTH: To supply the A.R.A. free of cost with the necessary gasoline and oil to operate its motor transportation and to transport such motor transportation by rail or otherwise as may be necessary.

NINETEENTH: To furnish at the request of the competent A.R.A. authorities all A.R.A. personnel, together with their impediments and supplies, free transportation in Russia.

TWENTIETH: To permit the A.R.A. to import and re-export free of duty and requisition such commissary, transport and office supplies as are necessary for its personnel and administration.

TWENTY-FIRST: That they will acquaint the Russian people with the aims and methods of the relief work of the A.R.A. in order to facilitate the rapid development of its efficiency and will assist and facilitate in supplying the American people with reliable and non-political information of the existing conditions and the progress of the relief work as an aid in developing financial support in America.

TWENTY-SECOND: That they will bear all expenses of the relief operation other than

A. Cost of relief supplies at port. (See paragraph 4).

B. Direct expenses of American control and supervision of relief work in Russia with exceptions as above. In general, they will give the A.R.A. all assistance in their power toward the carrying out of its humanitarian relief operations.

The A.R.A. agrees:—

TWENTY-THIRD: Within the limits of its resources and facilities, to supply, as rapidly as suitable organization can be effected, food, clothing and medical relief to the sick and particularly to the children within the age limits as decided upon by the A.R.A.

TWENTY-FOURTH: That its relief distribution will be to the children and sick without regard to race, religion or social or political status.

TWENTY-FIFTH: That its personnel in Russia will confine themselves strictly to the ministration of relief and will engage in no political or commercial activity whatever. In view of paragraph (1) and the freedom of American personnel in Russia from personal search, arrest and detention, any personnel contravening this will be withdrawn or discharged on the request of the Central Soviet Authorities. The Central Soviet Authorities will submit to the chief officer of the A.R.A. the reasons for this request and the evidence in their possession.

TWENTY-SIXTH: That it will carry on its operations where it finds its relief can be administered most efficiently and to secure best results. Its principal object is to bring relief to the famine stricken areas of the Volga.

TWENTY-SEVENTH: That it will import no alcohol in its relief supplies and will permit customs inspection of its imported relief supplies at points to be mutually agreed upon.

The Soviet authorities having previously agreed as the absolute sine qua non of any assistance on the part of the American people to release all Americans detained in Russia and to facilitate the departure from Russia of all Americans so desiring, the A.R.A. reserves to itself the right to suspend temporarily or terminate all of its relief work in Russia in case of failure on the part of the Soviet Authorities to fully comply with this primary condition or with any condition set forth in the above agreement. The Soviet Authorities equally reserve the right of cancelling this Agreement in case of non-fulfillment of any of the above clauses on the part of the A.R.A.

Made in Riga, August Twentieth, Nineteen Hundred and Twenty-One:

On behalf of Council of Peoples Commissaries of the Russian Socialist Federative Soviet Republic.

(signed) MAXIM LITVINOV
Assistant Peoples Commissary for Foreign Affairs.

On behalf of the American Relief Administration.

(signed) WALTER LYMAN BROWN
Director for Europe.

VIII

Resolution of thanks voted by the Council of Commissars at the Kremlin and sent to Mr. Hoover.

In the trying hour of a great and overwhelming disaster, the people of the United States, represented by the American Relief Administration, responded to the needs of the population, already exhausted by intervention and blockade, in the famine stricken parts of Russia and her Federated Republics.

Due to the enormous and entirely disinterested efforts of the American Relief Administration, millions of people of all ages were saved from death, and entire districts and even cities were saved from the horrible catastrophe which threatened them.

Now, when the famine is over and the colossal work of the American Relief Administration comes to a close, the Soviet of Peoples' Commissars, in the name of the millions of people saved and in the name of all the working people of Soviet Russia and the Federated Republics counts it a duty to express before the whole world its deepest thanks to this organization, to its leader, Herbert Hoover, to its representative in Russia, Colonel Haskell, and to all its workers, and to declare that the people inhabiting the Union of Soviet Socialist Republics will never forget the help given them by the American people.

IX

Excerpts from letter of Maxim Gorky to Herbert Hoover.

. . . In the past year you have saved from death three and one-half million children, five and one-half million adults, fifteen thousand students, and have now added two hundred or more Russians of the learned professions. I am informed that this charity cost America fifty-nine million dollars, figures which are sufficiently eloquent. In all the history of human suffering I know of nothing more trying to the souls of men than the events through which the Russian people are passing, and in the history of practical humanitarianism I know of no accomplishment which in terms of magnitude and generosity can be compared to the relief that you have actually accomplished. . . .

The generosity of the American people revives the dream of fraternity among people at a time when humanity greatly needs charity and compassion. Your help will be inscribed in history as a unique gigantic accomplishment worthy of the greatest glory and will long remain in the memory of millions of Russian children whom you saved from death.

X

Excerpts from statement by Herbert Hoover answering criticism of Russian Relief.

. . . What will bring real assistance to the Russian people in this time of their greatest need?

We could base help upon sentiment, which is charity. At best it is but a temporary expedient. We are providing charity to Russia today in a measure tenfold that coming from the rest of the world. We are saving the lives of ten million of their people. The solution cannot be found in charity alone. Unless productivity be restored, real and lasting help must be based upon cold economics or it will bring no real reconstruction or relief to Russia.

Some officials in Russia and their followers in the United States blame us for their situation. We are supposed to have incurred this responsibility by continuation of the blockade after the war was won. This blockade, imposed as a war measure against the co-operation of Russia with Germany, was continued for a year after peace.

I, myself, was one of those who strongly urged that this should not be done. I felt that whatever good could filter into Russia would relieve just so much individual misery, and that it would be well for the world to lift the curtain on this new experiment in economics.

We know now, however, that the economic troubles of Russia were from within and not from without, for Russian production was being destroyed in her social experiment. She had no commodities for exchange, even if exchange had been permitted. . . .

Some people believe, if we would go one step further in our relations with Russia, and receive in Washington a Soviet ambassador, then goods would begin to flow; but goods do not move in an economic vacuum.

XI

Excerpts from Harold G. Moulton, *Controlling Factors in Economic Development,* The Brookings Institution, Washington, D.C., 1949.

For the first time in industrial history the powers of government were extensively invoked to stem the tide of depression and to stimulate recovery. In part because of a growing belief that government could be a sort of balance wheel for the private economy, but more perhaps because of practical exigencies, governments everywhere were called upon to adopt remedial measures. Many of the earlier acts were primarily of a defensive nature intended merely to check the downward spiral of deflation or to bring relief to groups in acute distress. Other measures were, however, essentially offensive in character, designed to start the stalled economic engine and promote a new forward movement. In some cases primary reliance was placed upon monetary and fiscal policies; in others the emphasis was upon stimulating industrial and agricultural revival. Some of the measures were deflationary in character, directed toward reducing costs and prices as a means of establishing a sound basis for revival. Others were designed to raise prices, either by monetary policy or by increasing purchasing power in the hands of the public. A brief summary is necessary in order to reveal the widely divergent character of the policies adopted by leading countries. . . .

In the United States government intervention involved two stages. In the first stage, under the Hoover administration, the primary effort was directed toward arresting the depression. In early 1930 the administration obtained agreements from important industries, notably railroads and public utilities, to continue their production programs as usual, especially capital construction. In the same year the Federal Reserve lowered rediscount rates and engaged in extensive open-market operations with a view to easing the money market situation generally. The Railroad Credit Corporation was organized in late 1931, the Reconstruction Finance Corporation in February 1932, and the Home Loan Bank System in June 1932. Meanwhile, also, the Agricultural Marketing Act of June 15, 1929 provided a 500 million dollar revolving fund for the stabilization of agricultural prices. . . .

XII

"The Children's Charter," by Herbert Hoover.

I

For every child spiritual and moral training to help him to stand firm under the pressure of life.

II

For every child understanding and the guarding of his personality as his most precious right.

III

For every child a home and that love and security which a home provides; and for that child who must receive foster care, the nearest substitute for his own home.

IV

For every child full preparation for his birth, his mother receiving prenatal, natal and postnatal care; and the establishment of such protective measures as will make childbearing safer.

V

For every child health protection from birth through adolescence including: periodical health examinations and where needed, care of specialists and hospital treatment; regular dental examinations and care of the teeth; protective and preventive measures against communicable diseases; the insuring of pure food, pure milk and pure water.

VI

For every child from birth, through adolescence, promotion of health, including health instruction and a health program, wholesome physical and mental recreation, with teachers and leaders adequately trained.

VII

For every child a dwelling-place safe, sanitary, and wholesome, with reasonable provisions for privacy; free from conditions which tend to thwart his development; and a home environment harmonious and enriching.

VIII

For every child a school which is safe from hazards, sanitary, properly equipped, lighted, and ventilated. For younger children nursery schools and kindergartens to supplement home care.

IX

For every child a community which recognizes and plans for his needs, protects him against physical dangers, moral hazards and disease; provides him with safe and wholesome places for play and recreation; and makes provision for his cultural and social needs.

X

For every child an education which, through the discovery and development of his individual abilities, prepares him for life; and through training and vocational guidance prepares him for a living which will yield him the maximum of satisfaction.

XI

For every child such teaching and training as will prepare him for successful parenthood, homemaking, and the rights of citizenship; and, for parents, supplementary training to fit them to deal wisely with the problems of parenthood.

XII

For every child education for safety and protection against accidents to which modern conditions subject him—those to which he is directly exposed and those which, through loss or maiming of his parents, affect him indirectly.

XIII

For every child who is blind, deaf, crippled, or otherwise physically handicapped, and for the child who is mentally handicapped, such measures as will early discover and diagnose his handicap, provide care and treatment, and so train him that he may become an asset to society rather than a liability. Expenses of these services should be borne publicly where they cannot be privately met.

XIV

For every child who is in conflict with society the right to be dealt with intelligently as society's charge, not society's outcast; with the home, the school, the church, the court and the institution when needed, shaped to return him whenever possible to the normal stream of life.

XV

For every child the right to grow up in a family with an adequate standard of living and the security of a stable income as the surest safeguard against social handicaps.

XVI

For every child protection against labor that stunts growth either physical or mental, that limits education, that deprives children of the right of comradeship, of play, and of joy.

XVII

For every rural child a satisfactory schooling and health services as for the city child, and an extension to rural families of social, recreational, and cultural facilities.

XVIII

To supplement the home and the school in the training of youth, and to return to them those interests of which modern life tends to cheat children, every stimulation and encouragement should be given to the extension and development of the voluntary youth organizations.

XIX

To make everywhere available these minimum protections of the health and welfare of children, there should be a district, county, or community organization for health, education and welfare, with full-time officials, co-ordinating with a state-wide program which will be responsive to a nation-wide service of general information, statistics, and scientific research. This should include:

(a) Trained full-time public health officials, with public health nurses, sanitary inspection and laboratory workers.
(b) Available hospital beds.
(c) Full-time public welfare service for the relief, aid and guidance of children, in special need due to poverty, misfortune or behavior difficulties, and for the protection of children from abuse, neglect, exploitation or moral hazard.

FOR EVERY CHILD THESE RIGHTS, REGARDLESS OF RACE, OR COLOR, OR SITUATION, WHEREVER HE MAY LIVE UNDER THE PROTECTION OF THE AMERICAN FLAG.

On November 19, 1930, President Hoover opened the Children's Conference with one of the most notable addresses of his career:

I am satisfied that . . . your conference here will result in . . . a series of conclusions and judgments of unprecedented service in behalf of childhood, the benefits of which will be felt for a full generation.

The reward that accrues to you is the consciousness of something done unselfishly to lighten the burdens of children, to set their feet upon surer paths to health, well-being and happiness. For many years I have hoped for such a national consideration as this. You comprise the delegates appointed by our Federal departments and by the governors of our States, the mayors of our cities, and the representatives of our great national associations, our medical and public health professions. In your hands rest the knowledge and authority outside of the home itself.

I am mindful also of the unseen millions listening in their homes, who likewise are truly members of this conference, for these problems are theirs—it is their children whose welfare is involved, its helpful services are for them, and their co-operation is essential in carrying out a united and nation-wide effort in behalf of the children.

We approach all problems of childhood with affection. Theirs is the province of joy and good humor. They are the most wholesome part of the race, the sweetest, for they are fresher from the hands of God. Whimsical, ingenious, mischievous, we live a life of apprehension as to what their opinion may be of us; a life of defense against their terrifying energy; we put them to bed with a sense of relief and a lingering of devotion. We envy them the freshness of adventure and discovery of life; we mourn over the disappointments they will meet. . . .

The fundamental purpose of this conference is to set forth an understanding of those safeguards which will assure to them health in mind and body. There are safeguards and services to childhood which can be provided by the community, the state, or the Nation—all of which are beyond the reach of the individual parent. We approach these problems in no spirit of diminishing the responsibilities and values or invading the sanctities of those primary safeguards to child life—their homes and their mothers. After we have determined every scientific fact, after we have erected every public safeguard, after we have constructed every edifice for education or training or hospitalization or play, yet all these things are but a tithe of the physical, moral, and spiritual gifts which motherhood gives and home confers. None of these things carry that affection, that devotion of soul, which is the great endowment from mothers. Our purpose here today is to consider and give our mite of help to strengthen her hand that her boy and girl may have a fair chance.

These questions of child health and protection are a complicated problem requiring much learning and much action. And we need have great concern over this matter. Let no one believe that these are questions which should not stir a nation; that they are below the dignity of statesmen or governments. If we could have but one generation of properly born, trained, educated, and healthy children, a thousand other problems of government would vanish. We would assure ourselves of healthier minds in more vigorous bodies, to direct the energies of our Nation to yet greater heights of achievement. Moreover, one good community nurse will save a dozen future policemen.

Our problem falls into three groups: First, the protection and stimulation of the normal child; second, aid to the physically defective and handicapped child; third, the problems of the delinquent child. . . .

XIII

Excerpts from "The New Deal Further Explored," an address by Herbert Hoover before the John Marshall Republican Club, St. Louis, December 16, 1935.

. . . In 1930 by co-operation with the states, we secured the creation of state committees of leading citizens. With them we secured the creation of similar committees in every city, town, and county where relief was needed. These committees had no politics. They were men and women experienced in large affairs, sympathetic, understanding of the needs of their neighbors in distress. And they served without pay. In those days one did not enter into relief of his countrymen through the portals of a payroll. American men and women of such stature cannot be had as a paid bureaucracy, yet they will serve voluntarily all hours of the day and defer their own affairs to night.

These committees used the existing officials; they engaged their own tested organizations; they employed their own trusted citizens. They had the complete authority to determine the methods best adapted to their neighborhoods. They knew the problem of the man next door better than anybody in Washington. They themselves determined for their locality what method was to be used. They adapted these needs to the individual families. Their stewardship was under the limelight of their own community. They gave spiritual aid and encouragement.

At the start the relief in 1930 depended upon private giving. As times became more difficult, the committees co-operated in the use of county and municipal funds; and as it became still more difficult many of the state governments provided them with funds. Finally, as state resources weakened, we provided federal government funds to be distributed to the state governments and by them redistributed to the local organizations. That we built up no bureaucracy is evident from the fact that although the government had many new emergency tasks, yet during the Hoover administration the total number of all government officials decreased by ten thousand. That form of organization expressed in its noblest form the whole American ideal of local self-government, local responsibility, national co-operation, and the voluntary spirit of human service.

There was no important failure to provide for those in real need. There was no substantital complaint or suggestion of waste, politics, or corruption. Neither the Republican Party nor any of its agencies ever asked for votes or claimed that its administration deserved votes for it. That idea was repugnant to every decent sense of Americanism. . . .

XIV

Memorandum presented by Herbert Hoover to nation's financial leaders, October 31, 1931.

. . . the situation since the British collapse ten days ago is approaching disaster at an accelerated speed until it has reached a panic condition.

That while a similar situation due to the economic breakdown in Central Europe in the spring had been overcome by the action of the Government the rise of recovery therefrom had been again stifled by the fears over the British situation, those fears had been realized . . . we are again faced with a new and even worse emergency.

A survey shows at least twenty other countries will be forced off the gold standard with Great Britain . . . inevitably they would increase tariffs, quotas and other restrictions on their imports . . . their depreciated currencies make further barriers to our exports . . . our prices of agricultural commodities are again further demoralized . . .

current European attitude is that we will collapse next . . . a drain of at least one billion of the gold, hitherto here for refuge, by export and earmarking is in progress . . . [causing] the greatest withdrawal of all time. . . . The Federal Reserve system is expanding credit by every device to meet the sapping of our credit foundations . . . the fears of the people were, since the British failed ten days ago, expressed in unprecedented hoarding of currency . . . the volume of hoarding has reached $150,000,000 a week . . . it totalled over $500,000,000 since the middle of August and $900,000,000 over May 1st. . . . Security prices were demoralized by European selling and forced liquidations. . . . This with hoarding is breaking down an already weak banking system by compelling a sacrifice of their assets to meet withdrawals. . . . Bank failures in the twelve days since the British collapse already exceeded $500,000,000. . . . But beyond this, the banks in the large centers are calling interior loans to fortify themselves against foreign drains . . . the secondary banking centers being drained are fortifying themselves against it by calling loans from country banks and customers . . . the imminent collapse of banks threatens in many interior centers particularly in the south and mid-west . . . [and] the inability of farmers and home owners to meet mortgage requirements. . . . In all, a senseless "bankers' panic" and public fears are contributing to dragging the country down.

XV

Herbert Hoover's appraisal of the depression, as of spring, 1931.

. . . the financial systems of Europe were no longer able to stand the strain of their war inheritances and of their afterwar economic and political policies, an earthquake ran through forty nations. Financial panics; governments unable to meet their obligations; banks unable to pay their depositors; citizens, fearing inflation of currency, seeking to export their savings to foreign countries for safety; citizens of other nations demanding payment of their loans; financial and monetary systems either in collapse or remaining only in appearance. The shocks of this earthquake ran from Vienna to Berlin, from Berlin to London, from London to Asia and South America. From all those countries they came to this country, to every city and farm in the United States.

First one and then another of these forty nations either abandoned payment in gold of their obligations to other countries, or restricted payments by their citizens to foreign countries, so as practically to amount to at least temporary or partial repudiation of public and private debts. Every one of them in a frantic endeavor to reduce the expenditures of their citizens, imposed drastic restrictions upon their imports of goods. These events were not as children playing with blocks. They brought revolutions, mutinies, riots, downfalls of governments, and a seething of despair which threatened civilization.

The first effect of these shocks on us was from foreign dumping of American securities on our markets which demoralized prices upon our exchanges, foreign buying power stagnated because of their internal paralysis and this in turn stifled the markets for our farm and factory products, increased our unemployment and by piling up our surpluses demoralized our commodity prices. . . .

Before the end foreign countries drained us of nearly a billion dollars of gold and a vast amount of other exchange.

Then we had also to meet an attack upon our own flank by some of our own people, who, becoming infected with world fear and panic, withdrew vast sums from our own banks and hoarded it from the use of our own people, to the amount of $1,500,000,000. This brought its own train of failures and bankruptcies. Even worse, many of our less patriotic citizens started to export their money to foreign countries for fear we should be forced onto a paper money basis. . . .

Some of the reactionary economists urged that we should allow the liquidation to take its course until we had found bottom. Some people talked of vast issues of paper money. Some talked of suspending payments of government issues. Some talked of setting up a council of national defense. Some talked foolishly of dictatorship—any of which would have produced panic itself. Some assured me that no man could propose increased taxes in the United States to balance the budget in the midst of a depression and survive an election. . . .

XVI

Excerpts from Herbert Hoover's Fourth Annual Message to Congress. December 6, 1932.

There are three definite directions in which action by the government at once can contribute to strengthen further the forces of recovery by strengthening of confidence. They are the necessary foundations to any other action, and their accomplishment would at once promote employment and increase prices.

The first of these directions of action is the continuing reduction of all government expenditures, whether national, state, or local. The difficulties of the country demand undiminished efforts toward economy in government in every direction. Embraced in this problem is the unquestioned balancing of the federal budget. That is the first necessity of national stability and is the foundation of further recovery. It must be balanced in an absolutely safe and sure manner if full confidence is to be inspired.

The second direction for action is the complete reorganization at once of our banking system. The shocks to our economic life have undoubtedly been multiplied by the weakness of this system, and until they are remedied recovery will be greatly hampered.

The third direction for immediate action is vigorous and whole-souled co-operation with other governments in the economic field. That our major difficulties find their origins in the economic weakness of foreign nations requires no demonstration. The first need today is strengthening of commodity prices. That can not be permanently accomplished by artificialities. It must be accomplished by expansion in consumption of goods through the return of stability and confidence in the world at large and that in turn can not be fully accomplished without co-operation with other nations.

XVII

Extracts from the Fourth Annual Message to Congress, continued.

Conclusion.

It seems to me appropriate upon this occasion to make certain general observations upon the principles which must dominate the solution of the problems now pressing upon the nation. Legislation in response to national needs will be effective only if every such act conforms to a complete philosophy of the peoples' purposes and destiny. Ours is a distinctive government with a unique history and background, consciously dedicated to specific ideals of liberty and to a faith in the inviolable sanctity of the individual human spirit. Furthermore, the continued existence and adequate functioning of our government in preservation of ordered liberty and stimulation of progress depends upon the maintenance of state, local, institutional, and individual sense of responsibility. We have builded a system of individualism peculiarly our own which must not be forgotten in any governmental acts, for from it have grown greater accomplishments than those of any other nation.

On the social and economic sides, the background of our American system and the motivation of progress is essentially that we should allow free play of social and economic forces as far as will not limit equality of opportunity and as will at the same time stimulate the initiative and enterprise of our people. In the maintenance of this balance the Federal Government can permit of no privilege to any person or group. It should act as a regulatory agent and not as a participant in economic and social life. The moment the government participates, it becomes a competitor with the people. As a competitor it becomes at once a tyranny in whatever direction it may touch. We have around us numerous such experiences, no one of which can be found to have justified itself except in cases where the people as a whole have met forces beyond their control, such as those of the Great War and this great depression, where the full powers of the Federal Government must be exerted to protect the people. But even these must be limited to an emergency sense and must be promptly ended when these dangers are overcome.

With the free development of science and the consequent multitude of inventions, some of which are absolutely revolutionary in our national life, the Government must not only stimulate the social and economic responsibility of individuals and private institutions but it must also give leadership to co-operative action amongst the people which will soften the effect of these revolutions and thus secure social transformations in an orderly manner. The highest form of self-government is the voluntary co-operation within our people for such purposes.

But I would emphasize again that social and economic solutions, as such, will not avail to satisfy the aspirations of the people unless they conform with the traditions of our race, deeply grooved in their sentiments through a century and a half of struggle for ideals of life that are rooted in religion and fed from purely spiritual springs.

Herbert Hoover

Excerpts from Herbert Hoover's Fourth Annual Message to Congress, December 6, 1932—on banking reform.

The basis of every other and every further effort toward recovery is to reorganize at once our banking system. The shocks to our economic system have undoubtedly multiplied by the weakness of our financial system. I first called attention of the Congress in 1929 to this condition, and I have unceasingly recommended remedy since that time. The subject has been exhaustively investigated both by the committees of the Congress and the officers of the Federal Reserve System.

The banking and financial system is presumed to serve in furnishing the essential lubricant to the wheels of industry, agriculture, and commerce, that is, credit. Its diversion from proper use, its improper use, or its insufficiency instantly brings hardship and dislocation in economic life. As a system our banking has failed to meet this great emergency. It can be said without question of doubt that our losses and distress have been greatly augmented by its wholly inadequate organization. Its inability as a system to respond to our needs is today a constant drain upon progress toward recovery. In this statement I am not referring to individual banks or bankers. Thousands of them have shown distinguished courage and ability. On the contrary, I am referring to the system itself, which is so organized, or so lacking in organization, that in an emergency its very mechanism jeopardizes or paralyzes the action of sound banks and its stability is responsible for periodic dangers to our whole economic system. . . .

Excerpts from the Fourth Annual Message to Congress, December 6, 1932—on world co-operation.

. . . We have actively engaged in a World Disarmament Conference where, with success, we should reduce our own tax burdens and the tax burdens of other major nations. We should increase political stability of the world. We should lessen the danger of war by increasing defensive powers and decreasing offensive powers of nations. We would thus open new vistas of economic expansion for the world.

We are participating in the formulation of a World Economic Conference, successful results from which would contribute much to advance in agricultural prices, employment, and business. Currency depreciation and correlated forces have contributed greatly to decrease in price levels. Moreover, from these origins rise most of the destructive trade barriers now stifling the commerce of the world. We could by successful action increase security and expand trade through stability in international exchange and monetary values. By such action world confidence could be restored. It would bring courage and stability, which would reflect into every home in our land. . . .

XVIII

LET'S GO FISHIN'

By Herbert Hoover

Recently I made some suggestions for an economic and social tidying-up of our country in preparation for the return of our boys from overseas. As I wrote, I was depressed by the thousand mournful voices chanting daily of "post-war problems" in such powerful terms as recovery, reconstruction and regeneration.

But in their research efforts in speech and their labors in type, they all concern themselves solely with what we are to do while we are on their promised jobs. Civilization, however, is not going to depend so much on what we do when we are on the job, as what we do in our time off. The moral and spiritual forces do not lose ground while we are pushing "the instrumentalities of production and distribution." Their battle is in our leisure time.

When the guns cease firing, and the gas comes on again, some of us are going fishing. We American men and boys (and some women) are born fishermen—twelve million of us. We have proved it in bygone days by the annual licenses we took out from thrifty state governments.

We have had mostly to postpone the fishing beatitudes for the duration. Many of us are busy at the military front. Some of us on the home front could possibly get a day or a week off, but the fishing holes can only be approached by automobile or motorboats, and a stern government refuses to recognize that fish do not flourish near railway depots.

In the meantime, I suspect that Mother Nature is making the fish bigger and more plentiful by way of preparing to celebrate peace, and our paternal government is doing its duty to solve our postwar problems by running the hatcheries full blast, turning out billions of infant fish and trying to decrease infant mortality.

I have discussed this important subject in years past, but some review and extension of those remarks are not out of place in these days when we are groping for postwar regeneration. Nothing can stop these regenerative forces.

Even the Four Horsemen cannot stop them. War, murrain, famine, pestilence, dictators, the rise and fall of empires or republics may defeat the game fisherman temporarily, but he rises again to invade the streams and the sea. More people have gone fishing over more centuries than for any other human recreation.

Sometimes the uninstructed and the people who have bad "isms" scoff at the game fishermen and demand to know how they get that way. It is very, very simple. These regenerative impulses are physical, spiritual and economic—and they are strong.

The human animal originally came from out-of-doors. When spring begins to move in his bones, he just must get out again. One time, in the spring, our grandmothers used to give us nasty brews from herbs to purify our blood of the winter's corruptions. They knew something was the matter with the boys. They could have saved trouble by giving them a pole, a string and a hook. Some wise ones (among them my own) did just that.

The Call of the Open Spaces

Moreover, as civilization, cement pavements, office buildings, radios have overwhelmed us, the need for regeneration has increased, and the impulses are even stronger. When all the routines and details and the human bores get on our nerves, we just yearn to go away from here to somewhere else. To go fishing is a sound, a valid and an accepted reason for such an escape.

It is the chance to wash one's soul with pure air, with the rush of the brook, or with the shimmer of the sun on blue water. It brings meekness and inspiration from the decency of nature, charity toward tackle-makers, patience toward fish, a mockery of profits and egos, a quieting of hate, a rejoicing that you do not have to decide a darned thing until next week. And it is discipline in the equality of men—for all men are equal before fish.

Necessarily, fishermen are gregarious. Otherwise, the mighty deeds of the day or of a year ago or of ten years ago would go unsung. No one else will listen to them. Also, they are an optimistic class or they would not be fishermen. Therefore, as two or three are gathered together, the spiritual vitamins of faith, hope and charity have constant regeneration. And we need all that in these years of creaking civilization, and especially in the coming years of postwar tribulation.

Nor does this source of spiritual vitamins require any governmental bureau to administer it. All that is required of Congress is to restore our freedom from the fellows who restrict the use of gasoline, and the rugged individualism of the fisherman will do the rest.

His joys are not all confined to the hours near the water. I asserted years ago that one of the elements in the advance of civilization was the progress in the equipment to overcome the mysteries of fish. We have moved upward and onward from the primitive willow pole with a butcher-string line and hooks (ten for a dime) whose compelling lure was one segment of a worm and whose incantation was spitting on the bait. We have arrived at labor-saving devices and increased efficiency in tackle assembled from the bamboo of Burma, the steel of Sweden, the lacquer of China, the tin of Bangkok, the nickel of Madagascar, the silver of Nevada, and the feathers of Brazil—all compounded into mass production at Akron, Ohio.

For magic and incantations, we have moved forward to cosmetics for artificial flies, and wonders in special clothes, and bags with pigeonholes for everything, including mosquito repellents. We no longer call it a "pole," for it is a "rod," and we no longer say that a fish "bites," he now "strikes."

Out of all this progress, a good fisherman can secure many regenerative hours of winter, polishing up the rods and reels, greasing the lines, and discussing the relative merits of gay-colored flies and dead-sure lures—thereby recalling that Big One from the pool just below the rapids and the fly he rose to.

Nor is fishing a rich man's regeneration. That boy with the worm and a grin is always a reminder that men are equal before fish. However, that boy misses out in one particular that I hope to see attended to in our next era of national reform. There is regenerative joy in contemplating and fondling adequate tackle, which he cannot get out of a collection of angleworms. And his joys are more seasonal because he cannot put in the winter nights polishing up that tackle with its reminder of that Big One from that pool and thereby the renewed smell of battles to come.

New Deal for Young Anglers

I acknowledge to a prominent official an idea to reform this. All boys should be guaranteed from birth to manhood a quart of polish and a collection of tackle with an assortment of special flies. There has been sad neglect in this question of assuring artificial flies to the youth of our land, for flies proved their inspiring worth perhaps four hundred years ago—long before Izaak Walton.

When I was a boy and lived at the social level of worms, a true fisherman gave me three flies—a coachman, a gray hackle and a professor. I treasured them greatly and used them successfully for two or three years—until the wings were all worn off. But there were more fish in proportion to the water in those times.

There are some class distinctions among fishermen. The dry-fly devotees hold themselves a bit superior to the wet-fly fishermen; the wet-fly fishermen, superior to the spinner fishermen; and the spinners, superior to the bait fishermen. I have noticed, however, that toward the end of the day when there were no strikes each social level sometimes descends down the scale until it gets some fish for supper.

This class distinction may perhaps be ignored in the general reformation, for it is not based on the economic levels. The best dry fisherman I have known is a lady cook at a lumber camp in Montana. She scorned the wet-fly fisherman and rose to indignation at bait.

The swordfish and tarpon fishermen likewise have some social distinctions on the basis of the size of line and reel. The lower-thread line operators are the dukes and earls in that aristocracy. Also, the swordfish and marlin devotees are naturally superior to those who take mere mackerel, amberjacks or flounders. The bonefish fishermen claim a little superiority to the tarpon seekers. But again it is not economic status that counts in such good society so much as knowing what the fish bite.

Someone propounded the question to me: "Why have all Presidents in modern times been fishermen?" It seemed to me a worthy investigation, for the habits of Presidents are likely to influence the nation's youth. Some of us had been fishermen from boyhood and required no explanation. But others only became fishermen after entering the White House. In examining this national phenomenon, I concluded that the pneumatic hammering of demands on the President's mind had increased in frequency with the rising tide of economic and international complexity, and he just had to get away somehow, somewhere, and be alone for a few hours once in a while. But there are only two occasions when Americans respect privacy, especially in Presidents. Those are prayer and fishing. So that some have taken to fishing.

President Cleveland was both a stream and a sea fisherman from youth. His stiff trout rod is still preserved by a devoted fisherman, and it is recorded that his sea-fishing boatman was chosen for silence. Whether President Coolidge fished in his youth is uncertain. He was a good deal of a fundamentalist in economics, government and fishing, so he naturally preferred angleworms. But when the fly fishermen of the nation raised their eyebrows in surprise, he took to artificial flies. However, his backcast was so much a common danger that even the Secret Service men kept at a distance until they were summoned to climb trees to retrieve flies.

But I should return to expanding on postwar regeneration and its moral and spiritual values in a gloomy world. Statistics tell us that the gainfully employed have steadily decreased in hours of work during the whole of thirty years. And in shorter hours and long week ends and holidays, we have devoted more time to making merry and stirring the caldron of evil. Crime has increased. Yet nobody ever was in jail or plotted a crime when fishing. The increase of crime is among those deprived of those regenerations that impregnate the mind and character of fishermen.

Our standards of material progress include the notion and the hope that we shall still further lessen the daily hours of labor. We also dream of longer annual holidays as scientific discovery and mass production do our production job faster and faster. But when they do the job, they dull the souls of men unless their leisure hours become the period of life's real objective—regeneration by fishing.

The Problems of Leisure

Moreover, while we are steadily organizing increased production of leisure time, the production of what to do with it still lags greatly. We do have some great machinery of joy, some of it destructive, some of it synthetic, much of it mass production. We go to chain theatres and movies. We watch somebody else knock a ball over the fence or kick it over the goal post.

I do that and I believe in it. But these forms of organized joy are sadly lacking in the values which surround the fish. We gain none of the lift of soul coming from a return to the solemnity, the calm and inspiration of primitive nature.

Nor is it the fish that we get that counts, for they can be had in the market for mere silver. It is the break of the waves in the sun, the joyous rush of the brook, the contemplation of the eternal flow of the stream, the stretch of forest and mountain in their manifestation of the Maker, that soothes our troubles, shames our wickedness and inspires us to esteem our fellow men—especially other fishermen.

Reprinted by permission from *Colliers* magazine.

XIX

Excerpts from address by Herbert Hoover, Madison Square Garden, New York City, October 31, 1932.

. . . It is founded on the conception that only through ordered liberty, through freedom to the individual, and equal opportunity to the individual will his initiative and enterprise be summoned to spur the march of progress.

It is by the maintenance of equality of opportunity and therefore of a society absolutely fluid in freedom of the movement of its human particles that our individualism departs from the individualism of Europe. We resent class distinction because there can be no rise for the individual through the frozen strata of classes, and no stratification of classes can take place in a mass livened by the free rise of its particles. Thus in our ideals the able and ambitious are able to rise constantly from the bottom to leadership in the community.

This freedom of the individual creates of itself the necessity and the cheerful willingness of men to act co-operatively in a thousand ways and for every purpose as occasion arises; and it permits such voluntary co-operations to be dissolved as soon as they have served their purpose, to be replaced by new voluntary associations for new purposes.

There has thus grown within us, to gigantic importance, a new conception. That is, this voluntary co-operation within the community. Co-operation to perfect the social organization; co-operation for the care of those in distress; co-operation for the advancement of knowledge, of scientific research, of education; for co-operative action in the advancement of many phases of economic life. This is self-government by the people outside of Government; it is the most powerful development of individual freedom and equal opportunity that has taken place in the century and a half since our fundamental institutions were founded.

It is in the further development of this co-operation and a sense of its responsibility that we should find solution for many of our complex problems, and not by the extension of government into our economic and social life. The greatest function of government is to build up that co-operation, and its most resolute action should be to deny the extension of bureaucracy. We have developed great agencies of co-operation by the assistance of the Government which promote and protect the interests of individuals and the smaller units of business. The Federal Reserve System, in its strengthening and support of the smaller banks; the Farm Board, in its strengthening and support of the farm co-operatives; the Home Loan Banks, in the mobilizing of building and loan associations and savings banks; the Federal Land Banks, in giving independence and strength to land mortgage associations; the great mobilization of relief to distress, the mobilization of business and industry in measures of recovery, and a score of other activities are not socialism—they are the essence of protection to the development of free men.

The primary conception of this whole American system is not the regimentation of men but the co-operation of free men. It is founded upon the conception of responsibility of the individual to the community, of the responsibility of local government to the state, of the state to the National Government.

It is founded on a peculiar conception of self-government designed to maintain this equal opportunity to the individual, and through decentralization it brings about and maintains these responsibilities. The centralization of government will undermine responsibilities and will destroy the system.

Our government differs from all previous conceptions, not only in this decentralization but also in the separation of functions between the legislative, executive and judicial arms of government, in which the independence of the judicial arm is the keystone of the whole structure.

It is founded on a conception that in times of emergency, when forces are running beyond control of individuals or other co-operative action, beyond the control of local communities and of states, then the great reserve powers of the federal government shall be brought into action to protect the community. But when these forces have ceased there must be a return of state, local, and individual responsibility.

The implacable march of scientific discovery with its train of new inventions presents every year new problems to government and new problems to the social order. Questions often arise whether, in the face of the growth of these new and gigantic tools, democracy can remain master in its own house, can preserve the fundamentals of our American system. I contend that it can; and I contend that this American system of ours has demonstrated its validity and superiority over any other system yet invented by human mind.

It has demonstrated it in the face of the greatest test of our history—that is the emergency which we have faced in the past three years.

When the political and economic weakness of many nations of Europe, the result of the World War and its aftermath, finally culminated in collapse of their institutions, the delicate adjustment of our economic and social life received a shock unparalleled in our history. No one knows that better than you of New York. No one knows its causes better than you. That the crisis was so great that many of the leading banks sought directly or indirectly to convert their assets into gold or its equivalent with the result that they practically ceased to function as credit institutions; that many of our citizens sought flight for their capital to other countries; that many of them attempted to hoard gold in large amounts. These were but indications of the flight of confidence and of the belief that our government could not overcome these forces.

Yet these forces were overcome—perhaps by narrow margins—and this action demonstrates what the courage of a nation can accomplish under the resolute leadership in the Republican Party. And I say the Republican Party, because our opponents, before and during the crisis, proposed no constructive program; though some of their members patriotically supported ours. Later on the Democratic House of Representatives did develop the real thought and ideas of the Democratic Party, but it was so destructive that it had to be defeated, for it would have destroyed, not healed.

In spite of all these obstructions we did succeed. Our form of government did prove itself equal to the task. We saved this Nation from a quarter of a century of chaos and degeneration, and we preserved the savings, the insurance policies, gave a fighting chance to men to hold their homes. We saved the integrity of our government and the honesty of the American dollar. And we installed measures which today are bringing back recovery. Employment, agriculture, business—all of these show the steady, if slow, healing of our enormous wound.

I therefore contend that the problem of today is to continue these measures and policies to restore this American system to its normal functioning, to repair the wounds it has received, to correct the weaknesses and evils which would defeat that system. . . .

XX

Herbert Hoover's Commencement Day Address at Haverford College, Haverford, Pa., June, 1941, on the subject of the need for research in pure and applied science—

It is a great pleasure at last to be able to accept an invitation to come to Haverford. And for two reasons. It was founded and has been sustained by the faith in which I was reared. And when I was yearning to go to college my stern Quaker managers insisted that my spiritual welfare would be unsafe in a non-sectarian institution. They therefore secured for me a scholarship in this college and an alternate one at Earlham. But my ambitions then were in sciences and engineering—and Haverford, at that time, was not strong in that branch. That deficiency has long since been overcome and Haverford now turns out its quota of first quality men in those branches.

I wish to take this occasion to urge again the immediate expansion of our research facilities in pure and applied science, and the more systematic application of what we already know in these fields. That is at all times the highway to increased efficiency and increased productivity. And this action is the more urgent today because through it we can contribute to alleviate the hardships of our American people both during and after this war.

However, as Huxley insists, let me first define my terms. For the practical purposes of this discussion, pure science research means the search for fundamental natural law. That is the search for truth. That is a good exercise any time.

Applied science research is the application of such discoveries to practical use. That is invention. Pure science is thus the raw material of applied science.

For this discussion national industrial efficiency means producing more goods and services per capita.

I do not want you to think that I am building a rigid wall between pure and applied science. Their purposes and borders are much blended. I might mention another distinction between them. There are no big money-rewards to the pure scientists. Sometimes they get an obituary notice on the fourth page inside.

I am not one who believes that the whole of civilization is founded upon scientific discovery and the inventions. I could complain of a thousand economic and social ills that have come from the industrial revolution, including the increased capacity for mass-murder. But because of this war I can also tell you that unless we quickly have more of this same discovery and invention and a more efficient application of what we already know our standard of living and even our civilization will degenerate.

First—Whatever the outcome of these present wars, there is one thing certain—we shall have to divert a large segment of national energy to armament for years to come. That at once decreases the output of articles for public consumption. Unless we can by some parallel action increase our production of consumption goods, it means an immediate reduction in our standard of living. And there is nothing that can so contribute to make up that deficiency as new discovery in pure science and new inventions. From that source we can get more labor-saving devices, and better methods which increase production. We can get new materials to substitute for those we have to take from the people for munitions. Nor do we need depend wholly upon new discovery and new invention to increase our national productivity. We can organize to better apply what we already know—and that can produce immediate results.

Second—There is another and immediate purpose of enlarged research. The airplane has revolutionized warfare. It has made the aggressor far more powerful. It has made small nations helpless to defend their liberties. It has made the butchering of women and children a part of war. The world has not yet found the defensive answer. The airplane was born from the science of physics. The answer might come from there. And it imperatively demands research and more research—and at once. For if that answer could come and come quickly it would turn the whole fate of the world.

Third—Whatever the outcome of this war one more thing is certain—this whole world and our own country will be greatly impoverished and smothered with debt. There is only one certain road to rapid recuperation. That is to increase the technological power of the nation.

It is increased productivity at lower costs that the nation will need. In the past we have always reaped such advances from important discovery, invention and organized application.

There is, of course, the commonly proposed idea that we could increase production and alleviate scarcity in goods by longer working hours. But it is far better that we accomplish this by more scientific discoveries, new labor-saving devices, new methods, or the more vigorous organization and use of what we already know.

I do not need to be told that all the old arguments that invention puts men out of jobs. That ghost is as old as when Eli Whitney invented the cotton gin. That ghost should have been laid when it saw the effect of the gas engine. For every man in the livery stable yesterday there are 20 in garages today.

Nor is there justification for that other truculent ghost which wails about more pressure upon individual workers. It only means that we work our machines and heads harder.

Our pure science research is dependent largely upon our universities and a few specially endowed institutions. Their research work is decreasing rather than increasing. The reduced interest return on the endowments of our institutions is driving them to cut into research rather than teaching. I doubt that even without curtailment their total resources for pure science research amount to $20,000,000 a year. Thus we allow pure science a national expense account of about 5 per cent of what we allow for cosmetics.

We make a better showing in applied science. Governmental and industrial research, including agriculture, is supplied with probably $200,000,000 a year. That is not equal to our cosmetics allowance by a good deal.

And now under the pressure of preparedness as we need more new methods, more new inventions, more new labor-saving devices, and more new materials, let me explore the processes by which we got them.

I have said elsewhere that there was a time when invention came from the starving genius in the garret. We got the steam engine that way. These gifts now come from long years of patient experiment in great laboratories. Like the growth of plants cell by cell, of fact upon fact, some day there comes forth the blossom of discovery, the illuminating hypothesis or the great generalization. And finally it fruits into a multitude of inventions. Moreover, poverty does not essentially clarify thought. Nor does it provide laboratory equipment. Bread and water diet has been discarded by the mother of invention.

I can easily illustrate the movement of pure science from discovery to invention. Our electrical industries today are the result of search into pure science. They are the result of a half-century of step-by-step advance in the realms of pure physics and mathematics. It is from these realms that Faraday extracted the transformation of mechanical energy into electricity through induction. It is an old story that Gladstone was induced to visit Faraday's physics laboratory to see this new scientific contraption. When Gladstone, a practical man, inquired whether it would be of any use to mankind, Faraday opined, "I think some day you will be able to tax it." But it was long years afterward that Edison, Thompson, Siemens and the other engineers translated Faraday's discovery into power and light. And today it moans and groans with taxation. But it pays the taxes.

And taxes are not the major achievement of electricity. Rivers of sweat have been saved from the backs of men. Watt and Faraday did more to reduce the 84-hour week to a 44-hour week and to give more good jobs to men than all the laws and all the organizations which have been embattled in this cause.

Infinite drudgery has been lifted from the hands of women. The electric light alone has relieved the human race from the curse of always cleaning oil lamps, scrubbing up candle drips, and everlastingly carrying one or the other of them about.

And its benefits are not all economic. They lift the spirit. It adds cheer to life—enables us to postpone our spectacles for a few years longer. It has made reading in bed infinitely more comfortable. By merely pushing a button we have introduced the element of surprise in dealing with burglars. The goblins who lived in dark corners and under the bed have now been driven to the outdoors. The doctors now peer into the recesses of our insides. Our electric light enables our cities and towns to clothe themselves in gaiety by night, no matter how sad their appearance may be by day. It has lengthened the hours of our active lives and enabled us to read the type in the telephone book. It has become the friend of man and child.

But now to return to my illustration of the progress of skilled research in electrical physics. From Faraday we could move on to Maxwell's formulation of the electrical wave theory by pure mathematics. Hertz confirmed Maxwell in experiment and proved the radiation of waves through the air. It was the engineers Marconi and DeForest who transformed these discoveries of pure physics into the radio communication. Out of that we get jazz by night and war scares by day. Between them it diverts our minds from other woes.

And now somebody will say that all this is in the past. What of the future? Are there any great fields to explore from which such benefits can spring again? The answer is that never in the whole history of fundamental science have there been so many vistas opened before us as right now. Discovery and invention expand in geometrical progression. Inventive minds play upon every new invention and breed a dozen more.

Much of our progress comes from the invention of new instruments —that is, new tools for research. They are born from long hypothesis and prior experiment. Out of the discoveries in atomic structure and radiation have come new tools, new instruments, which open still wider avenues for research.

By use of these laboratory tools or instruments comes a multitude of discoveries and inventions. Every time we get a new one we have some addition to human progress. And in the very recent past our scientists have evolved a number of these instruments, the possibilities of which stretch our imagination to the breaking point.

The harnessing of the cathode ray through the cathode tube was the key to television. And a great industry has been born. From that application the cathode tube was further developed to the astonishing new electron microscope. Today we have photographs of red blood corpuscles as large as dish pans. We are actually able to photograph some molecules. A dime could be enlarged to a mile in diameter if we possessed a big enough film.

And from all of this we will know more of how to limit the conduct of bacteria and increase the energies of men. We will know far more about cellular structure and the make up of molecules which will improve our industrial processes. The field of discovery with this instrument has hardly been entered. There are only two or three of these microscopes in use. Shortly there will be scores of these in the hands of our scientists—provided someone furnishes the money to build and operate them.

And there are the cyclotron and the mass spectrograph, and their opening of the whole vistas of atomic structure. Actually atomic power here has been experimentally produced.

All these instruments are revolutionary. All advance in laboratory instruments is not so sensational. Minor ones happen every day which contribute to progress. The spectroscope was for years just a tool for the astronomer. Today it has been transformed into an instrument for accurate metallurgical analysis to control our steel furnaces and thus the methods of industry improve.

The invention of the steam engine did not appear in the headlines of a world then engaged in the Napoleonic Wars. Yet it saved the world for much of the impoverishment of those wars. History may yet record that the headlines of today should have been devoted to the inventions around the electron rather than war news.

And now I come again to the question of men and money for these explorations. I believe every physical scientist in this country today could name new paths, new fields, that wait for the money to mobilize men and equipment. Many of their results may be sterile but somewhere something comes—an improved instrument, a new path opens and in the end an increase in the standard of living.

Someone will say that these great discoveries of fundamental law cannot be forced—that we must wait for them. I do not contend you can go out and buy a genius and have him produce every morning. But I do say that he cannot perform without equipment and support.

Nor do we have to wait for pure science research to give birth to new laws, new instruments, new methods, new power, and new labor-saving devices. In many directions we sorely need support for research in the application of pure science discoveries we already know.

One of the greatest of our problems right now is to develop more industrial raw materials which our farmers can produce in substitution for their overproduction of food. I doubt whether we are spending five millions a year looking for them. And we are compelled to subsidize the farmer with a billion a year and to regiment him besides until we find some such solution as this.

And in the realm of industry there are further vast possibilities in synthetic fibers, rubber, in the plastics, or new sources and methods of making and use of cellulose and a score of other things. There is the field of metallurgical treatment of low-grade ores. If we developed such methods we could free ourselves from depending upon imports of chrome and manganese. We need substitutes for materials needed for defense. I doubt that actually three millions a year are being spent in such research laboratories.

Nor to improve our national efficiency do we have to wait for even these better applications of science.

Under the pressures of emergency we can increase national efficiency through the elimination of existing industrial waste of motion and materials. That requires that we remove every sort of restriction both by capital and labor which impedes or penalizes the use of better methods and better machines or the working of these machines full time.

At once someone will rise up and say that these are fine generalities; that they lack an exact and particular action which will bring results right now while we are in the middle of this preparation for defense. If you will go back to the last war and examine the methods which we then adopted for the elimination of waste, the simplification of methods, the substitution of materials for continuous operation, you will find an immediate and enormous field already pioneered. If the armed forces need to take 20 per cent of our shoes by such devices we can at once increase the output of our existing factories and thus save a cramp in our supply of shoes.

We will spend 20 billions a year on armament. We will pile most of it up in national debt. If we would invest 1 per cent of this in an insurance policy called research and elimination of waste, we might save some of the bankruptcy when these wars die.

It is possible that the aggressive superiority of the airplane in war may be checked. And that becomes vital to the freedom of nations and to stop the massacre of women and children.

And it is not beyond human imagination that the quiet, unobtrusive scientist and engineer in their laboratories might make all nations self-contained in raw materials and their production of goods. And what a holocaust that would be for international quarrels and international thinking—and for much of the causes of war.

And that brings me to another phase. We have been told with monotonous repetition by the collectivists and left-wingers that our frontiers are gone. They say our industrial plant is built. They claim there is no safety valve for human energies. They assure us that we have come to an age of humdrum problems of under-consumption, over-production, and the division of the existing pot. They say that new opportunity for youth has shrunken.

That is not so. There was never in history a more glorious frontier for youth than today. Adventure and opportunity beckon in every avenue of science. They beckon from the great profession of men trained to research. They beckon from its thousands of applications. From it springs tens of thousands of new services and industries. In them human courage, character, and ability have an outlet that never came even with the two-gun frontiers. Just as the new villages followed the stockades of the frontier, so do new cities follow every new mastery of technology and power.

And let those who lament the loss of frontier life not forget the adventures along every mile of highway and even with the traffic cop. That all emanated from the discovery of the combustion engine.

But research can bring far more than defense from aggression, or the opening of new frontiers, discoveries, adventures, inventions, labor-saving devices, more power or increased standards of living. There also lies in these fields a contribution to the moral and spiritual welfare of mankind. Here is the lifting of men's minds beyond the depressing incidents of the day. Here lies the unfolding of beauty, the ever-widening of the boundaries of knowledge. Here is the "inculcation of veracity of thought" in a world sodden with intellectual dishonesty. Here is the harmonizing of the individual to the pattern of his environment. Here is the confirmation of a Supreme Guidance in the universe far above man himself.

And today we need more of these things to help save and build a great nation.

XXI

Excerpts from Herbert Hoover's address to graduating class, Stanford University, June 16, 1935.

First of social securities is freedom—freedom of men to worship, to think, to speak, to direct their energies, to develop their own talents and to be rewarded for their effort. Too often plans of social security ignore these the primary forces which make for human progress without which America as we know it could not exist. Freedom is a spiritual need and a spiritual right of man. We can get security in food, shelter, education, leisure, music, books, and what not, in some jails. But we don't get freedom. Those who scoff that individual liberty is of no consequence to the under-privileged and the unemployed are grossly ignorant of the primary fact that it is through the creative impulses of liberty that the redemption of these sufferings and that social security must come.

The second of social securities is the capacity to produce a plenty of goods and services with which to give economic security to the whole of us. Scientific discovery, this vast technology and mechanical power, are the achievement of personal and intellectual freedom. Creativeness, intellectual accomplishments, initiative, and enterprise are the dynamic forces of civilization. They thrive alone among free men and women. It is these impulses which have built this capacity to produce a plenty that society must now learn to employ more effectively. This freedom and this plenty came into western civilization hand in hand—they are inseparable. This vastly complicated mechanism is not alone a mass of machines. These engines and machines are inert materials which require every hour of the day new human initiative, new enterprise, and new creative action, or they will not work. No other group of impulses would have produced this productivity. No other method but that of orderly personal liberty can operate or improve it. Economic security is lost the moment that freedom is sacrificed.

Any system which curtails these freedoms or stimulants to men destroys the possibility of the production which we know we must have to attain economic security. Social security will never be attained by an economy of scarcity. That is the economy of fear. Not out of scarcity or restriction but out of abundance can society make provision for all its members and support the unemployed, the sick, the aged, and the orphan. That is the economy of hope.

The safeguards of freedom lie in self-government. There never has been nor ever will be freedom when powers of government are lodged in a man or a group of men. Moreover, all history teaches us that even majorities cannot be trusted with the ark of freedom without checks.

Constitutional government, the division of powers, are the only successful protections the human race has devised. To transgress or to override them will weaken and finally destroy freedom itself. . . .

The doors of freedom must be kept open wide to initiative, to honest enterprise, to effort. The windows must be kept bright with hope and confidence in the future. These are the standards and tests which may be applied to every social proposal made to you. . . .

. . . The functioning of any economic system is peculiarly based upon faith in the future and confidence in certain constants in life. Without that faith all effort slackens. They are not only liberty in the broad sense but these constants include the detail of sanctity of contracts which are not unconscionable, the stability of the currency and credit, the maintenance of legitimate competition, government by specific laws, not by the uncertainties of administrative fiat. Without security in those constants, confidence and faith are impossible. Indeed, today our daily life and the whole world are seized with fears. There are within our ranks defeatists who in despair abandon all confidence in the race, in our accomplishment hitherto, and all hope that upon this rich experience we can further advance.

XXII

Excerpts from an address by Herbert Hoover in San Diego, California, September 17, 1935 on the Bill of Rights.

Our Constitution is not alone the working plan of a great Federation of States under representative government. There is embedded in it also the vital principles of the American system of liberty. That system is based upon certain inalienable freedoms and protections which not even the government may infringe and which we call the Bill of Rights. It does not require a lawyer to interpret those provisions. They are as clear as the Ten Commandments. Among others the freedom of worship, freedom of speech and of the press, the right of peaceable assembly, equality before the law, just trial for crime, freedom from unreasonable search, and security from being deprived of life, liberty, or property without due process of law, are the principles which distinguish our civilization. Herein are the invisible sentinels which guard the door of every home from invasion of coercion, of intimidation and fear. Herein is the expression of the spirit of men who would be forever free.

These rights were no sudden discovery, no over-night inspiration. They were established by centuries of struggle in which men died fighting bitterly for their recognition. Their beginnings lie in the Magna Charta at Runnymede five hundred and seventy years before the Constitution was written. Down through the centuries the Habeas Corpus, the "Petition of Rights," the "Declaration of Rights," the growth of the fundamental maxims of the Common Law, marked their expansion and security. Our forefathers migrated to America that they might attain them more fully. When they wrote the Declaration of Independence they boldly extended these rights. Before the Constitution could be ratified patriotic men who feared a return to tyranny, whose chains had been thrown off only after years of toil and bloody war, insisted that these hard-won rights should be incorporated in black and white within the Constitution—and so came the American Bill of Rights.

In the hurricane of revolutions which have swept the world since the Great War, men, struggling with the wreckage and poverty of that great catastrophe and the complications of the machine age, are in despair surrendering their freedom for false promises of economic security. Whether it be Fascist Italy, Nazi Germany, Communist Russia, or their lesser followers, the result is the same. Every day they repudiate every principle of the Bill of Rights. Freedom of worship is denied. Freedom of speech is suppressed. The press is censored and distorted with propaganda. The right of criticism is denied. Men go to jail or the gallows for honest opinion. They may not assemble for discussion. They speak of public affairs only in whispers. They are subject to search and seizure by spies and inquisitors who haunt the land. The safeguards of justice in trial or imprisonment are set aside. There is no right in one's savings or one's own home which the government need respect.

Here is a form of servitude, of slavery—a slipping back toward the Middle Ages. Whatever these governments are, they have one common denominator—the citizen has no assured rights. He is submerged into the State. Here is the most fundamental clash known to mankind

—that is, free men and women, co-operating under orderly liberty, as contrasted with human beings made pawns of dictatorial government; men who are slaves of despotism, as against free men who are the masters of the State.

Even in America, where liberty blazed brightest and by its glow shed light on all the others, it is besieged from without and challenged from within. Many, in honest belief, hold that we cannot longer accommodate the growth of science, technology and mechanical power to the Bill of Rights and our form of government. With that I do not agree. Men's inventions cannot be of more value than men themselves. But it would be better that we sacrifice something of economic efficiency than to surrender these primary liberties. In them lies a spiritual right of men. Behind them is the conception which is the highest development of the Christian faith—the conception of individual freedom with brotherhood. From them is the fullest flowering of individual human personality. . . .

Those who proclaim that by the Machine Age there is created an irreconcilable conflict in which Liberty must be sacrificed should not forget the battles for these rights over the centuries, for let it be remembered that in the end these are undying principles which spring from the souls of men. We imagine conflict not because the principles of Liberty are unworkable in a machine age, but because we have not worked them conscientiously or have forgotten their true meaning.

Nor do I admit that sacrifice of these rights would add to economic efficiency or would gain in economic security, or would find a single job or would give a single assurance in old age. The dynamic forces which sustain economic security and progress in human comfort lie deep below the surface. They reach to those human impulses which are watered alone by freedom. The initiative of men, their enterprise, the inspiration of thought, flower in full only in the security of these rights.

And by practical experience under the American system we have tested this truth. And here I may repeat what I have said elsewhere. Down through a century and a half this American concept of human freedom has enriched the whole world. From the release of the spirit, the initiative, the co-operation, and the courage of men, which alone comes of these freedoms, has been builded this very machine age with all its additions of comfort, its reductions of sweat. Wherever in the world the system of individual liberty has been sustained, mankind has been better clothed, better fed, better housed, has had more leisure. Above all, men and women have had more self-respect. They have been more generous and of finer spirit. Those who scoff that liberty is of no consequence to the under-privileged and the unemployed are grossly ignorant of the primary fact that it is through the creative and the productive impulses of free men that the redemption of those sufferers and their economic security must come. Any system which curtails these freedoms and stimulants to men destroys the possibility of the full production from which economic security can alone come.

These rights and protections of the Bill of Rights are safeguarded in the Constitution through a delicate balance and separation of powers in the framework of our government. That has been founded on the experience over centuries including our own day.

Liberty is safe only by a division of powers and upon local self-government. We know full well that power feeds upon itself—partly from the greed of power and partly from the innocent belief that utopia can be attained by dictation or coercion.

Nor is respect for the Bill of Rights a fetter upon progress. It has been no dead hand that has carried the living principles of liberty over these centuries. Without violation of these principles and their safeguards we have amended the Constitution many times in the past century to meet the problems of growing civilization. We will no doubt do so many times again. Always groups of audacious men in government or out will attempt to consolidate privilege against their fellows. New invention and new ideas require the constant remolding of our civilization. The functions of government must be readjusted from time to time to restrain the strong and protect the weak. That is the preservation of liberty itself. We ofttimes interpret some provisions of the Bill of Rights so that they override others. They indeed jostle each other in course of changing national life—but their respective domains can be defined by virtue, by reason, and by law. And the freedom of men is not possible without virtue, reason, and law.

Liberty comes alone and lives alone where the hard-won rights of men are held inalienable, where governments themselves may not infringe, where governments are indeed but the mechanisms to protect and sustain these principles. It was this concept for which America's sons have died on a hundred battlefields.

The nation seeks for solution of many difficulties. These solutions can come alone through the constructive forces which arise from the spirit of free men and women. The purification of Liberty from abuses, the restoration of confidence in the rights of men, from which come the release of the dynamic forces of initiative and enterprise, are alone the methods through which these solutions can be found and the purpose of American life assured.

XXIII

Excerpts from address by Herbert Hoover in St. Louis, Missouri, December 16, 1935 in which he corrected certain inaccurate statements of the Roosevelt administration.

In speaking at Atlanta two weeks ago the President's first basis of defense for his gigantic spending, deficits, and debts was the assertion that "The mechanics of civilization came to a dead stop on March 3, 1933."

What happened on March 3, 1933, was an induced hysteria of bank depositors. The banking structure at large subsequently proved to be sound. That is scarcely a dead stop to civilization.

I have always believed that the newspapers are one of the mechanisms of civilization. They did not quit. At that time I saw no headlines that the farmers had ceased to till the fields. Most of you did not detect that the delivery of food to your doors had stopped. Railway managers apparently did not know that their trains had stalled. Somebody failed to inform us that the hum of our factories was silent. We still had to jump out of the way of the twenty-three million automobiles. Our churches, schools, and courts are a part of the mechanics of civilization. They did not close. And the Supreme Court seems to be functioning yet. If civilization came to a dead stop the press missed a great piece of news that day.

If this notion is to be the excuse for this spending and other vagaries of the New Deal, we had better examine into it further.

The truth is that the world-wide depression was turned in June-July, 1932, all over the world. That was before the election of the

New Deal. That is supported by scores of leading American economists, business men, and public leaders. It is supported by the economic publications throughout the world.

That turning was aided by the measures of our Republican government. These measure were within the Constitution of the United States. They were not that futile financial jiggling which has violated economic law, morals, the Constitution, and the structure of American liberty. The turning was aided by the efforts of foreign governments. Every commercial country, including the United States, surged forward. Prices rose, employment increased, the whole agricultural, financial, and business structure grew in strength. After election of the New Deal we began a retreat. Only in the United States was there an interruption. We were the strongest and should have led the van. And we lagged behind for two years. The other countries of the world went forward without interruption. They adopted no New Deal. Apparently those nations did not hear that the mechanics of civilization came to a dead stop on March 3, 1933.

It did not come to a stop even in the United States. It was meddled with. We have not got over it yet. But why did we have a panic of bank depositors in 1933? Because they were scared. We had no bank panic from the crash of the boom in 1929. We had no panic at the financial collapse in Europe in 1931. We had no panic at the most dangerous point in the depression when our banks were weakest in the spring of 1932. There was no panic before the election of November, 1932. When did they become frightened? They became scared a few weeks before the inauguration of the New Deal on March 4, 1933.

What were they frightened of? They could not have been scared by the outgoing administration which had only a few days to run. They were frightened at the incoming New Deal. Why were they scared at the New Deal? Because soon after the election large numbers of people awoke to the fact that promises given in the campaign would be violated. Among other things it gradually spread that the gold standard would be abandoned or that the currency would be tinkered with. It was evident that a wholesale orgy of spending public money would be undertaken. Business slackened its energies. Shrewd speculators shipped their money abroad at fabulous profits. Bankers tried to protect themselves. The public in blind fear demanded gold and the "covenants" of the United States which called for gold. Some of them were scared at the banks by the destructive publication of RFC loans. *The banking structure was not insolvent. After the banks were closed it was found that the solvent banks, measured by deposits, comprised 92 per cent of the banking strength of the country. The President himself stated they were sound. Subsequently more banks were found sound and reopened. And beyond this, important banks wrongfully closed . . . such as in the Detroit area, are now paying out 100 per cent to the depositors. It was the most political and the most unnecessary bank panic in all our history. It could have been prevented. It could have been cured by simple co-operation.* (Italics author's.)

The President in further elucidation of the stop of civilization says: "At that time our national balance sheet, the wealth versus the debts of the American public, showed we were in the 'red.'" The value of America is not the quotations in the market place—either the highs of inflation booms or the lows made in anticipation of the New Deal. He informs us, however, that some great bankers told him that the country could safely stand an increase in the national debt to between fifty-five and seventy-five billions. He adds "remember this was in the spring of 1933." Thus we are to believe that when our wealth was less than our debts we were so strong we could still borrow fifty-five billions. It certainly is a confusing thought. It indicates some little excess of assets and at the same time great restraint on the part of the New Deal. . . .

Let me say one thing right at the outset. There is no disagreement upon the public obligation to relieve distress which flows from national calamity. The support of that comes from the conscience of a people. It comes from their fidelity to the Sermon on the Mount. The American people know that the genuine sufferers on relief are not slackers. They know the weary days of tramping the streets in search for a chance to work. They know the discouragement and despair which have stalked those homes. There is not a real man or woman whose heart does not warm to them, who will not sacrifice for them.

Some five years ago I stated that, "as a nation we must prevent hunger and cold to those of our people who are in honest difficulties." I have never heard a disagreement with that. And I wish to emphasize that there is no humor in relief. It is grim human tragedy.

I believe I can without egotism claim to have had some special experience in relief. At one time or another it became my task to organize and administer relief to over one hundred and fifty million people who had been reduced to destitution by war or by famine or by flood both at home and abroad. I gave some years to that service in the aspiration to save life, to allay suffering, to restore courage and faith in humanity.

It also became my duty in 1930 to see that relief was organized for our unemployed. Organization of relief upon a nation-wide basis was practically unknown in the world before those experiences. It therefore fell to me and my colleagues to pioneer in methods. We had to learn what basis would best and most sympathetically protect those in distress and still place the least burden on those who had to pay for it. I spent long, weary days listening to arguments whether to have direct money relief, or relief in kind, or public works, or made-work or "boon-doggling," or centralized administration, or decentralized responsibility. We tried out these alternatives. Out of those poignant experiences we learned certain fundamentals. We quickly learned that there were four types of persons who rush into relief. There were the starry-eyed who periodically discover that relief is needed and that everything up to date is wrong. There were those whose major passion was sociological experiment upon a mass of distress. There were those who would make profit from misery. There were always those present who do not neglect the political possibilities of relief. But there were the sterling, solid men and women in every city and hamlet who willingly served and sacrificed.

We learned that relief was an emergency operation, not a social experiment; that the object was to serve the people in genuine distress and nobody else. We learned that the dreamers cannot effectually conduct the grinding tasks of relief; that politics must be shunned as a plague. We learned that centralized bureaucracy gives the sufferers more red tape than relief. We learned that we must mobilize on a voluntary basis the best hearts and brains of every community to serve their neighbors. We learned that there must be complete decentralization to them of both authority and administration. We did not have to learn that local self-government and local responsibility was the basis of American life.

In 1930 by co-operation with the States, we secured the creation of State committees of leading citizens. With them we secured the creation of similar committees in every city, town, and county where relief was needed. These committees had no politics. They were men and women experienced in large affairs, sympathetic, understanding of the needs of their neighbors in distress. And they served without pay. In those days one did not enter into relief of his countrymen through the portals of a payroll. American men and women of such stature cannot be had as a paid bureaucracy, yet they will serve voluntarily all hours of the day and defer their own affairs to night.

These committees used the existing officials; they engaged their own tested organizations; they employed their own trusted citizens. They had the complete authority to determine the methods best adapted to their neighborhoods. They knew the problem of the man next door better than anybody in Washington. They themselves determined for their locality what method was to be used. They adapted these needs to the individual families. Their stewardship was under the limelight of their own community. They gave spiritual aid and encouragement.

At the start the relief in 1930 depended upon private giving. As times became more difficult, the committees co-operated in the use of county and municipal funds; and as it became still more difficult many of the State governments provided them with funds. Finally, as State resources weakened, we provided Federal Government funds to be distributed to the State governments and by them redistributed to the local organizations. That we built up no bureaucracy is evident from the fact that although the government had many new emergency tasks, yet during the Hoover administration the total number of all government officials decreased by ten thousand. That form of organization expressed in its noblest form the whole American ideal of local self-government, local responsibility, national co-operation, and the voluntary spirit of human service.

There was no important failure to provide for those in real need. There was no substantial complaint or suggestion of waste, politics, or corruption. Neither the Republican party nor any of its agencies ever asked for votes or claimed that its administration reserved votes for it. That idea was repugnant to every decent sense of Americanism.

However, all this was forgotten on March 3, 1933. We may accept that the date of Creation was moved to March 4, and we may examine what sort of a world has been made.

At that moment good men appeared who were certain that before their advent everything was done wrong. Also came the visionaries, the profit-maker, and, above all, the politician. They all yearned to serve their fellowmen. . . .

In conclusion, I should like to say a word to the young men and women among my listeners. Some of us have not much more span of life. We have seen America grow in greatness. Except the cost of war we have seen increasing security to the average man. Our interest is for those who will carry the burden and create the glories of America after us. We will continue fighting. But you have to live the years, you have to carry America on. It is your pockets into which the government will reach deeper and deeper if this goes on. It is you whose opportunities are being limited. I have but one suggestion. That you study the history of your country. That you survey its scene today. That you debate every phase of this government. That you carry this debate to every street corner, every school-house, every shop, and every counting room. What you decide will be final for our country. You will have the burdens. And may the Divine Being guide you aright.

XXIV

Excerpts from an address by Herbert Hoover in Spokane, Washington, November 5, 1938 on the subject of free enterprise.

What do we want as a minimum standard of American living for all the people? We want American children born in health. We want them brought up with plenty of vitamins in the sunshine. We want our race physically stronger with every generation. We want our youth high in ideals and resolute in character. We want them inspired with the spirit of human brotherhood. We want them trained to make their own living, to contribute to the advancement of the nation. We want every one of them to have a job to start in life. And we want them to have constructive joy all through the process.

We want old age serene in security from poverty or the fear of it.

And we want profitable work for the great middle groups between youth and old age, for they must support the whole. The focus of their lives is in the home. We want them to own their own homes. We want the gadgets that replace drudgery and give joy in these homes. We want each home to have a job or to own a farm or its own business. We want Americans to be secure in that job and get living and comfort out of it. And above all we want them to have that American personal liberty which makes the rest worth having. This is no impossible ideal. I am for whatever economic system will bring it about.

How are we to attain all this? The question is which is the right road? Which road leads to danger?

In all the history of the world mankind has found only two ways of doing the work of feeding, clothing, housing and providing comforts for the people. One is the way of liberty in which every man and woman is free to plan his own life, choose his own calling, start his own adventures, secure in reward of his effort and ability. That is the system of free enterprise.

The other way is the way of compulsion by which men work for slave-drivers or governments, or as dictated by governments. The dictators of Europe have softened that rough statement by calling it Planned Economy. And right here we come to the first quality of free enterprise. It has been proved in all history and is proved again in 16 nations today that you cannot have free criticism, free speech and free worship with a coercive economic system. For free men will fight coercion. And coercion to live must crush free men.

And let me emphasize that when I speak of free enterprise I do not mean that men can abuse or destroy the freedom of others by monopolies or any other kind of privilege or exploitation of business, farmers or labor. That destroys freedom itself. No one pretends that ours is a perfect system. There will be no perfect system until men are perfect. And economic life requires constant progressive reform and change. The reason is simple. Free men constantly find new inventions and new ideas. Some of them find new varieties of wickedness. . . .

XXV

Excerpts from address by Herbert Hoover before the Republican National Convention, 1936.

In this room rests the greatest responsibility that has come to a body of Americans in three generations. In the lesser sense this is a convention of a great political party. But in the larger sense it is a convention of Americans to determine the fate of those ideals for which this nation was founded. That far transcends all partisanship.

There is a moral purpose in the universe. There are elemental currents which make or break the fate of nations. Those forces which affect the vitality and the soul of a people will control its destinies. They far transcend the importance of transitory even though difficult issues of national life. . . .

Great calamities have come to the whole world. These forces have reached into every calling and every cottage. They have brought tragedy and suffering to millions of firesides. I have great sympathy for those who honestly reach for short cuts to the immensity of our problems. While design of the structure of betterment for the common man must be inspired by the human heart, it can only be achieved by the intellect. It can only be builded by using the mold of justice, by laying brick upon brick from the materials of scientific research; by the painstaking sifting of truth from the collection of fact and experience. Any other mold is distorted; any other bricks are without straw; any other foundations are sand. That great structure of human progress can be built only by free men and women.

Here in America, where the tablets of human freedom were first handed down, their sacred word has been flouted. Today the stern task is before the Republican party to restore the Ark of that Covenant to the temple in Washington.

Does this issue not transcend all other issues? Is it not alone the ground of Republican unity but unity beyond all partisanship? . . .

There's something vastly bigger than payrolls, than economics, than materialism, at issue in this campaign. The free spirit of men is the source of self-respect, of sturdiness, of moral and spiritual progress. With the inspirations of freedom come fidelity to public trust, honor and morals in government. The social order does not rest upon orderly economic freedom alone. It rests even more upon the ideals and character of a people. Governments must express those ideals in frugality, in justice, in courage, in decency, and in regard for the less fortunate, and above all in honor. Nations die when these weaken, no matter what their material prosperity.

Fundamental American liberties are at stake. Is the Republican party ready for the issue? Are you willing to cast your all upon the issue, or would you falter and look back? Will you, for expediency's sake, also offer will-o'-the-wisps which beguile the people? Or have you determined to enter in a holy crusade for liberty which shall determine the future and the perpetuity of a nation of free men? That star shell fired today over the no man's land of world despair would illuminate the world with hope. . . .

XXVI

This Crisis in American Life

Address before the Republican National Convention at Philadelphia, June 22, 1948.

Republican Convention and your guests:

It is indeed difficult to express to you my appreciation for your heart-warming welcome.

Those who have already addressed you in this Convention have emphasized the continuing grave crisis which envelopes our own country and the world. And this crisis is deeper than some may think. Every important government including our own has broken its promises to mankind. But civilization moves forward only on promises that are kept. And from these disasters faith has been hurt; hope has been diminished; thinking has been corrupted, and fear has been spread—all over the world.

The problems which confront us far transcend partisan action and I do not propose to speak in that sense tonight. I shall speak but a few moments and that as an appraisal of the responsibilities you face.

What is done here, what you do here, will affect the destiny of our country beyond any estimation of this moment. For you are more than ever before, the trustees of a great cause, the cause for which this party was founded, the cause of human liberty.

The World Problem of Free Men

Liberty has been defeated in a score of nations. Those governments have revived slavery. They have revived mass guilt. They have revived government by hatred, by exile, by torture. Today the men in the

Kremlin hold in their right hands the threat of military aggression against all civilization. With their left hands they work to weaken civilization by boring from within.

These tyrants have created a situation new in all human experience. We saved them from Hitler but they refuse to co-operate with us to establish good will or peace on earth. Thus today a powerful nation, dominated by men without conscience, finds it useful to have neither peace or war in the world.

Whether some of us, who foresaw that danger and warned of it, were right or wrong, and whatever the terrible errors of American statesmanship that helped bring it about, we are today faced with a world situation in which there is little time for regrets.

The only obstacle to the annihilation of freedom has been the United States of America. Only as long as America is free and strong will human liberty survive in the world.

Our Aid to Free Men Abroad

It is in our interest and, above all, in the interest of liberty throughout the world, that we aid in giving strength and unity to the nations of Western Europe. It is only thus that we can restore a balance of power in the world able to resist the hordes from the Eurasian steppes who would ruin Western Civilization.

And we have also a huge burden of increased armament to assure that no hostile force will ever reach this hemisphere.

With all the good will in our hearts, our friends abroad should realize that our economy must not be exhausted or overstrained by these burdens, or the last hope of the world is lost. We should only be playing Stalin's game, for his expressed hope lies in our economic collapse for which his Fifth Columns are busily planning.

Our friends abroad should realize that we are today straining our American economy to the utmost. Warning signals already clang in our ears. Relief and defense will soon be costing us over 22 billion dollars a year. Our Federal budget threatens to increase to 50 billions a year, unless we delay many plans for internal social and economic improvement.

Even our present 40 odd billion taxes and the export of materials so drain the savings of our people that in the year 1947 we did not properly maintain and expand the great tools of production and distribution upon which our standard of living depends.

Nor is there any room for more taxes except by a cut in the standard of living of those who do the nation's work. Some will say that we can increase corporation taxes. That is easy to say. But any student of economics knows that, in the long run, such a tax will be passed on to the consumer—provided we want to maintain our real wages and great tools of production. Surely any American would seem to have the right to aspire to the income of a United States Senator—less taxes. However, if our remaining untaxed income above that level in the country were completely confiscated, the take would provide only 2½% of the budget.

There are other warning signs. Our reputed prosperity has begun to walk on two stilts: one is the forced draft of exporting more than our surplus through relief; the other is a great armament program. We cannot go higher on these stilts, or we will break a leg getting down.

We should have no illusions. To the devasting Four Horsemen of the Apocalypse, modern civilization has added two more. Their names are High Taxes and Inflation. These are close by.

Therefore, with full compassion for those nations in difficulties, certain matters in aid to them must be recognized on both sides of the world.

The first is that our task is solely to aid their reconstruction. We can provide only bare necessities. There is no room for non-essentials, for profligacy, or for inefficiency.

We must not create a perpetual dependence of Europe and Asia upon the United States. We must not soften their preparedness to meet their own dangers. Otherwise our sacrifices will only undermine their self-reliance and the contribution they must make themselves towards the saving of Western Civilization.

We must insist that reconstruction of Western Europe be as a whole. That must include the restoration of the productivity of Germany, or Europe will die. We need neither forget nor condone Nazi guilt, but a free world must not poison its concepts of life by accepting revenge and hatred as a guide. Otherwise, not only will our efforts fail, but the American taxpayer will be bled white supporting an idle and despairing German people.

Great Strikes Can Defeat All Freedom

And if we are to carry both these burdens of relief and armament, we must have uninterrupted operation of the major tools of production and distribution among all the participating nations.

We in America must face the fact that no citizen, or group of citizens, in this Republic can assure the power to endanger not only the health and welfare of our own people, but freedom of the world, by halting or paralyzing the economic life of this nation. Such men have not been elected by the people to have such powers. Representative government must be master in its own house, or it will perish. We fought that battle out once with arrogant business men. We can no more have economic tyranny, if freedom is to live, than we can have political tyranny. There are other ways for determining economic justice than war on our people.

The Battle for Liberty at Home

Nor does the battle for freedom all lie beyond our own borders. We also have been infected with the European intermittent fever of creeping totalitarianism. It has been a mingling of germs from Karl Marx and Mussolini, with sheers from the Communists. This collectivism has slowly inserted its tentacles into our labor unions, our universities, our intelligentsia, and our Government.

Our difficulty lies not so much with obnoxious Communists in our midst as with the fuzzy-minded people who think we can have totalitarian economics in the hands of bureaucracy, and at the same time have personal liberty for the people and representative government in the nation. Their confused thinking convinces them that they are liberals—but if they are liberals, they have liberalism without liberty. Nor are they middle-of-the-roaders as they claim to be: they are a half-way house to totalitarianism.

They should take note that in every one of the countries of Europe where 400,000,000 people are now enslaved by the Communists, it has been the totalitarian liberals who provided the ladders upon which the Communist pirates have boarded the Ship of State.

The whole world was steadily moving along these collectivist roads until two years ago. Then in our Congressional elections, by their votes for both the Republican and Democratic candidates, the people showed the first turn from collectivism that has been made by any important nation in recent years.

The 300-year-old roots of freedom in America showed their resistance to the collectivist blight. The influence of our rebirth of liberty has now echoed throughout the world. But the battle is still on.

The deep soil of these 300-year-old roots is the spiritual concept that the rights of man to freedom are personal to him from his Creator—not from the State. That is our point of departure from all others. This spiritual concept, whatever our faults may be, has guided our people to a life, not only of material abundance, but far more glorious, to a life of human dignity.

Today the American people have reached an historic stage which has come to a few strong nations in their ability to contribute to moral leadership in the world. Few such nations have come upon that task with so few liabilities. In these 30 years of war we alone have taken no people's land; we have oppressed no race of man. We have faced all the world in friendship, with compassion, with a genuine love and helpfulness for our fellow men. In war, in peace, in disaster, we have aided those whom we believed to be in the right and to require our aid. At the end of wars, we have aided foe as well as ally; and in each instance, even the children of those who would do us hurt. We have hated war; we have loved peace.

What other nation has such a record?

It is these concepts of your country that this Party must bear high as the banner of a marching army. From this room free men and women will cheer free men and women the world over. You can say to them that the day is not done, that night has not come—that human liberty lives—and lives eternally here upon this continent.

The Responsibilities of This Convention

My fellow Republicans, from the inevitable passing of years, this is indicated as probably the last time I will meet with you in Convention. That does not mean I shall spend my days with less concern and less watchfulness of the deep currents which will determine the future of American life. But this does warrant my speaking from my heart of this great concern.

There may be some of you who believe that you have come here only to pass upon a platform and to select candidates for President and Vice President. Your greater task by far is to generate a spirit which will rekindle in every American a love not only for his country but a devotion to American civilization. You are here to feed the reviving fires of spiritual fervor which once made the word, American, a stirring description of a man who lived and died for human liberty, who knew no private interest, no personal ambition, no popular acclaim, no advantage of pride or place which overshadows the burning love for the freedom of man.

Great as your problems are, they are no greater than Americans have met before your time. You are no less able or courageous than they were.

Therefore, I repeat, what you say and do here and in this campaign, is of transcendent importance.

If you produce nothing but improvised platitudes, you will give no hope.

If you produce no leadership here, no virile fighter for the right, you will have done nothing of historic significance.

If you follow the counsel of those who believe that politics is only a game to be played for personal advantage, you are wasting your time and effort.

If here, or in this campaign, you calculate what will please this or that little segment of our population, and satisfy this or that pressure group or sectional interest, you will be betraying your opportunity, and tragically missing the call of your time.

If you temporize with collectivism in any form, you will stimulate its growth and make certain the defeat of free men.

If, on the other hand, in this campaign, as a mature and inspired political party, you face the truth that we are in a critical battle to safeguard our nation and civilization which, under God, have brought to use a life of liberty, then you will be guided step by step to restore the foundations of right thinking, of morals and of faith. If you choose your leadership with full recognition that only those can lead you who believe in your ideals, who seek not only victory but the opportunity to serve in this fight, then you will issue from this hall a clarion call, in as pure a note, in as full a tone as that call to arms which your political ancestors issued at Ripon, Wisconsin, when this party was born to make all men free.

And so I bespeak to you tonight to make yourselves worthy of the victory.

XXVII

Address by Herbert Hoover at Stanford University, California, on his seventy-fifth birthday, August 10, 1949.

My first duty is to acknowledge your generous reception and these most generous gifts to the Library.

It is now thirty-four years since this Library on War, Revolution and Peace was founded. Over these years friends of the Library have contributed over $3,450,000 toward its support. And of priceless value have been the millions of documents and materials furnished freely by hundreds of individuals and three-score governments.

This institution is not a dead storage. It is a living thing which over the years will correct a vast amount of error in the history of these troubled times. It will also teach the stern lessons of how nations may avoid war and revolution.

Not being a government institution, it has never received a dime from government sources, and its scholars therefore can be as free as the Sierra winds in its use and in the expression of objective truth.

In the somber situation of the world I would be derelict if today I discussed the lighter side of life instead of the serious issues which weigh on my heart.

Some of you will know that during the past two years I have added somewhat to my previous knowledge of the currents of government in this Republic. Beyond the immediate problems of efficient organization of the Federal Departments, there arise from these investigations some grave questions as to our whole future as a nation.

Now, as never before, we need thinking on some of these questions. If America is to be run by the people, it is the people who must think. And we do not need to put on sackcloth and ashes to think. Nor should our minds work like a sundial which records only sunshine. Our thinking must square against some lessons of history, some principles of government and morals, if we would preserve the rights and dignity of men to which this nation is dedicated.

The real test of our thinking is not so much the next election as it is the next generation.

I am not going to offer you solutions to our national ills. But I shall list some items for thought. Perhaps in Japanese-English a subhead would be "Bring feet from clouds into swamp where we now are."

We must wish to maintain a dynamic progressive people. No nation can remain static and survive: But dynamic progress is not made with dynamite. And that dynamite today is the geometrical increase of spending by our governments—Federal, state and local.

Perhaps I can visualize what this growth has been. Twenty years ago, all varieties of government, omitting Federal debt service, cost the average family less than $200 annually. Today, also omitting debt service, it costs an average family about $1300 annually.

This is bad enough. But beyond this is the alarming fact that at this moment executives and legislatures are seriously proposing projects which if enacted would add one-third more annually to our spending. Add to these the debt service and the average family may be paying $2900 yearly taxes. They may get a little back if they live to over 65 years of age.

No doubt life was simpler about 147 years ago, when our government got well under way. At that time there was less than one government employee, Federal, state and local including the paid military, to each 120 of the population. Twenty years ago, there was one government employee to about 40 of the population. Today, there is one government employee to about every 22 of the population. Worse than this, there is today one government employee to about 8 of the working population.

Twenty years ago, persons directly or indirectly receiving regular monies from the government—that is, officials, soldiers, sailors, pensioners, subsidized persons and employees of contractors working exclusively for the Government—represented about one person in every 40 of the population.

Today about one person out of every 7 in the population is a regular recipient of government monies. If those of age are all married, they comprise about one-half the voters of the last Presidential election.

Think it over.

In the long run it is the Average Working Citizen who pays by hidden and other taxes. I have made up a little table showing the number of days which this kind of citizen must work on average to pay the taxes.

	Days' work
Obligations from former wars	11
Defense and Cold War	24
Other federal expenditures	12
State and local expenditures	14
Total thus far	61

But beyond this the seriously proposed further spending now in process will take another 20 days' work from Mr. and Mrs. Average W. Citizen.

Taking out holidays, Sundays, and average vacations, there are about 235 working days in the year. Therefore, this total of 81 days work a year for taxes is about one week out of every month.

You might want to work for your family instead of paying for a gigantic bureaucracy.

Think it over.

To examine what we are doing, we must get away from such sunshine figures as the gross national income. We must reduce our problem to the possible savings of the people after a desirable standard of living. If we adopt the Federal Government's estimate of such a desirable standard, then the actual, and the seriously proposed, national and local governmental spending will absorb between 75% to 85% of all the savings of the people. In practice it does not work evenly. The few will have some savings, but the many must reduce their standard of living to pay the tax collector.

And it is out of savings that the people must provide their individual and family security. From savings they must buy their homes, their farms and their insurance. It is from their savings finding their way into investment that we sustain and stimulate progress in our productive system.

One end result of the actual and proposed spendings and taxes to meet them is that the Government becomes the major source of credit and capital to the economic system. At best the small business man is starved in the capital he can find. Venture capital to develop new ideas tends to become confined to the large corporations and they grow bigger. Governments do not develop gadgets of improved living.

Another end result is to expose all our independent colleges and other privately supported institutions to the risk of becoming dependent upon the state. Then through politics we will undermine their independence which gives stimulus to government supported institutions.

No nation grows stronger by subtraction.

Think it over.

It is proposed that we can avoid these disasters by more government borrowing. That is a device to load our extravagance and waste onto the next generation. But increasing government debts can carry immediate punishment for that is the road to inflation. There is far more courage in reducing our debts than in increasing them. And that is a duty to our children.

And there is no room for this spending and taxes except to cut the standard of living of most of our people. It is easy to say increase corporation taxes. That is an illusion. The bulk of corporation taxes is passed on to the consumer—that is, to every family. It is easy to say increase taxes on the higher personal income brackets. But if all incomes over $5000 a year were confiscated, it would cover less than 10% of these actual and proposed spendings.

The main road is to reduce spending and waste and defer some desirable things for a while.

There are many absolute necessities and there are many less urgent meritorious and desirable things that every individual family in the nation would like to have but cannot afford. To spend for them or borrow money for them would endanger the family home and the family life. So it is with the national family.

So long as we must support the necessary national defense and cold war at a cost of 24 days work per year to Mr. Average W. Citizen there are many comforting things that should be deferred if we do not wish to go down this road to ruin of our national family life.

Think it over.

Along this road of spending, the Government either takes over, which is socialism, or dictates institutional and economic life which is fascism.

The American mind is troubled by the growth of collectivism throughout the world.

We have a few hundred thousand Communists and their fellow travelers in this country. They cannot destroy the Republic. They are a nuisance and require attention. We also have the doctrinaire socialists who peacefully dream of their utopia.

But there is a considerable group of fuzzy-minded people who are engineering a compromise with all these European infections. They fail to realize that our American System has grown away from the systems of Europe for 250 years. They have the foolish notion that a collectivist economy can at the same time preserve personal liberty and constitutional government.

The steady lowering of the standard of living by this compromised collectivist system under the title "austerity" in England should be a sufficient spectacle. It aims at a fuller life but it ends in a ration.

Most Americans do not believe in these compromises with collectivism. But they do not realize that through governmental spending and taxes, our nation is blissfully driving down the back road to it at top speed.

In the end these solutions of national problems by spending are always the same—power, more power, more centralization in the hands of the state.

We have not had a great socialization of property, but we are on the last mile to collectivism through governmental collection and spending of the savings of the people.

Think it over.

A device of these advocates of gigantic spending is the manipulation of words, phrases and slogans to convey new meanings different from those we have long understood. These malign distortions drug thinking. They drown it in emotion. We see government borrowing and spending transferred into the soft phrase "deficit spending." The slogan of a "welfare state" has emerged as a disguise for the totalitarian state by the route of spending. Thomas Jefferson would not recognize this distortion of his simple word "welfare" in the Constitution. Jefferson's idea of the meaning of welfare lies in his statement, "To preserve our independence . . . we must make a choice between economy and liberty or profusion and servitude. . . . If we can prevent government from wresting the labors of the people under the pretence of caring for them we shall be happy."

Another of these distortions is by those who support such a state and call themselves "liberals." John Morley would not recognize them.

Out of these slogans and phrases and new meanings of words come vague promises and misty mirages, such as "security from the cradle to the grave," which frustrate those basic human impulses to production which make a dynamic nation.

Think it over.

It is customary to blame the Administrations or the legislatures for this gigantic increase in spending, these levies on the nation's workdays, and this ride to a dead-end of our unique and successful American system. A large cause of this growing confiscation of the work of the people by our various Governments is the multitude of great pressure groups among our citizens. Also the state and municipal governments pressurize the Federal Government. And within the Federal Government are pressure groups building their own empires.

Aggression of groups and agencies against the people as a whole is not a process of free men. Special privilege either to business or groups is not liberty.

Many of these groups maintain paid lobbies in Washington or in the State Capitols to press their claims upon the Administrations or the legislatures.

Our representatives must run for election. They can be defeated by these pressure groups. Our officials are forced to think in terms of pressure groups, not in terms of need of the whole people.

Perhaps some of my listeners object to somebody else's pressure group. Perhaps you support one of your own. Perhaps some of you do not protest that your leaders are not acting with your authority.

Think it over.

And finally, may I say that thinking and debate on these questions must not be limited to legislative halls. We should debate them in every school. We should resort to the old cracker barrel debate in every corner grocery. These phrases and slogans can be dissolved in common sense and integrity.

A splendid storehouse of integrity and freedom has been bequeathed to us by our forefathers. In this day of confusion, of peril to liberty, our high duty is to see that this storehouse is not robbed of its contents.

We dare not see the birthright of posterity to individual independence, initiative and freedom of choice bartered for a mess of a collectivist system.

My word to you, my fellow-citizens, on this seventy-fifth birthday is this: The Founding Fathers dedicated the structure of our government "to secure the blessings of liberty to ourselves and our posterity." We of this generation inherited this precious blessing. Yet as spendthrifts we are on our way to rob posterity of its inheritance.

The American people have solved many great crises in national life. The qualities of self-restraint, of integrity, of conscience and courage still live in our people. It is not too late to summon these qualities.

Emerson, Edwin. Hoover and His Times. Garden City Publishing Company. New York, 1932.
Gitlow, Benjamin. The Whole of Their Lives. Charles Scribner's Sons. New York, 1948.
Hard, William. Who's Hoover? Dodd, Mead & Co. New York, 1928.
Hendrick, Burton J. The Life and Letters of Walter Hines Page. Doubleday Doran & Co. New York, 1922.
Hinshaw, David. The Home Front. G. P. Putnam's Sons. New York, 1943.
Hoover, Herbert. Addresses Upon the American Road, 1933–1938. Charles Scribner's Sons. New York, 1938.
———. Addresses Upon the American Road, 1945–1948. D. Van Nostrand Co. New York, 1949.
———. American Ideals vs The New Deal. The Scribner Press. New York.
———. America's Way Forward. The Scribner Press. New York.
Hull, Cordell. The Memoirs of Cordell Hull. 2 vols. The Macmillan Co. New York, 1948.
Irwin, Will. Herbert Hoover: A Reminiscent Biography. The Century Co. New York, 1928.
Johnson, Walter (ed.). Selected Letters of William Allen White. Henry Holt & Co. New York, 1947.
Lyons, Eugene. Our Unknown Ex-President. Doubleday & Co. New York, 1948.
Moley, Raymond. 27 Masters of Politics. Funk & Wagnalls Co. New York, 1949.
Moulton, Harold G. Controlling Factors in Economic Development. The Brookings Institution. Washington, D. C., 1949.
Mullendore, William C. History of the United States Food Administration, 1917–1919. Stanford University Press. Stanford, 1941.
Myers, William Starr. The State Papers and Other Collected Writings of Herbert Hoover, 2 vols. Doubleday Doran & Co. New York, 1934.

Myers, William Starr and Newton, Walter H. The Hoover Administration, A Documented Narrative. Charles Scribner's Sons. New York, 1936.

Public Relations of the Commission for Relief in Belgium, 2 vols. Stanford University Press. Stanford, 1929.

Sullivan, Mark. Our Times: The Twenties. Charles Scribner's Sons. New York, 1935.

Surface, Frank M. and Bland, Raymond L. American Food in the World War and Reconstruction Period. Stanford University Press. Stanford, 1931.

Wilbur, Ray Lyman and Hyde, Arthur Mastic. The Hoover Policies. Charles Scribner's Sons. New York, 1937.

In addition to the foregoing books, I have studied or re-examined literally stacks of Congressional Records, magazine articles about Mr. Hoover, material in my personal files and government reports.

INDEX